Knowledge Discovery in Databases

Knowledge Discovery in Databases

Edited by **May Sanders**

New York

Published by Willford Press,
118-35 Queens Blvd., Suite 400,
Forest Hills, NY 11375, USA
www.willfordpress.com

Knowledge Discovery in Databases
Edited by May Sanders

International Standard Book Number: 978-1-68285-261-3 (Hardback)

Printed in the United States of America.

Contents

Preface

The world is advancing at a fast pace like never before. Therefore, the need is to keep up with the latest developments. This book was an idea that came to fruition when the specialists in the area realized the need to coordinate together and document essential themes in the subject. That's when I was requested to be the editor. Editing this book has been an honour as it brings together diverse authors researching on different streams of the field. The book collates essential materials contributed by veterans in the area which can be utilized by students and researchers alike.

Knowledge discovery in databases is an important element in developing the data as a whole. This book studies, analyzes and upholds the pillars of knowledge discovery and its utmost significance in modern times. State-of-the-art research and developments in this field have been presented herein in the most coherent manner through explanations of topics like dynamics and spatial distribution, online information, cascades, data sharing, networks, etc. Students, researchers, and professionals associated with knowledge discovery will benefit alike from this book.

Each chapter is a sole-standing publication that reflects each author´s interpretation. Thus, the book displays a multi-facetted picture of our current understanding of applications and diverse aspects of the field. I would like to thank the contributors of this book and my family for their endless support.

Editor

1

Effects of time window size and placement on the structure of an aggregated communication network

Gautier Krings[1*], Márton Karsai[2], Sebastian Bernhardsson[3], Vincent D Blondel[1] and Jari Saramäki[2*]

*Correspondence:
gautier.krings@uclouvain.be;
jari.saramaki@aalto.fi
[1]ICTEAM Institute, Université catholique de Louvain, Avenue Georges Lemaître, 4, 1348, Louvain-la-Neuve, Belgium
[2]Department of Biomedical Engineering and Computational Science, Aalto University School of Science, P.O. Box 12200, FI-00076, Aalto, Finland
Full list of author information is available at the end of the article

Abstract

Complex networks are often constructed by aggregating empirical data over time, such that a link represents the existence of interactions between the endpoint nodes and the link weight represents the intensity of such interactions within the aggregation time window. The resulting networks are then often considered static. More often than not, the aggregation time window is dictated by the availability of data, and the effects of its length on the resulting networks are rarely considered. Here, we address this question by studying the structural features of networks emerging from aggregating empirical data over different time intervals, focussing on networks derived from time-stamped, anonymized mobile telephone call records. Our results show that short aggregation intervals yield networks where strong links associated with dense clusters dominate; the seeds of such clusters or communities become already visible for intervals of around one week. The degree and weight distributions are seen to become stationary around a few days and a few weeks, respectively. An aggregation interval of around 30 days results in the stablest similar networks when consecutive windows are compared. For longer intervals, the effects of weak or random links become increasingly stronger, and the average degree of the network keeps growing even for intervals up to 180 days. The placement of the time window is also seen to affect the outcome: for short windows, different behavioural patterns play a role during weekends and weekdays, and for longer windows it is seen that networks aggregated during holiday periods are significantly different.

Introduction

Complex networks have become a standard tool for representing the interaction structure of complex systems [1, 2]. The strength of the network approach comes from its ability to cast the essential features of increasingly complex systems into a manageable form - in the simplest representation, interacting elements are mapped to nodes that are connected by links if they are known to interact. While this coarse-grained view has given a lot of insight into the key characteristics of such systems, it is evident that it entails several approximations and underlying assumptions. The first is the criterion for the existence of links - if the interactions are not binary (on/off) by nature, when is an interaction strong enough to be represented as a link? A common way of taking such strengths into account is to assign weights to the links of the network [3]. The second approximation is related to the time domain. Standard network theory deals with networks that are either static or only slowly changing in time. However, in reality, there are typically dynamical changes in the network structure on multiple time scales. Consequently, representing an empirical system as a static network involves aggregating or integrating over the network dynamics over some time interval. In addition, in many cases, the interactions of the system are not continuously active. While the microdynamics of link activations may be taken into account with the temporal network framework [4], for the aggregated network approach, the interaction frequencies are often used to define the edge weights. It is evident that when aggregating interactions over time, the choice of the aggregation window and its length have consequences on the characteristics of the resulting networks [5]. However, this issue has often been neglected in the literature; often, the aggregation interval has been dictated by the availability of data, while it would be beneficial to ensure that the network properties that one is interested in are captured by the aggregated networks.

In this paper, we address this question by monitoring and analyzing the features of network structure emerging from aggregation over different time intervals for an empirical data set human communication. We present a detailed study of the effects of the aggregation window on the structural features human communication networks that are known to display dynamics on multiple overlapping time scales. The data comes in the form of a time-stamped sequence of mobile telephone calls between anonymized customers of a Belgian mobile operator for a period of 6 months. This sequence is then aggregated over time to form links between customers, and key features of the resulting networks are studied. Although we only study a single set of data, we expect that our conclusions generally hold for similar data sets, as the mechanisms behind network formation are expected to be rather general for such communication networks (see Discussion).

There is an increasing number of studies of human social networks derived from telecommunication records. However, the networks analyzed in the literature have been constructed using very different time windows - a day [6], a week [7], one month [8], and several months (e.g. [9, 10]) - and therefore it is crucial to understand what features of the underlying system are captured by different aggregation intervals. For such social communication networks, there are several mechanisms that are expected to affect the resulting network structure. First, the distribution of link weights, *i.e.* call frequencies, is broad [9, 11]. Thus there are high-weight links that should on average be observed earlier on in the aggregation process, and many links of low weight that take a long time to be observed. Second, link weights are correlated with network topology, such that high-weight links are associated with denser network neighbourhoods [9]. Third, for links of any weight, it is known that the distributions of inter-call times are also broad, *i.e.* call sequences are bursty [12, 13], giving rise to longer-than-Poissonian waiting times between calls. Fourth, there are circadian patterns [14], where the overall level of call activity varies by hour, as well as weekly patterns where call behaviour depends on the day of the week. Fifth, there are changes in the network itself too - relationships grow and wane in strength, new links appear, and old ones are terminated. The aggregated network structure then reflects the joint effect of the above mechanisms that are associated with different time scales. Thus, one cannot expect that there is a proper aggregation interval that represents the true network; rather, different structural features emerge with different aggregation times. In order to understand what the network structure represents, it is important to understand this process.

This paper is structured as follows: first, we discuss the structural and temporal inhomogeneities that are expected to affect the features of aggregated networks. Then, we characterize the dependence of fundamental scalar measures of network structure on the aggregation interval, and address the properties of links added at different times during the aggregation procedure. We find that clustering of the network peaks at 9 days, as the strongest links associated with dense clusters are observed early on in the process. Another time scale is related to the stability of the aggregated networks - networks aggregated for around 30 days display the largest similarity between consecutive windows. Moving from scalar measures to distributions, we find that the degree and weight distributions become surprisingly stationary in 1-2 weeks of aggregation time. Finally, we investigate in detail the effects of different aggregation window placements, and show that the underlying behavioural patterns affect the aggregated networks: on short time scales, weekends differ from weekdays, and on longer scales, holiday periods give rise to anomalies in the aggregated network structure.

Data

Our data consist of the anonymized mobile telephone call records of the customers of a Belgian mobile operator from October 1, 2006 to March 31, 2007. Each customer is uniquely identified, and each call is associated with a time stamp and a duration. This data set has already been studied from a static perspective in several papers [10, 15, 16]. As our focus is on link dynamics, we filter out all customers who have modified their subscription plan during the data collection period. This removes new customers, and customers who have cancelled their subscription during the period. We also only concentrate on the customers of this specific operator (market share in Belgium ~30%), and discard all calls to/from customers of outside operators. The above filtering yields a network that has 2.1 million customers, making over 170 million calls during the collection period.

For reference, we also construct two randomized ensembles, based on two randomization techniques of the time stamps. For both cases, the resulting randomized reference sequences contain the same number of calls between the same individuals as the original data. In the first ensemble, the time stamps of all calls are generated uniformly at random over the complete time range, in order to remove the system-level call frequency pattern (daily and weekly pattern). In the second ensemble, the time stamps of all calls are randomly reshuffled, which retains the daily and weekly patterns, but removes other temporal correlations between the timings of calls of links. When aggregating over the entire observation period, the call sequences from both reference models produce networks that are equal to the network from aggregating the original data. In the remaining, we will refer to these references as respectively the "uniform" and the "shuffled" references.

Network growth

Structural and temporal inhomogeneities

We begin our investigations by addressing the inhomogeneities that are expected to play an important role in the evolution of the structural properties of networks aggregated over growing time intervals. The fundamental structural inhomogeneities are reflected in the standard statistical distributions for the call network, aggregated over the entire 6-month period of observation. In the aggregated network $G(t)$, a link is established between nodes i and j if a call is observed between them at any point during the aggregation interval

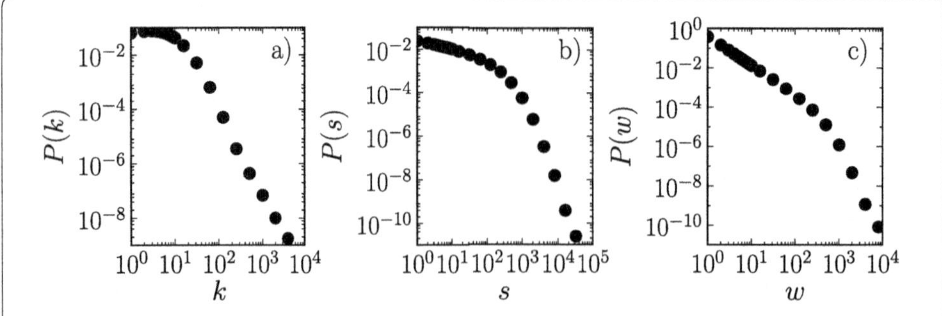

Figure 1 Degree, strength and weight distributions. The degree (**a**), strength (**b**) and weight (**c**) distributions of the aggregated network when the aggregation period covers the whole 6 months of data.

$(0, t)$; the weight w_{ij} of the link is defined as the total number of calls between i and j within the interval. The strength s_i of node i is then defined [3] as the total number of calls where i participates, and the degree k_i as usual as the number of links that node i has. As expected on the basis of earlier results [9–11], the probability density distributions of degree, strength, and link weights are all broad (see Figure 1). Thus there is a large number of nodes that make only infrequent calls, and a large number of links that carry only a few calls. When aggregating the network over shorter time intervals, one thus expects to first discover the high-strength nodes and high-weight links that are associated with the tails of these distributions.

In the time domain, the two main inhomogeneities are related to burstiness of calls forming the links, and the overall circadian pattern of the system-wide call frequency. Burstiness of the calls is reflected in the probability distribution $P(\tau)$ of the times τ between consecutive calls on individual edges. In Figure 2(a), it is seen that in line with earlier observations [12, 13, 17], the distribution $P(\tau)$ in our empirical data has a broader-than-

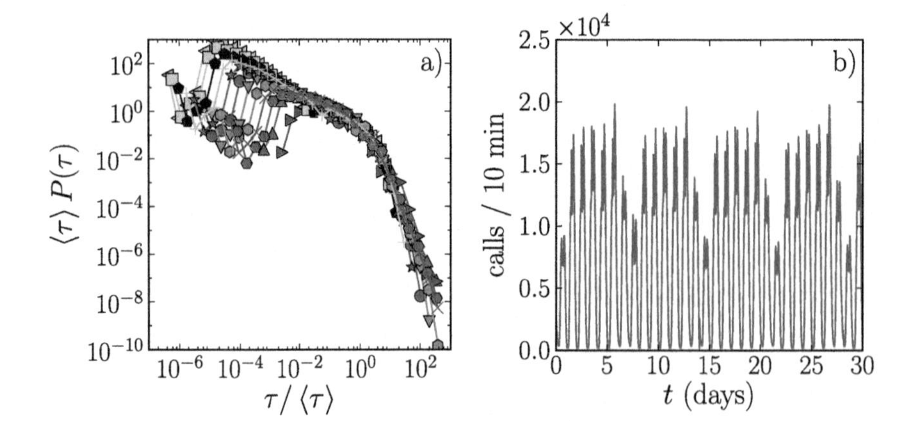

Figure 2 Temporal inhomogeneities. Temporal inhomogeneities affecting network growth. (**a**) The scaled inter-event time distribution of links $P(\tau)$, displaying a broader-than-Poissonian tail. For the plot, the edges have been divided into bins of different numbers of calls. The inter-event time distributions are then scaled by the average inter-event time $\langle\tau\rangle$ of each bin, following [12]. The non-scaling regime for low τ can be attributed to correlated calls, where an incoming call triggers an outgoing call within a short time period. (**b**) Total call rate in the network as a function of time, for the first 30 days, displaying the circadian and weekly patterns. Deep drops can be observed at night, while there are daily peaks, the highest of which appear on Friday evenings. Overall call activity is lower in the weekends, especially on Sundays.

Poissonian tail, a signature of burstiness. Such an inter-call time distribution gives rise to longer waiting times than expected if the calls were placed uniformly in time. Because of this, we expect to see slower network growth than for the uniform case. Further, as seen in Figure 2, the network-level call frequency clearly displays the usual daily and weekly pattern [13, 14], where the frequency shows two daily peaks followed by a decrease during nights. In addition, weekend activity is lower, especially for Sundays.

Evolution of network structure

All of the above features are expected to have an effect on the properties of networks aggregated over growing time intervals. Let us first monitor the growth of the aggregated network in terms of the numbers of nodes and links and the average degree, when the network $G(t)$ is aggregated up to a time t. As seen in Figure 3(a), the number of observed nodes $N(t)$ displays a rapid increase in the beginning of the aggregation process, such that the aggregated network contains 90% of the nodes after $t \sim 30$ days. This rapid increase is followed by slower growth as nodes with low call activity are gradually observed to make calls, joining them to the aggregated network. When compared to the uniform reference, where the time stamps of all calls are drawn uniformly at random from the entire 6-month interval, it is seen that the growth of $N(t)$ is slightly slower; however, for longer aggregation times, the difference can be considered negligible and thus the time-domain

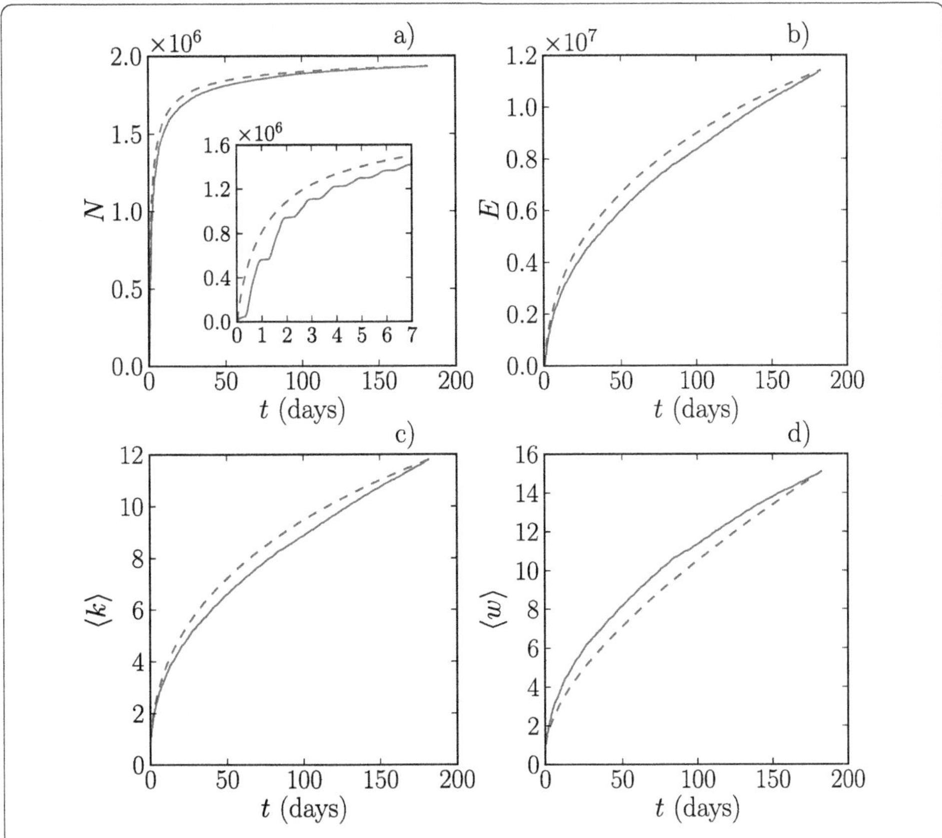

Figure 3 Basic distributions. Total numbers of (**a**) nodes and (**b**) edges and (**c**) the average degree and (**d**) the average edge weight in the aggregated network as a function of aggregation time. The solid (blue) line denotes original empirical data, while the dashed (red) line denotes the uniform reference. The inset in panel (a) displays the number of nodes for the first 7 days.

heterogeneities have a visible effect only for short time windows. For short time windows, in addition to the slowing-down effect of burstiness, the daily pattern is seen to give rise to a stepped shape of the $N(t)$ curve (see the inset of Figure 3(a)).

In contrast, the growth in the number of edges $E(t)$ is much more gradual, as seen in Figure 3(b). Here, an aggregation time of $t \sim 149$ days is required for catching 90% of the edges of the final 6-month aggregated network. In addition, unlike for the number of nodes, for long aggregation times, the number of edges keeps on growing steadily and no saturation in growth is observed. This is also reflected in the growth of the average degree (Figure 3(c)). Hence, even though the number of nodes becomes fairly stable in an aggregation period of 6 months, one cannot claim to have captured all the edges of the underlying network, and for longer windows, the average degree would still increase. This reflects the joint effect of several factors: first, as the edge weight distribution is broad, there are large numbers of edges with very low call frequencies, and observing those evidently takes a long time; there may be many edges where calls take place less frequently than once in six months. In addition, the ubiquitous burstiness that results in longer waiting times between calls slows down the growth in the number of links especially for the low-weight links - this effect is visible in Figure 3(b), although it is not very strong. Second, for such long observation periods, one can argue that the changes in the network structure should already have a visible effect: new social ties are formed while older ties wane in strength and may even cease to exist. Third, as the data contains all the calls made by the subscribers, many of the calls may be random in the sense that they do not reflect the structure of the underlying social network – as there is no background information on the nature of the calls, a random call to one's dentist or a call in response to an advertisement on used car sales are counted as links, just as calls to one's friends or relatives. This third mechanism would naturally result in an ever-growing number of links. The average link weights (Figure 3(d)) must necessarily keep on growing, since all new calls on existing edges are added to their link weight. This growth slows down towards the end of the observation period but does not become as linear-looking as the average degree growth; note that the new links giving rise to growing degrees also affect average weights. Comparison with the uniformly random times reference reveals the effect of burstiness - weights grow faster in the original data because of burstiness, where rapid sequences of calls following one another quickly increase link weights.

As a result of the interplay of the above mechanisms, the network keeps changing while it is being aggregated, and while some of its links are stable in the sense that they remain active for prolonged periods of time, others exist or can be detected only within limited time periods. Then, one may ask what should the aggregation window length be for obtaining representative, "backbone" networks that capture the stablest connections in the system? One way of obtaining a quantitative estimate of the characteristic time scale of network changes is to compare the similarity of networks aggregated for different periods of time when the observation period is divided into multiple consecutive aggregation windows. We calculate the similarity σ of two networks $G_1 = (V_1, E_1)$ and $G_2 = (V_2, E_2)$ as

$$\sigma(G_1, G_2) = \frac{|E_1 \cap E_2|}{|E_1 \cup E_2|}, \tag{1}$$

i.e. the size of the intersection of the sets E_1 and E_2 divided by the size of their union, such that $\sigma = 1$ if the networks are the same, and $\sigma = 0$ if they share no links. Figure 4

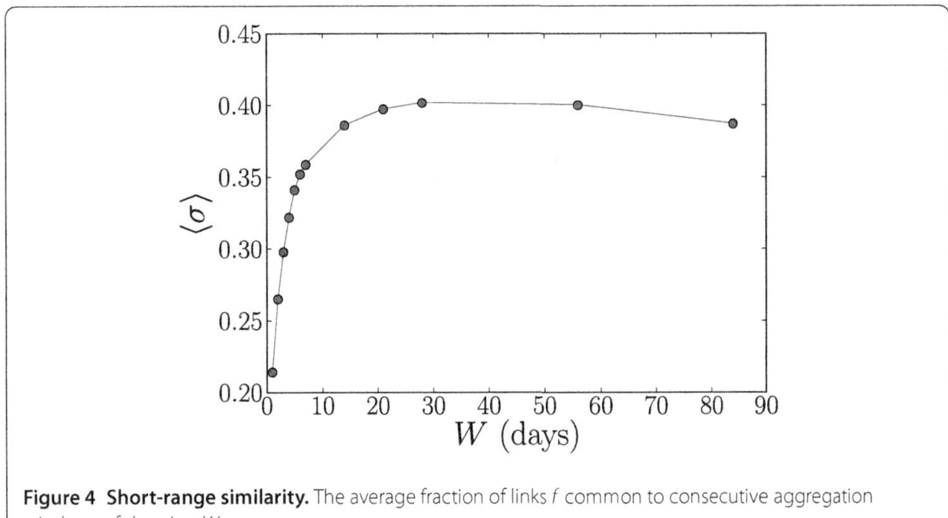

Figure 4 Short-range similarity. The average fraction of links f common to consecutive aggregation windows of duration W.

displays the average similarity σ of networks in consecutive windows of different durations W. When the windows are very short, the networks are very sparse and the number of common links is low. Then, the similarity increases with increasing window duration, reaching a maximum at ~30 days; subsequently, the similarity begins slowly decreasing as the aggregation process captures more and more of the very weak or random links.

As the growth of the number of links in Figure 3(b) does not saturate, it is of importance to understand the characteristics of links that emerge early on in the process. It is known from previous investigations [9] (with a different set of data) that link weights correlate with the network topology such that high-weight links are associated with dense network neighbourhoods, whereas low-weight links connect such neighbourhoods, in line with the Granovetter hypothesis [18]. This is directly related to the presence of *community structure* [19] in social networks; links within communities are stronger and have higher-than-average weights [20]. For the network aggregation, this means that clusters and communities containing high-weight links are likely to appear early on in the process. In order to investigate this effect, we measure the evolution of the network-level clustering coefficient $C(t)$, given by $3\times$ the number of triangles divided by the number of connected triplets in the network. As seen in Figure 5(a), the clustering coefficient does indeed show a rapid increase as a function of the aggregation interval length, and then decreases after a peak at around $t = 9$ days. This decrease can be attributed to the weak links observed later in the process: those links contribute less frequently to triangles. Hence, if short aggregation periods of around one week are used, the resulting network structure is dominated by strong links associated with dense clusters.

The fact that the edges observed early on in the aggregation process are related to the community structure is also visible when monitoring the *overlap* [9] of the added links. The overlap of a link connecting nodes i and j is defined as

$$O_{ij} = n_{ij} / \left[(k_i - 1) + (k_j - 1) - n_{ij}\right], \qquad (2)$$

where n_{ij} is the number of common neighbours of i and j, and k_i and k_j are their degrees. Thus the overlap measures the fraction of common neighbours out of all neighbours of

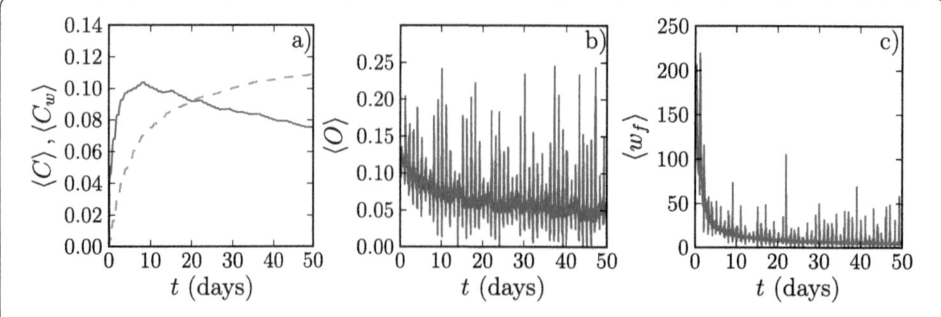

Figure 5 Clustering coefficient and topological overlap. (**a**) Global clustering coefficient of the network and (**b**) average final overlap of added edges as a function of aggregation time, for the first 2 months. The global clustering coefficient is computed as the number of triangles divided by the number of connected triplets. For the overlap, we calculate the final overlap of edges in the 6-month aggregated network, and average over the final overlap values of newly added links at each time point.

the two connected nodes. Figure 5(b) displays the average final 6-month overlap of the added links as a function of aggregation time. Here we have calculated the overlap of each link in the final 6-month aggregated network, and averaged over these values for links that are added to the network at time t. It is seen that the links that are added early on in the aggregation process have on average a higher overlap than those added later; the final overlap is a decreasing function. Hence, even when the aggregation times are short, the networks capture features of the community structure of the final aggregated networks. Interestingly, the overlap also shows a strong circadian and weekly pattern - its highest peaks correspond to the early morning when the overall call rate is very low. Thus, if calls are made during these hours, they are likely to be targeted towards people in the strongest clusters of friends and family.

In order to illustrate the network growth, we have visualized small subnetworks corresponding to different aggregation times t (Figure 6). Here, the subnetwork has been obtained by selecting all individuals whose subscriptions are associated with a certain postal code. This method of sampling yields better results than e.g. snowball sampling.[a] Panels (a) to (d) of Figure 6 show the growth of the network, such that edges that participate in triangles in the final 6-month aggregated network are coloured red. For the shortest aggregation periods (panels (a) and (b)), most of the added edges are in this set, reflecting the above observations on the early appearance of edges connected to communities and clusters. It should be noted that not all community-internal edges are discovered early on; rather, those links that appear early are associated with communities with a high probability.

Behaviour of statistical distributions

Above, it was seen that even for fairly long aggregation intervals, the average degree of the aggregated networks still keeps increasing as a function of the interval length. Likewise, because of how the aggregation process is defined, the average weight necessarily keeps on growing as well. Next, we turn to the statistical distributions of these quantities, and ask when they become descriptive of the underlying network. Evidently, as the averages keep increasing with the aggregation interval length, the probability density distributions of degrees and weights also change and shift towards higher degrees/weights. However, for such distributions to be meaningful descriptors of network structure, their under-

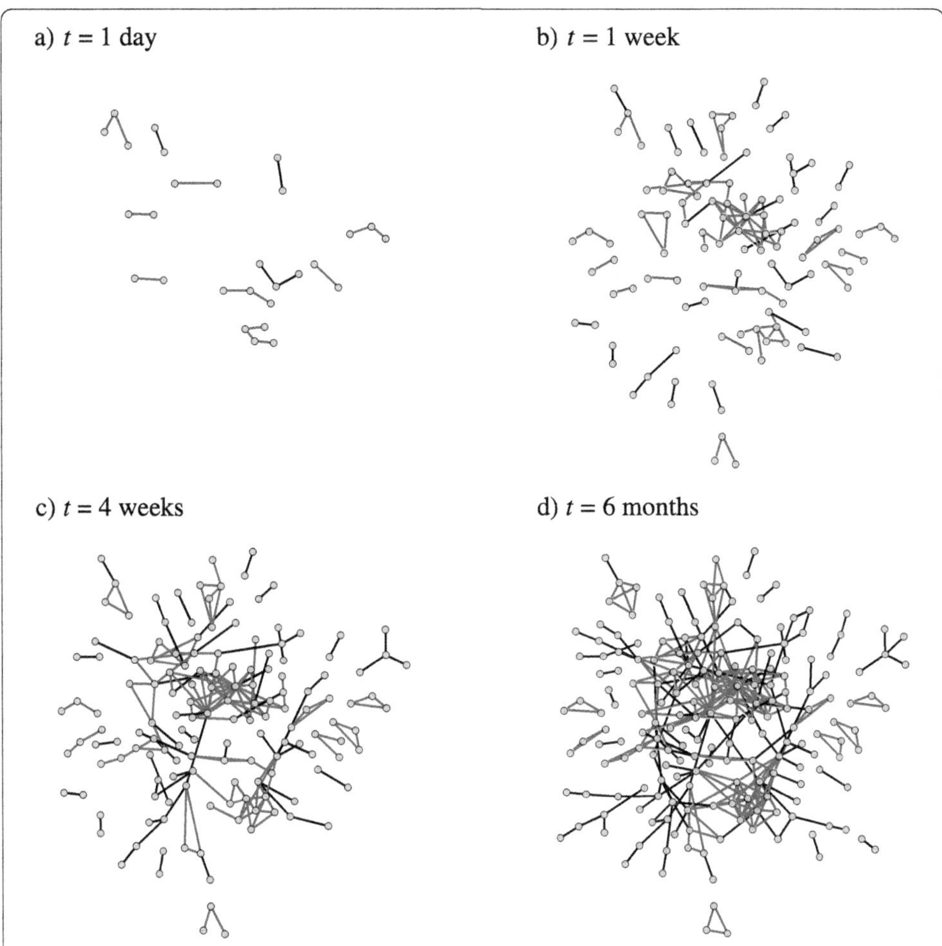

Figure 6 Aggregated network at different time scales. Series of aggregated networks with a growing aggregation interval. The network aggregated here represents a small subnetwork, obtained by picking individuals from a single postal code. Links that participate in triangles in the final 6-month aggregated network are coloured red, while the rest are black.

lying forms should for long enough intervals become stationary and depend only on their average values. In order to study the stationarity of the underlying dynamics one can compare such distributions by rescaling them as $P(x, \langle x \rangle) \sim \langle x \rangle P(x/\langle x \rangle)$, where $\langle x \rangle = \sum xP(x)$. Figure 7(a) and (b) display the PDF's for the degrees and weights, respectively, for different aggregation interval lengths. The bottom panels (c) and (d) display scaled versions of the distribution, rescaled with respect to their average value according to the above. For degrees, one sees that the rescaled distributions collapse onto a single curve, surprisingly already for aggregation intervals over a few days, while for the weights, the distributions converge slightly slower but eventually also collapse for window sizes of the order of weeks. The convergence of the rescaled degree distributions onto a single curve suggests that the underlying dynamics that is being aggregated has some stationary properties. A similar observation was made in [21] for different aggregation windows of the same length, with the conclusion that the underlying process is stationary. To quantify the convergence of the rescaled distributions to a single curve, we measure this convergence with the help of the L^2 distance between two distributions. The L^2 distance between two scalar functions

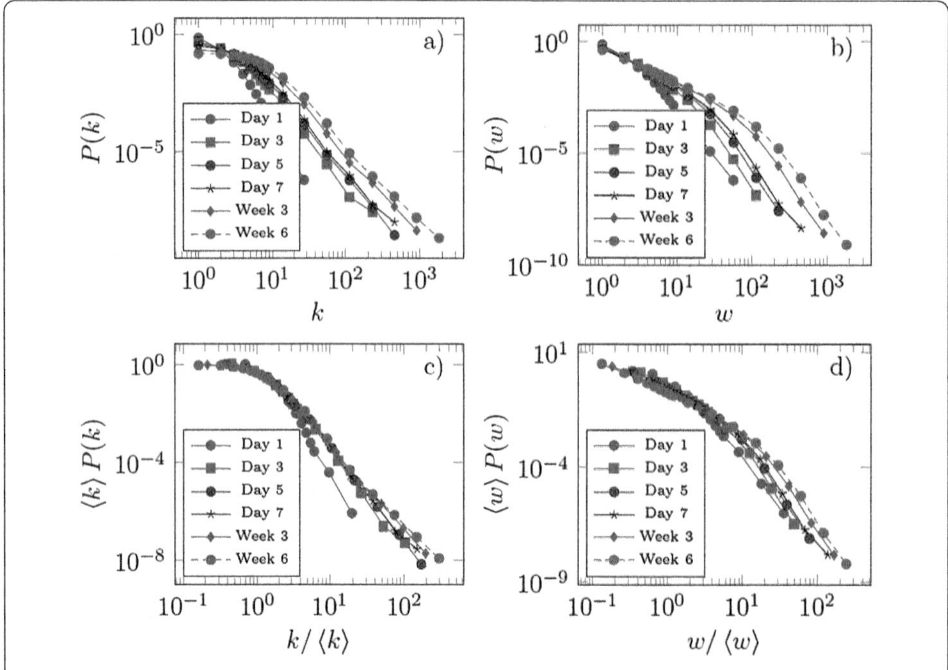

Figure 7 Unscaled and scaled distributions. (**a**) The degree distribution and (**b**) the weight distribution for different aggregation intervals, (**c**) the scaled degree distribution and (**d**) the scaled weight distribution. The distributions are rescaled with respect to their average value.

f and g defined over the same domain $D \subseteq R$ as

$$d(f,g) = \left(\int_D [f(x) - g(x)]^2 \, dx \right)^{\frac{1}{2}}. \tag{3}$$

To measure the convergence, we have successively calculated the distance between the rescaled degree (weight) distributions of networks aggregated over an interval of length t and networks aggregated over twice longer intervals of length $2t$. In Figure 8, it is seen

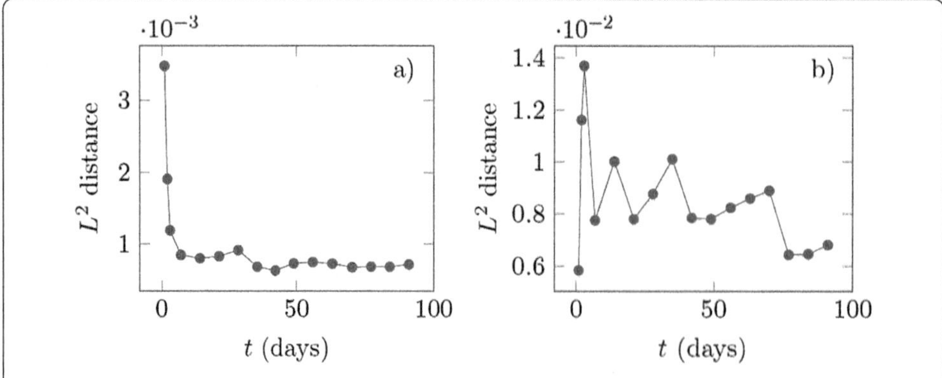

Figure 8 L^2 distance of rescaled distributions. The L^2 distance between the degree (**a**) and weight (**b**) distributions of the networks aggregated over a time interval of length t and $2t$. That is, the first point is the distance between the rescaled distributions of the network built with the first day and the network built with the two first days. The second point is the distance between the rescaled distributions of the two first days and the four first days, etc. The last point is the distance between the distributions of the network built with the 91 first days and the network built with the 182 first days.

that the L^2 distance between the degree distributions decreases and converges to a roughly constant value already for aggregation intervals longer than a few days. Hence, already after a short period, a sufficient amount of data has been collected to correctly estimate the stationary degree distribution of the network, and the shape of the degree remains similar for longer intervals. The weight distribution displays a slightly slower convergence, and is still slowly changing even for aggregation intervals of around 3 months; this is also related to the curvature seen in the evolution of the average link weight (Figure 3(d)). There are several possible explanations for this slower convergence: first, the number of links is increasing and each newly added link brings in a unit of weight. Second, the weights of existing links may display very different time dynamics, and third, the growth of link weights is affected by the burstiness of the call sequences and the resulting long inter-call times. Nevertheless, even the weight distributions do not change much, and care is needed only when interpreting the weight distributions of call networks aggregated over very short periods of time.

On the effects of aggregation window placement

In all analysis so far, we have assumed that the exact placement of the aggregation window, *i.e.* the time point of its beginning, plays no role in the results. However, as the characteristic daily and weekly patterns of Figure 2(b) indicate, the overall level of call activity in the network displays large variations by hour and day, and this is expected to have an effect on the aggregated networks, at least on shorter time scales. In addition, there may be less trivial effects if the actual behavioural patterns of individuals - affecting *who* they call - are also time-dependent. In this final section, we will address these issues.

Let us first focus on short time scales, and illustrate the growth of the network with a 2D heat map plot, displaying the number of nodes in aggregated networks as a function of the aggregation time and the beginning point of the aggregation window (Figure 9). The daily and weekly pattern is clearly visible in the plot - the network grows fastest during weekdays, especially Fridays. The growth is slowest when the aggregation begins on Saturdays and especially Sundays; the difference between Saturdays and Sundays is fairly large. However, this observation might be explained by the network-wide variation of the call frequency alone.

In order to have a closer look at the actual call patterns of individuals, we monitor the growth of the giant connected component of the network. As seen in Figure 5(b), the links that emerge early on in the aggregation process typically have high overlap, *i.e.* are associated with dense network neighbourhoods; however, the overlap also displays a time-dependent pattern. Roughly speaking, if the majority of calls in a given window is directed towards high-overlap individuals that are part of the same neighbourhood or cluster, the giant component should grow more slowly than if the calls are directed towards far-away nodes. We measure this effect by monitoring the average size of the emerging largest connected component; for reference, we also calculate their size relative to those in the time-shuffled reference ensemble. In this ensemble, the exact times of all calls are randomly reshuffled, so that the links of the reference ensemble networks have the same number of calls as the original networks, but their timings are now uncorrelated, with the exception of the daily/weekly call frequency pattern at the network level. Figure 10 displays the absolute and relative size of the giant component similarly to the 2D heat map plot for nodes. The absolute size displays a clear daily and weekly pattern much akin to that seen for the

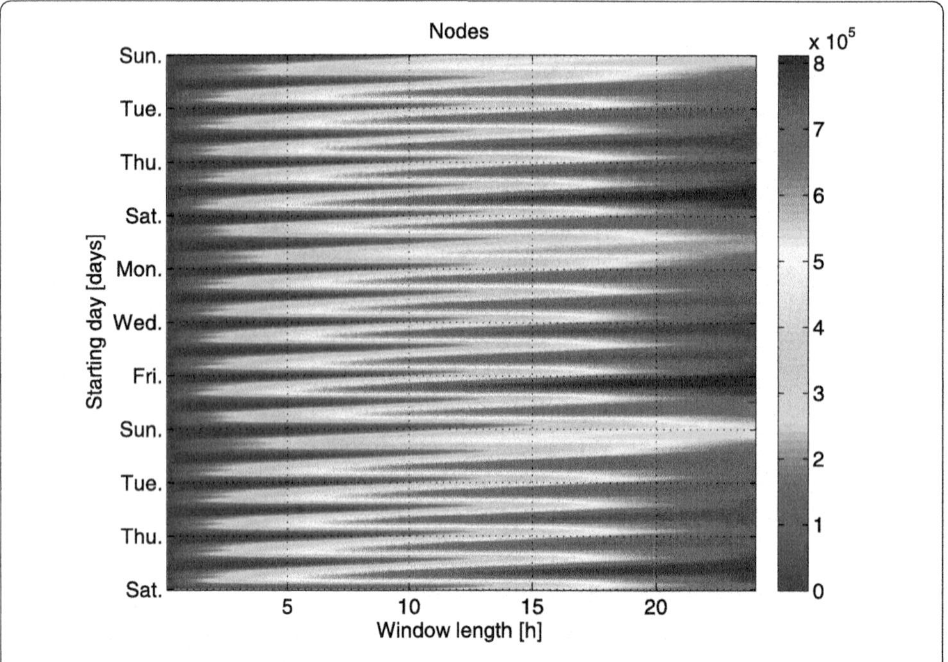

Figure 9 Number of nodes in the network. The number of nodes in the aggregated networks as a function of the aggregation interval length (horizontal axis, in hours) and the beginning point of aggregation (vertical axis). The vertical axis runs from top to bottom, and the first time point is early Sunday, just after midnight.

number of nodes in Figure 9. However, the behaviour of the average giant component size relative to the time-shuffled reference ensemble (lower panel) reveals an interesting feature: when the aggregation begins in the weekends, especially Sundays, the giant component grows more slowly than it does in the reference. Likewise, for weekdays, it grows far faster than it does in the reference. This points towards different behavioural modes - weekday calls are frequently related to links joining nodes that would otherwise remain disconnected within the aggregation window, whereas weekend calls appear to relate to high-overlap links and dense clusters and thus contribute less to the growth of the largest connected components. In other words, friends and relatives with shared social circles are called more frequently in the weekends.

Changes in behaviour very similar to the daily and weekly patterns also appear on longer time scales, as human communication patterns are affected *e.g.* by holiday periods. In order to observe such behavioural changes in the aggregated networks, we divide the data into non-overlapping time windows of 1 day, 1 week, and 2 weeks. We then aggregate networks corresponding to each time window, and monitor the similarity of the networks in two consecutive windows as a function of time. For this, we employ a weighted generalization of the Jaccard index of Equation 1:

$$\sigma_w = \frac{\sum_{(i,j)\in E} \min(w_{ij}^1, w_{ij}^2)}{\sum_{(i,j)\in E} \max(w_{ij}^1, w_{ij}^2)}, \tag{4}$$

where w_{ij}^1 and w_{ij}^2 are the weights of links between nodes i and j in the consecutive windows ($w_{ij} = 0$ if there is no link). Figure 11 displays the weighted network similarities for the three different window sizes as a function of time. No long-term trends can be observed in the similarities that fluctuate around roughly constant values. The 1-day similarity displays

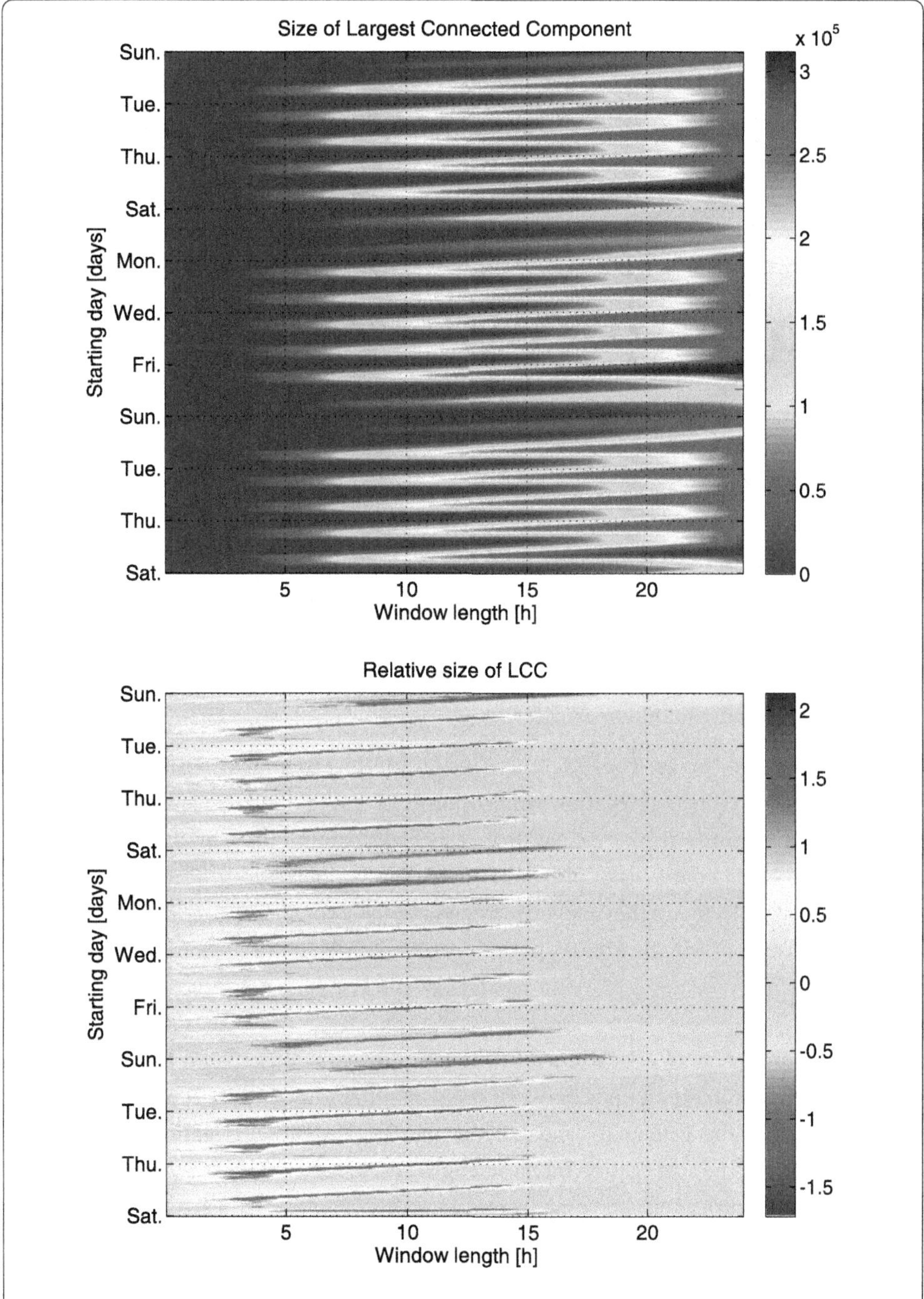

Figure 10 Largest connected component size. The absolute (top) and relative (bottom) size of the largest connected component as a function of the aggregation time (horizontal axis) and the beginning point of aggregation (vertical axis). The relative values of the bottom panel are the logarithm of the ratio between the observed largest connected component and the shuffled reference model, where call times do not correlate with network structure.

a clear daily and weekly pattern, in line with our observations on the connected component sizes. Here, for each week, the consecutive windows corresponding to Monday to Thursday have highest similarities, while similarities are far smaller between the 1-day networks for Friday, Saturday and Sunday. Some larger changes can be seen already for the 1-day measure during the holiday periods (autumn holiday, Christmas season) indi-

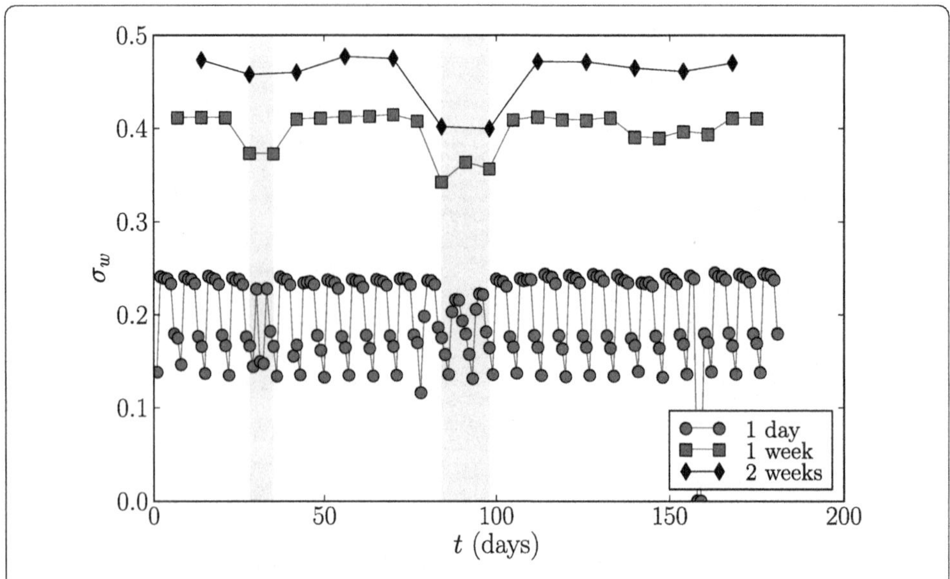

Figure 11 Long-range similarity. Similarity between networks corresponding to two consecutive aggregation windows of 1 day, 1 week, and 2 weeks. The two shaded areas correspond to national holiday periods: the autumn holiday (left), and holidays around Christmas and New Year (right). The zero-valued points for the 1-day curve are from missing data.

cated by the grey shaded areas. The differences corresponding to holiday periods become much more apparent when aggregation window sizes of 1 week and especially 2 weeks are used, as both measures display a clear drop, especially around the Christmas holiday season. Thus, the calling patterns of individuals are clearly different during such holiday seasons, and this is reflected in the respective aggregated networks that are different from networks aggregated outside the holiday periods.

Conclusions

In many cases, complex networks studied in the literature are constructed by aggregating links or sequences of interactions between the constituent nodes over some period of time, often limited by the availability of data, and their static structural features are then studied. The effects of the aggregation interval length and placement have been discussed only rarely [5, 21]. In order to shed some insight into this problem, we have investigated the structural features of mobile telephone call networks aggregated over aggregation intervals of increasing length. To ensure that the results are not affected by churn, *i.e.* customers leaving and subscribing to the operator, we only considered customers whose subscriptions did not change over the entire data interval from Oct 1st, 2006 to March 31th, 2007.

Evidently, there several dynamical mechanisms and inhomogeneities that affect the features of networks aggregated over different time intervals, from broad distributions of numbers of calls on links to burstiness-related long inter-call times and dynamical changes in the network itself, and disentangling the effects of such features is not possible on the basis of time-stamped data alone. Thus the resulting networks display properties that arise from the interplay of such features associated with multiple time scales, and the question of a "correct" or proper aggregation interval length is ill-posed. However, on the basis of our analysis, some statements about the general emergence of network features can be made. First, because of the broad link weight distribution and Granovetterian weight-topology correlations, where strong links are associated with dense neighbourhoods, the seeds of the underlying community structure are visible in aggregated networks already for rather short aggregation intervals of ∼1 week: the clustering coefficient of the network peaks at around 9 days, and the earlier a link is observed, the more likely it is to participate in a dense neighbourhood in the final network aggregated over the available data period, as seen by monitoring the neighbourhood overlap of the links. However, at the same time, although the growth of the number of nodes saturates fairly early, the number of links and the average degree of nodes keep on growing even for long aggregation intervals. This suggests that for short windows, the cluster and community structures dominate, whereas for longer windows, the contribution of both "weak" links and links that are practically random, *i.e.* arise from one-off-calls, increases. When networks from consecutive windows of different lengths are compared, they are seen to be maximally similar at a length of ∼30 days; this can be considered as the time scale of the recurrent, stable links, beyond which the weaker links start to have a considerable effect on network structure. The scaled degree and weight distributions become stationary already for short time intervals of a few days or weeks, respectively.

As the above results are from one dataset only, it is worth considering how general they are. As there are common underlying features of social networks - broad tie strength distributions and the Granovetterian relationship between tie strengths and topology - we believe that the fast emergence of clusters of strong links followed by increasing numbers of weaker links not associated with triangles is a general feature that holds across different communication networks. Likewise, one may assume that the time scale for obtaining stablest networks (∼30 days in our case) should remain roughly similar. However, in both cases, the exact numbers for the characteristic time scales might differ as they may also be affected by the overall call activity level. We also believe that the collapse of scaled distributions, indicating stationarity in the underlying processes, should be observable in other data sets too.

In addition to the effects of the aggregation window length, we have shown that comparing networks aggregated over windows of different placement can yield insight into the dynamic features of the behavioural patterns of individuals. The differences in the growth of the largest connected component point towards different behavioural modes in the weekends and during weekdays, where weekend calls are more frequently related to high-overlap links and dense clusters, and thus build the largest connected component more slowly; weekday calls play the role of "topological shortcuts" in the aggregation process and more rapidly give rise to overall network connectivity. Additionally, we have observed very different calling patterns during holiday periods, giving rise to aggregated networks that significantly differ from the networks constructed from data outside the holiday periods. Thus, the aggregation interval placement matters, and care should be taken when interpreting the structural features of networks constructed from data that involves holidays or other special periods.

Competing interests
The authors declare that they have no competing interests.

Author's contributions
GK, MK, SB, VB and JS designed the research and analysis, GK prepared the data, GK and SB performed the analysis, GK, MK and JS wrote the paper.

Acknowledgements

MK and JS acknowledge financial support of the Future and Emerging Technologies (FET) programme within the Seventh Framework Programme for Research of the European Commission, under FET-Open grant number: 238597 (project ICTeCollective). GK acknowledges support from the Concerted Research Action (ARC) "Large Graphs and Networks" from the "Direction de la recherche scientifique - Communauté française de Belgique". The scientific responsibility rests with its authors.

Endnote

[a] Because social networks are geospatially embedded, zip-code-based geospatial sampling yields networks that preserve rather well the typical characteristics of social networks. On the contrary, in snowball sampling where all nodes at a chosen graph distance from the focal node are included in the sample, the majority of nodes are at the "surface" of the snowball, as the number of nodes grows exponentially with graph distance. This artifact results in low clustering and makes observing community structure difficult.

Author details

[1]ICTEAM Institute, Université catholique de Louvain, Avenue Georges Lemaître, 4, 1348, Louvain-la-Neuve, Belgium. [2]Department of Biomedical Engineering and Computational Science, Aalto University School of Science, P.O. Box 12200, FI-00076, Aalto, Finland. [3]Swedish Defence Research Agency, SE-147 25 Tumba, Sweden.

References

1. Newman M, Barabási AL, Watts DJ (2006) The structure and dynamics of networks. Princeton University Press, Princeton
2. Newman M (2011) Networks: an introduction. Oxford University Press, Oxford
3. Barrat A, Barthélemy M, Pastor-Satorras R, Vespignani A (2004) The architecture of complex weighted networks. Proceedings of the National Academy of Sciences 101(11):3747-3752
4. Holme P, Saramäki J (2011) Temporal networks. arXiv:1108.1780
5. Holme P (2003) Network dynamics of ongoing social relationships. EPL 64:427
6. Aiello W, Chung F, Lu L (2000) A random graph model for massive graphs. In: Proceedings of the 32nd annual ACM symposium on theory of computing. ACM, New York, pp 171-180
7. Nanavati A, Gurumurthy S, Das G, Chakraborty D, Dasgupta K, Mukherjea S, Joshi A (2006) On the structural properties of massive telecom call graphs: findings and implications. In: Proceedings of the 15th ACM international conference on information and knowledge management. ACM, New York, pp 435-444
8. Seshadri M, Machiraju S, Sridharan A, Bolot J, Faloutsos C, Leskovec J (2008) Mobile call graphs: beyond power-law and log-normal distributions. In: Proceedings of the 14th ACM SIGKDD international conference on knowledge discovery and data mining. ACM, New York, pp 596-604
9. Onnela J, Saramäki J, Hyvönen J, Szabó G, Lazer D, Kaski K, Kertész J, Barabási A (2007) Structure and tie strengths in mobile communication networks. Proceedings of the National Academy of Sciences 104(18):7332
10. Lambiotte R, Blondel V, de Kerchove C, Huens E, Prieur C, Smoreda Z, Van Dooren P (2008) Geographical dispersal of mobile communication networks. Physica A: Statistical Mechanics and its Applications 387(21):5317-5325
11. Onnela J, Saramäki J, Hyvönen J, Szabó G, de Menezes M, Kaski K, Barabási A, Kertész J (2007) Analysis of a large-scale weighted network of one-to-one human communication. New Journal of Physics 9(6):179
12. Candia J, González MC, Wang P, Schoenharl T, Madey G, Barabási AL (2008) Uncovering individual and collective human dynamics from mobile phone records. Journal of Physics A: Mathematical and Theoretical 41:224015+
13. Karsai M, Kivelä M, Pan RK, Kaski K, Kertész J, Barabási AL, Saramäki J (2011) Small but slow world: how network topology and burstiness slow down spreading. Phys Rev E 83:025102
14. Jo HH, Karsai M, Kertész J, Kaski K (2011) Circadian pattern and burstiness in human communication activity. http://arxiv.org/abs1101:0377
15. Krings G, Calabrese F, Ratti C, Blondel V (2009) Urban gravity: a model for inter-city telecommunication flows. Journal of Statistical Mechanics: Theory and Experiment 2009:L07003
16. Blondel V, Krings G, Thomas I (2010) Regions and borders of mobile telephony in Belgium and in the Brussels metropolitan zone. Brussels Studies 42:4
17. Miritello G, Moro E, Lara R (2011) The dynamical strength of social ties in information spreading. Phys Rev E 83:045102(R)
18. Granovetter MS (1973) The strength of weak ties. American Journal of Sociology 78:1360-1380
19. Fortunato S (2010) Community detection in graphs. Physics Reports 486:75-174
20. Tibély G, Kovanen L, Karsai M, Kaski K, Kertész J, Saramäki J (2011) Communities and beyond: mesoscopic analysis of a large social network with complementary methods. Physical Review E 83:056125+
21. Gautreau A, Barrat A, Barthélemy M (2009) Microdynamics in stationary complex networks. Proceedings of the National Academy of Sciences 106:8847-8852

2

Genetic flow directionality and geographical segregation in a *Cymodocea nodosa* genetic diversity network

A Paolo Masucci[1], Sophie Arnaud-Haond[2], Víctor M Eguíluz[3], Emilio Hernández-García[3*] and Ester A Serrão[4]

*Correspondence: emilio@ifisc.uib-csic.es
[3]IFISC (CSIC-UIB), Instituto de Física Interdisciplinar y Sistemas Complejos, Consejo Superior de Investigaciones Científicas - Universitat de les Illes Balears, Palma de Mallorca, Spain
Full list of author information is available at the end of the article

Abstract

We analyse a large data set of genetic markers obtained from populations of *Cymodocea nodosa*, a marine plant occurring from the East Mediterranean to the Iberian-African coasts in the Atlantic Ocean. We fully develop and test a recently introduced methodology to infer the directionality of gene flow based on the concept of geographical segregation. Using the Jensen-Shannon divergence, we are able to extract a directed network of gene flow describing the evolutionary patterns of *Cymodocea nodosa*. In particular we recover the genetic segregation that the marine plant underwent during its evolution. The results are confirmed by natural evidence and are consistent with an independent cross analysis.

Introduction

With the advances of sequencing technology and the availability of large datasets, evolutionary biology needs to employ novel techniques, which are akin to those developed within statistical physics [1], to analyse and understand patterns in population dynamics. An interesting question in evolutionary biology is how to trace the directionality in migration patterns, a problem of outstanding importance in conservation biology in general, including the management of threatened or exploited species and of invasion processes [2]. It is also related to the more general problem of infection and information propagation in networks [3, 4].

In this paper we tackle the indirect assessment of migratory transfers (by pollen, propagules, or plant fragments) among plant populations using molecular markers to retrace the exchange of genes, or *gene flow*, among them. This is done by fully developing a recently introduced methodology based on a directionality index [5]. This index finds its origins on the concept of *geographical segregation* [6], often related to social studies, to infer the evolutionary pathways from microsatellite datasets. Microsatellites [7] are portions of non-coding DNA with a variable number of repetitions of a motif consisting of a few bases. They are widely used in intraspecific genetic studies. Despite being non-coding, we will use eventually the word *genes* to denote the microsatellites, and *alleles* for their different varieties occurring at a particular position in the genome (a particular *locus*).

Classical population genetics analyses do not allow inferring the direction of migration using molecular data. Although some Bayesian analyses have been more recently developed to do so [8, 9], many require complex and time-consuming computing of the likelihood functions, restraining the ability to explore more than often too simple evolutionary scenarios and molecular models [10].

In the present study we analyse a dataset that presents evident cases of geographical segregation, such as island effects and we are able to show that the proposed methodology spots these islands, based on microsatellite data only and without any further geographical information or evolutionary assumption. In particular we use the information contained in microsatellite genetic markers from the entire geographic distribution of a marine plant species, *Cymodocea nodosa* (CN). This dataset has been selected because there is enough information to infer the past history of the gene flow based on the geographical distribution of genetic polymorphism [11], allowing the assessment of the usefulness of the new methods here described.

Understanding the pathways of gene flow along the Mediterranean-Atlantic transition zone was the main aim of this genetic dataset [11]. Based on presence/absence of alleles, this revealed that the flow of genetic information across the Mediterranean-Atlantic transition zone had most likely occurred westwards, because dominant Mediterranean alleles penetrate into the nearest Atlantic sites (Atlantic Iberia), but the opposite is not true, *i.e.* dominant Atlantic alleles are not found in any Mediterranean populations. This clear pattern of presence/absence of diagnostic alleles results in that this data set provides an ideal workbench to test and to develop a recently introduced method of inferring directionality of gene flow, here based on distances computed from the Jensen-Shannon divergence [12].

Network theory has already proved to be useful in the study of metapopulation systems dynamics [13]. In particular it has been shown that the analysis of topological relationships between different populations carries fundamental information for the understanding of evolutionary dynamics [13]. It is important to further develop and test methodologies to extract reliable information-flow networks from biological datasets.

The method considered in this work introduces some novelties with respect to classical approaches, which have been already underlined in [5]. The gene flow network is extracted by means of a model-independent measure, which is a normalised version of the Jensen-Shannon divergence. An interesting aspect of the application of this method is that we extract the *gamete space* from the allele sequences and we perform the analysis in that space. *Gametes* are the mother and father sexual cells that fuse in a sexual reproduction event. The nuclear genetic information from the two gametes remain mostly separated in the daughter cell (in the different chromosomes of each chromosome pair) and subsequent cells originating from it, but sequencing techniques cannot identify which gene is coming from which gamete. From the observed alleles in each individual in our dataset we construct the set of possible gametes that could have originated such individual, and we apply our techniques to such gamete pool. The distance measure in the gamete space has to be considered more detailed than the one in the allelic space, since it takes into account the possible correlations between different loci. An extension of the method to include mutation effects can be easily obtained as better explained below.

Here we advance the method beyond its first application [5], in fully developing and verifying the directionality index methodology by introducing a test for the detected directionality significance. This is done with an ad-hoc randomization test. This method is independent of the way the genetic flow is extracted and can then be applied independently of the genetic distance used. The present analysis reveals that the methodology is efficient in cases of evident geographical segregation, for which the method was designed, while it is not efficient in detecting the direction of the flows where geographical segregation is not present.

Moreover in the *Additional file 1*, we give a detailed comparison of the distance method applied here with some of the most used genetic distance measures based on microsatellite analysis, such as the Nei distance [14], the Cavalli-Sforza distance [15], the Goldstein distance [14] and the average square distance [16].

Data and results

The genetic flow network

Our dataset consists of 845 *ramets* of *Cymodocea nodosa*. A ramet is a single plant shoot, whereas a *genet* is a genetic individual, or clone, derived from a single event of sexual recombination (*i.e.*, from a single seed) and having given birth through clonal growth to a population of ramets therefore sharing the same genome [17]. Ramets were sampled from 60 different meadows, distributed geographically between the Mediterranean basin and the Atlantic Ocean, covering the entire plant distribution [11]. This dataset is the one discussed in [11] with the addition of a few populations more recently sampled, as for example from Morocco. Among the 40 ramets taken at each site, after removal of genet (*i.e.*, clonal) repetitions the number of ramets available in the data set ranged from 4 to 34 per meadow. Hence each of the 845 ramets of the dataset represents a different clone.

We characterize each ramet by some microsatellite markers [7]. In particular, each ramet has been genotyped to identify in it $n = 8$ pairs of alleles, *i.e.* pairs of microsatellites that occupy a specific position (locus) on the chromosomes, each element of the pair characterizing the same locus in the two homologous chromosomes arising from the maternal and paternal gametes in a sexual reproduction event. The number n of pairs of microsatellites used was selected for highest information content with minimum cost (see [11] and references therein), a standard microsatellite genotyping methodology.

To characterize the presence of gene flow between meadows we use the general network strategy [13, 18, 19], in which populations (here, the meadows) are nodes of a graph, and they are linked when significant relationships among them (indicating gene flow) are detected.

There are different ways to implement such inference of gene flow, mostly based on different types of distances [13, 18, 20]. Here we use a methodology based on information theory [5], which is especially suited to compare genetic data taken from populations of different sizes, taking into account not just properties of individual alleles but also the full information genotyped (including correlations among sites, linkage disequilibrium, for example).

We consider the set of meadows as a metapopulation system where each population is a meadow and each population element is an n-dimensional vector representing an equiprobable gamete of that meadow, where n is the number of loci.

To derive the gamete pool we notice that each ramet is characterised by a set of $n =$ 8 pairs (a, b) of alleles, each pair belonging to a given locus. Since it is not known *a-priori* which chromosome a given allele belongs to, we consider all the possible combinations of alleles between the n pairs, *i.e.* $2^n = 256$ equiprobable gametes representing a single ramet. In this way our system becomes represented by $845 \cdot 2^8 = 216{,}320$ points in an 8-dimensional space. Each meadow can be characterised by a discrete probability function

$P = P(\vec{x})$ assigning a relative weight to each of the possible gametes $\vec{x}$ in n-dimensional space, *i.e.* $P = P(\vec{x})$ is the probability to find the gamete $\vec{x}$ in that meadow.

For each pair of meadows characterised by probability distributions $P = P(\vec{x})$ and $Q = Q(\vec{x})$ we calculate the normalised Jensen-Shannon divergence

$$JSD(P\|Q) \equiv \frac{H(\pi_A P + \pi_B Q) - \pi_A H(P) - \pi_B H(Q)}{-\pi_A \ln \pi_A - \pi_B \ln \pi_B}, \qquad (1)$$

with $\pi_{A,B} = n_{A,B}/(n_A + n_B)$, n_i the sample size of meadow i and $H(F) = -\sum_{\vec{x}} F(\vec{x}) \ln F(\vec{x})$ the Shannon index or entropy of distribution F.

The information-theoretic meaning of *JSD* is discussed in detail in [5, 12, 21]. We stress that *JSD* is a measure of difference between P and Q that takes into account the information on the gametes which are shared by both populations as well as the ones which are exclusive to one of them. This second capability is not present in other information-theoretic distances, such as the Kullback-Leibler divergence [12].

In the *Additional file 1*, we illustrate in detail the relationships between Eq. (1) and other classical measures to calculate genetic divergence. We want to stress that Eq. (1) is independent of any evolutionary assumption, *i.e.* it just calculates the punctual correlations within the meadows' attribute probability distributions. Nevertheless it is possible to relax and extend such a measure to include mutation effects, just considering the computation of the probability distribution in an n-dimensional sphere of a given radius, surrounding the point $\vec{x}$. Varying such a radius, it is then possible to coarse-grain the system at different resolutions.

JSD distances are calculated among all pairs of meadows. Smaller distance implies stronger genetic identity among the meadows. By selecting a particular threshold value for the distance we can represent the genetic flow as a network [5, 13] in which meadows with smaller *JSD* distance appear linked. As we increase the threshold we observe how the different linked clusters of populations become larger and merge.

A convenient threshold to use is the percolation threshold [13], at which a connected path across the whole geographic area first appears. The network fragments for threshold values below the percolation threshold, while the genetic flow spanning the network remains robust above it. At this point different clusters, and subclusters, representing sets of meadows with important internal gene flow, and gene paths among them, can be identified.

In Figure 1 we show the network at the percolation threshold, when the major components in the network connect. As we can see the purely topological genetic flow network accurately reflects the geographical locations to which the different meadows belong. There are well connected clusters representing Senegal, Mauritania, Canaries and Madeira, then we have the other large cluster spanning within the Mediterranean meadows. Between those two big clusters we find the Atlantic Iberian meadows and the Moroccan meadows.

While this representation is interesting to understand the effectiveness of *JSD* as a genetic divergence measure, it also confirms the findings of [11] regarding the main evolutionary scenario for CN. To see that we plot in Figure 2 the connected clusters that form when increasing the distance threshold. We interpret that the first populations to merge when the genetic distance threshold is raised from zero are the ones that differentiated

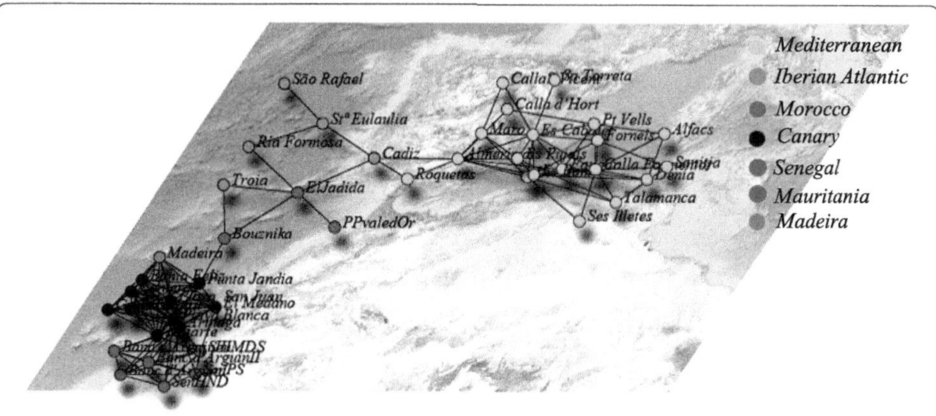

Figure 1 Genetic flow network for *Cymodocea nodosa*. Genetic flow network for *Cymodocea nodosa* meadows at the percolation threshold, obtained via the JSD measure applied to raw gamete data from the sampled meadows (the genetically very distant and disconnected Greek populations are not shown). Different colors indicate the different meadow origins. The network is displayed via a spring embedding algorithm, i.e. it does not contain geographical information. Nevertheless the genetic clusters well trace the different geographical origins, as it is possible to see by comparison with the approximately overlayed map displayed below.

more recently. Then small genetic divergences correspond to the most recent time of divergence. In our analysis we observe that the first meadows to be connected are the ones South of the Canaries, while the ones that are more distant are the ones in Greece (those do not appear in the figure, since they are not connected until higher distance thresholds), with a range of intermediate distances in between. Then we can infer an evolutionary dynamics that starts in the Greek Sea, goes to the main Mediterranean basin and then spreads in the Atlantic. This coincides with the ancient history of habitat colonization by this species inferred in [11], which proposes that the species originated in the eastern Mediterranean by divergence from its close relative in the Indian Ocean/Red Sea and colonized the western Mediterranean and Atlantic by spreading westwards. Moreover the fact that Senegal and Mauritania cluster strongly with the Canaries and Madeira, in respect to the weak clustering of the Canaries with Morocco and the Iberian Atlantic, is in agreement with the evolutionary scenario previously suggested on the basis of biogeographical information. These findings are also in agreement with the possible extinction of meadows in Morocco and Iberia during the last glacial maximum, that was accompanied by a drop in sea surface temperatures below the range at which CN commonly occurs, and by a drop of sea level that changed coastline morphology [22], that would have been followed by colonization of this region by an admixture of Atlantic and Mediterranean genetic types [11].

Inferring genetic flow directionality

The second part of the analysis is about inferring the directionality of the detected gene flows. The main question we pose is: 'is it possible to understand which is the source and which the sink in a given genetic channel?'. To understand this, we further develop the technique introduced in [5] based on geographical segregation [6]. We say that a population is segregated when it contains elements (gametes in our case, but this could equally be applied to alleles, as shown in the *Additional file 1*) quite exclusive and distinct from the rest of populations, and elements common in other populations are not so abundant

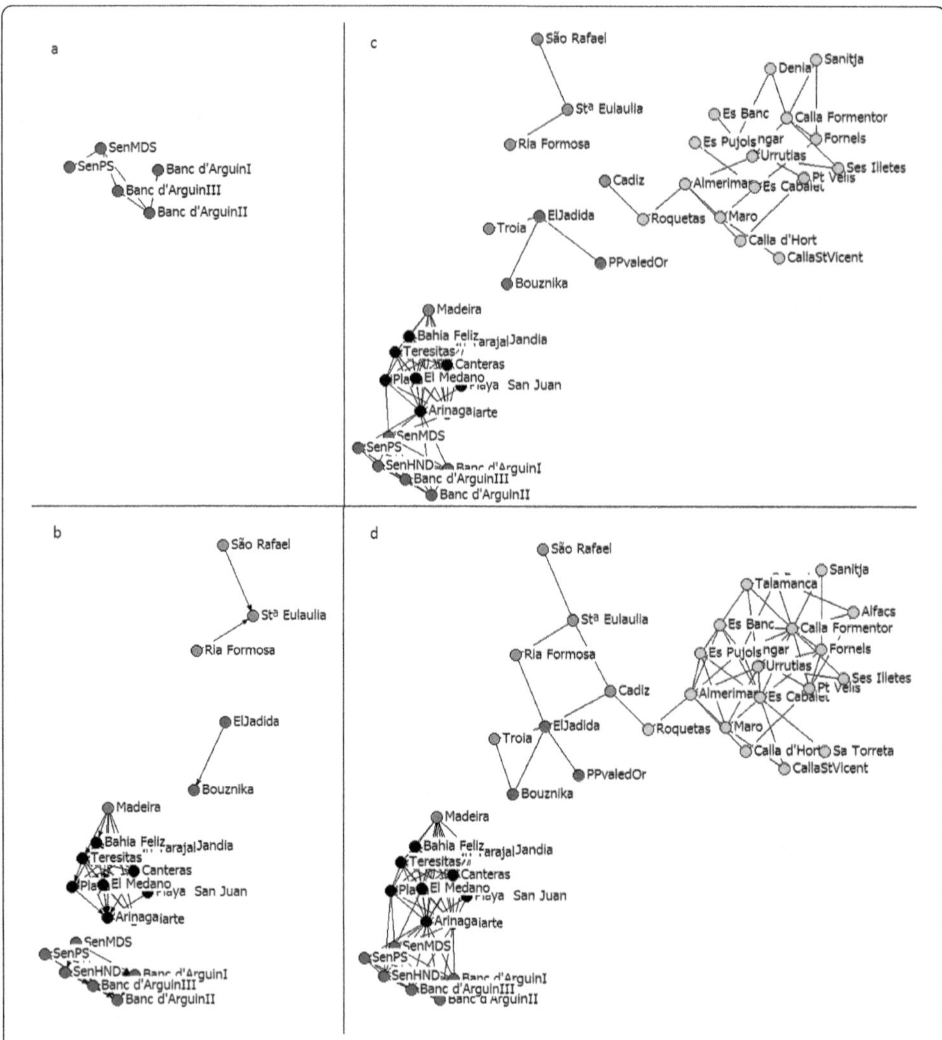

Figure 2 Genetic flow network for *Cymodocea nodosa* at growing values of the distance threshold. Clusters that appear when linking populations with a JSD distance smaller than a distance threshold T, for increasing values of T approaching from below the percolation threshold. (**a**) $T = 0.57$. (**b**) $T = 0.89$. (**c**) $T = 0.95$. (**d**) $T = 0.97$, just below the percolation threshold. The cluster colors are the same as in Figure 1.

here. The main reasoning resides on the observation that a population which is initially segregated will not maintain its character if it is open to receive gametes from other different ones. It will remain segregated only if there is no gene exchange or if there is some but the population acts as a source.

In terms of frequency distributions, these are peaked on particular elements in segregated populations, whereas distributions are more unstructured in those acting as sinks receiving genes from different sources. Between any pair of populations among which a genetic flow has been detected (as described in the previous section, this occurs when their genetic distance is smaller than the given percolation threshold), a directionality index I_{PQ} is defined between meadows characterized by gamete distributions P and Q. It takes into account the different segregation state of the pairs of populations by means of the respective Shannon information indices, corrected for their different sizes and number of common elements.

To be more precise, given the two populations characterized by P and Q let us denote by D_P the set of different gametes present in the first population, D_Q the ones present in the second, $X = D_P \cup D_Q$ the total set between both populations, and $J = D_P \cap D_Q$ the set of common gametes (that we assume to be non-empty). We denote by μ_P the fraction between the number of gametes common to both populations with respect to the total number of gametes in the first one, and analogously we define μ_Q as the fraction of common gametes between both populations with respect to the total number of gametes in the second one. We have $0 < \mu_{P,Q} \leq 1$ and if μ_P or μ_Q is close to one, it means that the shared alleles are the dominant part of the corresponding population. Let us denote by $P_J = P_J(\vec{x})$, with $\vec{x} \in J$, the frequency distribution of the alleles in the first population, normalized to unity when summing over all the common alleles (the J set), and analogously we define $Q_J = Q_J(\vec{x})$, with $\vec{x} \in J$.

With these definitions, the directionality index is defined as [5]:

$$I_{PQ} \equiv -\operatorname{sign}\left[\frac{H(P_J)}{\mu_P} - \frac{H(Q_J)}{\mu_Q}\right], \tag{2}$$

where H is the Shannon index of the distributions, as defined in the previous subsection.

If $I_{PQ} = 1$ we can infer a direction of the genetic flow from the first to the second population, whereas $I_{PQ} = -1$ indicates the reverse flow. The idea is that the net flow of gametes is from the less entropic (*i.e.*, less diverse, more segregated) populations towards the more entropic, properly adjusting for the different sizes and fraction of common alleles. Very diverse populations cannot be sources of only very specific gametes, and they are more likely to be sinks, whereas the reverse will be true for segregated populations. Large width of gamete distributions may be an indicator of large diversity, but it is better to use the Shannon information as a more robust indicator of diversity. For more information about our directionality indicator we refer to [5].

Significance test of the detected directions

The idea of tracing the directionality of gene flow via a measure of geographical segregation turns out to be a delicate point. First of all this method is applicable in case there are traces of segregation in the subset of shared gametes of the considered meadow. After that we have to understand if the difference in the segregation indexes between the two meadows in consideration is large enough to let us infer a direction for the genetic flow.

To address these points first we should remember that the data set used to infer directionality is not the whole set of gametes, as used for network construction, but just those gametes that are shared by the two samples in consideration. A convenient way to quantify the number of shared gametes is by means of the proportion μ_P of shared gametes between populations characterized by distributions P and Q, with respect to the total number of gametes in the population characterized by P. We emphasize that μ_P is not only a property of population P, but of the pair of populations being compared. This proportion should be non-negligible in order to infer reliable conclusions for the flow directionality.

Second, to understand if the detected directionality I_{PQ} between two meadows of size n_1 and n_2 is a sign of segregation or it is a random effect, we first measure the magnitude for the directionality index I_{PQ} and then we measure it again after having shuffled the sample. To shuffle the sample we consider two meadows of size n_1 and n_2 and we fill them randomly with the genets extracted from the original two meadows. We repeat this operation

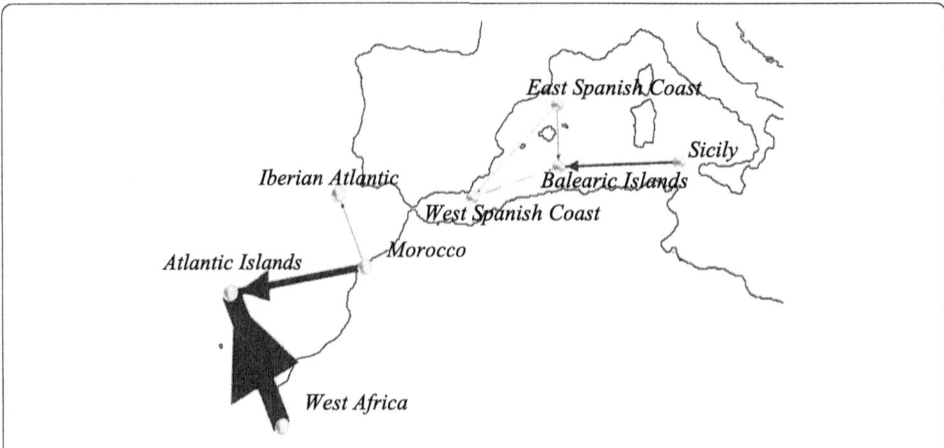

Figure 3 Gene flow directionality network. Gene flow directionality network for *Cymodocea nodosa* genetic flow network evaluated in the gamete space. Nodes represent populations of meadows grouped together by their geographical attributes. Arrows are directional genetic flows, their width is proportional to the value of R, quantifying the significance of the inferred directionality.

1,000 times, so to obtain an estimation of the distribution for the randomised directionality index, which turns out to be Gaussian. From there one gets the average randomised directionality index I^R_{PQ} and its standard deviation σ_R.

The ratio $R = |I_{PQ} - I^R_{PQ}|/\sigma_R$ gives us the number of standard deviations (sd) the measured segregation index is far from the expected one in a random situation. For instance obtaining a value of R larger than 2.58 has a probability $p < 0.01$ of being explained by randomness.

Results

To have a better statistical sample, we group the elements of the clusters shown in Figure 1 into single populations. Since we are interested in retrieving the directionalities of gene flow, we cluster the meadows according to their geographical origin. Nevertheless such a clustering is not significatively different from the one that would be obtained via a technique based, for example, on modularity minimization [23].

In Figure 3 we show the results for the directional analysis. The widths of the arrows are proportional to R, quantifying the significance of the relationship. The genetic flow directionality traces are found to be significant in terms of R and μ (see Table 1) from the Spanish Coast and Sicily to the Balearic Islands, from the African coast to the Canary Islands and Madeira, from the East (Mediterranean) Spanish Coast to the West (Mediterranean) Spanish Coast and from Morocco to the Iberian Atlantic. These results agree with expectations from inferences based on allele presence/absence by [11] and [24].

These results tell us that the method correctly identifies phenomena of geographical segregation. This phenomenon is typical for islands, where it is not easy for species to genetically mix with far away populations. Then we can see that all the islands in the studied sample are identified as sinks of the genetic flow. Also the main east toward west spread trend has been identified by this methodology.

In contrast with the recent events of gene flow, this method is not efficacious to trace the directionality from the Mediterranean basin to the Atlantic, a much more ancient process that took place before all the glacial range shifts and post-glacial recolonization migra-

Table 1 Results of the randomization test for the directionality analysis

Link P-Q	R	μ_P	μ_Q
WA-AI	442.48	0.26	0.01
MO-AI	159.16	0.03	0.004
SI-BI	65.45	0.02	0.008
ESC-BI	15.64	0.17	0.06
SI-BI	65.45	0.02	0.008
MO-IA	13.61	0.07	0.03
ESC-WSC	4.92	0.09	0.07
WSC-BI	4.4	0.24	0.13

Only the significant ($p < 0.01$) directionalities are listed. In the first column the population pairs, in the second column the value of R calculated over 1000 replicas, in the third column μ_P, in the fourth column μ_Q. The acronyms stand for: WA: West African coast, AI: Atlantic islands, MO: Morocco, SI: Sicily, BI: Balearic Islands, ESC: East Spanish coast, IA: Iberian Atlantic, WSC: West Spanish coast.

tions, since there is no trace of segregation in that case. Directionality of the genetic flow, at such ancient scales, cannot be spotted with this technique.

Discussion

The directional network resulting from this analysis is in agreement with diverse and converging information on historical fluctuation of species ranges along the Mediterranean-Atlantic transition zone, associated to paleoclimatic events, putative recolonization pathways and secondary contact zones inferred from biogeographic analysis on various taxa, and expectation derived from oceanographic modeling.

The directed network (Figure 3) reveals a clear trend of gene flow of South-Western preferential migration pathways from the Western and central Mediterranean meadows towards the Almeria-Oran front (an oceanographic feature east of the Gibraltar strait). This coincides with the gene flow paths that were previously hypothesized on the basis of many private alleles found in the Atlantic that do not enter this transition zone, whereas Mediterranean polymorphism was much more shared with populations from the transition zones [11]. Modeled Lagrangian dispersal trajectories across the East-West Mediterranean divide [25]) from March to June, the fruit dispersal season for *Posidonia oceanica* (which flowers in the winter), support a main trend of particle exchange toward West in the Mediterranean [26]. This was associated to a lack of dispersal expected toward Sicily and the Eastern part of the Mediterranean, as predicted from the prevailing current directions. Despite having a different reproductive season (flowering in spring, seeds produced in summer) and seeds that develop buried in the sediment and are not expected to disperse with currents, CN is likely to disperse via reproductive plant fragments, drifting along these same current directions, in agreement with the inferences of the present directionality flow network analysis, from Sicily westwards.

Besides this direction of the Mediterranean flow toward the Almeria-Oran populations, a second major result with the presented methodology is the confirmed lack of input of the Atlantic into the Mediterranean. Preferential pathways of migration within the Atlantic show strong directionality of flow from Western Africa and Morocco toward the Canary Islands, and from Morocco toward Iberian Atlantic populations of the transition zone, with no sign of any entrance of Atlantic flow into the Mediterranean.

In summary, the directed network built here confirms a dominant direction of fluxes with an East-West direction in the Mediterranean from Sicily and Spain toward South

Western meadows and Almeria-Oran Front, and the lack of mirror exchange from the Atlantic toward the Mediterranean.

A phenomenon that can confound some of our techniques is that of a genetic bottleneck. This consists of a large reduction of population size, which leads also to a much decreased diversity because of genetic drift [27]. This happens for example if only a few individuals colonize a new island (founder effect) and expand there. The recovered new population has small diversity, with the potential to be identified as a 'source' although in fact it has been the receiver of the gene flow. Fortunately this is not a problem because our methodology does not compute the directionality index for all pairs of populations, but only among those with a strong similarity, as measured by the JSD distance. Our measure of genetic flow will give a very small value in the case mentioned above. In addition, even if a recent and strong bottleneck (*i.e.* contemporary to the sampling) or a recent re-expansion post-bottleneck may transitorily induce 'source-like' characteristics in the distributions, such distributions would display a characteristic lack of polymorphism in the first case, and a typical genetic signature on the distribution of polymorphism and divergence in the latter that will be easily detected by available population genetics tools [28, 29]. A careful examination of data should thus allow discarding such confounding factor or pointing it as a possible alternative explanation of directionally detected with our methods.

We stress that the data treatment presented in this paper is independent of evolutionary assumptions, but that it can be easily extended to include mutation. This can be done, as we already point out, coarse-graining the probability space in function of a simple parameter indicating the resolution with which we distinguish different gametes. Then varying this parameter it is possible to study the evolutionary paths at different time windows, but further research in this direction is needed to better implement these points.

While the present research is about genetic flow dynamics, the whole information flow/directionality index method has a wider range of application, from metapopulation systems to social dynamics and more in general it can be relevant whenever a given population can be represented by vectors of attributes in a symbolic space.

A set of Matlab routines implementing the network analysis described here can be found in [30].

Competing interests

The authors declare that they have no competing interests.

Authors' contributions

APM developed the methodology and performed the analyses. SAH and EAS provided the data and the biological interpretations. VME and EHG contributed to the methods and to the analyses. All authors participated in the writing of the paper.

Author details

[1]Centre for Advanced Spatial Analysis, University College of London, London, UK. [2]Département Étude des Ecosystèmes Profonds-DEEP, Laboratoire Environnement Profond-LEP, Institut Français de Recherche pour l'Exploitation de la MER, Centre de Brest, France. [3]IFISC (CSIC-UIB), Instituto de Física Interdisciplinar y Sistemas Complejos, Consejo Superior de Investigaciones Científicas - Universitat de les Illes Balears, Palma de Mallorca, Spain. [4]CCMAR, CIMAR-Laboratório Associado, Universidade do Algarve, Gambelas, Faro, 8005-139, Portugal.

Acknowledgements

We thank Filipe Alberto for supplying the data, and discussing the results. Supported by Ministerio de Economía y Competitividad (Spain) and Fondo Europeo de Desarrollo Regional through projects FISICOS (FIS2007-60327) and MODASS (FIS2011-24785). SAH acknowledges support from the ANR Clonix project (ANR-11-BSV7-007). Publication fee has been covered partially by the CSIC Open Access Publication Support Initiative through its Unit of Information Resources for Research (URICI).

References

1. Drossel B (2001) Biological evolution and statistical physics. Adv Phys 50(2):209-295
2. Travis J, Park K (2004) Spatial structure and the control of invasive alien species. Anim Conserv 7:321-330
3. Haydon D, Cleaveland S, Taylor L, Laurenson M (2002) Identifying reservoirs of infection: a conceptual and practical challenge. Emerg Infect Dis 8:1468-1473
4. Vespignani A (2012) Modelling dynamical processes in complex socio-technical systems. Nat Phys 8:32-39
5. Masucci AP, Kalampokis A, Eguíluz VM, Hernández-García E (2011) Extracting directed information flow networks: an application to genetics and semantics. Phys Rev E 83:026103
6. Duncan OD, Duncan B (1955) A methodological analysis of segregation indexes. Am Sociol Rev 20(2):210-217
7. Messier W, Li S, Stewart C (1996) The birth of microsatellites. Nature 381(6582):483
8. Beerli P, Felsenstein J (1999) Maximum-likelihood estimation of migration rates and effective population numbers in two populations using a coalescent approach. Genetics 152(2):763-773
9. Guillemaud T, Beaumont M, Ciosi M, Cornuet J, Estoup A (2010) Inferring introduction routes of invasive species using approximate Bayesian computation on microsatellite data. Heredity 104:88-99
10. Csilléry K, Blum MG, Gaggiotti OE, François O (2010) Approximate Bayesian Computation (ABC) in practice. Trends Ecol Evol 25(7):410-418
11. Alberto F, Massa S, Manent P, Diaz-Almela E, Arnaud-Haond S, Duarte CM, Serrao EA (2008) Genetic differentiation and secondary contact zone in the seagrass Cymodocea nodosa across the Mediterranean-Atlantic transition region. J Biogeogr 35(7):1279-1294
12. Lin J (1991) Divergence measures based on the Shannon entropy. IEEE Trans Inf Theory 37(1):145-151
13. Rozenfeld AF, Arnaud-Haond S, Hernández-García E, Eguíluz VM, Serrão EA, Duarte CM (2008) Network analysis identifies weak and strong links in a metapopulation system. Proc Natl Acad Sci USA 105(48):18824-18829
14. Goldstein DB, Linares AR, Cavallisforza L, Feldman M (1995) An evaluation of genetic distances for use with microsatellite loci. Genetics 139(1):463-471
15. Nei M (1972) Genetic distance between populations. Am Nat 106(949):283-292
16. Goldstein DB, Linares AR, Cavallisforza L, Feldman M (1995) Genetic absolute dating based on microsatellites and the origin of modern humans. Proc Natl Acad Sci USA 92(15):6723-6727
17. Arnaud-Haond S, Duarte CM, Alberto F, Serrão EA (2007) Standardizing methods to address clonality in population studies. Mol Ecol 16(24):5115-5139
18. Dyer R, Nason J (2004) Population graphs: the graph theoretic shape of genetic structure. Mol Ecol 13(7):1713-1727
19. Dale M, Fortin MJ (2010) From graphs to spatial graphs. Annu Rev Ecol Evol Syst 41:21-38
20. Fortuna MA, Albaladejo RG, Fernandez L, Aparicio A, Bascompte J (2009) Networks of spatial genetic variation across species. Proc Natl Acad Sci USA 106(45):19044-19049
21. Grosse I, Bernaola-Galvan P, Carpena P, Roman-Roldan R, Oliver J, Stanley H (2002) Analysis of symbolic sequences using the Jensen-Shannon divergence. Phys Rev E 65:041905
22. Thiede J (1978) A glacial Mediterranean. Nature 276:680-683
23. Newman M (2006) Modularity and community structure in networks. Proc Natl Acad Sci USA 103(23):8577-8582
24. Alberto F, Arnaud-Haond S, Duarte C, Serrão E (2006) Genetic diversity of a clonal angiosperm near its range limit: the case of *Cymodocea nodosa* in the Canary Islands. Mar Ecol Prog Ser 309:117-129
25. Pinardi N, Allen I, Demirov E, De Mey P, Korres G, Lascaratos A, Le Traon P, Maillard C, Manzella G, Tziavos C (2003) The Mediterranean ocean forecasting system: first phase of implementation (1998-2001). Ann Geophys 21(1):3-20
26. Serra IA, Innocenti AM, Di Maida G, Calvo S, Migliaccio M, Zambianchi E, Pizzigalli C, Arnaud-Haond S, Duarte CM, Serrao EA, Procaccini G (2010) Genetic structure in the Mediterranean seagrass Posidonia oceanica: disentangling past vicariance events from contemporary patterns of gene flow. Mol Ecol 19(3):557-568
27. Ewens W (2004) Mathematical population genetics I. Theoretical introduction. Interdisciplinary applied mathematics. Springer, Berlin
28. Luikart G, Cornuet JM (1998) Empirical evaluation of a test for identifying recently bottlenecked populations from allele frequency data. Conserv Biol 12:228-237
29. Luikart G, Allendorf F, Cornuet JM, Sherwin W (1998) Distortion of allele frequency distributions provides a test for recent population bottlenecks. J Heredity 89(3):238-247
30. Masucci AP (2012) Matlab code for genetic flow analysis. http://sites.google.com/site/apmasucci/home/genetic_flow. Accessed 16 November 2012

3

Probing crowd density through smartphones in city-scale mass gatherings

Martin Wirz[1*], Tobias Franke[2], Daniel Roggen[1], Eve Mitleton-Kelly[3], Paul Lukowicz[2] and Gerhard Tröster[1]

*Correspondence: martin.wirz@ife.ee.ethz.ch
[1]Wearable Computing Laboratory, ETH Zürich, Zürich, Switzerland
Full list of author information is available at the end of the article

Abstract

City-scale mass gatherings attract hundreds of thousands of pedestrians. These pedestrians need to be monitored constantly to detect critical crowd situations at an early stage and to mitigate the risk that situations evolve towards dangerous incidents. Hereby, the crowd density is an important characteristic to assess the criticality of crowd situations.

In this work, we consider location-aware smartphones for monitoring crowds during mass gatherings as an alternative to established video-based solutions. We follow a participatory sensing approach in which pedestrians share their locations on a voluntary basis. As participation is voluntarily, we can assume that only a fraction of all pedestrians shares location information. This raises a challenge when concluding about the crowd density. We present a methodology to infer the crowd density even if only a limited set of pedestrians share their locations. Our methodology is based on the assumption that the walking speed of pedestrians depends on the crowd density. By modeling this behavior, we can infer a crowd density estimation.

We evaluate our methodology with a real-world data set collected during the Lord Mayor's Show 2011 in London. This festival attracts around half a million spectators and we obtained the locations of 828 pedestrians. With this data set, we first verify that the walking speed of pedestrians depends on the crowd density. In particular, we identify a crowd density-dependent upper limit speed with which pedestrians move through urban spaces. We then evaluate the accuracy of our methodology by comparing our crowd density estimates to ground truth information obtained from video cameras used by the authorities. We achieve an average calibration error of 0.36 m^{-2} and confirm the appropriateness of our model. With a discussion of the limitations of our methodology, we identify the area of application and conclude that smartphones are a promising tool for crowd monitoring.

Keywords: crowd sensing; pedestrian behavior; crowd density estimation; participatory sensing; smartphone

1 Introduction

City-scale mass gatherings attract hundreds of thousands of attendees. On 25 April 2011, an estimated number of 1.2 million spectators congregated in London for the wedding of Prince William and Catherine Middleton [1]. Around 2 million people gathered on 25 May 2010 in Buenos Aires to attend several concerts and street art parades celebrating the Bicentennial of the May Revolution [2]. Up to 2 million people got together in Madrid, Spain for a parade celebrating the success of the Spanish national football team winning the 2010 FIFA World Cup [3]. Such events with many visitors but with a restricted area and complex architectural configurations like narrowings and intersections bear the risk of dangerous crowd incidents [4, 5]. It is therefore a top priority for organizers of such events to maintain a high level of safety and to minimize the risk of crowd incidents. Hereby, guidelines on planning help minimize the risk by deploying adequate safety measures [6, 7]. The raise of pedestrian simulation tools has enabled the identification of critical locations where dangerous crowd behaviors may emerge [8, 9]. Simulation tools help to design and proactively deploy crowd control mechanisms before mass gatherings to mitigate the risk of dangerous crowd incidents. However, despite a proper preparation, the behavior of the crowd during an event remains highly unpredictable [10, 11]. Hence, emerging critical crowd situations need to be detected at an early stage in order to mitigate the risk of a situation evolving towards a dangerous incident. Crowd density, *i.e.* the number of people per unit area, has been identified as one important measure to assess the criticality of a situation [12, 13] and there is a need to obtain this information during an event [14].

In our ongoing research effort, we want to turn pedestrians' smartphones into a reliable sensing tool for measuring the crowd density during city-wide mass gatherings. In a previous study [14], we introduced a participatory sensing system for crowd monitoring by tracking the location of attendees of mass gatherings via their smartphones. Attendees of such a mass gathering can download a smartphone App to record the user's location at regular intervals. This information is collected from all App users and used to infer the users' current spatial distribution. To motivate as many attendees as possible to download the App and share their locations, the App offers a set of features including an interactive festival program and maps of the venue as an incentive to all. Nevertheless, by following a participatory sensing approach, we expect only a fraction of all attendees to participate and hence, the location of only a limited set of pedestrians is known. Therefore, the explanatory power of the obtained distribution is limited as these numbers do not provide direct evidence of the actual crowd density.

In this work, we address this challenge and present a methodology to infer the crowd density by tracking the locations of a subset of all event attendees. Our methodology relies on a calibration approach that provides a relation between the distribution of App users and the crowd density. Hereby, we make use of the characteristic that pedestrians exhibit a distinct behavior which depends on the crowd density in the vicinity. By assessing the behavior of the App users and applying our model, we obtain a crowd density estimation. Evaluation of our approach is performed with a real-world data set collected during the Lord Mayor's Show 2011 in London, a festival attracting around half a million spectators. We use this data set to confirm the suitability of our methodology and evaluate the accuracy of our crowd density estimation by comparing our results to results from video footage obtained from CCTV cameras. We conclude our work by addressing the limitations of our methodology and identifying next steps.

2 Related work

This section discusses related work. Section 2.1 introduces crowd characteristics relevant to assess the criticality of a situation during mass gatherings. Section 2.2 compares technologies and methods to measure such crowd characteristics with a focus on crowd density.

Table 1 Chart of crowd density

Dynamics	Density [m^{-2}]	Behavior and risk
Standing	7.1	Critical crowd density for static crowds
Walking	0.43	Stream of pedestrians can maintain normal walking speed and avoid one another
	2	Walking speed is reduced
	3.57	Involuntary contact is experienced between people
	5.55	Potentially dangerous crowd forces begin to develop

Chart derived from the findings of Fruin [23] to assess the criticality of a crowd density. The density of a static crowd can exceed the density of a moving crowd before a critical values is reached.

2.1 Crowd characteristics to assess the criticality of a situation during mass gatherings

Various empirical studies have analyzed crowd behaviors during mass gatherings and identified critical, potentially dangerous situations: A focus in literature has been the investigation of human stampedes [15–19]. Stampedes often occur if people start to rush towards a common target. Congestions, or clogging, at narrowings and counter flow of pedestrians have been identified as critical situations in which stampedes may occur [20, 21]. Irregular pedestrian flow is an additional risk which may cause turbulent motions in a crowd [20]. *Johansson et al.* [22] identified the transition from smooth pedestrian flow to stop-and-go waves as a warning sign of a critical situation.

Based on such observations, researchers have identified different crowd characteristics that may indicate potentially critical situations. One of the most important crowd characteristic is the local crowd density. *Au et al.* [13] report that one of the key aspects in developing and maintaining a crowd safety system is to identify areas where crowds build up. Areas where people are likely to congregate need careful observation during an event to provide crowd safety. *Nicholson et al.* [12] state the need for accurate crowd density estimation to correctly asses the criticality of a situation. Crowd density is also observed by police forces during the management of mass gatherings. Table 1 shows a chart derived from the findings of Fruin [23] to assess the criticality of a situation of a situation during a mass gathering.

The local crowd density alone does not allow for a complete assessment of the criticality of a situation. In addition to crowd density, the intention or behavior of a crowd is required for a correct situational understanding. As an example, a high crowd density in a static crowd is less critical than a high crowd density exhibiting counter flow. This distinction is also evident in Table 1. A critical crowd density is reached at 5.55 m^{-2} for a moving crowd. A static crowd, however, can exceed this value before a critical density is reached. *Helbing et al.* [20] introduce a measure that incorporates this aspect. They call this measure *crowd pressure* which is given as the local velocity variance multiplied by the local crowd density. In their work, they identified that crowd pressure can be seen as an early warning sign for critical crowd situations. They identified an increased crowd pressure value right before dangerous crowd turbulence emerges.

2.2 Monitoring crowds

Nowadays, video-based crowd monitoring tools are widely deployed. *Gong et al.* [24] review the state-of-the-art of vision-based systems for crowd monitoring. They conclude that currently deployed systems suffer from poor scalability to crowded public spaces due to deployment complexity and manually judging the criticality of a situation from the footage. Further, manually monitoring multiple video streams simultaneously requires lots of training for a person. To overcome these limitations, police forces use helicopters to gain an instantaneous overview and men in the field to obtain detailed information [14].

Recent developments such as multi-camera networks to fuse information from multiple cameras and computer vision algorithms to automatically monitor crowds can mitigate these issues. *Jacques et al.* [25] review state-of-the-art techniques. Hereby, the authors differ between *object-based approaches* and *holistic approaches*. In object-based approaches, single individuals are detected and tracked individually. Relevant information is fused to analyze group behaviors. As an example, *Mehran et al.* [26] use the social-force model introduced by *Helbing et al.* [27] to infer crowd patterns from pedestrian tracks. Object-based approaches have been used by *Johanssȯn et al.* [22] investigate crowd behaviors during the Hajj in Makkah. *Steffen et al.* [28] presented approaches for inferring crowd densities and other crowd behaviors based on pedestrian trajectories.

Holistic approaches do not rely on tracking individuals but follow a top-down methodology in which the crowd is considered as a single entity. These approaches obtain coarser-level information such as crowd density, the flow of the crowd and crowd turbulence but no local, individual-specific information. As an example, *Krausz et al.* [19] developed an optical flow-based method for an automatic detection of dangerous motion behaviors including congestions during mass gatherings. They used their method to study video-footage recorded during the Love Parade disaster of 2010 in Duisburg, Germany where 21 visitors died in a stampede. By comparing the two approaches, the authors of [25] write that while object-level analysis tends to produce more accurate results, the identification of individuals is challenging in high density crowds due to clutter and occlusion which makes it difficult to obtain an accurate estimation of the crowd density.

Despite the recent advances of computer vision and pattern recognition techniques, until now, it remains challenging to obtain an automated global situation awareness during mass gatherings from video footage [24]. Using alternative technologies for observing crowds has recently found interest in the research community. Hereby, thanks to their proliferation, mobile devices like smartphones have increasingly been considered as a viable tool for monitoring the behavior of a crowd. These sensor-rich devices offer various ways to obtain information about the whereabouts of their users and hence allow for monitoring the physical behavior of them [29]. By combining information from many people, the behavior of a collective can be monitored.

To infer crowd conditions like those mentioned in Section 2.1, the location of attendees of a mass gathering is required. There are different approaches to determine a smartphone's location which can broadly be divided into two classes: *in-network localization* and *on-device localization*. The in-network location methods utilize the fact that at any given time, a smartphone is connected to a cell tower in a network. The information which device is connected to which cell tower is being stored centrally in a database and updated constantly. Since the location of each cell tower is known, a position estimation of the mobile devices can be obtained. For on-device localization methods, on the other hand, the location is derived directly on the users' smartphones by means of GPS positioning, WiFi-fingerprinting or other comparable approaches [30]. The in-network localization approaches have the advantage that the locations of all subscribed devices are routinely being logged by the network operators. Thus, location information from a large number of devices can be obtained without any user interaction (and permission). Popular methods for obtaining in-network location estimation include the recording of network bandwidth usage by detecting how much communication is going on in a particular location. *Calabrese et al.* [31] used this measure to investigate crowd dynamics in the city of Rome. The obtained measure is an aggregated number which is highly dependent on communication behavior and is not necessarily correlated to the actual number of individuals in that location. Another method to capture in-network location information is to use Call Data Records (CDRs) [32, 33]. A single CDR tuple is generated for every voice call and Short Message Service (SMS) transaction and consists of the sender and receiver numbers together with a timestamp and the cell ID the sender is situated in. This data is routinely being collected by every network operator for operational and billing purposes. While being useful for many studies, CDR-based location data faces several limitations. Firstly, CDRs are sparse in time because they are generated only when a transaction occurs and not at fixed periodic intervals. Hence, as long as no communication takes place, a smartphone's location is not being revealed. Secondly, they are coarse in space as they record locations at the granularity of a cell tower sector resulting in a location uncertainty of around 300 meters [34].

Methods to obtain on-device location information include GPS positioning and WiFi/GSM-fingerprinting [35]. With these approaches a location accuracy of up to 5 m can be obtained for GPS and around 20 m for WiFi-based positioning, respectively [36, 37]. A further advantage is that in contrast to in-network methods, location updates of a user can be recorded at regular intervals and not sporadically, event-driven as in the case of CDRs. This makes it much simpler to extract movement trajectories and is less situational-biased as opposed to if positions are only recorded if communication is going on. *Koshak et al.* [38] use GPS positioning to track pedestrian movements in a crowded area in Makkah. With a post-event evaluation, they identified critical zones by evaluating the crowd flow obtained from the collected GPS updates. There are other means to track the location of smartphone users and estimate a crowd density. As an example, *Versichele et al.* [39] present an approach where Bluetooth beacons are placed in the environment in order to track smartphone users during a city-wide festival. The authors conduct a post-event evaluation to understand the spatial commuting pattern of the festival visitors. While Bluetooth can provide a fine-grained position estimation, it requires beacons placed in the environment to observe pedestrians and hence, people are only tracked at specific locations around deployed beacons. The work of Bandini discusses in [40] opportunities and challenges of different technologies for tracking pedestrians in crowded situations. Table 2 summarizes our literature review by listing different technologies and methods the assessment of the crowd density.

We conclude that determining the location of a person on a mobile device using GPS or any other localization approach can provide a much more accurate location estimation compared to in-network approaches. On-device localization methods also have advantages over vision-based approaches as limitations such as occlusion or the limitations in low-light conditions are inexistent and that the whole venue space can easily be covered. However, on-device localization approaches face a big challenge: In contrast to in-network methods, the location is determined on a user's smartphone. To collect this information, a user has to deliberately share it. This requires a dedicated piece software running on the device.

Table 2 Overview of technologies and methods for crowd density assessment

Sensor modality	Class	Method	Reference
Video	Holistic	Optical flow	[19]
		Fractal dimension	[41]
		Pixel counting	[42]
		Machine learning	[43]
	Object-based	Trajectories	[22, 28]
		Supervised classification	[44]
		Unsupervised clustering	[45]
		Social force model	[26]
Smartphone	In-network	CDR	[32, 33]
		Network bandwidth usage	[31, 46]
	On-device	Trajectories	[14, 38]
	Other	Bluetooth beacons	[39, 47]

Overview of technologies and methods to automatically to assess crowd density. Different video-based approaches have been investigated, a selection of methods is given here. Thanks to the location-awareness of modern smartphones, they have increasingly been considered as an alternative platform for crowd monitoring.

We present in the next section methods to infer crowd characteristics from location information as provided by smartphones. Afterwards, in Section 3, we will address the implications on-device localization approaches face by requiring people to run a piece of software on the smartphones. We then present our method to mitigate the influence.

2.3 Measures of local crowd characteristics and their relation

2.3.1 Crowd density and speed of the crowd

The density and speed of a crowd are important local characteristics to assess the criticality of a crowd situation. In this section, we present methods to derive these measures from position information of pedestrians and discuss their relation.

Local crowd density *Johansson et al.* [22] introduce the notation of local density $\rho(\vec{r}, t)$. The local density is determined by considering the location $\vec{r}_i$ of all pedestrians i at time t and is given as:

$$\rho(\vec{r}, t) = \frac{1}{\pi R^2} \sum_i \exp[-\|\vec{r}_i(t) - \vec{r}\|^2 / R^2], \tag{1}$$

where R is the kernel radius and defines the smoothing around the location $\vec{r}$.

Local crowd speed The local crowd speed is calculated in an analogous fashion as the crowd density [22]. To obtain a crowd speed value v, a weighted mean function is applied on the speed measures of the pedestrians around the location $\vec{r}$. Hence, the local speed is given as

$$v(\vec{r}, t) = \frac{\sum_i v_i \exp[-\|\vec{r}_i(t) - \vec{r}\|^2 / R^2]}{\sum_i \exp[-\|\vec{r}_i(t) - \vec{r}\|^2 / R^2]}, \tag{2}$$

where v_i is the speed of pedestrian i at location $\vec{r}_i$ and time t. Again, R is the kernel radius.

2.3.2 The fundamental diagram: relation between crowd density and speed

The influence of the crowd density on the walking speed of pedestrians has been investigated intensively for the purpose of dimensioning pedestrian facilities with respect to

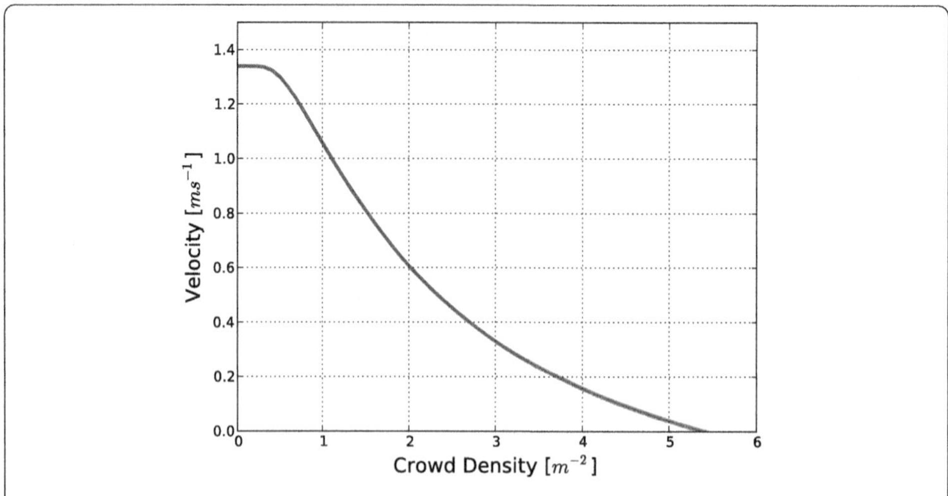

Figure 1 Weidmann's fundamental diagram. Plot of the density-speed relation according to Weidmann's fundamental diagram function of Equation 3 [48].

comfort and safety. For low crowd density situations, pedestrians will be able to maintain free flow speed and are not interrupted by their neighbors. However with increasing density, the speed will decrease as the influence of the neighboring pedestrians force speed adjustments. This is similar to the situations in vehicular traffic [49]. This speed-density relationship is termed *Fundamental Diagram.* Weidmann [48] was one of the first to look at this relationship for pedestrians and proposed an analytical description from empirical data. He proposed to describe the relation between local density and speed as follows:

$$v(\rho) = v_0 \left\{ 1 - \exp\left[-\gamma \left(\frac{1}{\rho} - \frac{1}{\rho_{\max}} \right) \right] \right\}, \tag{3}$$

where $v_0 = 1.34\ \mathrm{ms}^{-1}$ is the free speed at low densities (free flow), $\rho_{\max} = 5.4\ \mathrm{m}^{-2}$ the maximal pedestrian density from which onward movement is not possible anymore and $\gamma = 1.913\ \mathrm{m}^{-2}$ a fit parameter. Figure 1 shows a plot of the fundamental diagram given by Equation 3 and the listed parameters. The work of Weidmann stimulated successive contributions focusing on verifying and understanding this relationship. Several reports focus on the influence of various architectural configurations [50, 51], different crowd patterns [52] as well as demographics and cultural aspects [53, 54] on the fundamental diagram. Other works use the fundamental diagram to model pedestrian behaviors [55–57], investigate microscopic behavior patterns [58] and discuss and compare variations found across fundamental diagrams from different works [55, 59]. By comparing the results with other empirical data sets, it was found that the fundamental diagram is highly cultural dependent and needs to be adjusted for different venues. Weidmann's equation relies on fitting the fundamental diagram's analytical function to the recorded data set. Johansson addresses this issue in [55] and presents a generalized model. It relies on measurable parameters only and not on arbitrary fit parameters. Johannson showed that the model fits for different data sets. It can be tuned to follow existing models derived from various empirical data sets. Hence, the methods is believed to be sufficiently generic to be applied to various real-life situations. Johannson's method only relies on the maximum local crowd density and the free speed of pedestrians in unrestricted conditions. Both parameters are highly cultural and demographic specific and hence are expected to vary significantly for different events. Nevertheless, the parameters are measurable and can be determined based on values from literature, expert knowledge or empirical measurements [53, 60].

3 Considering App users as probes to infer crowd characteristics

3.1 Challenges in participatory sensing systems

Section 2.2 discusses the advantages of on-device localization methods for tracking pedestrians and identifies a major challenge: In contrary to in-network approaches, people have to deliberately share their position information. This requires a dedicated piece of software running on a user's smartphone. At first sight, such an approach may appear undesirable, as it can be assumed that the majority of people is not willing to install such an application and constantly send their current position to a remote server for various reasons, including privacy concerns and energy considerations. In the case of a mass gathering, this may imply that only a fraction of all attendees would run such an application and many would opt for not having their location tracked. However, in a preceding study, we verified that people are willing to share privacy-sensitive location information if they receive some benefits or if they realize that sharing such information is for their own good and safety [61]. Thus, we believe such an approach is still viable and promising by following a participatory sensing scheme where users are motivated to deliberately share their location information by providing them with incentives and making it very transparent what the data is being used for. In [14] we introduce the concept of a smartphone App that tracks pedestrian's movements and offers attendees of a mass gathering a set of features which users regard as useful to them, *e.g.* an interactive program guide, a map superimposing the location of points of interest, or background information about the mass gathering. During the event, users of the App can receive location-dependent messages from the police. Through the users' smartphones, the police can inform users situated in a particular area with targeted information on how to behave in case of an emergency.

3.2 Considering App users as probes

Even by deploying an attractive App to reach a large user base, we can only expect to receive position information from a fraction of all event attendees. Our concept to infer crowd conditions by only tracking a limited number of event attendees is to consider the App users who share data as so called *probes* and extrapolate crowd information based on their behaviors. This is comparable to approaches in zoology where scientists monitor schools of fish or packs of mammals by equipping some of the members with tracking sensors to monitor and study interaction patterns and conclude about the whole group's social behavior and habitats. Following such an approach imposes a set of assumptions which we will discuss in the following:

1. Unknown ratio of App users: The ratio of event attendees using the App at any given moment is unknown. While the absolute number of App users is known, it is usually not possible to obtain the exact number of event attendees at a certain point in time.
2. Spatial distribution of App users corresponds to the distribution of event: Throughout the whole event we consider a spatial distribution of App users that corresponds to the spatial distribution of event attendees. This means that among

the event attendees, the App users are equally distributed. This is important, as it helps us to discover trends. While it does not allow us to directly infer how many people resist at one location, we can identify that a certain percentage of users, and hence event attendees, situates themselves in a given area.

3. Natural behaviors and interaction patterns: App users behave naturally and interact with the environment and other persons in a similar way as non-App-users. Hence, the averaged behavior of the App users at one specific location corresponds to the averaged behavior of the event attendees in this area. By accepting this assumption, we can infer certain crowd characteristics at a given location even if not every person is being tracked. We simply infer the behavior by considering the behavior of the App users. This is possible because pedestrians in crowds are likely to mimic the behavior of the neighboring pedestrians, *e.g.* by adjusting their walking speed and direction [62, 63]. By looking at a single individual, this assumption may not hold as a person may always decide independently on their behavior, *e.g.* stand still, walk in another direction, *etc.* However, by averaging over the App users, we assume that the averaged App user behavior corresponds to that of the crowd at a given location.

The more pedestrians participate and share their location, the more reliable we can conclude about occurring crowd characteristics. However, the obtained App user distribution does not reflect the actual crowd density. In the following section, we briefly cover the data collection platform and present the data set used for evaluation. Afterwards, we verify the assumptions introduced in this section and focus on the density-speed relation in our data set. Based on the obtained findings, in Section 5.6 we present our methodology to automatically infer a crowd density estimation from the collected position data and evaluate it against ground truth information obtained from video footage.

4 Data collection framework and data set

4.1 CoenoSense data collection framework

To collect location updates from pedestrians, we developed a generic App for mobile devices which can be tailored to a specific mass gathering and provides the users with event-related information and features. These features are designed to be attractive and useful during the event to reach a large user base. While a user's smartphone is running the App, the current location of the device is sampled at 1 Hz using the integrated GPS sensor. Such a high sampling rate was chosen to capture as much of the motion dynamics as possible. Besides the user's current location, the recorded GPS information also reveals the current velocity and heading direction of a user. This information is logged too. The recorded data is periodically sent a server running the *CoenoSense* framework. *CoenoSense* is a data collection backend infrastructure to collect and store arbitrary context information received from potentially thousands of mobile devices simultaneously. It allows for real-time processing of the collected data.

To ensure a user's privacy, data is sent anonymously and our App offers users full control over data sharing and data recording. It can be disabled by the user at any time.

4.2 Data set

We deployed the App and the *CoenoSense* platform during the Lord Mayor's Show 2011 which took place in London on November the 12th between 11 am and 6 pm. The Lord Mayor's Show is a street parade in the City of London, the historic core of London and the present financial centre. The App offers a festival program, a map indicating points of interest and additional background information about the event. In collaboration with the event organizers, we event's official iPhone App and distributed it for free. It was advertised on the Lord Mayor's Show website and available through Apple's iTunes App store.

GPS location updates were collected between 00:01 on November 12th and 23:59 the same day and only if a user was in a specific geographical area around the venue the event takes place.

Within the collaboration with the event organizers and police forces, we obtained access to the CCTV video footage recorded during the Lord Mayor's Show. These are the same video recordings as used by the police to monitor the event. We consider this footage as ground truth information and is used in the following sections to verify our assumptions and evaluate our methods. We used video footage from four cameras placed at different locations. These locations have been identified by the police as being critical with respect to occurring crowd behaviors. For each camera, we defined an area of approximately 10 m^2 within which the crowd density is being extracted.

5 Empirical findings

In this section, we report on various spatio-temporal behavior properties that can be discovered in our data set. We start by investigating general statistics and put a special focus on aspects which help to support the assumptions stated in Section 3.2. Afterwards, we focus on the density-velocity relation.

5.1 Spatio-temporal distribution of App users

We collected a total of 3,903,425 location updates from 828 different users. During the parade, location updates from up to 244 users were received simultaneously, at any one time. On average, 4,719 location updates were recorded per user. This corresponds to a running time of 78.65 minutes. A few users shared more than 10,000 samples which requires them to run the application for more than 2.7 hours. Figure 2 shows this by illustrating the distribution of time the application was running for each user. To understand the temporal usage pattern, Figure 3 shows the number of active users throughout the event. The axis of abscissae represents the time of the day. The axis of ordinate indicates the number of active users that share location updates at each point in time. Periods in which important event-related activities took place are indicated with a colored background. The first procession happens between 11:00 and 12:30 (Interval (a)). After a break, the second procession takes place between 13:00 and 14:30 (Interval (b)). Before the end of the event, a firework display takes place between 17:00 and about 17:30 (Interval (c)). Figure 4 shows the spatial usage pattern. Superimposed is a heat map representation of the spatial distribution of the collected data samples throughout the whole event. The heatmap visualizes the density of the reported location updates. The more data has been collected at a location, the 'hotter' (*i.e.* more yellow) it is colored. From this plot we can deduce that data collection is not uniform across space but concentrated to specific areas. These areas correspond to the locations in which event-related activities took place. However, in this plot, temporal information is lost. It does not allow to distinguish whether there is a high concentration of pedestrians for a short time or a few users stationary for a long time. To better understand spatio-temporal dynamics, Figure 5 shows the heat maps of four different time intervals. Hereby, Figure 5(a) shows the distribution of reported locations during the first procession (Interval (a)), Figure 5(b) during the second procession (Interval (b)) and Figure 5(c)

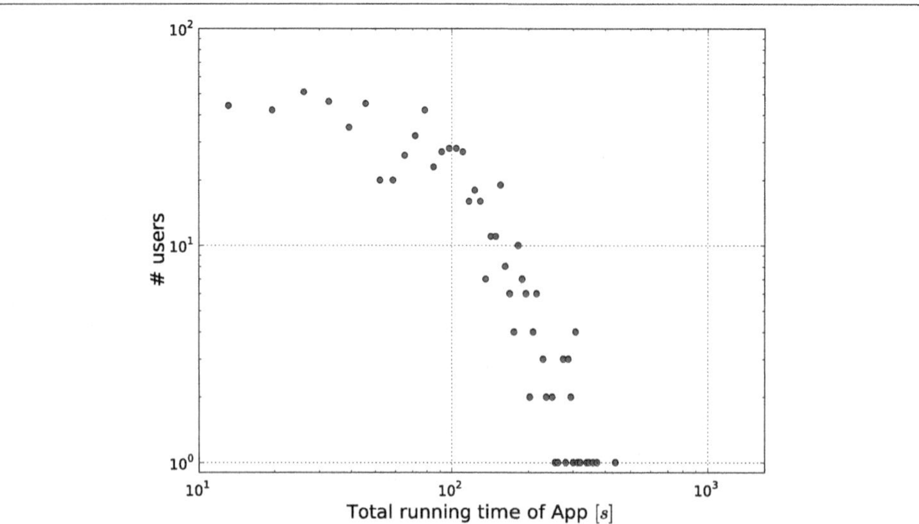

Figure 2 Distribution of time the application was running for each user. The distribution of time the application was running for each user. During the parade, location updates from up to 244 users were received simultaneously, at any one time. On average, 4,719 location updates were recorded per user. This corresponds to a running time of 78.65 minutes. A few users shared more than 10,000 samples which requires them to run the application for more than 2.7 hours.

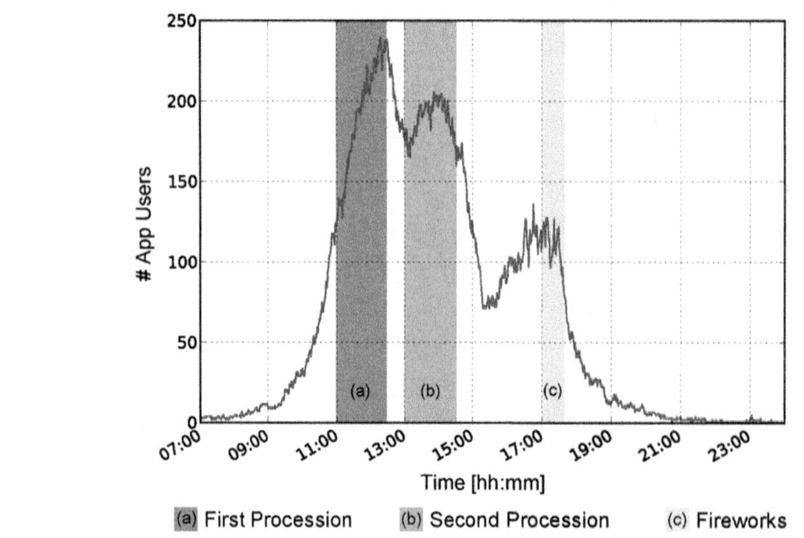

Figure 3 App users over time. Number of App users during the Lord Mayor's Show 2011. Colored intervals represent event-related activities. The first procession takes place between 11:00 and 12:30 (Interval **(a)**). The second procession takes place between 13:00 and 14:30 (Interval **(b)**). The firework display takes place between 17:00 and 17:30 (Interval **(c)**). About the event: A new Lord Mayor of the City of London is appointed every year and this public parade is organized to celebrate his inauguration. The Lord Mayor participates in a procession from the City of London to the Royal Courts of Justice in the City of Westminster. As in the Middle Ages, he is accompanied by military displays, marching bands, acrobats, dancers, displays of pomp and charity and symbols of London's ancient strength and resolve. The annual one-day event attracts about half a million spectators each year and is one of the City's longest established and best known annual events dating back to 1535. The event starts at 11:00 and the processional route goes from the Mansion House via Bank, St. Paul's Cathedral and Fleet Street to the Aldwych; the tail of the procession will reach the Royal Courts at about 12.30. There is a short break during the ceremony, then the whole procession sets off again at 13:00 to take the new Lord Mayor back to Mansion House. The procession finally ends at about 14:30 when the last floats reach the City.

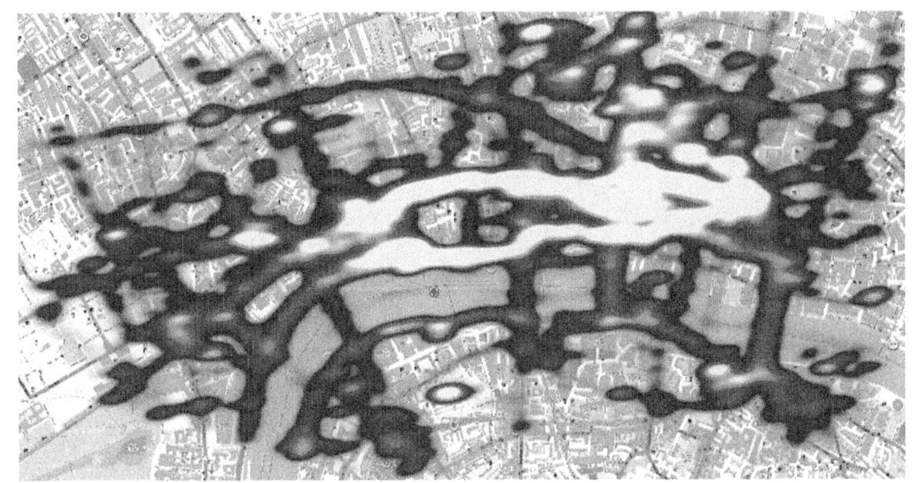

Figure 4 Heat map of user distribution. Map of the data recording zone. Superimposed is a heat map representation of the distribution of all recorded location updates. The 'hotter' an area is colored (*i.e.* the more yellow it is), the more data points have been colected in this area. It is visible that more data has been collected around locations where event-related activities took place.

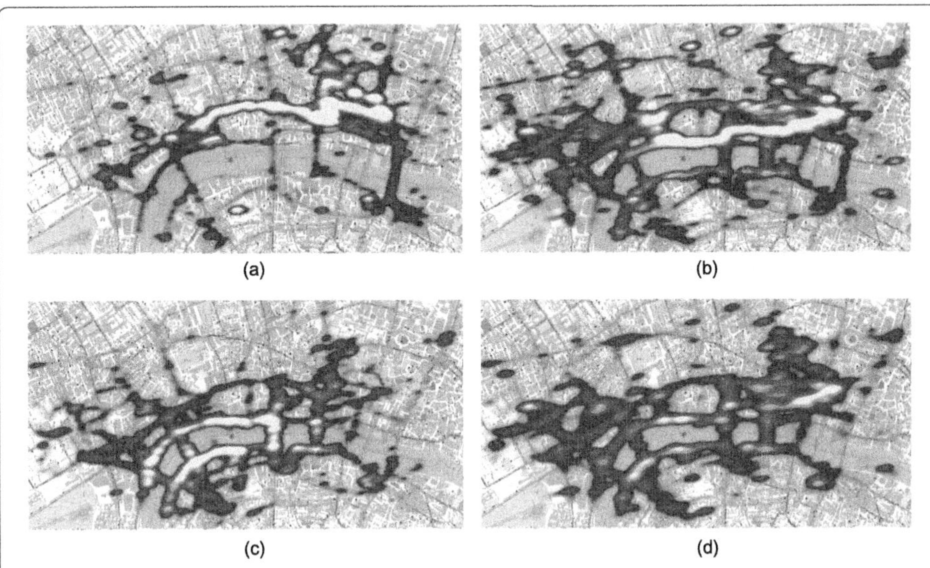

Figure 5 Spatio-temporal distribution of users. Spatio-temporal distribution of user: **(a)** Distribution of users during the first procession between 11:00 and 12:30 (Interval (a)); **(b)** Distribution during the second procession between 13:00 and 14:30 (Interval (b)); **(c)** Distribution during the firework display between 17:00 and 17:30 (Interval (c)); **(d)** Distribution during the break between 14:30 and 17:00. It is visible that people amass along streets where the processions take place and around the river basin during the fireworks. During the break, however, the accumulation is much lower and concentrated around bus and metro stations.

during the firework display (Interval (c)). Figure 5(d) shows the distribution of reported locations during the break between 14:30 and 17:00. Although temporal information is not present, these heat maps reveal an expected spatial distribution of event attendees: people amass along streets where the processions take place and around the river basin during the fireworks. During the break, however, the accumulation is much lower and concentrations around bus and metro stations are visible.

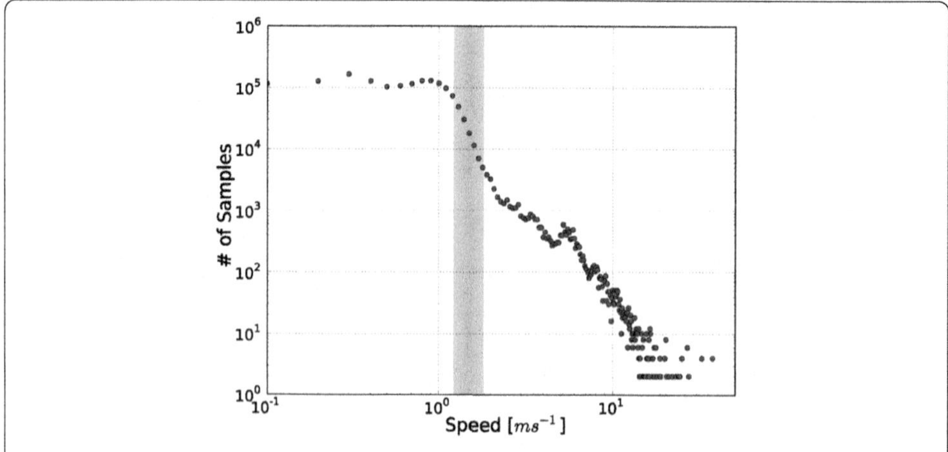

Figure 6 Velocity distribution. Velocity distribution of the collected samples. The orange region indicates the unrestricted walking velocity range of pedestrians in urban spaces [64].

5.2 Velocity distribution

App users do not necessarily walk around by foot but may travel by any means of available transportation. By recording a user's location, the GPS sensor also provides the current velocity the device travels. Figure 6 shows the velocity distribution of the collected data. The orange-colored area indicates the walking velocity range of pedestrians in urban spaces. The mean value is 1.47 ms^{-1} with a variance of 0.3 ms^{-1} according to *Willis et al.* [64]. Walking velocity is affected by cultural influences, demographics and even time of the day and weather conditions. However, these influences lie within the indicated area. The plot reveals that the majority of the collected samples were recorded at a velocities between 0 ms^{-1} and 2 ms^{-1} while only a few data samples were recording at higher velocities. In the following, we are interested in pedestrian dynamics and hence, unless stated otherwise, we only consider data samples where the corresponding velocity lies between $0\ ms^{-1} \leq v \leq 1.47 + 0.3\ ms^{-1}$ ($=1.77\ ms^{-1}$).

5.3 Relation between user density and crowd density

We assume that the spatial distribution of App users corresponds to the actual spatial distribution of event attendees (Assumption 2). This implies that for a given point in time, the ratio of App users to event attendees is constant for every location. To verify this assumption, we compare the actual crowd density at a specific location to the App user density at the same location. The crowd density is obtained from video footage recorded by CCTV video cameras (see Section 4.2). We use recordings from three different locations and for each of these locations defined an area of approximately 10 m^2 within which the pedestrians are manually counted at certain points in time. Given these counts, the crowd density ρ_{Crowd} is obtained by dividing the number of people N in the area by the size A of the area. Hence:

$$\rho_{\text{Crowd}} = \frac{N}{A}. \tag{4}$$

The corresponding user density ρ_{User} is obtained from the GPS location data using Equation 1. Figure 7(a) shows a scatter plot of the $(\rho_{\text{User}}, \rho_{\text{Crowd}})$-tuples. In total, we obtained 154 density tuples.

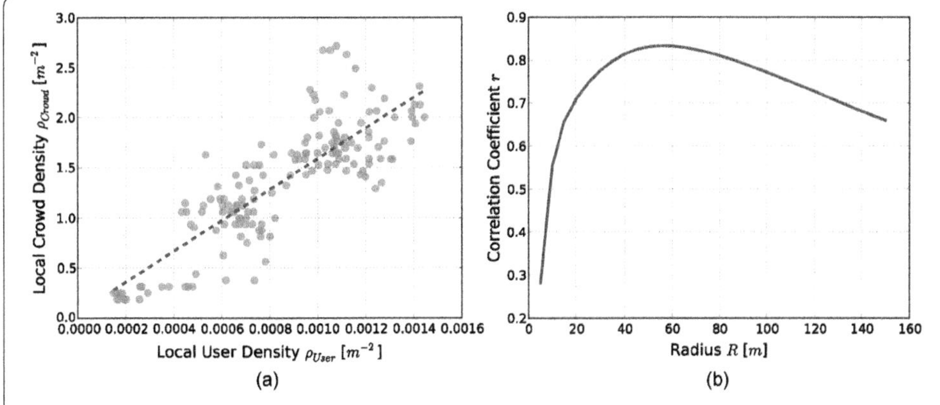

Figure 7 User density (GPS) vs. crowd density (CCTV). (a) Scatter plot of (ρ_{User}, ρ_{Crowd})-tuples. This data was obtained throughout the whole event at three distinct locations. The green fit line indicates the linear regression. **(b)** influence of the kernel radius R of Equation 1 on the correlation coefficient r of the linear regression.

To fulfill Assumption 1, we assume a linear relation between ρ_{Crowd} and ρ_{User}. With a linear regression analysis, we can assess the quality of the linear relation. The linear regression is depicted in Figure 7(a). The user density ρ_{User} depends on the kernel radius R of Equation 1. To understand the influence, we vary the kernel radius R between $5 \text{ m} < R < 150 \text{ m}$. Figure 7(b) depicts the influence of the kernel radius on the correlation between the crowd density and the user density. We obtain a low correlation coefficient for small values of R. The correlation coefficient increases to a maximum of $r = 0.833$ for $R = 55$ m followed by a decline for larger values of R. The observed behavior can be explained in the following way: This variation is getting smoothed out for larger values of R as the area to determine the density is increased. Hence, small variations in the number of available sample points do not affect the density estimation as greatly resulting in lower variations. By exceeding some value of R, the considered area is so large that the estimated density does not capture the local variation anymore. Local variations are smoothed out and large deviations between the user density and the crowd density can be observed. This causes a drop in the correlation coefficient.

A further error might be introduced by the localization errors due to sub-optimal GPS fixes in urban spaces, where often only a limited number of GPS satellites are visible at the street level. It has been shown in [65] that this error is lower than 24 m for 95% of all samples recorded in urban spaces and that the median error is 8 m.

5.4 Behavioral similarity with respect to density

We assess whether Assumption 3 holds by comparing a user's own velocity to the velocity of their neighbors. For this we determine a user's location and velocity and compare it to the crowd velocity at this location. We calculate the crowd velocity at the user's location using Equation 2 without including the user's own velocity. The velocity difference Δv_k is given by the difference between the user's velocity and the crowd velocity. Hence,

$$\Delta v_k = \left| v_k - \frac{\sum_{i \in \{N \setminus k\}} |\vec{v}_i| \exp[-\|\vec{r}_i(t) - \vec{r}\|^2 / R^2]}{\sum_{i \in \{N \setminus k\}} \exp[-\|\vec{r}_i(t) - \vec{r}\|^2 / R^2]} \right|, \tag{5}$$

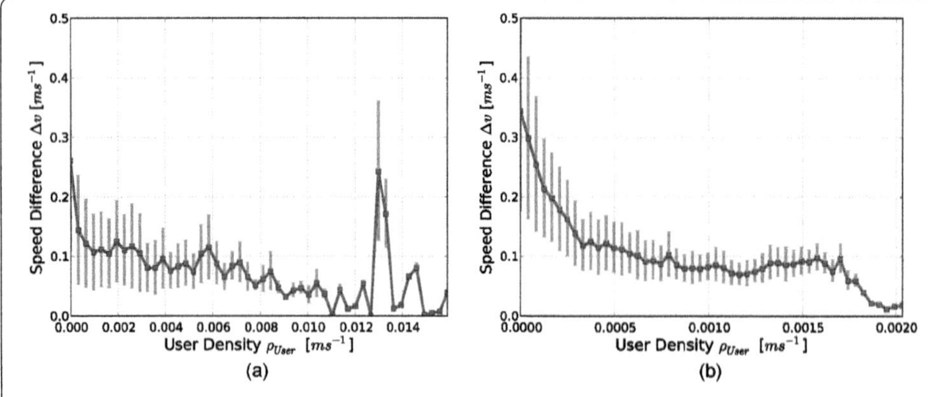

Figure 8 Walking speed similarity. Relation between the difference of a user's velocity and the velocity of the crowd in their vicinity in dependence of the crowd density. Plot **(a)** shows the relation for a kernel radius of $R = 10$ m and **(b)** for $R = 55$ m, respectively. The plots depict that for low densities, the mean value is around 0.3 ms^{-1} which corresponds to the variance in pedestrian walking velocity in unrestricted environments [64]. The differences decay towards 0 by increasing the crowd density.

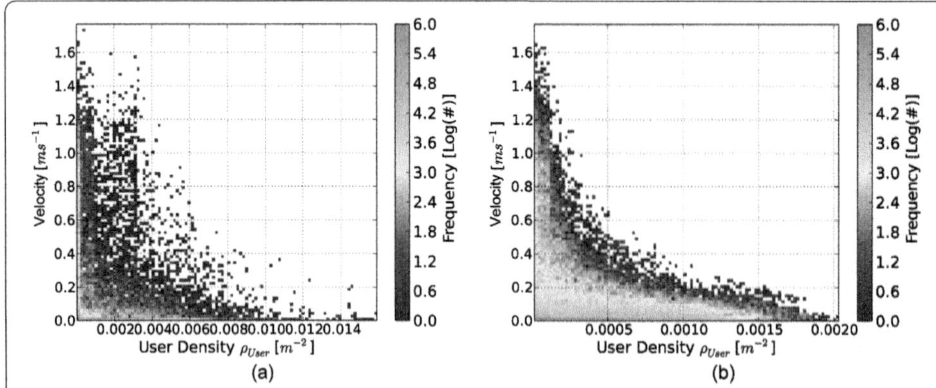

Figure 9 Histogram of density-speed tuples. Histogram of the density-velocity relation of our data set the kernel radii **(a)** $R = 10$ m and **(b)** $R = 55$ m, respectively. The plots depict a two-dimensional histogram of all obtained density-velocity tuples (logarithmic scale). The color values indicate the occurrence frequency of a tuple. It is observable that the walking velocity covers the whole range from 0 ms^{-1} up to a maximal value for a given density. This upper limit is depends on the crowd density and decays for larger crowd densities.

with v_k the velocity of user k and N the set of all users. We calculate the velocity difference at each time step for each user together with the local density at that location. The two plots in Figure 8 show the obtained relationship by plotting the velocity difference versus the user density. Plot (a) is obtained with a kernel parameter of $R = 10$ m and (b) with $R = 55$ m, respectively. We see that in both cases, for small densities, the mean value is around 0.3 ms^{-1} which corresponds to the variance in pedestrian walking velocity in unrestricted environments [64]. Additionally, a trend can be observed that the velocity differences tend to get smaller for larger densities. This supports Assumption 3.

5.5 The fundamental diagram: relation between density and velocity

We want to investigate towards which extent the density-velocity relation found in our data set corresponds to existing fundamental diagram models. Figure 9(a) and Figure 9(b) show a histogram of the density-velocity relation for a kernel radius of $R = 10$ m and $R = 55$ m, respectively. To obtain these plots, we divided time into intervals of one second and calculated for each interval t and for each user that was active in this interval the local density $\rho(\vec{r}, t)$ using Equation 1 and the crowd velocity $v(\vec{r}, t)$ using Equation 2. The plots depict a two-dimensional histogram of all obtained density-velocity tuples (logarithmic scale). The color values indicate the occurrence frequency of a tuple. The two plots reveal some general aspects of the density-velocity relation found in our data sets:

- both plots exhibit a clear trend that with higher densities, the velocity range decreases;
- for low densities, the whole walking velocity range between 0 ms^{-1} and 1.77 ms^{-1} is observed;
- low velocity values can be observed for all densities.

By comparing the obtained results to the density-velocity relation discussed in Section 2.3.2, we see that our data does not look like the plot of the function provided by Weidmann. Our data is scattered across a region as opposed to the bijective mapping of the fundamental diagram. This difference can be explained as follows: The model derived by Weidmann assumes that the pedestrians want to reach a target location. This assumption is not given in our situation. Not every pedestrian has a target location to reach and might decide to walk with his own pace or even decides to stand still. Thus, we can observe walking velocities covering the whole range from 0 ms^{-1} up to a maximal value for a given density. It is, however, observable that this maximal value depends on the crowd density and decreases for higher densities. Therefore, we can conclude that the crowd density value at a given location imposes a restriction on the maximal walking velocity that is possible.

5.6 Calibration of crowd density estimates

Based on the findings deduced in the previous section, we introduce and evaluate a methodology to estimate a crowd density from the spatial distribution of App users. Our method relies on Assumption 2. Section 5.3 shows the existence of a linear relation between the crowd density and the user density. By knowing the parameters of the linear regression, a crowd density can be estimated from the user density. The regression parameters, however, are unknown. Thus, a calibration method is required to obtain these parameters.

5.6.1 Calibrating the spatial distribution of App users to obtain crowd density estimates

By using Equation 1, we obtain a local user density ρ_{User} from the spatial distribution of App users. Making use of the linear relation, we obtain a local crowd density estimation $\hat{\rho}_{\text{Crowd}}$ from the measured local user density ρ_{User}:

$$\hat{\rho}_{\text{Crowd}}(\vec{r}, t) = \frac{m}{k}\rho_{\text{User}}(\vec{r}, t) + \frac{q}{k}, \tag{6}$$

where m, q and k are unknown regression parameters and depend on the ratio of App users to event attendees.

Section 2.3.2 presents Weidmann's analytical equation to model the fundamental diagram (Equation 3). This equation describes the crowd speed as a function of the crowd density. It can be transformed so that the crowd density is a function of the crowd speed:

$$\rho_{\text{Crowd}}(\vec{r}, t, v) = \frac{\gamma \cdot \rho_{\max}}{\rho_{\max} \cdot \ln(\frac{-v_0}{v(\vec{r},t) - v_0}) + \gamma} \quad \text{with } v(\vec{r}, t) \neq v_0. \tag{7}$$

The speed of the crowd $v(\vec{r},t)$ is obtained using Equation 2. Hence, we can obtain a crowd density estimates $\tilde{\rho}_{\text{Crowd}}$ by combining Equation 2 and Equation 7. The parameters $\rho_{\max}$ and v_0 are cultural dependent and can be taken from literature (*e.g.* [48, 53, 55]). The fitting parameter γ, however, remains unknown.

For a given time at a given location, Equation 6 and Equation 7 should provide the same crowd density estimates $\hat{\rho}_{\text{Crowd}}$ and $\tilde{\rho}_{\text{Crowd}}$. Hereby, Equation 6 considers the local user density and Equation 7 the local crowd speed. We define an error measure e:

$$e = \left(\hat{\rho}_{\text{User}}(\vec{r},t) - \rho_{\text{User}}(\vec{r},t)\right)^2 \tag{8}$$

with

$$\begin{aligned}\hat{\rho}_{\text{User}}(\vec{r},t) &\overset{(6)}{=} \frac{k \cdot \hat{\rho}_{\text{Crowd}}(v) - q}{m} = \frac{k \cdot \tilde{\rho}_{\text{Crowd}}(v) - q}{m} \\ &\overset{(7)}{=} \frac{\frac{k \cdot \gamma \cdot \rho_{\max}}{\rho_{\max} \cdot \ln\left(\frac{-v_0}{v(\vec{r},t) - v_0}\right) + \gamma} - q}{m}, \quad m \neq 0.\end{aligned} \tag{9}$$

The missing calibration parameters m, q and γ can now be found by minimizing the error e with a least square method. The minimization criteria we used is

$$S(m,q,\gamma) = \sum_{i=1}^{N} \left[\hat{\rho}_{\text{User}}(m,q,\gamma,v,k) - \rho_{\text{User}}\right]^2. \tag{10}$$

5.6.2 Modeling the fundamental diagram from the recorded density-speed information

With the previous approach, we can obtain the optimal calibration parameters m and q by using Weidmann's equation to fit the user density to the corresponding crowd speed. However, the density-speed tuples do not represent the fundamental diagram well as there is a great amount of variation in the walking behavior of pedestrians (Section 5.5). We found in our data set that pedestrians walk with a speed between 0 ms^{-1} and a density-dependent upper limit. We consider this upper limit as the speed with which pedestrians' walking behavior gets restricted by the surrounding crowd. Increasing the personal walking speed would conflict with the social forces acting on a pedestrian [27]. Our assumption is that pedestrians walking with the upper limit speed for a given density behave according to the fundamental diagram. Hence, we perform a calibration with only these upper limit values. To obtain the upper limit values, we introduce $\tau(\rho)$, the 0.99-percentile value. $\tau(\rho)$ is the threshold speed for a given density ρ for which 99% of all measured speed values are smaller. Figure 10 shows again the frequency plot of the $(\rho_{\text{User}}(\vec{r},t), v(\vec{r},t))$-tuples together with the 0.99-percentile values $\tau(\rho)$. These percentile values $\tau(\rho)$ can now be used to minimize Equation 10 to obtain the calibration parameters m and q. The green curve in Figure 10 shows the calibrated fundamental diagram. Hereby, we set $\rho_{\max} = 3.5$ m^{-2} (According to Weidmann [48]) and $v_0 = 1.77$ ms^{-1} (according to *Willis et al.* for UK [64]). Table 3 lists the calibration parameters obtained by our minimization process for different kernel radii R.

5.6.3 Evaluation of the calibration methodology

To gain insight into the accuracy of our calibration methodology, we calibrate all user density measure ρ_{User} where a CCTV-based reference crowd density is available. This is the

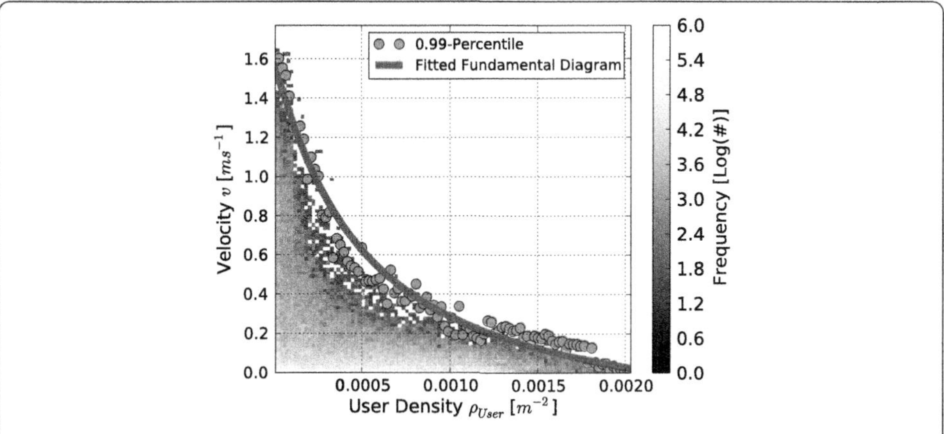

Figure 10 Threshold speed and fitted fundamental diagram. Histogram of the user density-speed tuples (gray) and the 0.99-percentile values $\tau(\rho)$. The green line is a plot of the fundamental diagram fitted through these 0.99-percentile points by following our calibration method.

Table 3 Overview of calibration parameter

R	*m*	*q*	*γ*	*k*
10	550	0	1.6	1.7
15	624	0.1	1.1	1.4
20	757	0	0.6	1.5
25	1,176	0.1	0.6	1.9
30	1,262	0.2	0.5	1.7
35	618	0.1	0.5	0.7
40	1,972	0.3	0.5	1.9
45	1,312	0.2	0.5	1.1
50	1,339	0.2	0.5	1.0
55	1,177	0.2	0.5	0.8

Calibration parameters obtained through our calibration method for different kernel radii.

same data as used in Section 5.3. We compare the outcome to the CCTV-based reference data. Ideally, the estimated crowd density $\hat{\rho}_{\text{Crowd}}$ obtained from the calibrated App user distribution should be identical to the observed crowd density ρ_{Crowd} from the video footage. We apply a linear regression trough the data tuples to understand the calibration accuracy. Figure 11 shows the linear regressions for different kernel radii. A perfect regression would correspond to the diagonal axis. We see that all regressions are situated around the diagonal axis.

We perform a residual analysis to assess the appropriateness of the chosen model. A residual is defined as follows:

$$\epsilon = \hat{\rho}_{\text{Crowd}} - \rho_{\text{Crowd}}. \quad (11)$$

Figure 12(a) is a plot of the residuals for the kernel radii $R = 10$ m and $R = 55$ m dependent on the crowd density. Figure 12(b) shows the normal probability plot. The normal probability plot helps to determine whether or not it is reasonable to assume that the random errors in a statistical process can be assumed to be drawn from a normal distribution. The normal probability plot shows a strongly linear pattern. With a linear regression fitted through the data (dashed lines), we obtain a correlation coefficient of 0.985 for $R = 10$ m and 0.969 for $R = 55$ m, respectively. These correlation coefficients indicate that there are

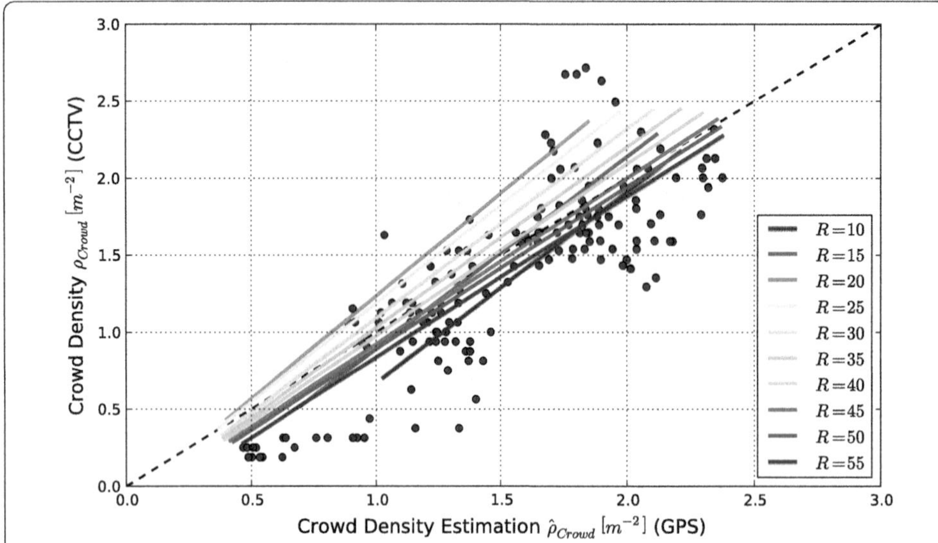

Figure 11 Calibration regression. Linear regressions of the calibrated crowd densities $\hat{\rho}_{\text{Crowd}}$ and the crowd densities ρ_{Crowd} obtained from video footage. Results are shown for different kernel radii R. A perfect regression would correspond to the diagonal axis. Additionally, the figure also shows the scatter plot of the calibrated data points for the case of $R = 55$ m.

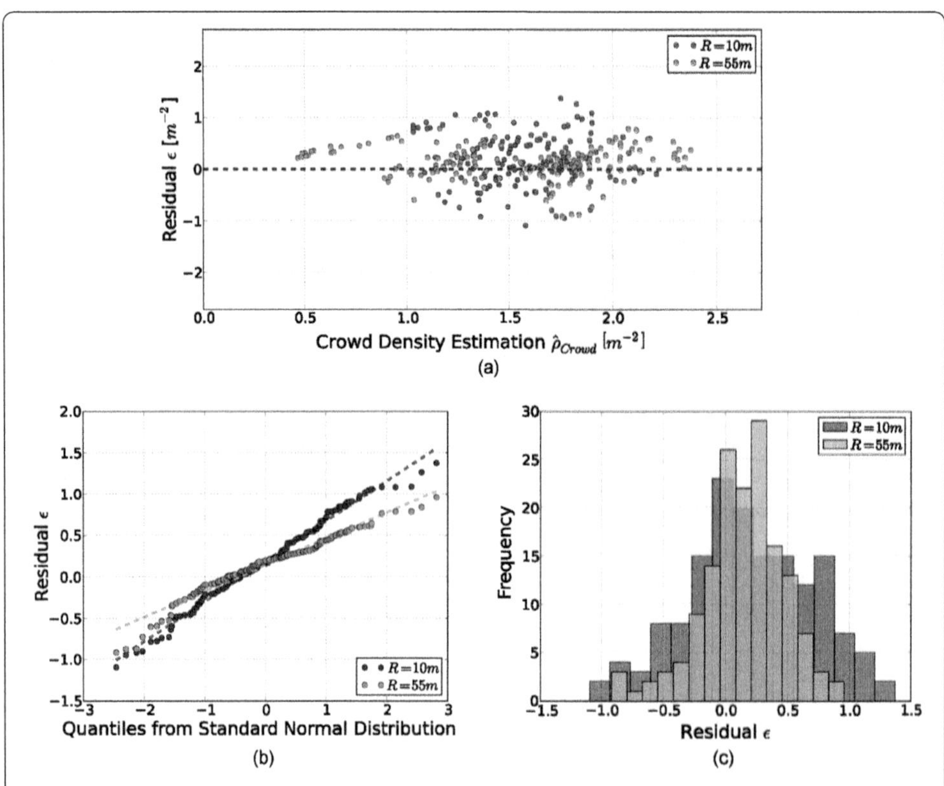

Figure 12 Residual analysis. (a) Residual plot of the estimated crowd density to the actual crowd density for the two kernel radii $R = 10$ m and $R = 55$ m. **(b)** The normal probability plot of the residuals. The good linearity of the regression supports the chosen model. **(c)** The histogram of the residuals shows a normal distribution.

Table 4 Correlation coefficient and calibration error

R [m]	*r*	σ (RMSE) [m^{-2}]
10	0.56	0.54
15	0.66	0.46
20	0.71	0.51
25	0.75	0.46
30	0.78	0.41
35	0.80	0.37
40	0.81	0.35
45	0.82	0.34
50	0.83	0.35
55	0.83	0.36

Results of the crowd density calibration method by comparing the obtained crowd density estimates to ground truth information extracted from CCTV video footage. The density estimates rely on the kernel radius R which is used to determine the user density. Results for different values of R are listed. The correlation coefficient r indicates how well the crowd density estimates correlate to the ground truth measures. The crowd density estimation error σ is the average estimation error.

only minor deviations from the line fit to the points on the probability plot. Hence, the chosen model appears to be suitable to model the data. This finding is also supported by the histogram depicted in Figure 12(c) which shows that the residuals have a normal distribution.

To understand how well we can estimate the crowd density from the distribution of App users, we determine the overall calibration error by calculating the root mean squared error (RMSE) σ as follows:

$$\begin{aligned}\sigma &= \sqrt{\frac{\sum_i^N(\rho_{\text{Crowd}} - \hat{\rho}_{\text{Crowd}})^2}{N}}\\ &= \sqrt{\frac{\sum_i^N(\rho_{\text{Crowd}} - (\frac{m}{k}\cdot\rho_{\text{User}} + \frac{q}{k}))^2}{N}}.\end{aligned} \tag{12}$$

Table 4 lists σ for different kernel radii. The table also lists the obtained correlation coefficients r of a linear regression through the actual crowd density ρ_{Crowd} and the estimation $\hat{\rho}_{\text{Crowd}}$.

Given all these findings, we conclude:

- The residual analysis reveals that the error is normal distributed which suggests that the chosen model fits the data well and that the error is not introduced by the model but inherently present in the data,
- we achieve a correlation coefficient of $r = 0.56$ for $R = 10$ m and $r = 0.83$ for $R = 55$ m, respectively. This implies that there is some predicting power for obtaining a crowd density estimation, and
- the calibration error is $\sigma = 0.54\ \text{m}^{-2}$ for $R = 10$ m and $\sigma = 0.36\ \text{m}^{-2}$ for $R = 55$ m, respectively.

6 Conclusion

A participatory sensing approach for crowd monitoring faces a major limitation: Participation is based on a voluntary base. Regardless of the incentivization strategy, we expect that only a small fraction of all attendees of a mass gathering is being tracked. This makes it challenging to conclude about the crowd density. This work addressed this limitation. We presented a methodology which allows to infer a crowd density even if only a small number of crowd members is being tracked. The principle behind our methodology is that the walking speed of pedestrians depends on the crowd density. By measuring the location and speed, we can calibrate the distribution of tracked pedestrians to the distribution of all attendees of a mass gathering using the fundamental diagram. With this, we can infer crowd density estimates.

We used a data set recorded during a city-scale mass gathering to evaluate our methodology. We compared crowd density estimates to ground truth information obtained from video footage: For a kernel radius of $R = 55$ m, the average calibration error is 0.36 m^{-2}. Further, a correlation coefficient of 0.83 indicates that a linear relation between the crowd density and the user density can be assumed. The residual analysis revealed that the model fits the data well.

Besides these results, the work presents another finding: We could verify that the walking speed of pedestrians depends on the crowd density. Hereby, we found a similar relation between the speed of a crowd and the density as related work suggests. In particular, we identified a crowd density dependent upper limit speed with which pedestrians move through urban spaces. These upper speed limit values follow existing fundamental diagram models closely.

There are several factors to consider:

- The reason for not reaching a higher correlation coefficient than the maximum value of $r = 0.83$ might stem from the unequal spatial distribution of App users and event attendees at certain time steps. However, there are also other factors: It was sometimes difficult to count the correct number of attendees in the predefined area from the video footage as some pedestrians were occluded by others. Therefore, the crowd density extracted from the video is also error-prone.
- We obtained the highest correlation coefficient and lowest calibration error for a kernel radius $R = 55$ m. This is a large radius to infer local characteristics. We believe this is due to the sparsity in our data set. We were tracking less than 1% of all attendees. A smaller kernel radius could provide more accurate local crowd information [20] but would require a much larger user base. Providing more attractive incentives, making the App available on different mobile platforms and having a good advertisement campaign in place could stimulate a higher participation.
- We obtained best results with a radius of 55 m. This seems to be like a big area to cover for monitoring crowd. However, as we use a Gaussian weighting scheme to calculate our measures, the influence of the users decays rapidly the further away they are from the center of the circle. Further, we believe that this radius can be smaller by having a larger ratio of App users.

The location sampling rate of 1 Hz was chosen to capture as much of the pedestrian dynamics as possible. However, such a high sampling rate is very energy consuming. Besides privacy considerations, also the heavy battery consumption of such an App might have a detrimental effect on participation. Therefore, it is important to incorporate an efficient energy conserving sampling strategy. This can be achieved by lowering the sampling frequency but also by only reading location updates from GPS if needed. Hereby, low-power acceleration sensors can help to determine if a user is stationary or not and only switch on the GPS if motion is being detected.

Another important issue that has not been addressed in this work is to obtain a confidence measure giving indication about the reliability of the inferred crowd density. It may be that due to a small percentage of users compared to the total number of attendees, the inferred crowd density may even become null. Hereby, a plausibility check *e.g.* by comparing the active number of users to a roughly estimated number of attendees by the security personnel could give confidence about the inferred crowd density.

This work is one of the first addressing the challenges arising by crowd sensing through a participatory sensing approach with smartphones. We believe the results are promising to stimulate successive contributions. In particular, we see the following next steps to investigate some of the aspects not addressed in this work:

- We evaluated our approach on data from only one mass gathering. To generalize the findings, our method has to be applied to data collected during different mass gatherings and the results have to be compared. The type of the gathering and cultural aspects may have an influence.
- A sensitivity analysis investigating the relation between the ratio of App users and the accuracy of crowd density estimation helps to understand how many pedestrian need to be tracked to obtain a significant estimation accuracy.
- An evaluation of the online performance of our method reveals the required amount of data to estimate a crowd density. The required amount of data is closely connected to the required amount of pedestrians. These two aspects should be investigated jointly.
- We used the analytical model of Weidmann to represent the fundamental diagram. As noted in Section 2.3.2, other models exist which consider additional information. The suitability of alternative models for our calibration method remains to be investigated.
- A possible demographic bias in our App usage was not taken into consideration. However, such factors influence the behavior of pedestrians. Considering the age or gender distribution or the cultural background could further tune the model parameters.
- We did not consider to include spatial characteristics into our model. As the behavior of pedestrians depends on the architectural configuration, such information could be considered to increase the estimation accuracy.

This work shows on the example of crowd density that a participatory sensing approach can give insight into crowd characteristics and provide information relevant to assess the criticality of a situation during city-scale mass gatherings. Given our results and the many advantages of on-device localization (localization accuracy, user control over privacy, multitude of sensor modalities, low deployment cost, *etc.*), we suggest that smartphones are a viable tool for crowd monitoring.

Competing interests
The authors declare that they have no competing interests.

Authors' contributions
This work is a joint effort between ETH Zürich, DFKI Kaiserslautern and the London School of Economics. Collaboration has been established within the FP7 ICT SOCIONICAL project. The different partners have contributed to different parts of this work. All authors were heavily involved in the data recording part which includes system design and deployment but also management and coordination task and establishing the required contacts. All authors have contributed to this document and given the final approval. Detailed contributions (inn alphabetic order): Experiment planning: TF, PL, EMK, DR, MW. System deployment: TF, PL, EMK, DR, MW. Evaluation: MW. Manuscript: TF, PL, EMK, DR, GT, MW. Acquisition of funding: PL, EMK, DR, GT.

Author details
[1]Wearable Computing Laboratory, ETH Zürich, Zürich, Switzerland. [2]Embedded Intelligence Group, DFKI Kaiserslautern, Kaiserslautern, Germany. [3]Complexity Research Programme, London School of Economics and Political Science, London, United Kingdom.

Acknowledgements
This work is supported under the FP7 ICT Future Enabling Technologies programme of the European Commission under grant agreement No. 231288 (SOCIONICAL).

References

1. BBC News (2011) Royal wedding: in numbers. http://www.bbc.co.uk/news/uk-13248642
2. Clarin.com (2010) Dos millones de personas, en un cierre inolvidable. http://edant.clarin.com/diario/2010/05/25/um/m-02199900.htm
3. RTVE (2010) Dos millones de personas recibieron a la Selección Española de Fútbol en Madrid. http://www.rtve.es/alacarta/videos/television/dos-millones-personas-recibieron-a-seleccion-espanola-futbol-madrid/828627/
4. Helbing D, Mukerji P (2012) Crowd disasters as systemic failures: analysis of the love parade disaster EPJ Data Sci 1:7. http://www.epjdatascience.com/content/1/1/7
5. Sime J (1995) Crowd psychology and engineering. Saf Sci 21:1-14
6. Tarlow P (2002) Event risk management and safety, vol 4. Wiley, New York
7. Getz D (2007) Event studies: theory, research and policy for planned events. Elsevier, Amsterdam
8. Johansson A, Batty M, Hayashi K, Al Bar O, Marcozzi D, Memish ZA (2012) Crowd and environmental management during mass gatherings. Lancet Infect Dis 12(2):150-156
9. Helbing D, Buzna L, Johansson A, Werner T (2005) Self-organized pedestrian crowd dynamics: experiments, simulations, and design solutions. Transp Sci 39:1-24
10. Hughes RL (2003) The flow of human crowds. Annu Rev Fluid Mech 35:169-182. http://www.annualreviews.org/doi/abs/10.1146/annurev.fluid.35.101101.161136.
11. Smelser NJ (1963) Theory of collective behavior
12. Nicholson C, Roebuck B (1995) The investigation of the Hillsborough disaster by the health and safety executive. Saf Sci 18(4):249-259
13. Au S, Great Britain H, Staff SE, Health GB, Executive S, Ltd RC (1993) Managing crowd safety in public venues: a study to generate guidance for venue owners and enforcing authority inspectors. HSE contract research report, HSE Books. http://books.google.ch/books?id=3osbPwAACAAJ
14. Wirz M, Franke T, Roggen D, Mitleton-Kelly E, Lukowicz P, Tröster G (2012) Inferring and visualizing crowd conditions by collecting GPS location traces from pedestrians' mobile phones for real-time crowd monitoring during city-scale mass gatherings. In: Collaboration technologies and infrastructures (WETICE), 21st international conference on. IEEE Press, New York
15. Batty M, Desyllas J, Duxbury E (2003) The discrete dynamics of small-scale spatial events: agent-based models of mobility in carnivals and street parades. Int J Geogr Inf Sci 17(7):673-697
16. Lee R, Hughes R (2005) Exploring trampling and crushing in a crowd. J Transp Eng 131:575
17. Hsieh Y, Ngai K, Burkle F Jr, Hsu E (2009) Epidemiological characteristics of human stampedes. Disaster Med Public Health Prep 3(4):217
18. Burkle F, Hsu E (2011) Ram Janki temple: understanding human stampedes. Lancet 377(9760):106-107
19. Krausz B, Bauckhage C (2012) Loveparade 2010: automatic video analysis of a crowd disaster. Comput Vis Image Underst 116(3):307-319
20. Helbing D, Johansson A, Al-Abideen H (2007) Dynamics of crowd disasters: an empirical study. Phys Rev E 75(4):046109
21. Krausz B, Bauckhage C (2011) Analyzing pedestrian behavior in crowds for automatic detection of congestions. In: Computer vision workshops (ICCV workshops), 2011 IEEE international conference on. IEEE Press, New York, pp 144-149
22. Johansson A, Helbing D, Al-Abideen HZ, Al-Bosta S (2008) From crowd dynamics to crowd safety: a video-based analysis. ArXiv e-prints
23. Fruin J (1981) Crowd disasters - a systems evaluation of causes and countermeasures. Inc. US National Bureau of Standards, pub. NBSIR, 81-3261
24. Gong S, Loy CC, Xiang T (2011) Security and surveillance. In: Moeslund TB, Hilton A, Krüger V, Sigal L (eds) Visual analysis of humans. Springer, London
25. Jacques J Jr, Musse S, Jung C (2010) Crowd analysis using computer vision techniques. IEEE Signal Process Mag 27:66-77
26. Mehran R, Oyama A, Shah M (2009) Abnormal crowd behavior detection using social force model. In: Computer vision and pattern recognition. IEEE Press, New York
27. Helbing D, Molnar P (1995) Social force model for pedestrian dynamics. Phys Rev E 51:4282-4286
28. Steffen B, Seyfried A (2010) Methods for measuring pedestrian density, flow, speed and direction with minimal scatter. Phys A, Stat Mech Appl 389(9):1902-1910
29. Eagle N, Pentland A (2006) Reality mining: sensing complex social systems. Pers Ubiquitous Comput 10(4):255-268
30. LaMarca A, Chawathe Y et al (2005) Place lab: device positioning using radio beacons in the wild. In: Pervasive computing
31. Calabrese F, Colonna M, Lovisolo P, Parata D, Ratti C (2011) Real-time urban monitoring using cell phones: a case study in Rome. IEEE Trans Intell Transp Syst 12:141-151
32. Becker R, Caceres R, Hanson K, Loh J, Urbanek S, Varshavsky A, Volinsky C (2011) A tale of one city: using cellular network data for urban planning. IEEE Pervasive Comput 10(4):18-26
33. Couronne T, Olteanu Raimond A, Smoreda Z (2011) Looking at spatiotemporal city dynamics through mobile phone lenses. In: Network of the future, international conference on the. IEEE Press, New York
34. Calabrese F, Pereira F, Di Lorenzo G, Liu L, Ratti C (2010) The geography of taste: analyzing cell-phone mobility and social events. In: Pervasive computing. Lecture notes in computer science, vol 6030. Springer, Berlin, pp 22-37
35. Kim D, Kim Y, Estrin D, Srivastava M (2010) Sensloc: sensing everyday places and paths using less energy. In: Proc. of the 8th ACM conference on embedded networked sensor systems. ACM, New York

36. Van Diggelen F (2009) A-GPS: assisted GPS, GNSS, and SBAS. Artech House, Norwood
37. Azizyan M, Constandache I, Choudhury RR (2009) SurroundSense: mobile phone localization via ambience fingerprinting. In: Proceedings of the 15th annual international conference on mobile computing and networking, MobiCom '09. ACM, New York, pp 261-272
38. Koshak N, Fouda A (2008) Analyzing pedestrian movement in mataf using gps and gis to support space redesign. In: The 9th international conference on design and decision support systems in architecture and urban planning
39. Versichele M, Neutens T, Delafontaine M, de Weghe NV (2012) The use of bluetooth for analysing spatiotemporal dynamics of human movement at mass events: a case study of the Ghent festivities. Appl Geogr 32(2):208-220
40. Bandini S, Federici ML, Manzoni S (2007) A qualitative evaluation of technologies and techniques for data collection on pedestrians and crowded situations. In: Proceedings of the 2007 summer computer simulation conference, SCSC. Society for Computer Simulation International, San Diego, pp 1057-1064
41. Marana A, Da Fontoura Costa L, Lotufo R, Velastin S (1999) Estimating crowd density with Minkowski fractal dimension. In: Acoustics, speech, and signal processing, IEEE international conference on, vol 6, pp 3521-3524
42. Ma R, Li L, Huang W, Tian Q (2004) On pixel count based crowd density estimation for visual surveillance. In: Cybernetics and intelligent systems, IEEE conference on, vol 1. IEEE Press, New York, pp 170-173
43. Wu X, Liang G, Lee K, Xu Y (2006) Crowd density estimation using texture analysis and learning. In: Robotics and biomimetics, ROBIO'06, IEEE international conference on. IEEE Press, New York, pp 214-219
44. Jones M, Snow D (2008) Pedestrian detection using boosted features over many frames. In: Pattern recognition, ICPR 2008, 19th international conference on. IEEE Press, New York, pp 1-4
45. Brostow G, Cipolla R (2006) Unsupervised Bayesian detection of independent motion in crowds. In: Computer vision and pattern recognition, IEEE computer society conference on, vol 1. IEEE Press, New York, pp 594-601
46. Reades J, Calabrese F, Sevtsuk A, Ratti C (2007) Cellular census: explorations in urban data collection. IEEE Pervasive Comput 6(3):30-38
47. Morrison A, Bell M, Chalmers M (2009) Visualisation of spectator activity at stadium events. In: Information visualisation, 13th international conference. IEEE Press, New York, pp 219-226
48. Weidmann U (1992) Transporttechnik der Fussgänger: Transporttechnische Eigenschaften des Fussgängerverkehrs (Literaturauswertung). IVT, Zürich
49. Helbing D (2009) Derivation of a fundamental diagram for urban traffic flow. Eur Phys J B, Condens Matter Complex Syst 70(2):229-241
50. Jelić A, Appert-Rolland C, Lemercier S, Pettré J (2011) Properties of pedestrians walking in line-fundamental diagrams. Arxiv preprint arXiv:1111.5708
51. Daamen W, Hoogendoorn S (2003) Experimental research of pedestrian walking behavior. Transp Res Rec 1828:20-30
52. Zhang J, Klingsch W, Schadschneider A, Seyfried A (2012) Ordering in bidirectional pedestrian flows and its influence on the fundamental diagram. J Stat Mech Theory Exp 2012:P02002
53. Chattaraj U, Seyfried A, Chakroborty P (2009) Comparison of pedestrian fundamental diagram across cultures. ArXiv e-prints
54. Smith R (1995) Density, velocity and flow relationships for closely packed crowds. Saf Sci 18(4):321-327
55. Johansson A (2009) Constant-net-time headway as a key mechanism behind pedestrian flow dynamics. Phys Rev E 80(2):026120
56. Seyfried A, Steffen B, Lippert T (2006) Basics of modelling the pedestrian flow. Phys A, Stat Mech Appl 368:232-238
57. Fang Z, Lo S, Lu J (2003) On the relationship between crowd density and movement velocity. Fire Saf J 38(3):271-283
58. Seyfried A, Steffen B, Klingsch W, Boltes M (2005) The fundamental diagram of pedestrian movement revisited. J Stat Mech Theory Exp 2005:P10002
59. Schadschneider A, Klingsch W, Klüpfel H, Kretz T, Rogsch C, Seyfried A (2008) Evacuation dynamics: empirical results, modeling and applications. Arxiv preprint arXiv:0802.1620
60. Wiseman R (2008) Quirkology: the curious science of everyday lives. Pan, London
61. Wirz M, Roggen D, Tröster G (2010) User acceptance study of a mobile system for assistance during emergency situations at large-scale events. In: Human-centric computing (HumanCom), 3rd international conference on. IEEE Press, New York, pp 1-6
62. Warburton K, Lazarus J (1991) Tendency-distance models of social cohesion in animal groups. J Theor Biol 150(4):473-488
63. Moussaid M, Garnier S, Theraulaz G, Helbing D (2009) Collective information processing and pattern formation in swarms, flocks, and crowds. Top Cogn Sci 1(3):469-497
64. Willis A, Gjersoe N, Havard C, Kerridge J, Kukla R (2004) Human movement behaviour in urban spaces: implications for the design and modelling of effective pedestrian environments. Environ Plan B, Plan Des 31(6):805-828
65. Wirz M, Schläpfer P, Kjærgaard M, Roggen D, Feese S, Tröster G (2011) Towards an online detection of pedestrian flocks in urban canyons by smoothed spatio-temporal clustering of GPS trajectories. In: Proceedings of the 3rd ACM SIGSPATIAL international workshop on location-based social networks. ACM, New York

4

Social dynamics of Digg

Tad Hogg[1] and Kristina Lerman[2*]

*Correspondence: lerman@isi.edu
[2]USC Information Sciences Institute, Marina del Rey, CA, USA
Full list of author information is available at the end of the article

Abstract

Online social media provide multiple ways to find interesting content. One important method is highlighting content recommended by user's friends. We examine this process on one such site, the news aggregator Digg. With a stochastic model of user behavior, we distinguish the effects of the content visibility and interestingness to users. We find a wide range of interest and distinguish stories primarily of interest to a users' friends from those of interest to the entire user community. We show how this model predicts a story's eventual popularity from users' early reactions to it, and estimate the prediction reliability. This modeling framework can help evaluate alternative design choices for displaying content on the site.

1 Introduction

The explosive growth of the Social Web hints at collective problem-solving made possible when people have tools to connect, create and organize information on a massive scale. The social news aggregator Digg, for example, allows people to collectively identify interesting news stories. The microblogging service Twitter has created a cottage industry of third-party applications, such as identifying trends from the millions of conversations taking place on the site and notifying you when your friends are nearby. Other sites enable people to collectively create encyclopedias, develop software, and invest in social causes. Analyzing records of complex social activity can help identify communities and important individuals within them, suggest relevant readings, and identify events and trends.

Effective use of this technology requires understanding how the social dynamics emerges from the decisions made by interconnected individuals. One approach is a stochastic modeling framework, which represents each user as a stochastic process with a few states. As an example, applying this approach to Digg successfully described observed voting patterns of Digg's users [1–3]. However, quantitative evaluation of the model was limited by the poor quality of data, which was extracted by scraping Digg's web pages.

In this paper we present two refinements to this modeling approach for Digg. First, we explicitly allow for systematic differences in *interest* in news stories for linked and unlinked users. This distinction is a key aspect of social media where links indicate commonality of user interests. We also include additional aspects of the Digg user interface in the model, thereby accounting for cases where the existing model identified anomalous behaviors. As the second major contribution, we describe how to measure confidence intervals of model predictions. We show that confidence intervals are highly correlated with the error between the predicted and actual votes stories accrue. Thus the confidence intervals indicate the quality of the model's predictions on a per-user or per-story basis.

This paper is organized as follows. The next section describes Digg and our data set. We then present a stochastic model of user behavior on Digg that explicitly includes dependencies on social network links. Using this model, we quantify these dependencies and discuss how the model predicts eventual popularity of newly submitted content. Finally, we compare our approach with other studies and discuss possible applications of stochastic models incorporating social network structure.

2 Digg: a social news portal

At the time data was collected, Digg was a popular news portal with over 3 million registered users. Digg allowed users to submit and rate news stories by voting on, or 'digging,' them. Every day Digg promoted a small fraction of submitted stories to the highly visible *front page*. Although the exact promotion mechanism was kept secret and changes occasionally, it appears to use the number of votes the story receives. Digg's popularity was largely due to the emergent front page created by the collective decisions of its many users. Below we describe the user interface that existed at the time of data collection.

2.1 User interface

Submitted stories appear in the *upcoming* stories list, where they remain for about 24 hours or until promoted to the front page. By default, Digg shows upcoming and front page stories in recency lists i.e., in reverse chronological order with the most recently submitted (promoted) story at the top of the list. A user may choose to display stories by popularity or by some broad topic. Popularity lists show stories with the most votes up to that time, e.g., the most popular stories submitted (promoted) in the past day or week. Each list is divided into pages, with 15 stories on each page, and the user has to click to see subsequent pages.

Digg allows users to designate friends and track their activities. The friend relationship is asymmetric. When user A lists user B as a *friend*, A can follow the activities of B but not vice versa. We call A the *fan*, or follower, of B. The *friends interface* shows users the stories their friends recently submitted or voted for.[a]

In this paper, we focus on the recency and 'popular in the last 24 hours' lists for all stories and the friends interface list for each user. These lists appear to account for most of the votes a story receives.

2.2 Evolution of story popularity

Most Digg users focus on front page stories, so upcoming stories accrue votes slowly. When a story is promoted to the front page, it becomes visible to many more users and accrues votes rapidly. Figure 1 shows the evolution of the number of votes for a story submitted in June 2009. The slope abruptly increases at promotion time (dashed line). As the story ages, accumulation of new votes slows down, and after a few days stories typically no longer receive new votes.

The final number of votes varies widely among the stories. Some promoted stories accumulate thousands of votes, while others muster only a few hundred. Stories that are never promoted receive few votes, in many cases just a single vote from the submitter, and are removed after about 24 hours.

A challenge for understanding this variation in popularity is the interaction between the stories' *visibility* (how Digg displays them) and their *interestingness* to users. Models

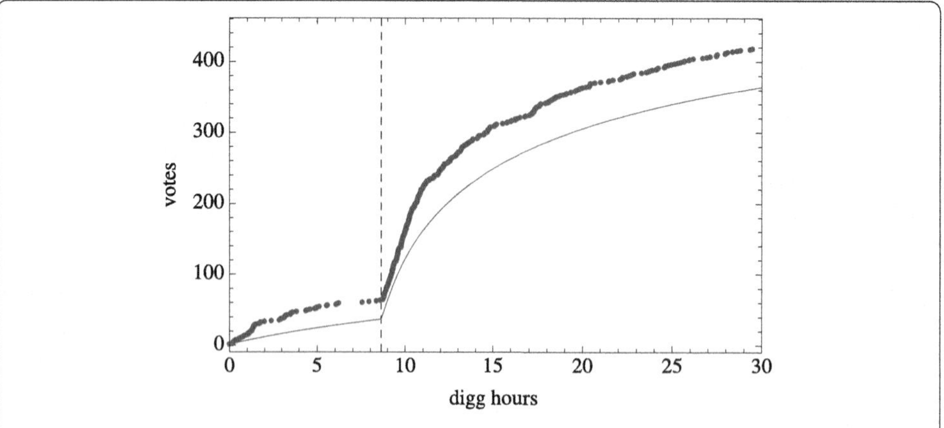

Figure 1 Voting behavior: the number of votes vs. time, measured in Digg hours, for a promoted story. The curve shows the corresponding solution from our model and the dashed vertical line indicates when the story was promoted to the front page. This story eventually received 452 votes.

accounting for the structure of the Digg interface can help distinguish these contributions to story popularity.

2.3 Data set

We used Digg API to collect complete (as of 2 July 2009) voting histories of all stories promoted to the front page of Digg in June 2009.[b] For each story, we collected story id, submitter's id, and the list of voters with the time of each vote. We also collected the time each story was promoted to the front page. The data set contains over 3 million votes on 3,553 promoted stories. We did not retrieve data about stories that were submitted to Digg during that time period but were never promoted. Thus, in contrast to prior models that included promotion behavior [2], our focus is on the behavior of promoted stories, which receive most of the attention from Digg users.

We define an *active user* as any user who voted for at least one story on Digg during the data collection period. Of the 139,409 active users, 71,367 designated at least one other user as a friend. We extracted the friends of these users and reconstructed the fan network of active users, i.e., a directed graph of active users who are following activities of other users.

Over the period of a month, some of the voters in our sample deleted their accounts and were marked 'inactive' by Digg. Such cases represent a tiny fraction of all users in the data set; therefore, we take the number of users to be constant.

2.4 Daily activity variation

Activity on Digg varies considerably over the course of a day, as seen in Figure 2. Adjusting times by the cumulative activity on the site accounts for this variation and improves predictions. Following [4, 5] we define the 'Digg time' between two events (e.g., votes on a story) as the total number of votes made during the time between those events. With our data, this only counts votes on stories that were eventually promoted to the front page. In our data set, there are on average about 4,000 votes on front page stories per hour, with a range of about a factor of 3 in this rate during the course of a day. This behavior is similar to that seen in an extensive study of front page activity in 2007 [4], and as in that study we

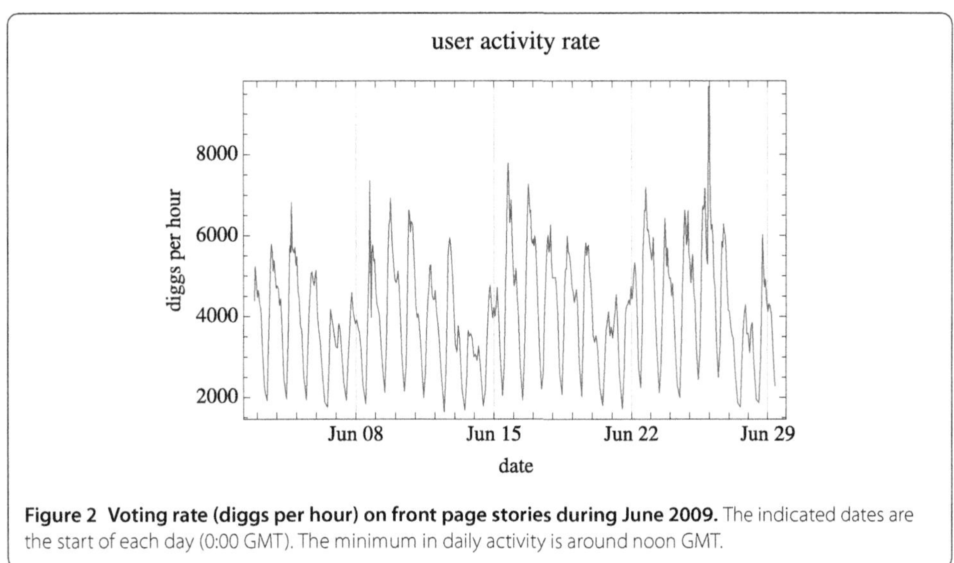

Figure 2 Voting rate (diggs per hour) on front page stories during June 2009. The indicated dates are the start of each day (0:00 GMT). The minimum in daily activity is around noon GMT.

scale the measure by defining a 'Digg hour' to be the average number of front page votes in an hour.

3 Social dynamics of Digg

A key challenge in stochastic modeling is finding a useful combination of simplicity, accuracy and available data to calibrate the model. Stochastic models of online social media describe the joint behavior of their users and content. Since these web sites receive much more content than users have time or interest to examine, one important property to model is how readily users can find content. A second key property is how users react to content once they find it. Thus an important modeling choice for social media is the level of detail sufficient to distinguish user behavior and content visibility. Following the practice of population dynamics [6] and epidemic modeling [7] we consider groups of users and content. We assume that individuals within each group have sufficiently similar behavior that their differences do not affect the main questions of interest. In the case of Digg, one such question is the number of votes a story receives over time. In our approach, we focus on how a single story accumulates votes, based on the combination of how easily users can find the story and how interesting it is to different groups of users.

Following Refs. [1, 2], we start with a simple model in which story visibility is determined primarily by its location on the recency and friends lists, and use a single value to describe the story's interestingness to the user community. We use the 'law of surfing' [8] to relate location of the story to how readily users find it. This model successfully captured the qualitative behavior of typical stories on Digg and how that behavior depended on the number of fans of the story's submitter [2, 9].

However, the simple model did not quantitatively account for several behaviors in the new data set. These included the significant daily variation in activity rates seen in Figure 2 and systematic differences in behavior between fans of a story's submitter and other users. In particular, the new data was sufficiently detailed to show users tend to find stories their friends submit as more interesting than stories friends vote on but did not submit. Another issue with the earlier model is a fairly large number of votes on stories far down the recency list. This is especially relevant for upcoming stories where the large rate of

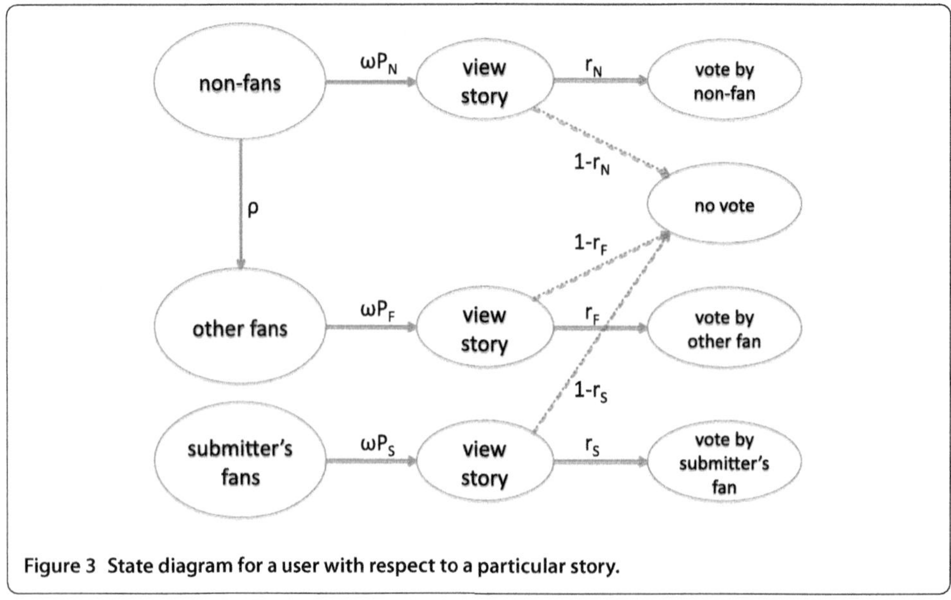

Figure 3 State diagram for a user with respect to a particular story.

new submissions means a given story remains near the top of the recency list for only a few minutes. To account for such votes, the model's estimated 'law of surfing' parameters indicated users browse an implausibly large number of pages while visiting Digg.

These observations motivate the more elaborate model described in this paper. This model includes systematic differences in interestingness between fans and other users and additional ways Digg makes stories visible to users.

3.1 User model

We allow for differences between users by separating them into groups, and assume that visibility of stories and voting behavior of users within each group is statistically the same. We refine the previous stochastic model of Digg [2] by not only distinguishing votes from fans and non-fans [5], but also allowing for differences between fans of the *submitter* and fans of *other* voters who are not also fans of the submitter. The state diagram Figure 3 shows the resulting user model. The state `submitter's fans` includes all users who are fans of the submitter and have not yet seen the story; the `other fans` state includes all users who are fans of other voters but not the submitter, who have not yet seen the story; and the `non-fans` state includes all users who are neither fans of the submitter nor other voters, and have not yet seen the story. The state `no vote` includes all users who have seen the story and decided not to vote for it. With respect to votes on a given story treated in this model, users visit Digg according to a Poisson process with average rate ω in terms of Digg time.

Users transition between states stochastically by browsing Digg's web pages and voting for stories. The submitter provides a story's first vote. All of her fans start in the `submitter's fans` state, and all other users start in the `non-fans` state. Each vote causes non-fan users who are that voter's fans and who have not yet seen the story to transition from the `non-fans` state to the `other fans` state. A user making this transition is not aware of that change until later visiting Digg and seeing the story on her friends list.

Once a user sees a story, she will vote for it with probability given by how interesting she finds the story. Nominally people become fans of those whose contributions they consider

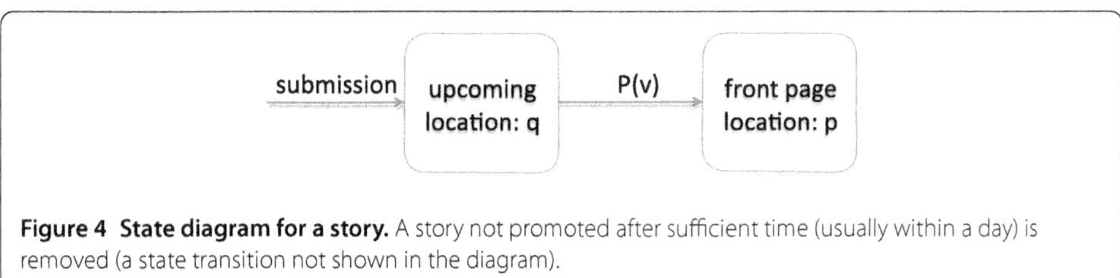

Figure 4 State diagram for a story. A story not promoted after sufficient time (usually within a day) is removed (a state transition not shown in the diagram).

interesting, suggesting fans have a systematically higher interest in stories than non-fans. Our model accounts for this by having the probability a user votes on a story depend on the user's state. Users in each state also have a different probability to see stories, which is determined by the story's *visibility* to that category of users. Users vote at most once on a story, and our focus is on the final decision to vote or not after the user sees the story.

The visibility of stories changes as stories age and accrue votes. Figure 4 shows the state diagram of stories. A story starts at the top of the upcoming stories recency list. The location increases with each new submission. A promoted story starts at the top of the front pages. The location increases as additional stories are promoted.

These state diagrams lead to a description of the average rates of growth [3] for votes from submitter fans, other fans and non-fans of prior voters, v_S, v_F and v_N, respectively:

$$\frac{dv_S}{dt} = \omega r_S P_S S, \tag{1}$$

$$\frac{dv_F}{dt} = \omega r_F P_F F, \tag{2}$$

$$\frac{dv_N}{dt} = \omega r_N P_N N, \tag{3}$$

where t is the Digg time since the story's submission and ω is the average rate a user visits Digg (measured as a rate per unit Digg time). We find only a small correlation between voting activity and the number of fans. Thus we use the average rate users visit Digg, rather than having the rate depend on the number of fans a user has. v_N includes the vote by the story's submitter. P_S, P_F and P_N denote the story's *visibility* and r_S, r_F and r_N denote the story's *interestingness* to users who are submitter fans, other fans or non-fans of prior voters, respectively. Visibility depends on the story's state (e.g., whether it has been promoted), as discussed below. Interestingness is the probability a user who sees the story will vote on it.

These voting rates depend on the number of users in each category who have not yet seen the story: S, F and N. The quantities change as users see and vote on the story, with average rate of change given by

$$\frac{dS}{dt} = -\omega P_S S, \tag{4}$$

$$\frac{dF}{dt} = -\omega P_F F + \rho N \frac{dv}{dt}, \tag{5}$$

$$\frac{dN}{dt} = -\omega P_N N - \rho N \frac{dv}{dt}, \tag{6}$$

with $v = v_S + v_F + v_N$ the total number of votes the story has received. The quantity ρ is the probability a user is a fan of the most recent voter, conditioned on that user not having

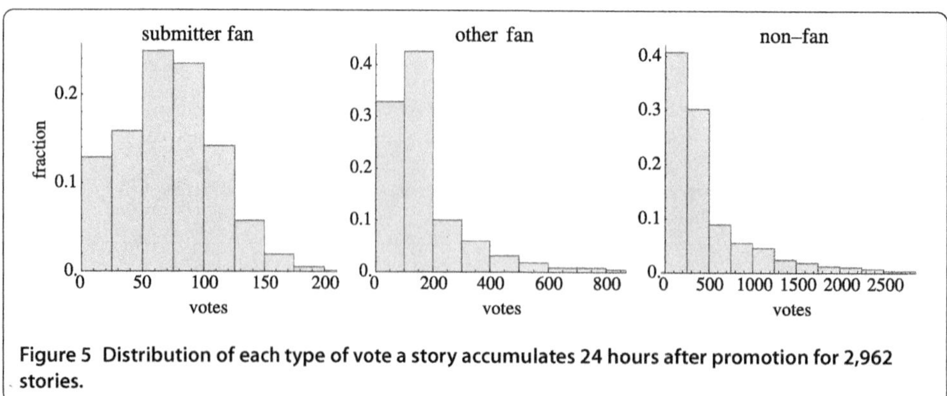

Figure 5 Distribution of each type of vote a story accumulates 24 hours after promotion for 2,962 stories.

seen the story nor being a fan of any voter prior to the most recent voter. For simplicity, we treat this probability as a constant over the voters, thus averaging over the variation due to clustering in the social network and the number of fans a user has. The first term in each of these equations is the rate the users see the story. The second terms arise from the rate the story becomes visible in the friends interface of users who are not fans of previous voters but are fans of the most recent voter.

Initially, the story has one vote (from the submitter) and the submitter has S_0 fans, so $v_S(0) = v_F(0) = 0$, $v_N(0) = 1$, $S(0) = S_0$, $F(0) = 0$ and $N(0) = U - S_0 - 1$ where U is the total number of active users at the time the story is submitted. Over time, a story becomes less visible to users as it moves down the upcoming or (if promoted) front page recency lists, thereby attracting fewer votes and hence fewer new fans of prior voters. If the story gathers more votes than other stories, it is moved to the top of the popularity list, so becomes more visible.

Figure 5 shows the range of votes the stories receive by 24 hours after promotion. Generally, stories have most votes from non-fans, somewhat fewer from other fans and a relatively small number from submitter's fans. The number of votes from submitter's fans is weakly correlated with the numbers from other fans (correlation coefficient 0.11) and non-fans (0.12). The numbers from other fans and non-fans are highly correlated (0.95).

3.2 Story visibility

A fan easily sees the story via the friends interface, so we take $P_S = P_F = 1$ for front page stories. While the story is upcoming, it appears in the friends interface but users do not necessarily choose to view upcoming stories friends liked. Users can readily make this choice because the friends interface distinguishes upcoming from front page stories. We characterize the lower visibility of upcoming stories with constants c_S and c_F which are less than 1. The corresponding visibility is then $P_S = c_S$ and $P_F = c_F$.

Users who are not fans of prior voters must find the story on the front or upcoming pages. Thus P_N depends on how users navigate through these pages and the story's location at the time the user visits Digg. This navigation is not given by our data. Instead, we use a model of user navigation through a series of web pages in which users estimate the value of continuing at the site, and leave when that value becomes negative [8]. This 'law of surfing' leads to an inverse Gaussian distribution of the number of pages m a user visits before leaving the web site,

$$e^{-\lambda(m-\mu)^2/(2m\mu^2)}\sqrt{\frac{\lambda}{2\pi m^3}} \tag{7}$$

with mean μ and variance μ^3/λ [8]. We use this distribution for user navigation on Digg [2].

The visibility of a story on the mth front or upcoming page is the fraction of users who visit *at least m* pages, i.e., the upper cumulative distribution of Equation (7). For $m > 1$, this fraction is

$$f_{\text{page}}(m) = \frac{1}{2}\left(F_m(-\mu) - e^{2\lambda/\mu}F_m(\mu)\right), \tag{8}$$

where $F_m(x) = \text{erfc}(\alpha_m(m-1+x)/\mu)$, erfc is the complementary error function, and $\alpha_m = \sqrt{\lambda/(2(m-1))}$. For $m = 1, f_{\text{page}}(1) = 1$. The visibility of stories decreases in two distinct ways when a new story arrives. First, a story moves down the list on its current page. Second, a story at the 15th position moves to the top of the next page. For simplicity, we model these processes as decreasing visibility in the same way through m taking on fractional values within a page, e.g., $m = 1.5$ denotes the position of a story half way down the list on the first page.

Digg presents several lists of stories. We focus on two lists as the major determinants of visibility for front page stories: reverse chronological order ('recency') and most popular in the past 24 hours ('popularity'). Users can also find stories via other means. For instance, Digg includes other lists showing recent and popular stories in specific topics (e.g., sports or business) and popularity over longer time periods, e.g., the previous week. Stories on Digg may also be linked to from external web sites (e.g., the submitter's blog).

For front page votes, the recency and popularity lists provide the bulk of non-fan votes while the stories are close to the top of at least one of these lists, as illustrated in Figure 6.

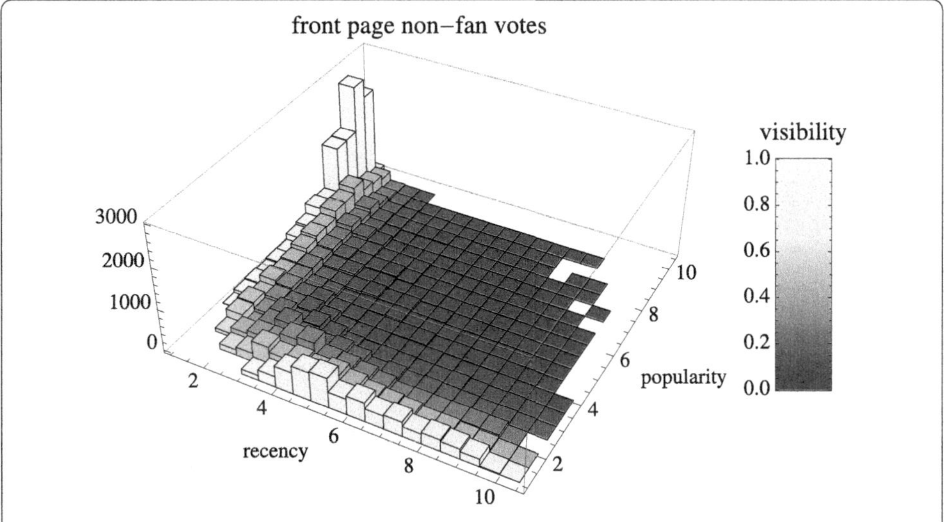

Figure 6 Distribution of front page non-fan votes by location of the story on recency and popularity lists (for votes within 24 hours of story promotion), for a sample of 100 stories with a total of 41,615 such votes. The colors indicate the visibility for each location predicted by the model parameters using Equation (9), ranging between 0 and 1 as indicated on the legend.

The rank on the recency list is the number of stories promoted more recently than that story and the rank on the popularity list is the number of stories, promoted within the 24 hours prior to the vote, with more votes. Since a page shows 15 stories, the location in terms of number of pages, as shown in the figure, is 1/15th the rank, starting from page 1. Some votes occur while stories are far down both the recency and popularity lists, so the user likely finds the story by another method.

From these observations, we account for three ways users who are not connected to prior voters find a story: via the recency list, via the popularity list or via one of the other methods described above. We combine visibility from these three methods assuming independent choices by users, giving the probability to see the story as

$$P_{\text{visibility}}(t,v) = 1 - \left(1 - f_{\text{page}}\left(p(t)\right)\right)\left(1 - f_{\text{page}}\left(p_{\text{popularity}}(v)\right)\right)(1-\beta), \tag{9}$$

where $p(t)$ and $p_{\text{popularity}}(v)$ are the locations of the story on the recency and popularity lists, respectively, and β is the probability to find the story by another method. Although the positions of the stories on these lists depend on the specific stories submitted or promoted shortly after the story, these locations are approximately determined by the time t and number of votes v the story has, as described below. For visibility by other methods, we take β to be a constant, independent of story properties such as time since submission or number of votes. That is, we do not explicitly model factors affecting the visibility of stories by other methods. Moreover, the data does not provide information on how users find a story nor the number who find the story but choose not to vote on it. These data limitations preclude a more detailed model of these other methods by which users find stories. For our focus on promoted stories, this is a minor limitation because the recency and popularity lists account for the bulk of the non-fan votes determined by our parameter estimates discussed below.

The location of a story on the recency and popularity lists could be additional state variables, which change as new stories are added and gain votes. Instead of modeling this in detail, we approximate these locations using the close relation between location and time (for recency) or votes (for popularity).

Position of a story in the recency list

Using Digg time to account for the daily variation in activity on the site, the rate of story submission and promotion is close to linear. Thus the page number of a story on either the upcoming or front page recency list is [2]

$$p(t) = \begin{cases} k_{\text{u}}t + 1 & \text{if } t < T_{\text{promotion}}, \\ k_{\text{f}}(t - T_{\text{promotion}}) + 1 & \text{otherwise}, \end{cases} \tag{10}$$

where $T_{\text{promotion}}$ is the time the story is promoted to the front page and the slopes are given in Table 1. Since each page holds 15 stories, these rates are 1/15th the story submission and promotion rates, respectively.

Position of a story in the popularity list

The position of a story on the popularity list is the number of stories submitted or promoted in the previous 24 hours with more votes, for stories on upcoming or front page

Table 1 Model parameters, with times in Digg hours

Parameter	Value
average rate each user visits Digg	$\omega = 0.16 \pm 0.01$/hr
number of active users	$U = 248{,}000 \pm 3{,}000$
page view distribution	$\mu = 0.92 \pm 0.04$
	$\lambda = 0.9 \pm 0.1$
visibility by other methods	$\beta = 0.05 \pm 0.01$
probability a user is a voter's fan	$\rho = 1.7 \times 10^{-5}$
upcoming stories location	$k_u = 59.8$ pages/hr
front page location	$k_f = 0.31$ pages/hr
fraction viewing upcoming pages	
submitter fans	$c_S = 0.57 \pm 0.03$
other fans	$c_F = 0.10 \pm 0.01$
non-fans	$c_N = 0.11 \pm 0.01$
story specific parameters	
interestingness to submitter fans	r_S
interestingness to other fans	r_F
interestingness to non-fans	r_N
number of submitter's fans	S_0
promotion time	$T_{\text{promotion}}$

Error ranges are 95% confidence intervals for the parameter estimates.

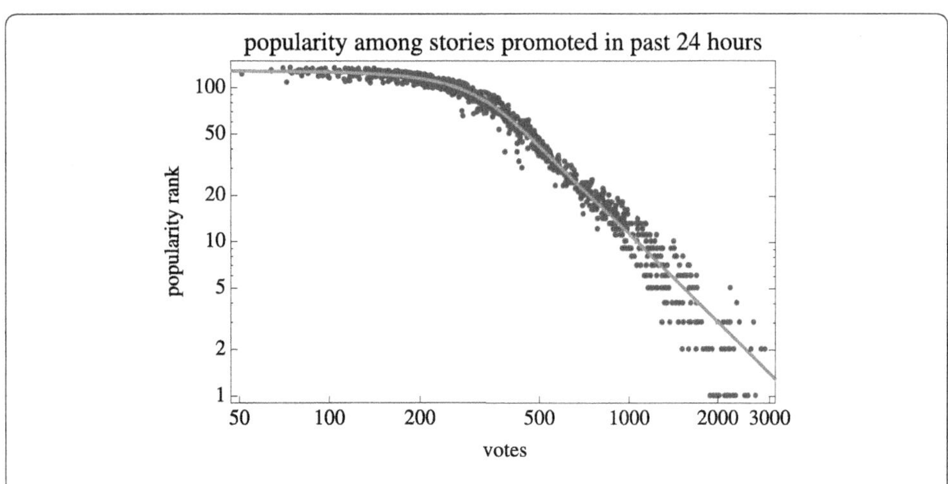

Figure 7 Relation between rank on the popularity list and number of votes for front page stories on a log-log plot. The curve is the fit to a double-Pareto lognormal distribution.

lists, respectively. The distribution of votes among stories in a 24 hour period is similar from day to day. Thus we expect that a story's position on the popularity list, determined by the location of its number of votes in this distribution, is approximately a function of its number of votes alone, with only minor variation depending on the time (i.e., the set of other stories from the past 24 hours). To evaluate this expectation, we determined the popularity rank of a sample of front page votes within 24-hours of story promotion and compared the rank to the number of votes, as shown in Figure 7. As we expected, the figure shows that the rank is well-determined by the number of votes. Thus we model the position of a story on the popularity list as depending only on the number of votes the story has at the time, i.e., consider $p_{\text{popularity}}(v)$ as a function of the number of votes the story has. This gives a simple, approximate relation between the actual location and number of votes - ignoring the minor variations due to the specific stories promoted at different times.

To identify a suitable functional approximation for $p_{\text{popularity}}(v)$, we note that a story typically accumulates votes at a rate proportional to how interesting it is to the user population. From a prior analysis of votes in 2006 on Digg [2] we expect the interestingness to be approximately lognormally distributed. Thus if we observe a sample of votes on stories over the same time interval for each story, the distribution of votes, and hence location on the popularity list, would follow a lognormal distribution. However, the popularity list includes stories of various times up to 24 hours since submission or promotion. Thus some stories of high interest will have few votes because they were just recently submitted or promoted, and conversely some stories with only moderate interestingness will have relatively many votes because they have been available for votes for nearly 24 hours. The combination of lognormal distribution of rates for accumulating votes and this variation in the observation times modifies the tails of the lognormal to be power-law, i.e., a double-Pareto lognormal distribution [10].

Such a distribution fits the observed positions on the front page popularity list, as indicated in Figure 7. The fit for the rank (i.e., number of stories above the given one in the popularity list, so the story promoted in the past 24 hours with the most votes has rank 0) is

$$\text{rank} = S(1 - \Lambda(a, b, \nu, \sigma; v)), \tag{11}$$

where $S = 129.0 \pm 0.1$ is the average number of stories promoted in 24 hours and $\Lambda(\ldots; v)$ is the cumulative distribution of a double-Pareto lognormal distribution, i.e., fraction of cases with fewer than v votes. The parameters $a = 1.90 \pm 0.005$ and $b = 2.50 \pm 0.03$ are the power-law exponents for the upper and lower tails of the distribution, respectively, and the parameters $\nu = 5.88 \pm 0.002$ and $\sigma = 0.16 \pm 0.004$ characterize the location and spread of the lognormal behavior in the center of the distribution. This fit captures the power-law tail relating stories near the top of the popularity list with the number of votes the story has. These are the cases for which the popularity list contributes significantly to the overall visibility of a story. More precisely, the Kolmogorov-Smirnov (KS) statistic shows the vote counts are consistent with this distribution (p-value 0.92). We use this distribution, combined with the rate stories are promoted, to relate the number of votes a story has to its position on the popularity list, providing a functional form for $p_{\text{popularity}}(v)$.

The popularity rank for upcoming stories submitted in the past 24 hours is more complicated than for the front pages due to the promotion. Nevertheless, the main factor determining a story's location on the popularity list is its number of votes, particularly after adjusting for most of the daily variation in activity by using Digg time described in Section 2.4. Stories with many votes are more likely to be promoted, and hence removed from the popularity list for upcoming stories. This removal alters the upper tail of the distribution and hence the numbers of votes for stories appearing near the top of the popularity list. Moreover, out of the $\approx$20,000 stories submitted each day, our data includes only the $\approx$100 stories per day eventually promoted. However, popularity significantly contributes to visibility only for stories near the top of the popularity list. Thus for our model, it is sufficient to determine the relation between votes and rank for upcoming stories with relatively many votes. Such stories are likely to be promoted eventually and hence included in our sample. Instead of a power-law tail, our data on the eventually promoted stories is better fit by an exponential for the upcoming stories with relatively many votes, and hence near the top of the popularity list:

$$\text{rank} = e^{c-dv} \tag{12}$$

with $c = 5.3 \pm 0.01$ and $d = 0.029 \pm 0.0002$. This fits well for upcoming stories submitted within the past 24 hours with more than 100 votes, corresponding to rank of about 20 or less on the upcoming popularity list. For stories with few votes, e.g., fewer than 10 or 20, this fit based on the stories eventually promoted substantially underestimates the rank. Nevertheless, the estimated rank for such stories is still sufficiently large that the law of surfing parameters we estimate indicate users do not find such stories via the popularity list. Thus this underestimate does not significantly affect our model's behavior for upcoming stories.

Friends interface

The fans of the story's submitter can find the story via the friends interface. As additional people vote on the story, their fans can also see the story. We model this with $F(t)$, the number of fans of voters on the story by time t who are not also fans of the submitter and have not yet seen the story. Although the number of fans is highly variable, we use the average number of additional fans from an extra vote, ρN, in Equation (4).

4 Parameter estimation

We estimate model parameters using 100 stories from the middle of our sample.

4.1 Estimating parameters from observed votes

In our model, story location affects visibility only for non-fan voters since fans of prior voters see the story via the friends interface. Thus we use just the non-fan votes to estimate visibility parameters, via maximum likelihood. Specifically, we use the non-fan votes to estimate the 'law of surfing' parameters μ and λ, as well as the probability for finding the story some other way, β.

This estimation involves comparing the observed votes to the voting rate from the model. As described above, the model uses rate equations to determine the average behavior of the number of votes. We relate this average to the observed number of votes by assuming the votes from non-fan users form a Poisson process whose expected value is $dv_N(t)/dt$, given by Equation (3).

For a Poisson process with a constant rate ν, the probability to observe n events in time T is the Poisson distribution $e^{-\nu T}(\nu T)^n/n!$. This probability depends only on the *number* of events, not the specific times at which they occur. Estimating ν involves maximizing this expression, giving $\nu = n/T$. Thus the maximum-likelihood estimate of the rate for a constant Poisson process is the average rate of the observed events.

In our case, the voting rate changes with time, requiring a generalization of this estimation. Specifically consider a Poisson process with nonnegative rate $\nu(t)$ which depends on one or more parameters to be estimated. Thus in a small time interval $(t, t + \Delta t)$, the probability for a vote is $\nu(t)\Delta t$, and this is independent of votes in other time intervals, by the definition of a Poisson process. Suppose we observe n votes at times $0 < t_1 < t_2 < \cdots < t_n < T$

during an observation time interval $(0, T)$. Considering small time intervals Δt around each observation, the probability of this observation is

$$
\begin{aligned}
&P\big(\text{no vote in } (0, t_1)\big)\nu(t_1)\Delta t \\
&\quad \times P\big(\text{no vote in } (t_1, t_2)\big)\nu(t_2)\Delta t \\
&\quad \ldots \\
&\quad \times P\big(\text{no vote in } (t_{n-1}, t_n)\big)\nu(t_n)\Delta t \\
&\quad \times P\big(\text{no vote in } (t_n, T)\big).
\end{aligned}
$$

The probability for no vote in the interval (a, b) is

$$\exp\left(-\int_a^b \nu(t)\,dt\right).$$

Thus the log-likelihood for the observed sequence of votes is

$$-\int_0^T \nu(t)\,dt + \sum_i \log \nu(t_i). \tag{13}$$

The maximum-likelihood estimation for parameters determining the rate $\nu(t)$ is a trade-off between these two terms: minimizing $\nu(t)$ over the range $(0, T)$ to increase the first term while maximizing the values $\nu(t_i)$ at the times of the observed votes. If $\nu(t)$ is constant, this likelihood expression simplifies to $-\nu T + n \log \nu$ with maximum at $\nu = n/T$ as discussed above for the constant Poisson process. When $\nu(t)$ varies with time, the maximization selects parameters giving relatively larger $\nu(t)$ values where the observed votes are clustered in time.

We combine this log-likelihood expression from the votes on several stories, and maximize the combined expression with respect to the story-independent parameters of the model, while determining the interestingness parameters separately for each story.

4.2 User activity

Our model involves a population of active users who visit Digg during our sample period and vote on stories. Specifically, the model uses the rate users visit Digg, ωU. We do not observe visits in our data, but can infer the relevant number of active users, U, from the heterogeneity in the number of votes by users. The data set consists of 139,409 users who voted at least once during the sample period, giving a total of 3,018,197 votes. Figure 8 shows the distribution of this activity. Most users have little activity during the sample period, suggesting a large fraction of users vote infrequently enough to never have voted during the time of our data sample. This behavior can be characterized by an activity rate for each user. A user with activity rate ν will, on average, vote on νT stories during a sample time T. We model the observed votes as arising from a Poisson process whose expected value is νT and the heterogeneity arising from a lognormal distribution of user activity rates [11]:

$$P_{\text{lognormal}}(\mu, \sigma; r) = \frac{1}{\sqrt{2\pi}\, r\sigma} \exp\left(-\frac{(\mu - \log(r))^2}{2\sigma^2}\right), \tag{14}$$

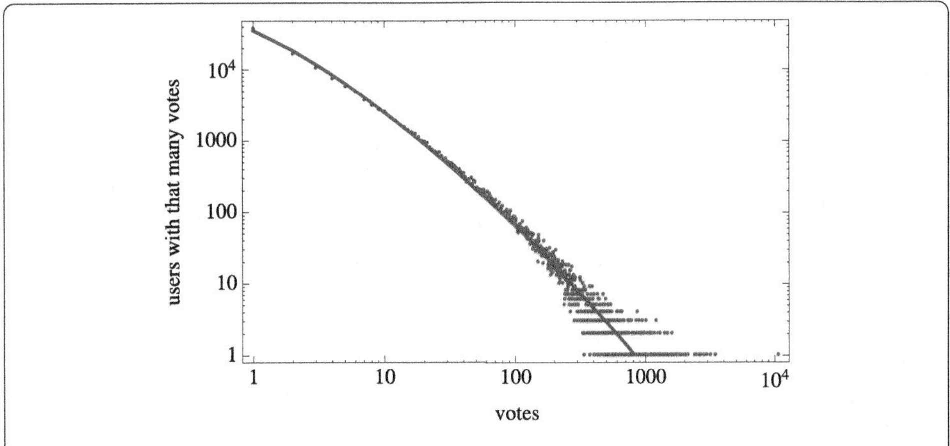

Figure 8 User activity distribution on logarithmic scales. The curve shows the fit to the model described in the text.

where parameters μ and σ are the mean and standard deviation of $\log(r)$.

This model gives rise to the extended activity distribution while accounting for the discrete nature of the observations. The latter is important for the majority of users, who have low activity rates and vote only a few times, or not at all, during our sample period.

Specifically, for n_k users with k votes during the sample period, this mixture of lognormal and Poisson distributions [12, 13] gives the log-likelihood of the observations as

$$\sum_k n_k \log P(\mu,\sigma;k),$$

where $P(\mu,\sigma;k)$ is the probability of a Poisson distribution to give k votes when its mean is chosen from a lognormal distribution $P_{\text{lognormal}}$ with parameters μ and σ. From Equation (14),

$$P(\mu,\sigma;k) = \frac{1}{\sqrt{2\pi}\,\sigma k!}\int_0^\infty \rho^{k-1} e^{-(\log(\rho)-\mu)^2/(2\sigma^2)-\rho}\, d\rho$$

for integer $k \geq 0$. We evaluate this integral numerically. In terms of our model parameters, the value of μ in this distribution equals νT.

Since we do not observe the number of users who did not vote during our sample period, i.e., the value of n_0, we cannot maximize this log-likelihood expression directly. Instead, we use a zero-truncated maximum likelihood estimate [14] to determine the parameters μ and σ for the vote distribution of Figure 8. Specifically, the fit is to the probability of observing k votes conditioned on observing at least one vote. This conditional distribution is $P(\mu,\sigma;k)/(1 - P(\mu,\sigma;0))$ for $k > 0$, and the corresponding log-likelihood is

$$\sum_{k>0} n_k \log P(\mu,\sigma;k) - U_+ \log\bigl(1 - P(\mu,\sigma;0)\bigr),$$

where U_+ is the number of users with at least one vote in our sample. Maximizing this expression with respect to the distribution's parameters μ and σ gives νT lognormally distributed with the mean and standard deviation of $\log(\nu T)$ equal to -0.10 ± 0.04 and

2.43 ± 0.02, respectively. Based on this fit, the curve in Figure 8 shows the expected number of users with each number of votes. This is a discrete distribution: the lines in the figure between the expected values serve only to distinguish the model fit from the points showing the observed values.

With these estimated parameters, $P(\mu, \sigma; 0) = 0.43$, indicating 43% of the users had sufficiently low, but nonzero, activity rate that they did not vote during the sample period. We use this value to estimate U, the number of active users during our sample period: $U = U_+/(1 - P(\mu, \sigma; 0))$.

4.3 Links among users

We observe $u = 258{,}218$ users with fans, and these users have a total of $c = 1{,}731{,}658$ connections. Our data has 139,409 distinct voters, of which 78,007 have no fans. There is little correlation between links and voting activity, so we estimate the fraction of users with zero fans from the ratio of these values, i.e., about 56%. Thus the average number of fans per user, including users without fans, is $c/(1.56u) \approx 4.3$.

We estimate the model parameter ρ of Equations (4) and (6) as the probability a fan link connects the first to the second user of a randomly selected pair of users, corresponding to the average number of fans per user divided by the number of active users U.

4.4 Visibility to submitter's fans

Because stories are always visible to fans and we know the number of fans of the story's submitter, the model behavior (Equations (1) and (4)) can be solved without reference to the rest of the model. We have $P_S = 1$ when the story is on the front page and $P_S = c_S < 1$, reflecting users' preference for front page stories. Thus, these equations have two story-independent parameters, i.e., the rate users visit Digg (ω) and the probability users view upcoming stories submitted by their friends (c_S), and two story-dependent parameters, i.e., the interestingness (r_S) and number of fans of the submitter (S_0). S_0 is given in our data, while we estimate the other parameters from the data, i.e., votes by fans of the stories' submitters.

4.5 Visibility to non-fans

In our model, story location affects visibility only for non-fan voters since fans of prior voters see the story via the friends interface. Thus we use just the non-fan votes to estimate visibility parameters, via maximum likelihood. A story typically receives only a few dozen votes before promotion, mostly from fans. With the value of ρ, estimated as described above, Equation (6) gives $N(t) \approx U$ up to a few hours after promotion. Over this time period, Equation (3) simplifies to $dN/dt \approx \omega U r_N P_N$ with P_N depending on story location on the recency and popularity lists. r_N is constant for a given story, so P_N determines the time variation in the voting rate by non-fans.

For front page stories, in our model $P_N = P_{\text{visibility}}(t, v)$ from Equation (9), which has three parameters: μ and λ characterizing the browsing behavior for the recency and popularity lists, and the probability to find the story by other methods, β. We estimate these parameters by maximizing the likelihood of observing the non-fan front page votes according to the model, as described above for estimating a Poisson process with a time-dependent rate in Equation (13). This estimation also determines r_N for each story.

For upcoming stories, we take $P_N = c_N P_{\text{visibility}}(t, v)$, giving a single additional parameter, c_N, to estimate, since we assume browsing behavior on the upcoming pages is the same as for front pages. This assumption has little effect on the model behavior because of the large number of submissions and relatively few non-fan votes for upcoming stories. A submitted story remains near the front of the recency list for only about a minute after submission and stories reaching the front of the popularity list (due to having many votes) are soon promoted to the front page. Thus moderate variations in how deeply users browse the upcoming recency or popularity lists (i.e., the values for μ and λ) have little effect on the non-fan votes. Instead, the relatively few non-fan upcoming votes arise mainly through users finding the story by other means. That is, in most cases $P_{\text{visibility}} \approx \beta$ for upcoming stories. Thus $P_N = c_N P_{\text{visibility}}(t, v) \approx c_N \beta$ and any difference between β for upcoming and front page stories would merely rescale the value of c_N. This parameter is readily estimated using Equation (13) with the upcoming non-fan votes.

4.6 Visibility to other fans

From Equation (2), dv_F/dt changes abruptly when the story is promoted since P_F changes from c_F to 1 upon promotion. Thus we estimate c_F by the change in voting rate by fans other than those of the submitter by comparing the votes a story receives one hour before promotion and the votes received during the hour after promotion.

With all story-independent parameters estimated, we can then solve the full model for a story to determine dv_F/dt as a function of time. This gives the expected rate of other fan votes as a function of time. We determine r_F for the story as the value maximizing the log-likelihood (Equation (13)) for the other fan votes the story receives.

4.7 Summary

Table 1 lists the estimated parameters. All of these parameters, except the three story interestingness parameters r_S, r_F and r_N, are either known (e.g., the number of submitter's fans) or estimated from data from a sample of stories and then used for all stories. The interestingness parameters are estimated individually for each story from its votes.

5 Results

Figure 1 compares the solution of the rate equations with the actual votes for one story. This illustrates that the model captures the main qualitative features of the vote dynamics: an abrupt jump in votes after promotion followed by a slowing of the voting rate.

Figure 6 shows how visibility estimated by our model (indicated by color) compares with the distribution of front page votes. Many votes occur when the story is recently promoted (so near the top of the recency list) or has received many votes within 24 hours after promotion (so near the top of the popularity list). This is consistent with our model, which predicts higher visibility for stories in these positions on the lists.

5.1 Interestingness for fans and non-fans

We use the model to evaluate systematic differences in story interestingness between fans and non-fans. The estimated r values indicate the stories have a wide range of interestingness to users, as shown in Figure 9, along with fits to lognormal distributions. The figure shows r_N values tend to be much smaller than the interestingness for fans, as also seen in an earlier study with a smaller data set from 2006 [5]. The r-values are weakly correlated, with Spearman rank correlation between r_S and r_F of 0.17, between r_S and r_N of 0.03, and between r_F and r_N of 0.39. Moreover, there is a large range in the ratio of interestingness

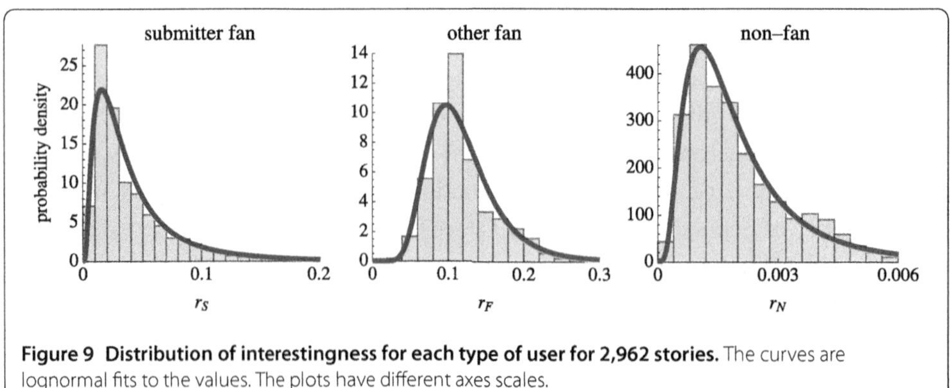

Figure 9 Distribution of interestingness for each type of user for 2,962 stories. The curves are lognormal fits to the values. The plots have different axes scales.

Table 2 Parameters for lognormal distribution of interestingness for 2,962 stories

Vote type	μ	σ
submitter fan	-3.48 ± 0.04	0.84 ± 0.03
other fan	-2.20 ± 0.02	0.37 ± 0.01
non-fan	-6.41 ± 0.03	0.66 ± 0.02

Error ranges are 95% confidence intervals for the parameter estimates.

to fans and non-fans, suggesting stories with particularly large ratios are mainly of niche interest.

Table 2 summarizes the lognormal distribution parameters. The lognormal fits provide a concise description of the distribution of interestingness values and are useful as prior distributions for prediction from early votes, as discussed in Section 5.2. However bootstrap tests [15] based on the Kolmogorov-Smirnov (KS) statistic show the estimated r-values are unlikely to arise from these distributions (p-values all less than 0.02). This test and the others reported in this paper account for the fact that we fit the distribution parameters to the data [16].

The relationship between interestingness for fans and other users indicates a considerable variation in how widely stories appeal to the general user community. Moreover, we find other fans have somewhat higher interest in stories than submitter fans, i.e., r_F tends to be larger than r_S. Since we have $c_S > c_F$ (Table 1), we find submitter fans are more likely to view the story while upcoming, but less likely to vote for it, compared with other fans. This suggests people favor the submitter as a source of stories to read, while the fact that a friend, not the submitter, voted for the story makes it more likely the user will vote for the story. Identifying these possibilities illustrates how models can suggest subgroups of behaviors in social media for future investigation.

5.2 Predicting popularity from early votes

In this section we use the model to predict popularity of Digg stories. We focus on the 89 of the 100 stories in the calibration data set that were promoted within 24 hours of submission. Most stories are promoted within 24 hours of submission (if they are ever promoted) and this restriction simplifies the model's use of the 'popular in last 24 hours' list by not requiring it to check for removal from the list if the story is still upcoming more than 24 hours after submission.

Predicting popularity in social media from intrinsic properties of newly submitted content is difficult [17]. However, users' early reactions provide some measure of predictability

[4, 11, 18, 19]. The early votes on a story allow estimating its interestingness to fans and other users, thereby predicting how the story will accumulate additional votes. These predictions are for expected values and cannot account for the large variation due, for example, to a subsequent vote by a highly connected user which leads to a much larger number of votes.

We can improve predictions from early votes by using the lognormal distributions of r-values, shown in Figure 9, as the prior probability to combine with the likelihood from the observations according to Bayes theorem. Specifically, instead of maximizing the likelihood of the observed votes, $P(r|\text{votes})$, as discussed above, this approach maximizes the posterior probability, which is proportional to $P(r|\text{votes})P_{\text{prior}}(r)$ where P_{prior} is taken to be the lognormal distribution $P_{\text{lognormal}}$ in Equation (14) with parameters from the fits shown in Figure 9.

For a prediction at time T, we use the votes up to time T to estimate the r values by finding the values that maximize

$$L = \log\big(P(r_S, r_F, r_N|\text{votes})\big) + \log\big(P_{\text{prior}}(r_S)P_{\text{prior}}(r_F)P_{\text{prior}}(r_N)\big). \tag{15}$$

We then solve the model starting at time T and use the values from that solution as the predictions at later times. Solving the model equations starting at time T requires initial values, i.e., the number of votes $v_S(T)$, $v_F(T)$, $v_N(T)$ and the size of the user groups who have not yet seen the story: $S(T)$, $F(T)$, $N(T)$. The numbers of votes is available in our data but the sizes of the user groups is not. Instead, we estimate user group sizes from the voting *rates* and the estimated r values. That is, at the prediction time T we use the times of recent votes to estimate the derivative in number of each type of vote at time T. With estimates of the r values and voting rates, we use the model equations to estimate the group size at time T. For instance, Equation (1) gives

$$S(T) = \frac{1}{\omega r_S P_S}\frac{dv_S}{dt}. \tag{16}$$

We estimate the voting rates from the number of votes in the 15 minutes prior to time T, except if there are fewer than five votes in this time we extend the time interval to include the five previous votes. For simplicity, to avoid treating the discontinuity in visibility at promotion, we based this estimate on front page votes when T is after the promotion time. This approach to estimating user group sizes is reasonable while the story is accumulating votes rapidly, i.e., when it is recently promoted. In that case the story is highly visible and we have a good estimate of the voting rate. This is the situation of interest for prediction based on users' early response to a story. On the other hand, old stories have low visibility and accumulates votes slowly, if at all, as seen in Figure 1. In that case, the group size estimate, based on the ratio of voting rate and visibility, will be highly uncertain.

We focus on behavior after promotion. Figure 10 compares predicted to actual votes for one story 24 hours after promotion. Votes from submission to promotion are used to estimate r values for the three groups of users. The model solutions extend from the time of these estimates, i.e., the story's promotion time, to $t = 24$ Digg hours after promotion. The model quantitatively reproduces the observed votes for this story.

Generalizing from this example for a single story, Figure 11 shows the prediction errors for each type of vote the story receives 24 Digg hours after promotion, based on estimating

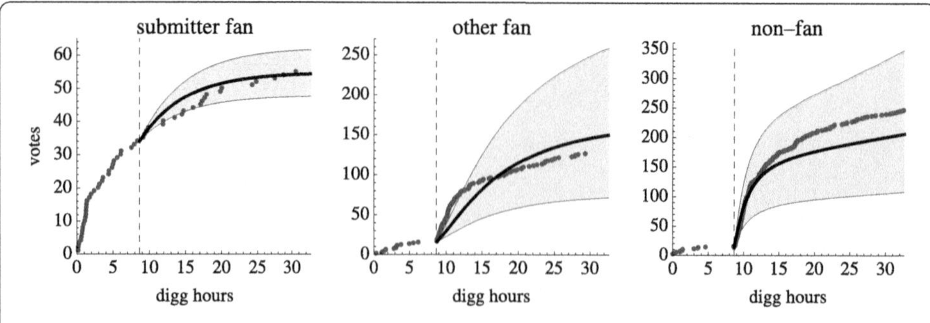

Figure 10 Predictions compared to actual votes (dots) for each type of user for one story. The figure shows predictions made at promotion (black line) and the growth in the 95% confidence interval of the prediction up to 24 hours after promotion. The dashed vertical line shows the story's promotion time.

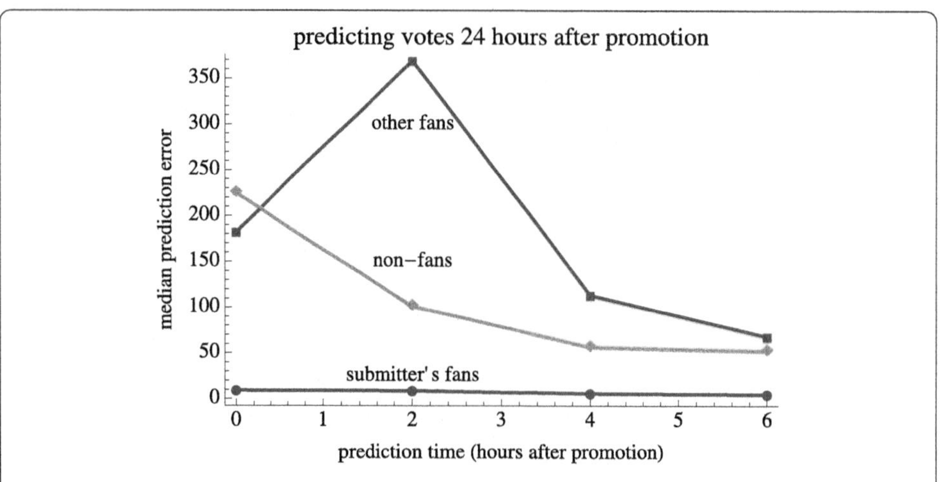

Figure 11 Median error between predicted and observed votes 24 Digg hours after promotion for predictions made 0, 2, 4 and 6 Digg hours after promotion for 500 stories.

r-values from votes received by time T for various times T at and shortly after promotion. For context of the size of these errors, Figure 5 shows the range of number of votes the stories have at the times of these predictions, i.e., 24 hours after promotion.

As expected, errors generally decrease when predictions are made later. Of more interest is the difference among the type of votes, particularly for votes from other fans. Early votes are mainly from submitter's fans and non-fans, so the ability to predict differences in behavior for those groups based on early votes could be useful in quickly distinguishing stories likely to be of broad or niche interest to the user community.

Overall, the model reasonably predicts votes from submitter's fans and non-fans, but is much less accurate for votes from other fans. One reason for this difference is the relatively small number of other fan votes while a story is upcoming. Specifically, the number of other fans F starts at zero. Only a vote by a non-fan can increase F, and upcoming stories have low visibility to non-fan voters. Even after a number of other fans becomes available, it takes some time for those users to return to Digg. Thus there are relatively few early other fan votes, leading to poor estimates for r_F values. Moreover, the relatively small number of other fans means a single early voter with many fans can significantly change F away from its average value used in the model. These factors lead to the relatively large

Table 3 Spearman rank correlation between predicted and observed number of each type of votes 24 Digg hours after promotion, for predictions made at various times T after promotion (measured in Digg hours) for 500 stories

$T - T_{\text{promotion}}$	Correlation		
	Submitter fan	Other fan	Non-fan
0	0.86	0.29	0.42
2	0.94	0.74	0.91
4	0.97	0.78	0.93
6	0.97	0.81	0.95

Table 4 Classification errors on whether a story receives more than the median number of votes from each type of voter received by 24 Digg hours after promotion, for predictions made at various times T after promotion (measured in Digg hours) for 500 stories

$T - T_{\text{promotion}}$	Classification error		
	Submitter fan	Other fan	Non-fan
0	0.12	0.41	0.37
2	0.09	0.45	0.16
4	0.07	0.33	0.11
6	0.07	0.30	0.10

errors in predicting the other fan votes. As a direction for future work, this observation suggests predictions would benefit from including measurements of the social network of the voters to determine the value of F at the time of prediction rather than using an estimate based on the model.

Another view of prediction quality is how well the model predicts the rank ordering of stories, i.e., whether the story is likely to be relatively popular. We measure this with the Spearman rank correlation between the model's prediction and the observed number of votes 24 Digg hours after promotion, as shown in Table 3. Even for other fan votes, where the absolute prediction error is relatively large, the predicted values give a good indication of the relative rank of the stories.

Predicting whether a story will attract a large number of votes, rather than the precise number of votes, is a key issue for web sites such as Digg. Such predictions form the basis of using crowd sourcing to select a subset of submitted content to highlight [19]. As an example of this distinction, we predict whether a story will receive more than the median number of votes of each type of user based on votes received up to various times. This amounts to a binary classification task. Table 4 compares predictions made at different times. The classification error rate is the fraction of stories for which prediction of whether the story receives more than the median number of votes differs from the actual value.

5.3 Confidence intervals

We can use the model to estimate how well it predicts future votes. For a given set of parameter values, prediction variability comes from differences in estimated r values. If r is poorly determined, predictions will be unreliable.

To quantify this behavior, we numerically evaluate the second derivative matrix D of the log-likelihood combined with the priors based on votes on the story up to time T, $L(r)$ given in Equation (15), at the maximum $r = r_{\max}$, where $r = (r_S, r_F, r_N)$. This gives

$$L(r) = L(r_{\max}) + \frac{1}{2}(r - r_{\max})D(r - r_{\max}) \tag{17}$$

to second order in $|r - r_{max}|$. To this order of expansion, the likelihood is

$$\exp\big(-(r - r_{max})D(r - r_{max})/2\big). \tag{18}$$

This corresponds to a multivariate normal distribution for r with mean r_{max} and covariance matrix $-D^{-1}$. Since we are expanding around a maximum, the 2nd derivative matrix is negative definite so this gives a well-defined normal distribution, i.e., with a positive definite covariance matrix. This covariance includes both individual variances in the values of r_S, r_F and r_N and correlations among their variations around the maximum.

If $L(r)$ is a fairly flat function of r around the maximum, then maximum likelihood poorly constrains the values, corresponding to large variances in the normal distribution. Conversely, if $L(r)$ is sharply peaked, the distribution will be narrow.

We apply this observation to estimate confidence intervals for the predictions. We first numerically evaluate the second derivative matrix D at the maximum. We then generate random samples of r from the multivariate normal distribution. For each of these samples, we solve the model starting from the time T to any desired time for predicting the votes, e.g., 24 hours after promotion. After collecting these predictions from many samples, we use quantiles of their ranges as the confidence intervals. In the examples presented here, we generate 1,000 random samples and determine the 95% confidence interval from the variation in r values as the range between the 2.5% and 97.5% quantiles of these samples.

As one example, Figure 10 shows how confidence intervals grow with time after the prediction for predictions made from votes at the time a story is promoted. Predictions made at later times, when more votes are available, generally have smaller confidence intervals. More generally, Figure 12 shows the relation between 95% confidence interval and prediction error 24 Digg hours after promotion, based on prediction made at the time of promotion. Large errors tend to be associated with large confidence intervals. To quantify this relationship, correlations between prediction error and confidence interval size for the stories shown in Figure 12 are 0.76, 0.96 and 0.66 for submitter fans, other fans and non-fans, respectively. Thus the confidence intervals, which are computed from the vote information available at the time of prediction, indicate how well the model can predict votes. However, the confidence intervals based on variation in the estimate of r values do not account for all the sources of error. For instance, Figure 12 shows some cases where the error is considerably larger than the confidence interval. Furthermore, only about a third

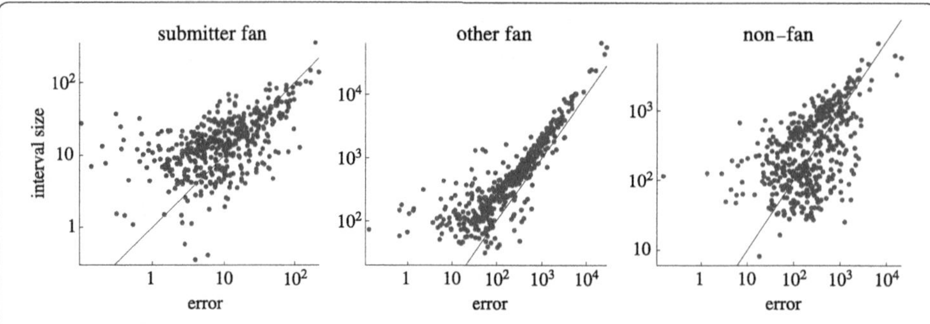

Figure 12 Size of 95% confidence interval vs. prediction error 24 Digg hours after promotion for predictions based on votes up to each story's promotion time, for 500 stories. The diagonal lines correspond to errors equal to the size of the confidence interval.

of the actual votes 24 hours after promotion are within the confidence intervals, whereas we would expect about 95% of the stories to be within the intervals. Additional variation could be due, for instance, to votes by exceptionally well-connected users that significantly increase the story's visibility compared to the average value assumed with the model. Large prediction errors can also arise from poor estimates of the sizes of the groups of each type of user at the time of prediction.

6 Related work

Models of social dynamics can help explain and predict the popularity of online content. The broad distributions of popularity and user activity on many social media sites can arise from simple macroscopic dynamical rules [20]. A phenomenological model of the collective attention on Digg describes the distribution of final votes for promoted stories through a decay of interest in news articles [21]. Likewise, a model that accounted for shifts in public attention, e.g., brought about by exogenous events, reproduced in simulation the aggregate distribution of popularity of Web pages [22], but did not model dynamics of individual items. Yet another study [23] offered a qualitative explanation for the observed dynamics of popularity of individual news stories in terms of the dueling effects of preference for recent stories and those already featured in the news; however, no attempt was made to connect this model to empirical data. Stochastic models [1, 2] offer an alternative explanation for the popularity distribution of Digg news stories. Rather than novelty decay (or bias for recent news), they explain the votes distribution by the combination of variation in the stories' inherent interest to users and effects of user interface, specifically decay in visibility as the story moves to subsequent pages. Stochastic modeling framework explains both the dynamics of popularity of an individual news story, as well as the distribution of final popularity of many stories. Crane and Sornette [24] found that collective dynamics was linked to the inherent quality of videos on YouTube. From the number of votes received by videos over time, they could separate high quality videos from junk videos. This study is similar in spirit to our own in exploiting the link between observed popularity and content quality. We assume all users explore stories using the same parameters for the 'law of surfing' [8]. More generally, such models could be adjusted to accommodate a range of surfing persistence among different groups of users [25]. Web-based experiments allow directly manipulating visibility to distinguish its effect from social influence and content quality, e.g., by reversing the order in which content is shown to users [26]. State-based models, such as we used here, apply to forecasting user behavior in a wide variety of contexts, including web searches [27] which are one mechanism by which users could find content without relying on visibility explicitly provided by the social media site. However, while these studies aggregated data from thousands of individuals, our method focuses instead on the *microscopic* dynamics, modeling how individual behavior contributes to content popularity.

Statistically significant correlation between early and late popularity of content is found on Slashdot [18], Digg and YouTube [4]. Specifically, similar to our study, Szabo and Huberman [4] predicted long-term popularity of stories on Digg. Through large-scale statistical study of stories promoted to the front page, they were able to predict stories' popularity after 30 days based on its correlation with popularity one hour after promotion. Similarly, Lerman and Hogg [9] predicted popularity of stories based on their pre-promotion votes. We also quantitatively predict stories' future popularity, but unlike earlier works, we also estimate confidence intervals of these predictions for each story.

Previous works found social networks to be an important component to information diffusion. Niche interest content tends to spread mainly along social links in Second Life [28], in blogspace [29], as well as on Digg [19], and does not end up becoming very popular with the general audience. Models based on biased random walks to select actions [30] provide more detailed descriptions of information diffusion in social media [31] than used in our modeling approach. Aral et al. [32] found that social links between like-minded people, rather than causal influence, explained much of information diffusion observed on a network. Our modeling approach allows us to systematically distinguish users who are linked to those who are not linked and study diffusion separately for each group.

Commercial recommendation systems, such as those used by Amazon and Netflix, use collaborative filtering [33] to highlight new products for users. They ask users to rate products and compare ratings to identify users with similar opinions and recommend to them new products other users with similar opinions liked. Researchers have recognized that links between users in a recommender system can be induced from the declarations of user interest, and that these links can used to make new recommendations [34]. However, unlike social media sites, collaborative filtering-based systems do not allow users to explicitly declare their social links. Nevertheless, such techniques can be useful in automatically helping social media users find others with similar interests [35–37] and thereby encourage users to make implicit links explicit in social media web sites. In our context, such methods could increase the visibility of similar users to each other, thereby improving the sorting of users between the fan and non-fan categories studied in our model.

7 Discussion

Highlighting friends' contributions is a common feature of social media sites, including Digg. To evaluate the effects of this behavior, we explicitly distinguish votes from submitter's fans, other fans and non-fans in our model, while separating the effects of differences in visibility and interestingness among these groups of users. This identifies that submitter's fans are, on average, far more likely to find the story interesting. Our model adjusts for the higher visibility of stories to fans, thereby identifying that increased attention from fans is not just due to the increased visibility. Identifying stories of particularly high interest to fans could be a useful guide for highlighting stories in the friends interface, i.e., emphasizing those with relatively large interestingness to friends as reflected in the early votes. Moreover, this information could be useful to recommend new fans to users, based on visibility-adjusted similarity in voting rather than, as commonly done in collaborative filtering [33], just using the raw score of similar votes. This could be particularly important for users with relatively infrequent votes, where variations due to how visible a story is could significantly affect the similarity of the vote pattern with that of other users.

For more precise estimates, the web site could track the fraction of users seeing the story that vote for it, thereby directly estimating interestingness and accounting for the large variability in number of fans among the voters, in contrast to our model which used an average value. Exploiting such details of user behavior becomes more important as the complexity of the web site interface increases, offering many ways for users to locate content. Recording which method leads each user to find the story can aid in identifying any systematic differences in interests among those users.

We find a wide range of interestingness ratios between fans and non-fans. This explains prior observations of the effect of relatively high votes from fans on indicating popularity to the general user population, and also suggests stories that are of niche interest to the fans rather than the general user population. Our assumption that fans of prior voters easily see the story is reasonable for users with relatively few friends, so only a few stories will appear in their friends interface. For users with many friends, visibility of a story would decrease when many newer stories appear on the friends interface. This possibility could be included in the model using the 'law of surfing' for the stories appearing in each users' friends interface.

For prediction, we find the largest errors with votes from other fans. This likely arises from the relatively small number of such votes, especially while the story is upcoming. In that case, the large variation in number of fans per user can have a dramatic effect not accounted for in the model. This suggests the main source of the prediction error arises from the long-tail distribution of fans per user, which the model treats as a single average value based on the parameter ρ. We could test this possibility by collecting additional data on the actual fans of each voter, thereby using the observed value of $F(t)$ at the time of prediction when estimating r-values. In cases where $F(t)$ is particularly large, e.g., due to an early vote by a user with many fans, this will result in a smaller estimated value for r_F and hence smaller predicted number of other fan votes.

Models can suggest improved designs for user-contributory web sites. Our results suggest it may be useful to keep popular stories visible longer for users who return to Digg less often - giving them more chance to see the popular stories before they lose visibility. This would be a fine-tuned version of 'popular stories' pages, adjusted for each user's activity rate. That is, instead of showing stories in order of recency only, selectively move less popular stories down the page (once there are enough votes to determine popularity), thereby leaving the more popular ones nearer the top of the list for users who come back to Digg less often.

We examined behavior over a relatively short time (e.g., up to a day after promotion). Over longer times, additional factors could become significant, particularly a decrease in the interestingness as news stories submitted to Digg become 'old news' [21].

Modeling visibility depends on how the web site user interface exposes content. This highlights a challenge for modeling social media: continual changes to the user interface can alter how visibility changes for newly submitted content. Thus accurate models require not only data on user behavior but also sufficient details of the user interface at the time of the data to determine the relation between visibility and properties of the content.

The lognormal distribution of interestingness seen here and in other web sites [11] is useful as a prior distribution for estimating interestingness from early behavior on web sites. The use of such priors will be more important as models make finer distinctions among groups of users, e.g., distinguishing those who find the content in different ways as provided by more complex interfaces. In such cases, many groups will not be represented among the early reaction to new content and use of priors will be especially helpful.

User-contributory web sites typically allow users to designate others whose contributions they find interesting, and the sites highlight the activity of linked users. Thus our stochastic model, explicitly distinguishing behavior of users based on whether they are linked to users who submitted or previously rated the content, could apply to many such web sites.

Competing interests
The authors declare that they have no competing interests.

Authors' contributions

KL collected the data, TH performed the model parameter estimation. Both authors developed the model, wrote the paper, and approved the final manuscript.

Author details

[1]Institute for Molecular Manufacturing, Palo Alto, CA, USA. [2]USC Information Sciences Institute, Marina del Rey, CA, USA.

Acknowledgements

This work is supported in part by the Air Force Office for Scientific Research under contract FA9550-10-1-0102 and by the National Science Foundation under grant IIS-0968370. Any opinions, findings, and conclusions or recommendations expressed in this material are those of the authors and do not necessarily reflect the views of the funding agencies. Authors thank Suradej Intagorn for collecting and processing data.

Endnotes

[a] At the time of data collection Digg offered a social filtering feature which recommended stories, including upcoming stories, that were liked by users with a similar voting history. It is not clear how often users employed these features and we do not explicitly include them in our model.

[b] The data set is available at http://www.isi.edu/~lerman/downloads/digg2009.html.

References

1. Lerman K (2007) Social information processing in social news aggregation. IEEE Internet Comput 11(6):16-28
2. Hogg T, Lerman K (2009) Stochastic models of user-contributory web sites. In: Proc. of the third international conference on weblogs and social media (ICWSM2009). AAAI Press, Menlo Park, pp 50-57
3. Lerman K, Hogg T (2012) Using stochastic models to describe and predict social dynamics of web users. ACM Transactions on Intelligent Systems and Technology (to appear)
4. Szabo G, Huberman BA (2010) Predicting the popularity of online content. Commun ACM 53(8):80-88
5. Hogg T, Lerman K (2010) Social dynamics of Digg. In: Proc. of the fourth international conference on weblogs and social media (ICWSM2010). AAAI Press, Menlo Park, pp 247-250
6. Haberman R (1987) Mathematical models: mechanical vibrations, population dynamics, and traffic flow. Classics in Applied Mathematics. SIAM, Philadelphia
7. Hethcote HW (2000) The mathematics of infectious diseases. SIAM Rev 42(4):599-653
8. Huberman BA, Pirolli PLT, Pitkow JE, Lukose RM (1998) Strong regularities in World Wide Web surfing. Science 280:95-97
9. Lerman K, Hogg T (2010) Using a model of social dynamics to predict popularity of news. In: Proc. of the 19th intl. World Wide Web conference (WWW2010). ACM, New York, pp 621-630
10. Reed WJ, Jorgensen M (2004) The double Pareto-lognormal distribution: a new parametric model for size distributions. Commun Stat, Theory Methods 33:1733-1753
11. Hogg T, Szabo G (2009) Diversity of user activity and content quality in online communities. In: Proc. of the third international conference on weblogs and social media (ICWSM2009). AAAI Press, Menlo Park, pp 58-65
12. Bulmer MG (1974) On fitting the Poisson lognormal distribution to species-abundance data. Biometrics 30:101-110
13. Miller G (2007) Statistical modelling of Poisson/log-normal data. Radiat Prot Dosim, 124:155-163
14. Hilbe JM (2008) Negative binomial regression. Cambridge Univ. Press, Cambridge
15. Efron B (1979) Bootstrap methods: another look at the jackknife. Ann Stat 7:1-26
16. Clauset A, Shalizi CR, Newman MEJ (2009) Power-law distributions in empirical data. SIAM Rev 51:661-703
17. Salganik M, Dodds P, Watts D (2006) Experimental study of inequality and unpredictability in an artificial cultural market. Science 311:854
18. Kaltenbrunner A, Gomez V, Lopez V (2007) Description and prediction of Slashdot activity. In: Proc. 5th Latin American web congress (LA-WEB 2007)
19. Lerman K, Galstyan A (2008) Analysis of social voting patterns on Digg. In: Proceedings of the 1st ACM SIGCOMM workshop on online social networks
20. Wilkinson DM (2008) Strong regularities in online peer production. In: EC'08: Proceedings of the 9th ACM conference on electronic commerce. ACM, New York, pp 302-309
21. Wu F, Huberman BA (2007) Novelty and collective attention. Proc Natl Acad Sci USA 104(45):17599-17601
22. Ratkiewicz J, Fortunato S, Flammini A, Menczer F, Vespignani A (2010) Characterizing and modeling the dynamics of online popularity. Phys Rev Lett 105(15):158701+. http://prl.aps.org/pdf/PRL/v105/i15/e158701
23. Leskovec J, Backstrom L, Kleinberg J (2009) Meme-tracking and the dynamics of the news cycle. In: KDD'09: Proceedings of the 15th ACM SIGKDD international conference on knowledge discovery and data mining, ACM, New York, pp 497-506. http://www.cs.cornell.edu/home/kleinber/kdd09-quotes.pdf
24. Crane R, Sornette D (2008) Viral, quality, and junk videos on YouTube: separating content from noise in an information-rich environment. In: Lerman K et al (eds) Proc. of the AAAI symposium on social information processing, pp 18-20
25. Levene M, Borges J, Loizou G (2001) Zipf's law for web surfers. Knowl Inf Syst 3:120-129
26. Salganik MJ, Watts DJ (2008) Leading the herd astray: an experimental study of self-fulfilling prophecies in an artificial cultural market. Soc Psychol Q 71:338-355
27. Radinsky K, Svore K, Dumais S, Teevan J, Brocharov A, Horvitz E (2012) Modeling and predicting behavioral dynamics on the web. In: Proc. of the 21st intl. World Wide Web conference (WWW2012)
28. Bakshy E, Karrer B, Adamic LA (2009) Social influence and the diffusion of user-created content. In: Proc. of the 10th ACM Conf. on electronic commerce (EC09), ACM, New York, pp 325-334
29. Colbaugh R, Glass K (2010) Early warning analysis for social diffusion events. In: Proceedings of IEEE international conferences on intelligence and security informatics

30. Bogacz R et al (2006) The physics of optimal decision making: a formal analysis of models of performance in two-alternative forced-choice tasks. Psychol Rev 113:700-765
31. Götz M, Leskovec J, McGlohon M, Faloutsos C (2009) Modeling blog dynamics. In: Proc. of the third international conference on weblogs and social media (ICWSM2009). AAAI Press, Menlo Park, pp 26-33
32. Aral S, Muchnik L, Sundararajan A (2009) Distinguishing influence-based contagion from homophily-driven diffusion in dynamic networks. Proc Natl Acad Sci USA 106(51):21544-21549. http://dx.doi.org/10.1073/pnas.0908800106
33. Konstan JA, Miller BN, Maltz D, Herlocker JL, Gordon LR, Riedl J (1997) GroupLens: applying collaborative filtering to Usenet news. Commun ACM 40(3):77-87. citeseer.ist.psu.edu/konstan97grouplens.html
34. Perugini S, Goncalves MA, Fox EA (2004) Recommender systems research: a connection-centric survey. Journal of Intelligent Information Systems 23(2):107-143
35. Backstrom L, Leskovec J (2011) Supervised random walks: predicting and recommending links in social networks. In: Proc. of the 4th ACM intl. conf. on web search and data mining (WSDM)
36. Bringmann B, Berlingerio M, Bonchi F, Gionis A (2010) Learning and predicting the evolution of social networks. IEEE Intell Syst 25(4):26-34
37. Schifanella R, Barrat A, Cattuto C, Markines B, Menczer F (2010) Folks in folksonomies: social link prediction from shared metadata. In: Proc. of the 3rd ACM intl. conf. on web search and data mining (WSDM2010)

5

Urban magnetism through the lens of geo-tagged photography

Silvia Paldino[1], Iva Bojic[2], Stanislav Sobolevsky[2*], Carlo Ratti[2] and Marta C González[3]

*Correspondence: stanly@mit.edu
[2]SENSEable City Laboratory, Massachusetts Institute of Technology, 77 Massachusetts Avenue 9-209, Cambridge, MA 02139, USA
Full list of author information is available at the end of the article

Abstract

There is an increasing trend of people leaving digital traces through social media. This reality opens new horizons for urban studies. With this kind of data, researchers and urban planners can detect many aspects of how people live in cities and can also suggest how to transform cities into more efficient and smarter places to live in. In particular, their digital trails can be used to investigate tastes of individuals, and what attracts them to live in a particular city or to spend their vacation there. In this paper we propose an unconventional way to study how people experience the city, using information from geotagged photographs that people take at different locations. We compare the spatial behavior of residents and tourists in 10 most photographed cities all around the world. The study was conducted on both a global and local level. On the global scale we analyze the 10 most photographed cities and measure how attractive each city is for people visiting it from other cities within the same country or from abroad. For the purpose of our analysis we construct the users' mobility network and measure the strength of the links between each pair of cities as a level of attraction of people living in one city (i.e., origin) to the other city (i.e., destination). On the local level we study the spatial distribution of user activity and identify the photographed hotspots inside each city. The proposed methodology and the results of our study are a low cost mean to characterize touristic activity within a certain location and can help cities strengthening their touristic potential.

Keywords: city attractiveness; big data; human mobility; urban planning; tourism study; smart city; complex systems; collective sensing; geo-tagged Flickr

1 Introduction

The traces of communication and information technologies are currently considered to be an efficient and consolidated way of collecting useful and large data sources for urban studies. There are in fact various ways to electronically track human behavior and the most diffuse one is collecting data from mobile phones [1, 2]. It was already demonstrated that this technique can be used as an accurate method for understanding crowds [1] and individual mobility patterns [3–5], to classify how the land is used [6–9] or to delineate the regional boundaries [10–12]. Moreover, it was shown how to identify some of user characteristics from mobile call patterns, for example how to determinate if a user is a tourist or a resident [13]. However, when it comes to studying human mobility patterns, exploring detailed call records is not the only possibility - other sources of big data collected from digital maps [14], electronic toll systems [15], credit cards payments [16, 17], Twitter [18], circulation of bank notes [19], vehicle GPS traces [20] and also using geotagged photographs [21–23] can be successfully applied.

The focus of this paper is on geotagged photographs that provide novel insights into how people visit and experience a city, revealing aspects of mobility and tourism, and discovering the attractions in the urban landscape. In the past, photography was already considered as a good mean of inquiry in architecture and urban planning, being used for understanding landscapes [24]. Moreover, Girardin et al. showed that it was possible to define a measure of city attractiveness by exploring big data from photograph sharing websites [25]. They analyzed two types of digital footprints generated by mobile phones that were in physical proximity to the New York City Waterfalls: cellular network activity from AT&T and photographic activity from Flickr. They distinguished between attractiveness and popularity. Regarding attractiveness they defined the Comparative Relative Strength indicator to compare the activity in one area of interest with respect to the overall activity of the city. They measured the attractiveness of a particular event in New York City. In this study we consider the attractiveness in the overall area of the city during three years, comparing the attractiveness and spatial distribution of activities in different cities.

Discovering how to increase the global city attractiveness or the local attractiveness of hotspots requires knowing the differences in the visits made by residents and tourists. While both residents and tourists take photographs at locations that they consider important, the reasons why they are taking photographs are different. This knowledge helps us to understand the different usages of the urban infrastructure in people spare time. The overall goal is to find the ways how passively collected data can be used for low cost applications that inform urban innovation. These information trends can be of interest for planning, forecasting of economic activity, tourism, or transportation [26]. Finally, a comparative study of cities from different parts of the world is a relevant objective to discern how the patterns of human behavior largely depend on a particular city [27].

In this paper we define city global attractiveness as the absolute number of photographs taken in a city by tourists, while local attractiveness of hotspots within a city is defined by the spatial distribution of photographs taken by all users (either local residents or tourists). In our analysis we are using a dataset that consist of more than 100 million publicly shared geotagged photographs took during a period of 10 years. The dataset is divided into 8,910 files denoting 3,015 different locations (e.g., cities or certain areas of interest such as Niagara Falls) where for almost every location three different labels are given: *resident, tourist* and *unknown*, to denote people who are living in the area, visiting the area or are uncategorized.

2 Data

For each photograph in the dataset, which is publicly available on the website sfgeo.org, the following data is given: user id, timestamp, geo coordinates and link from which the photograph can be downloaded. From the given dataset we omitted duplicates (9.33% of the dataset in total) together with the photographs with incorrect timestamps (0.01% of the dataset in total). In the end we were left with more than 90 million photographs. Figure 1 shows how the number of taken photographs and users changed over the period of 10 years. We can see that almost 75% of the photographs were taken from 2007 until 2010. In the further analysis we are thus considering only photographs taken during those three years (about 70 million of photographs in total).

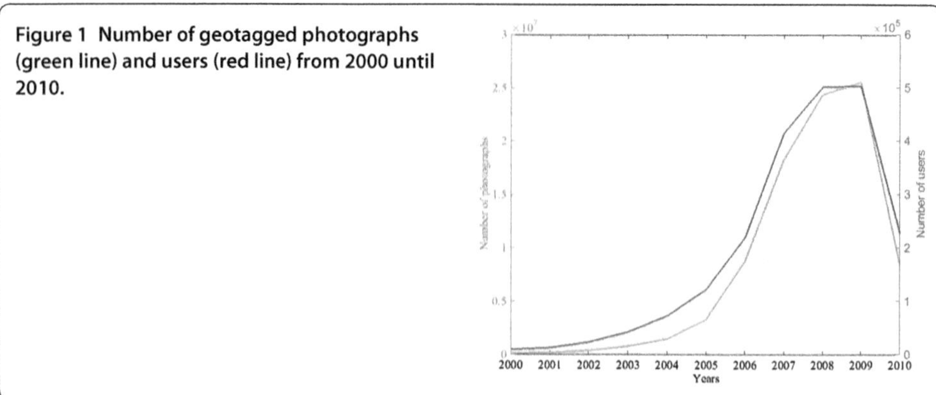

Figure 1 Number of geotagged photographs (green line) and users (red line) from 2000 until 2010.

3 Definition of user home cities and countries

In order to determinate if there is any difference between how residents vs. tourists are attracted to a certain location, for each user in the dataset we have to determinate his/her home city and country. Even though the dataset has tags for: *resident, tourist* and *unknown,* the given categorization is not comprehensive and in some cases is not consistent. For instance, for more than 85% of users in the dataset their home city is not defined (i.e., their photographs are always in *unknown* files). In addition, for almost 25% of users for who their home city is defined at least two or more cities are listed as their home cities making the proposed categorization inconsistent.

Due to the aforementioned reasons, we used our own criteria to determinate if a person is living in the area where he/she took a photograph or not. We are considering that a person is a resident if at that location he/she took the highest number of the photographs (at least 10 of them) over the longest period of time (at least longer than 180 days) calculated as the time between the first and last photograph taken at the location. Once when we determinate a user home city, he/she is automatically becoming a tourist in all other cities in the dataset. A category 'tourist' in this sense denotes many different kinds of visitors including business visitors. However, most of people taking photographs at locations other than their home cities in fact act like tourists during this particular instance of time.

From almost 1 million users that took photographs between 2007 and 2010, for only 11% of them we were able to determinate their home city and country using our criteria. However, these users took more than 40% of all photographs (i.e., almost 30 million). Our classification was not consistent with the initial categorization (i.e., users whose photographs were listed in only one *resident* file) for only less than 2% of users. Moreover, for every city in the dataset we identified its country code allowing us to classify tourists as domestic or foreign ones, where domestic tourists are coming from the same country as the considered city, while foreign tourists are all the others - visitors from different countries. Finally, for every city all the observed activity is assigned to residents, domestic tourists or foreign tourists and for each of these categories, we keep the following data: user id, geo coordinates and for tourists their home city id together with their country code and continent id.

4 Attractiveness

4.1 Global attractiveness

Considering our original question what attracts people to a certain location, we start our analysis looking at different locations and their absolute global attractiveness that is quantified by the number of photographs taken in them by either domestic or foreign tourists, leaving out the contribution that was made by their residents. Once we determined user home cities and countries, in order to calculate global attractiveness for different locations, we ranked locations by the total number of photographs taken in them by tourists (i.e., people residing outside the considered city) from all over the world. We find that the first 10 ranked cities by photographs are: New York City, London, Paris, San Francisco, Washington, Barcelona, Chicago, Los Angeles, Rome and Berlin. In order to see how strong might be the impact of short-distance domestic visitors on this ranking on this classification, we compared it with the ranking built based just on the activity of foreign users in a city. Surprisingly the difference is not that high - New York and London are still the two leading cities (just switching order), Paris and San Francisco are still within top 5, while Rome having the lowest place in this new ranking among all the cities mentioned is still the 23rd world most photographed city with respect to the activity of foreign tourists. That is why the cities we picked up are the important destinations not only for all (including domestic), but also for the foreign visitors.

This ranking is also highly consistent with the one presented in [22] - all of our top 10 cities happen to be among the first 15 cities they mention. Another two global rankings of city visitor attractiveness worth mentioning in that context are the ones presented by Euromonitor[a] and MasterCard[b]. Although one should not really expect them to be consistent with our ranking, as those rankings are built on diverse (and sometimes heterogeneous) sources of data trying to include all the visits and not necessary only tourists who are willing to take photographs as we do it in our study, we will compare them against our ranking. One could often expect one city to attract more people, but another one, attracting less, being more picturesque, and motivating those fewer people attracted for taking more photos, which would result in a higher total photographic activity. However all 10 of our top cities are included in Euromonitor's top destinations list. Worth mentioning is that this is already not the case for a newer version Euromonitor's ranking from 2015[c] - for example Washington falls out of the top 100 world destinations according to their recent estimate. This serves as a good example of how dynamic the world is, while it is not too surprising that our ranking built based on the data before 2010 happens to be more consistent with the older version of Euromonitor's report. Moreover, we found that our top 3 cities - New York, London and Paris - are also the top 3 (the order is different however) in MasterCard's ranking, while in total 7 of out top 10 cities (besides Berlin, Washington and Chicago) are mentioned among the 'Global Top 20 Destination Cities by International Overnight Visitor Spend' in 2014.

Further, we focus this study on the global attractiveness of these 5 US cities and 5 European Union cities (EU), and add together the remaining information as the rest of Europe, the rest of the US and the rest of world.

From the aforementioned ranking we were able to extract the origin-destination (O/D) network between 10 most photographed cities, the rest of the US, and Europe as well as the rest of the world. Figure 2 shows O/D flows among the top 10 city-to-city estimated flows of visitors. Colors of the ribbons correspond to destination cities and origin cities are marked with a thin stripe at the end of a ribbon (visualization method based on Krzywinski [28]). With this visualization it is evident that the most attractive cities are London and New York City, followed by San Francisco, Washington and Paris. It is interesting to point out that the most important flows happen exactly between these cities and New York City

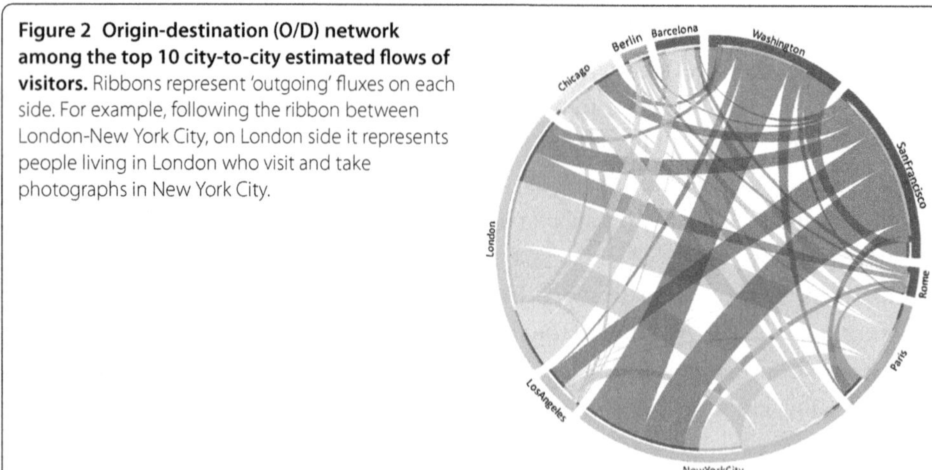

Figure 2 Origin-destination (O/D) network among the top 10 city-to-city estimated flows of visitors. Ribbons represent 'outgoing' fluxes on each side. For example, following the ribbon between London-New York City, on London side it represents people living in London who visit and take photographs in New York City.

Table 1 Heterogeneity of Flickr usage: total number of photographs taken worldwide by residents of different areas versus their official population in 2008

City	Population (mln)	Photographs taken	Photographs per 1,000 residents
New York City	8.36	1,026,199	122.75
London	7.81	1,151,799	147.48
Paris	2.23	534,092	239.50
San Francisco	0.81	851,425	1,051.14
Washington	0.59	525,313	890.36
Barcelona	1.62	255,038	157.43
Chicago	2.85	412,246	144.65
Los Angeles	3.83	289,810	75.67
Rome	2.71	126,011	46.50
Berlin	3.43	182,325	53.16
Rest of EU	482.61	8,637,148	17.90
Rest of the US	287.61	7,347,003	25.55
Rest of the world	5,905.14	6,877,894	1.16

(New York City-Washington, New York City-San Francisco, New York City-London, New York City-Paris), while London and Paris have the strongest flow between each other. The less active cities are Berlin and Rome.

The dependence between the number of users and the number of photographs they took is quite close to linear, having $R^2 \cong 0.87$ for the linear approximation. Therefore, the analysis based on the number of taken photographs is to some extent also a good proxy for the number of active users; further we will use the number of photographs as the main measure of attractiveness. However, using this measure one should also be aware of the heterogeneity of Flickr activity belonging to users coming from different parts of the world. As shown in Table 1 this heterogeneity is quite noticeable - number of photographs taken worldwide by users originating from different cities across the globe varies from 1.16 for the rest of the world to more than 1,000 for San Francisco. In many places across the world people are almost never using geotagging location services (e.g., Flickr) and are not sharing their photographs publicly because of different reasons: e.g., technical, cultural or even political ones. Among the top 10 ranked cities this activity varies in a magnitude of 20 times between people living in San Francisco (the most active population) and Rome (the least active).

In order to use the O/D flows of geotagged photography as a proxy for actual human mobility between cities across the globe, the appropriate normalization for the above heterogeneity is required. One way of doing it is by normalizing the O/D flows shown in Figure 2 by the number of photographs taken per 1,000 of residents of the origin location reported in Table 1. However, this would require further assumptions about the homogeneity of the dataset representativeness for different modes of people travel behavior that would be a questionable assumption given the dataset sparsity and heterogeneity. Therefore, in the further analysis we will refrain from extrapolating the original values of O/D flows defined by the actual number of photographs taken to represent actual human mobility. In this way we will focus our analysis on the actual photographic activity of the users, keeping in mind that flows of the activity from different origins might actually have different representativeness across the entire human population and might not represent the entire variety of types of human activity from the considered origins in the considered destinations. However, we believe that photographic activity by itself is an important component of visitor behavior and might serve as a relevant proxy for measuring city visual attractiveness for the visitors.

The cumulative incoming flow for each destination in the O/D network from all the origins other than the considered destination represents the destination's total global attractiveness in terms of geotagged photographic activity of tourists. Normalized by the population of destination, this measure becomes a relative global attractiveness of the destination stating how much visitors per capita of residential population the location has.

Figure 3(a) shows the relative global attractiveness in relation to the population of the city (with additional distinction by domestic and foreign tourists). This gives a completely different city ranking from the initial one (e.g., New York City, London, Paris, San Francisco, Washington, Barcelona, Chicago, Los Angeles, Rome and Berlin) - now the top relative attractiveness is observed in San Francisco and in Washington for domestic tourists, while the top destination by relative attractiveness for the foreign tourists is observed in Paris. Zooming into the relative structure of photographic activity within each city (Figure 3(b)), a clearly distinctive pattern between European and American cities can be observed. Namely, in American cities the city residents take most of the photographs; followed by the domestic tourists mostly taking the rest, while in EU cities the activity within the cities is much more diverse showing a higher fraction of touristic and specifically foreign touristic activity. The borderline cases from both groups are London and New York City, the former having the highest fraction of residential activity among European cities making it more similar to the American cities, while the latter has the highest fraction of foreign activity among American cities, making it more similar to European ones. One of the possible explanations could be that the observed pattern is attributed to the cultural similarities going back in the history of British-American ties.

Additionally, for every city we can define a measure that shows how mobile its residents are (i.e., if their activity is home-oriented or not) by looking at the ratio of loop edges to the total outgoing weights from the O/D matrix (i.e., user activities in their home cities compared to their total activities). We depict these results in Figure 3(c). Although this ratio is nearly flat varying between 50-60%, an interesting pattern appears when looking at the destinations of activities. Again, American and European patterns are surprisingly distinctive - while the American tourists seem to be mostly engaged in domestic tourism, EU citizens' travel more abroad. This difference can be explained because the US is much

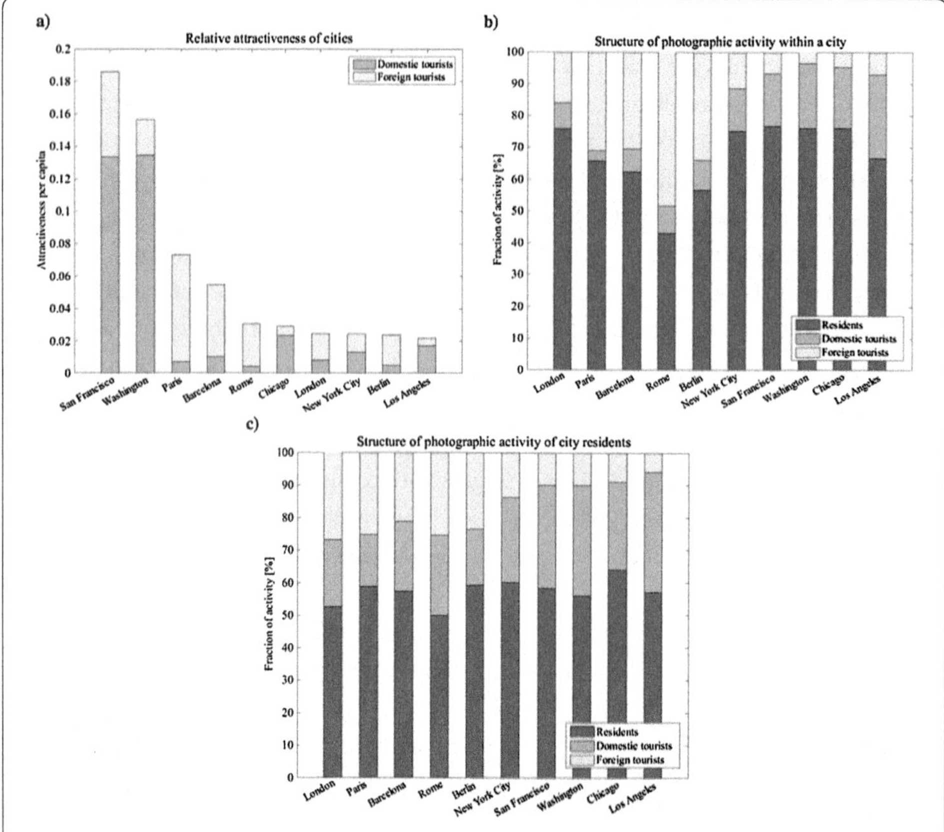

Figure 3 Relative attractiveness. (a) A relative global attractiveness of top 10 cities measured as the estimated amount of touristic activity per capita of urban population, it is plotted in the decreasing order of total attractiveness, **(b)** the structure of photographic activity within a city and **(c)** the structure of photographic activity of city residents. Figure 3(a) shows the number of domestic and foreign photographs divided by the city population (i.e., attractiveness per capita for domestic and foreign tourists). Figure 3(b) shows the percentage of photographs within each city depending on the type of user, while Figure 3(c) shows the share of activity type of users that reside in the particular city. For example, as depicted in Figure 3(b), Rome receives the largest amount of foreign tourist activity and Washington DC the smallest. And as depicted in Figure 3(c) people living in Washington DC have the largest share of domestic tourists while Parisians have the smallest.

bigger and at the same time much more geographically diverse when compared to the EU countries of our studied cities. American users thus have more options when engaged in domestic tourism and are consequently less likely to travel to foreign destinations.

When considering the strength of each particular O/D flow $a(i,j)$ between the origin i and destination j (i.e., a number of photographs taken by the residents of i when visiting city j), one should expect that the number of people travelling between larger or more significant cities is higher. Therefore, in order to estimate the qualitative strength of each particular O/D flow beyond just the effect of scale, we compare all the non-loop edges of the normalized network versus the homogenous null-model where all the outgoing mobility is distributed in the relative proportion to the destination attractiveness, i.e., for each non-loop edge ($i \neq j$) the null model is:

$$\text{model}(i,j) = \frac{w^{\text{out}*}(i)w^{\text{in}*}(j)}{\sum_{k\neq i}(w^{\text{in}*}(k))},$$

Table 2 Relative strength of the links between each pair of cities, normalized by the null-model estimation

O/D ->	New York City	London	Paris	San Francisco	Washington	Barcelona	Chicago	Los Angeles	Rome	Berlin
New York City	-	0.99	0.88	1.11	2.08	0.32	1.60	0.79	0.61	0.53
London	0.92	-	1.57	0.73	0.35	1.59	0.31	0.44	1.50	1.37
Paris	0.76	2.44	-	0.60	0.21	1.60	0.13	0.24	1.41	1.60
San Francisco	1.58	0.83	0.44	-	0.86	0.45	1.46	2.43	0.41	0.32
Washington	1.70	0.38	0.77	1.40	-	0.75	1.07	0.89	0.67	0.51
Barcelona	0.67	2.40	1.29	0.20	0.05	-	0.12	0.19	1.24	3.32
Chicago	1.25	0.77	0.78	1.37	1.62	0.58	-	1.37	0.41	0.34
Los Angeles	1.31	0.56	0.24	3.31	0.39	0.50	1.07	-	0.31	0.31
Rome	0.76	1.63	1.70	0.21	0.29	2.25	0.36	0.07	-	1.69
Berlin	0.64	1.79	1.15	0.61	0.37	2.15	0.16	0.09	2.22	-

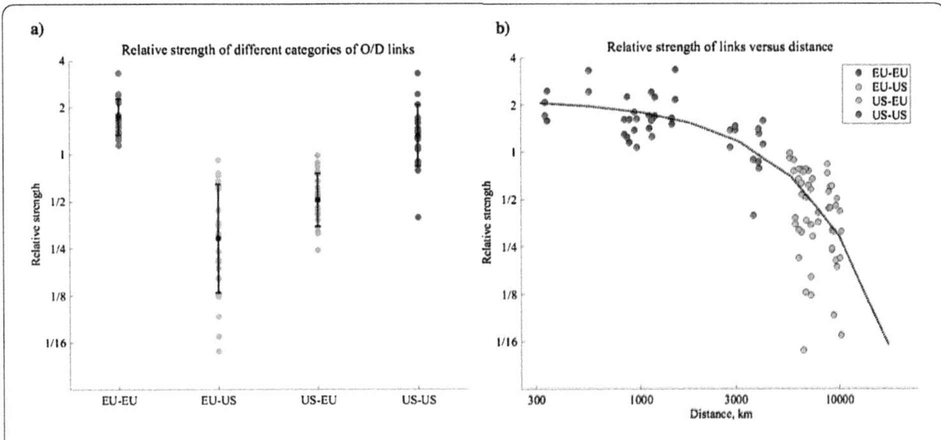

Figure 4 Relative strength of different types of links (a) grouped by continents, (b) ordered by distance.

where $w^{out/in*}(i) = w^{out/in}(i) - a(i,i)$, $w^{in}(c)$ is the total number of photographs taken in city c and $w^{out}(c)$ is the total number of photographs taken worldwide by city c residents. Using the aforementioned model, we compute the fraction $a(i,j)/\text{model}(i,j)$ (see Table 2) in order to see how qualitatively strong the links between each pair of cities are, i.e., how people from each origin are attracted to each destination beyond just the effect of scale.

One clear pattern, which can be immediately recognized, is a high level of attractiveness between pairs of American cities, as well as a lower level of connectivity between American cities and EU ones (see Figure 4(a)). This pattern was rather expected, as trans-Atlantic links are likely to be weaker than more local ones. To a certain extent it could be attributed to a general decay of links with distances (similar to Krings [29]) - indeed the overall trend is well approximated by an exponential function (Figure 4(b)) going sharply down once when crossing the ocean. However, an interesting finding shown in both Figures 4(a) and 4(b) is that the links going from the US to EU are stronger than same distance links going in the reciprocal direction from EU to the US (see Figure 4(a)). According to this, Americans are more attracted by EU destinations than Europeans are by the US cities.

4.2 Local attractiveness

Until this point, cities have been considered only as aggregated spatial units. However, cities all around the world are not spatially homogenous and there are always relatively more attractive areas within them to which one can refer as 'hotspots.' Moreover, attrac-

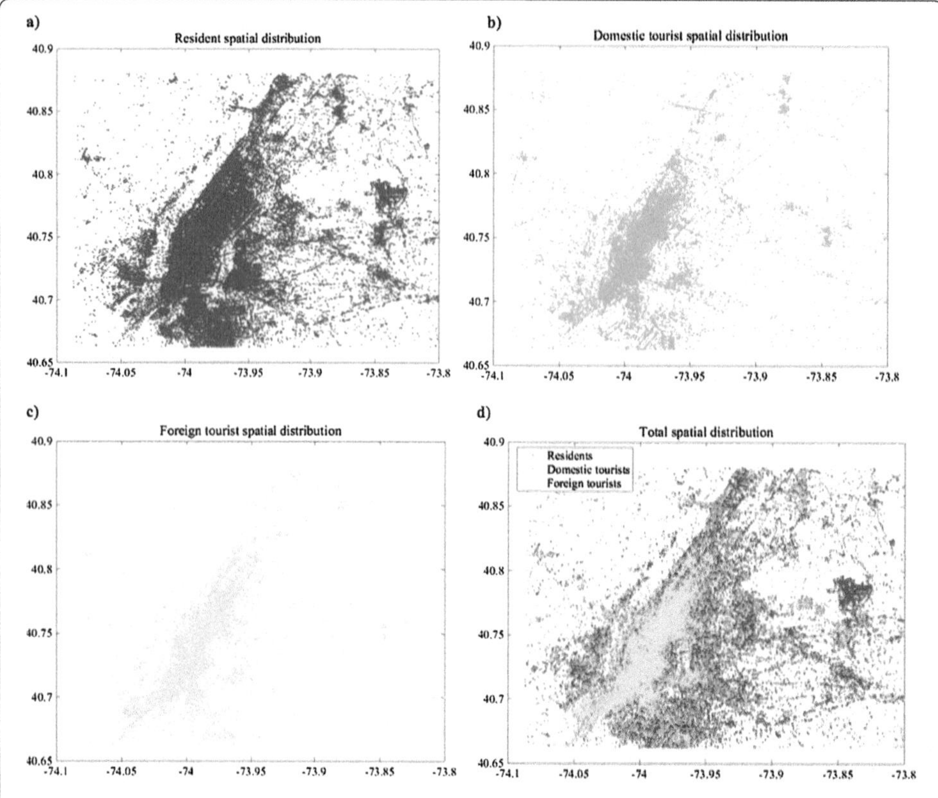

Figure 5 Spatial distribution in New York City. Dots represent photographs taken by New York City **(a)** residents, **(b)** domestic tourists, **(c)** foreign tourists creating a map of attractiveness for three different categories, while **(d)** is the map of attractiveness for the three contributions together.

tiveness of different locations across the city could vary for different categories of users. In order to investigate this local attractiveness, we identified spatial distribution of photographs taken by users belonging to resident, domestic or foreign tourist groups. Visualizing them on the map, where each dot represents a photograph taken, Figure 5 shows different spatial patterns of how different categories of users take photographs in New York City, which was taken as an example. As expected, tourists in general take more photographs in central areas within the city while residents take photographs at locations that are much more spatially distributed - scattered all over the city. By putting those dots onto the map, we can create 'maps of attractiveness' for every city and for its residents and tourists.

In order to analyze the spatial activity we use 500×500 m rectangular grids covering each city. First we start with a standard analysis of the distribution functions of the activity density values across the grid cells for different categories of users - residents, domestic and foreign visitors, as well as for the total activity. All of activities can be fitted to truncated lognormal distributions (distribution truncation is an important consideration from a technical standpoint as by its definition the cells covered by user activity cannot have less than one photograph taken inside of them) as shown in Figure 6 for New York City. We took New York City just as an example as patterns for the other cities are similar with the only difference in the relative position of the curves corresponding to the foreign and domestic visitors.

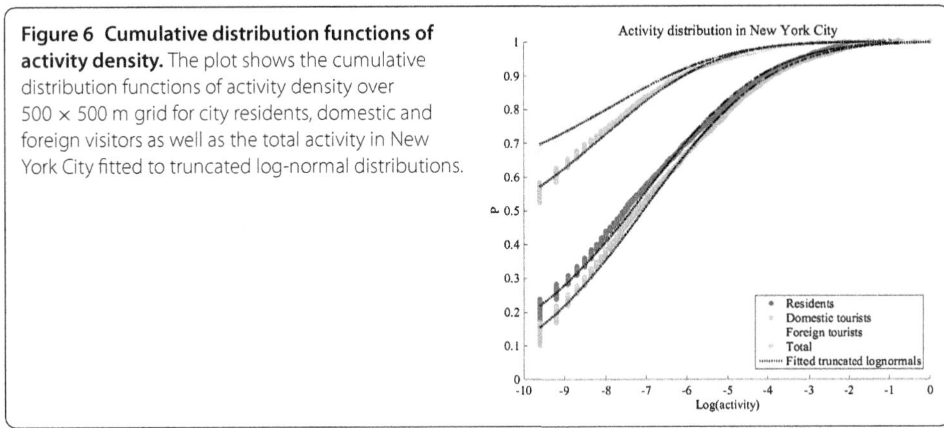

Figure 6 Cumulative distribution functions of activity density. The plot shows the cumulative distribution functions of activity density over 500 × 500 m grid for city residents, domestic and foreign visitors as well as the total activity in New York City fitted to truncated log-normal distributions.

Table 3 Variance of the fitted lognormal distributions

City	Residents	Domestic tourists	Foreign tourists	Total activity
New York City	2.37	2.17	2.26	2.44
London	1.86	1.89	2.22	1.92
Paris	2.24	1.62	2.33	2.39
San Francisco	2.19	2.07	2.09	2.22
Washington	2.21	2.10	2.17	2.22
Barcelona	2.20	1.77	2.42	2.38
Chicago	2.17	2.03	2.08	2.23
Los Angeles	1.86	1.84	1.71	1.91
Rome	2.04	1.88	2.95	2.39
Berlin	1.86	1.78	2.04	2.07

Variance of the fitted lognormal distributions to the activity density is shown in 500 × 500 m grid for city residents, domestic and foreign visitors, as well as for the total activity in the different cities.

Log-normal distribution is characterized by its mean and variance. While means vary for different types of users due to the differences of their total activity level, variance characterizes how broad or narrow the distribution is, i.e., how strongly the activity density varies over the area of the city covered by the considered user activity. The values of variance for all 10 cities and different categories of users reported in Table 3 show a consistent pattern - with the only exception of Los Angeles variance of domestic visitor where their spatial activity is always the lowest one, while variance of the foreign activity is higher for all the EU cities compared to the residential activity and lower for all the American cities. Variance of the total activity is usually the highest one with the exception of three EU cities - London, Barcelona and Rome.

Another perspective of user activity spatial distribution across different cities can be expressed by considering the dimensions of the areas covered by different quintiles of the top density cells. Figure 7 visualizes the shape of the curve characterizing those distributions (normalization is performed by the number of cells covering 50% of the total activity in order to bring different distributions on the same scale) in all 10 cities for all types of users (i.e., residents, domestic and foreign tourists). The curve shows how large is the most photographed area covering a given quintile of the total activity within the city in relation to the total area covered. Interestingly, curves for all 10 cities and three different types of users nearly follow one single shape which seems to represent a universal pattern of spatial distribution of the photographic activity across the city.

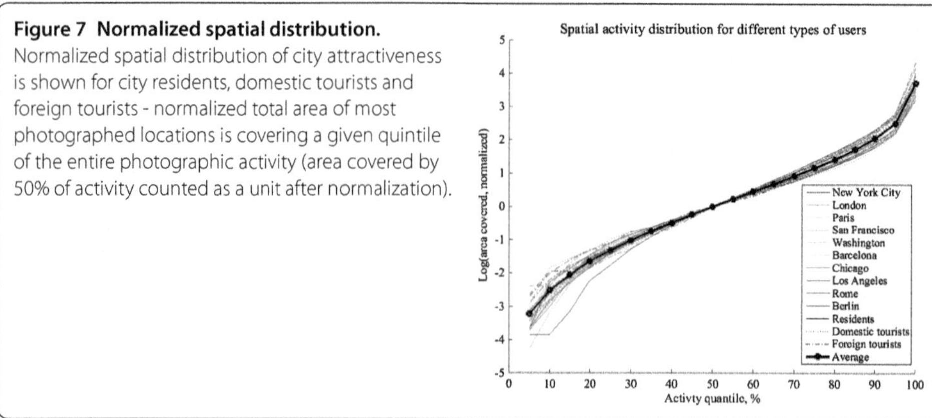

Figure 7 Normalized spatial distribution. Normalized spatial distribution of city attractiveness is shown for city residents, domestic tourists and foreign tourists - normalized total area of most photographed locations is covering a given quintile of the entire photographic activity (area covered by 50% of activity counted as a unit after normalization).

Table 4 Top photographed area

City	Domestic tourists	Foreign tourists
New York City	0.47	0.35
London	0.40	0.25
Paris	0.33	0.27
San Francisco	0.64	0.48
Washington	0.45	0.32
Barcelona	0.45	0.26
Chicago	0.37	0.21
Los Angeles	1.32	0.74
Rome	0.47	0.33
Berlin	0.25	0.26

Relative size of the top photographed area is covered by the activity of domestic and foreign visitors versus the corresponding area covered by residents in the different cities.

However, quantitatively the areas covered by the activity of city residents, domestic and foreign visitors within each city are quite different. Considering an average ratio between the size of areas covered by different activity quintiles (given the similarity of the spatial distribution shapes) for domestic/foreign tourists vs. the corresponding areas covered by the activity of residents for each city, we can see that these values vary largely from one city to another (see Table 4). The pattern is always the same - foreign tourist activity (in any given quintile) covers smaller areas compared to that one of domestic (the only exception is Berlin where those are almost the same) and, with the only exception of Los Angeles, the areas covered by both types of visitors are always smaller compared to the areas covered by the activity of residents. Once more, a very clear difference between the US and EU cities can be noticed - tourists visiting the US cities (with the exception of Chicago) explore more extensively the area compared to the ones visiting EU cities.

The existing spatial activity coverage in each city is not homogenous as people are often initially attracted by its main destinations that become 'must visit' locations consequentially getting the highest photographic activity. For city residents those locations, which are often called 'hotspots,' include parks, squares or sport facilities, while tourists are usually more attracted to the key places for the city identity (e.g., Times Square in New York City, Big Ben in London). The overall tourist activity in the New York City is visualized in Figure 8 by grouping coordinates of taken photographs into cells and creating a 3D map of the city perception. Our findings of New York City 'hotspots' are similar to those previously identified in [22].

Figure 8 A tourist density attractiveness map of New York City. The most photographed place in the city is Times Square. In Bronx, which does not attract many people, tourists are mostly taking photographs of Yankees Stadium.

Further we give a definition of the hotspots as spatially connected areas on the rectangular grid which consist of the high-density cells and possess the highest cumulative activity. The given algorithm allows us to define a given number of spatial hotspots in all types of user activity, ordering them according to their cumulative activity level. Specifically we identify the top n activity hotspots within each city using a following algorithm:

1. Consider top n density cells in the grid and let a be the lowest activity level among them.
2. Select all the cells with activity higher or equal to a and divide them into spatially connected components (considering cells having at least one common vertex to be connected).
3. If resulting number of connected components is equal or higher than n (could be higher if a number of cells has the same activity level a) stop the algorithm defining selected connected components as the hotspots.
4. Otherwise, if the number of components is $t < n$, select $n - t$ top activity cells from the remaining ones (not covered by selected components) and let a be the lowest activity level among them. Repeat from Step 2.

Figure 9 reports the average total percentage of activity covered by n hotspots in our 10 cities depending on n. In the further analysis we will be considering $n = 12$ hotspots for each city on average covering around 30% of the total photographic activity of all users in the city, as a reasonable trade-off between having enough hotspots to represent important locations across the city and draw reliable conclusions from one hand, and the intent to have those hotspots cover just the major areas of interest across the city, but not majority of them from the other.

In Figure 10 we show examples of the resulting maps for the total user activity (including residents and tourists) in one US city (i.e., New York City) and one EU city (i.e., Rome). In both cities the most active area is their downtown and moreover, one hotspot represents their stadiums - Yankee Stadium in New York City and Olimpico in Rome. Another similarity is that in both cities among their top 12 hotspots are their squares and parks, mean-

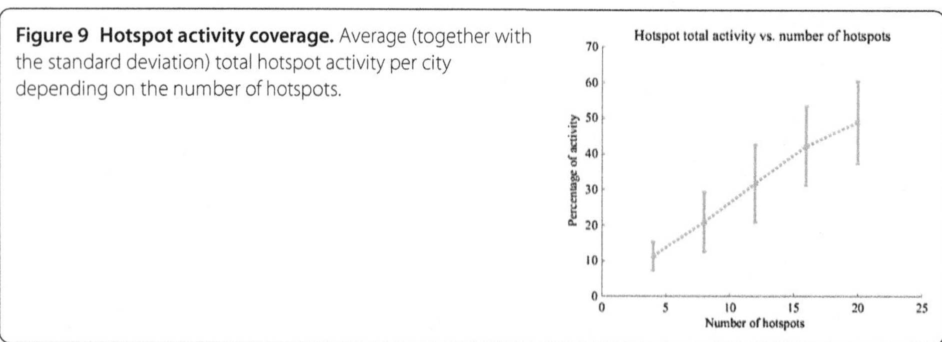

Figure 9 Hotspot activity coverage. Average (together with the standard deviation) total hotspot activity per city depending on the number of hotspots.

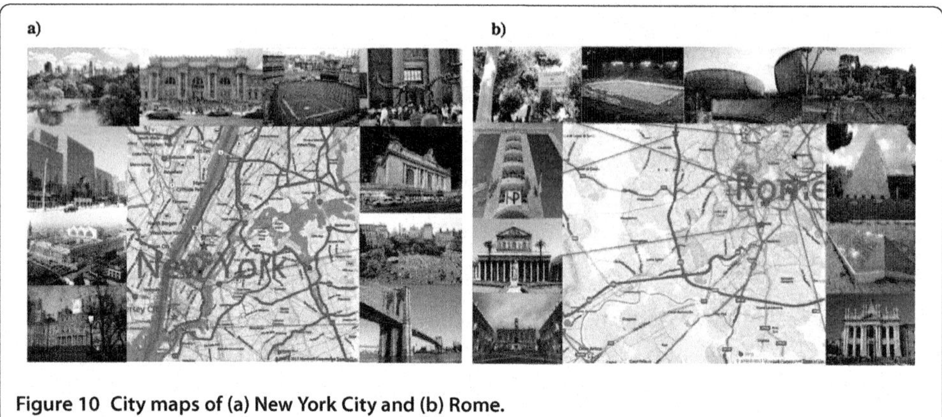

Figure 10 City maps of (a) New York City and (b) Rome.

Table 5 Hotspots in New York City and Rome

Hotspot rank	New York City	Rome
1	Downtown	Downtown
2	New York City Hall	San Giovanni in Laterano square
3	Metropolitan Museum of Art	Olimpico Stadium
4	Union Square	Auditorium Parco della Musica
5	Citi Field	Caio Cestio Pyramide
6	Yankee Stadium	IED - Istituto Europeo di Design
7	American Museum of Natural History	Papillo Hotel
8	Penn Station	Capitolium
9	Grand Central Terminal	Villa Torlonia
10	Javitz Center	Church San Paolo Fuori Le Mura
11	Brooklyn Bridge	Parco dei Caduti
12	Central Park	Passeggiata del Gianicolo

ing that outside of their downtowns and besides their most famous attractions, people take photographs and spend their time at locations where they can meet and talk with other people. The only two cultural hotspots outside the downtown of Rome are the Church San Paolo Fuori le Mura and the Capitolium. Similarly, in New York City hotspots that are outside downtown are two museums located close to Central Park - the Metropolitan Museum of Art and the American Museum of Natural History. Table 5 gives the complete list of top 12 hotspots in Rome and New York City.

Once that we identified the first dozen of the most photographed spatial hotspots for each city for all types of users, we define the cumulative activity within each of them separately for residents, domestic and foreign visitors and rank them in the decreasing order by the number of photographs taken. We then plot that number vs. the hotspot rank (similar

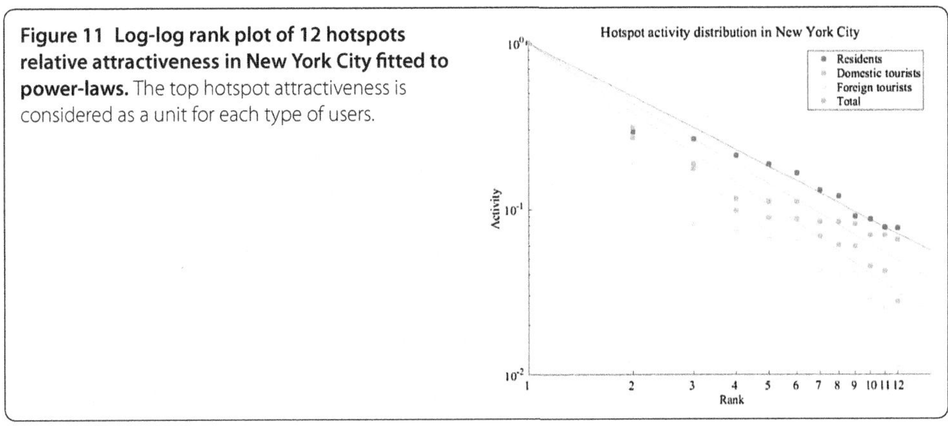

Figure 11 Log-log rank plot of 12 hotspots relative attractiveness in New York City fitted to power-laws. The top hotspot attractiveness is considered as a unit for each type of users.

Table 6 Values of *q* exponents for residents and tourists in the different cities

City	Residents	Domestic tourists	Foreign tourists	Total activity
New York City	1.06	1.39	1.63	1.21
London	1.29	1.35	1.61	1.25
Paris	1.25	1.38	1.43	1.23
San Francisco	1.10	1.12	1.21	1.02
Washington	1.21	2.51	2.81	1.42
Barcelona	1.65	2.18	2.26	1.69
Chicago	1.48	1.91	2.71	1.54
Los Angeles	1.25	1.46	1.84	0.92
Rome	2.37	2.77	3.17	2.61
Berlin	1.60	2.19	1.60	1.56

q exponent is a measure of how concentrated or distributed people activity is across different 'hotspots.' Namely, a higher value means that people are more focused on just visiting major attractions.

to the approach used in González et al. [3]). Approximating these rank plots with power law dependences $hotspotActivity(\mathrm{rank}) = c\,\mathrm{rank}^{-q}$ (by doing so we get R^2 above 90% on average) gives us another important quantitative relative characteristic of how concentrated or distributed between the key destinations across the city is the activity of different types of people. Figure 11 shows those distributions on an example of New York City where the distribution is more flat (i.e., lower q) for the residents and sharper for domestic and especially foreign tourists (i.e., higher q).

Detailed comparison of q exponents for different cities is presented in Table 6. From the values of q we can see how concentrated or distributed resident and tourist activity is within them. If the value of q exponent is higher, then it means that people are more focused on just visiting the major attractions, while a lower exponent means that people attention is more equally distributed among different attractions. By quantifying q separately for residents, domestic and foreign tourists, we can conclude that their values largely vary from one city to another, corresponding to the unique city spatial layout. However, we can still discover additional strongly consistent pattern in human behavior across different cities: the distribution always becomes sharper for the visitors and especially for the foreign visitors with the only exception of Berlin where foreign activity has almost the same exponent as the activity of the city residents.

5 Summary and conclusion

The importance of cities in our society is well founded and it is evident that cities play a crucial role as more than half of world population lives in them. 'Rethinking' cities is thus the key component of the world sustainable development paradigm. The first and the most direct way of doing that is by rethinking the way we plan them. In order to become a better planner, one needs to start considering people needs. Not only do people need efficiency, better transportation and green energy, but also do they need a better experience of living in cities enjoying the things that they have interest in and that they find attractive. In this study we thus conducted an analysis of cities through the city attractiveness and derived patterns. The novelty of the study is in the kind of data that was used in it: geotagged photographs from publicly available photograph sharing web sites (e.g., Flickr).

Over the last decade big data analyses have being increasingly utilized in urban planning (e.g., analysis of cell phone records for the transportation planning). However, information from geotagged photographs was not very often analyzed although they can provide us with an additional layer of information useful for the urbanism in general. Namely, taken photographs indicate places in cities important enough for people to visit them and to decide to leave their digital trails there. By analyzing the global dataset of geotagged photographs we identified 10 most photographed cities, which happened to be distributed evenly between the US and EU. Focusing on the top 10 selected destinations, we studied spatial patterns of visitor attraction versus behavior of the residential users together with analyzing people mobility between those 10 cities and other places all around the world.

Although intercity origin/destination fluxes in a rather predictable way depend on the distance between two cities, links between American and European cities are surprisingly asymmetric. Namely, links going from American origins to EU destinations are on average stronger than the ones going in the opposite direction. Another clearly distinctive pattern between EU and American cities is related to the structure of the photographic activity within them. The results showed that in the US cities their residents take most of the photographs while the domestic tourists mostly cover the rest leaving not much for foreigners. The activity that happens in the EU cities is much more diverse showing a higher fraction of touristic and specifically foreign activity. Finally, when investigating the qualitative structure of destinations, again American and EU patterns are surprisingly distinctive - while Americans seem mostly engaged in domestic tourism, the Europeans travel more abroad than within their own home countries.

Moreover, we extracted the photographic activity at the local scale comparing attraction patterns for residents, domestic and foreign tourists within a city. Spatial distribution of photographic activity of all those user categories follows the same universal pattern - activity density distributions of all types of users follow log-normal law pretty well while the shapes of the curves for area size vs. activity quintile appear to be strongly consistent. However, the areas covered by tourist activities are always smaller compared to the areas covered by residents with the only exception of Los Angeles where domestic tourist activities cover larger areas compared to city residents. The ratio between areas covered by tourists and city residents is different for domestic and foreign tourists and is always higher for domestic tourists with only exception of Berlin where those factors are almost the same.

Once again, we find the activities within American and European cities are different from the quantitative standpoint. First, tourists visiting American cities (with the exception of Chicago) explore them more extensively, covering more of the areas of residential activity. More strikingly, the variance of the foreign activity density distribution is always higher for all the European cities compared to the residential activity and lower for all the American cities. Finally, we identified the hotspots in each city focusing on the most photographed places of each city. We noted that hotspot attractiveness follows a power-law distribution where the exponent of this distribution serves as an indicator of how focused people's attention is on the major attractiveness compared to how distributed it is among a number of objectives. For all cities with the exception of Berlin, activity of the tourists and especially foreign tourists appeared to be more concentrated on the major attractions.

To conclude, by showing differences between people visiting the US and EU cities our study revealed interesting patterns in human activity. The results of our study are useful for understanding of what has to be enhanced in cities and where it can be appropriate to increase services targeting different categories of users. In past those questions were traditionally answered by analyzing different available datasets such as hotel information or survey data. However, collecting or getting the access to such datasets usually requires significant efforts and/or expenses, while geotagged photography is publicly available while providing a unique global perspective on addressing many research questions at both global and local scale. In future work we will also consider the longitudinal perspective of data analysis by showing how the observed human patterns evolve over time.

Competing interests

The authors declare that they have no competing interests.

Authors' contributions

MG, SS and CR defined the research agenda, SP and IB processed the data, SP, IB and SS analyzed the results, SP, IB and SS wrote the manuscript, all authors edited the manuscript.

Author details

[1]Department of Physics, University of Calabria, Via Pietro Bucci, 87036 Arcavacata, Rende CS, Italy. [2]SENSEable City Laboratory, Massachusetts Institute of Technology, 77 Massachusetts Avenue 9-209, Cambridge, MA 02139, USA. [3]Department of Civil and Environmental Engineering, Massachusetts Institute of Technology, 77 Massachusetts Avenue, Cambridge, MA 02139, USA.

Acknowledgements

The authors wish to thank MIT SMART Program, Accenture, Air Liquide, BBVA, The Coca Cola Company, Emirates Integrated Telecommunications Company, The ENEL foundation, Ericsson, Expo 2015, Ferrovial, Liberty Mutual, The Regional Municipality of Wood Buffalo, Volkswagen Electronics Research Lab, UBER and all the members of the MIT Senseable City Lab Consortium for supporting the research. We further thank MIT research support committee via the NEC and Bushbaum research funds, as well as the research project 'Managing Trust and Coordinating Interactions in Smart Networks of People, Machines and Organizations', funded by the Croatian Science Foundation. Finally, we would like to thank Eric Fisher for providing the dataset for this research, Alexander Belyi for some help with the visualizations and also Jameson L Toole, Yingxiang Yang, Lauren Alexander for useful recommendations at the early stage of this work.

Endnotes

[a] http://blog.euromonitor.com/2010/01/euromonitor-internationals-top-city-destination-ranking.html.

[b] http://newsroom.mastercard.com/wp-content/uploads/2014/07/Mastercard_GDCI_2014_Letter_Final_70814.pdf.

[c] http://blog.euromonitor.com/2015/01/top-100-city-destinations-ranking.html.

References

1. Ratti C, Pulselli RM, Williams S, Frenchman D (2006) Mobile landscapes: using location data from cell-phones for urban analysis. Environ Plan B, Plan Des 33(5):727-748
2. Reades J, Calabrese F, Sevtsuk A, Ratti C (2007) Cellular census: explorations in urban data collection. IEEE Pervasive Comput 6(3):30-38
3. González MC, Hidalgo CA, Barabási AL (2008) Understanding individual human mobility patterns. Nature 453:779-782
4. Kung KS, Greco K, Sobolevsky S, Ratti C (2014) Exploring universal patterns in human home-work commuting from mobile phone data. PLoS ONE 9(6):e96180. doi:10.1371/journal.pone.0096180
5. Hoteit S, Secci S, Sobolevsky S, Ratti C, Pujolle G (2014) Estimating human trajectories and hotspots through mobile phone data. Comput Netw 64:296-307

6. Reades J, Calabrese F, Ratti C (2009) Eigenplaces: analysing cities using the space-time structure of the mobile phone network. Environ Plan B, Plan Des 36(5):824-836
7. Toole JL, Ulm M, González MC, Bauer D (2012) Inferring land use from mobile phone activity. In: Proceedings of the ACM SIGKDD international workshop on urban computing. ACM, New York, pp 1-8
8. Grauwin S, Sobolevsky S, Moritz S, Godor I, Ratti C (2014) Towards a comparative science of cities: using mobile traffic records in New York, London and Hong Kong. In: Computational approaches for urban environments. Geotechnologies and the environment, vol 13, pp 363-387
9. Pei T, Sobolevsky S, Ratti C, Shaw SL, Li T, Zhou C (2014) A new insight into land use classification based on aggregated mobile phone data. Int J Geogr Inf Sci 28(9):1-20
10. Ratti C, Sobolevsky S, Calabrese F, Andris C, Reades J, Martino M, Claxton R, Strogatz SH (2010) Redrawing the Map of Great Britain from a Network of Human Interaction. PLoS ONE. doi:10.1371/journal.pone.0014248
11. Sobolevsky S, Szell M, Campari R, Couronné T, Smoreda Z, Ratti C (2013) Delineating geographical regions with networks of human interactions in an extensive set of countries. PLoS ONE 8(12):e81707. doi:10.1371/journal.pone.0081707
12. Amini A, Kung K, Kang C, Sobolevsky S, Ratti C (2014) The impact of social segregation on human mobility in developing and industrialized regions. EPJ Data Sci 3:6. doi:10.1140/epjds31
13. Furletti B, Gabrielli L, Renso C, Rinzivillo S (2012) Identifying users profiles from mobile calls habits. ACM SIGKDD International Workshop on Urban Computing
14. Fisher D (2007) Hotmap: looking at geographic attention. IEEE Trans Vis Comput Graph 13(6):1184-1191
15. Houée M, Barbier C (2008) Estimating foreign visitors flows from motorways toll management system. In: 9th international forum on tourism statistics
16. Sobolevsky S et al (2014) Mining urban performance: scale-independent classification of cities based on individual economic transactions. ASE BigDataScience 2014, Stanford, CA, preprint. arXiv:1405.4301
17. Sobolevsky S, Sitko I, Tachet des Combes R, Hawelka B, Murillo Arias J, Ratti C (2014) Money on the move: big data of bank card transactions as the new proxy for human mobility patterns and regional delineation. The case of residents and foreign visitors in Spain. In: 2014 IEEE international congress on big data, Anchorage, AK
18. Hawelka B, Sitko I, Beinat E, Sobolevsky S, Kazakopoulos P, Ratti C (2014) Geo-located Twitter as proxy for global mobility patterns. Cartogr Geogr Inf Sci 41(3):260-271
19. Brockmann D, Hufnagel L, Geisel T (2006) The scaling laws of human travel. Nature 439:462-465
20. Kang C, Sobolevsky S, Liu Y, Ratti C (2013) Exploring human movements in Singapore: a comparative analysis based on mobile phone and taxicab usages. In: Proceedings of the 2nd ACM SIGKDD international workshop on urban computing. ACM, New York, p 1
21. Girardin F, Calabrese F, Dal Fiore F, Ratti C, Blat J (2008) Digital footprinting: uncovering tourists with user-generated content. IEEE Pervasive Comput 7(4):36-43
22. Crandall DJ, Backstrom L, Huttenlocher D, Kleinberg J (2009) Mapping the world's photos. In: WWW'09: proceedings of the 18th international conference on world wide web. ACM, New York, pp 761-770
23. Zheng YT, Zha ZJ, Chua TS (2012) Mining travel patterns from geotagged photos. ACM Trans Intell Syst Technol 3(3):1-18
24. Spirn A (1998) The language of landscape, pp 3-81
25. Girardin F, Vaccari A, Gerber A, Biderman A, Ratti C (2009) Quantifying urban attractiveness from the distribution and density of digital footprints. Int J Spat Data Infrastruct Res 4:175-200
26. Sinkiene J, Kromolcas S (2010) Concept, direction and practice of city attractiveness improvement. Public Policy Adm 31:147-154
27. Van den Berg L, Van der Meer J, Otgaar AHJ (2007) The attractive city: catalyst of sustainable urban development. In: Ache P, Lehtovuori P (eds) European urban and metropolitan planning. Proceedings of the first openings. Seminar 12th October 2007 YTK-espoo. Centre for urban and regional studies publication C67, pp 48-63
28. Krzywinski M, Schein J, Birol I, Connors J, Gascoyne R, Horsman D, Jones SJ, Marra MA (2009) Circos: an information aesthetic for comparative genomics. Genome Res 19(9):1639-1645. doi:10.1101/gr.092759.109
29. Krings G, Calabrese F, Ratti C, Blondel VD (2009) Urban gravity: a model for inter-city telecommunication flows. J Stat Mech Theory Exp 2009(07):L07003

6

The distorted mirror of Wikipedia: a quantitative analysis of Wikipedia coverage of academics

Anna Samoilenko and Taha Yasseri*

*Correspondence:
taha.yasseri@oii.ox.ac.uk
Oxford Internet Institute, University of Oxford, 1 St Giles', Oxford, OX1 3JS, UK

Abstract

Activity of modern scholarship creates online footprints galore. Along with traditional metrics of research quality, such as citation counts, online images of researchers and institutions increasingly matter in evaluating academic impact, decisions about grant allocation, and promotion. We examined 400 biographical Wikipedia articles on academics from four scientific fields to test if being featured in the world's largest online encyclopedia is correlated with higher academic notability (assessed through citation counts). We found no statistically significant correlation between Wikipedia articles metrics (length, number of edits, number of incoming links from other articles, *etc.*) and academic notability of the mentioned researchers. We also did not find any evidence that the scientists with better WP representation are necessarily more prominent in their fields. In addition, we inspected the Wikipedia coverage of notable scientists sampled from Thomson Reuters list of 'highly cited researchers'. In each of the examined fields, Wikipedia failed in covering notable scholars properly. Both findings imply that Wikipedia might be producing an inaccurate image of academics on the front end of science. By shedding light on how public perception of academic progress is formed, this study alerts that a subjective element might have been introduced into the hitherto structured system of academic evaluation.

Keywords: Wikipedia; online reputation; altmetrics; scientometrics; peer-production; crowd-scouring; bibliometrics; *h*-index

Introduction

Modern scholarship is undergoing a revolutionary process of transformation triggered by the advances in information and communication technology. In growing numbers, scholars are moving their everyday work to the Web, creating diverse digital footprints galore. Recent studies show that social media have become indispensable in supporting research related activities [1, 2]. According to an analysis of STI conference presenters, 84% of scholars have web pages, 70% are on LinkedIn, 23% have public Google Scholar profiles, and 16% are on Twitter. Online reputation management is becoming essential in academic circles [3]: 77% of researchers monitor their personal online images, and 88% guard the reputation of their work online [4]. Researchers are advised to establish a Web presence on social media websites such as Twitter and Google+ so that they appear higher in the search results and thereby become more visible [5].

These developments in the research enterprise, affect both formal (among scholars) and informal (with the wider public) scholarly communication [6, 7], and create new possibilities as well as challenges, in the evaluation of the contribution of the individual researchers and the scholarly progress in general [8, 9]. Modern research communities are under increasing pressure to justify their scientific and societal value to the general public, funding agencies, and other stakeholders, and online presence plays an important role in this competitive race [9]. These days citation analysis, which involves counting how many times a paper or a researcher is referred to by other researchers, along with analyzing authors' citation networks, is increasingly used to quantify the importance of scientists across the disciplines [10]. Direct citation counts and their functions like h-index [11] and g-index [12] are widely employed for scientific impact evaluation and measuring researchers' visibility [13]. They can be of fundamental importance in decisions about hiring [14] and grant awards [15], and often are the only way for non-specialists from different fields or non-academic institutions to judge the impact of a scientific publication or a scholar [13].

Although citation counts are universally acknowledged as the indicator of academic prestige, they are loosely correlated with the future scientific impact of scientists [16]. Previous research admits their biases associated with (1) negative or ceremonial citations [13], (2) geographical gravity laws in citation practices [17], (3) incomparability of citation counts across fields [10] and bibliographical databases [13, 18–20]. Finally, subject to delays caused by publishing and peer review procedures, citation counts accumulate slowly and lag behind by several years. Along with citation counts, public engagement is another factor essential for scientists' future funding, promotions, and academic visibility [5, 21]. Increasingly often, this engagement is happening online through different social media, and can be measured with the number of 'likes', clicks, comments, downloads, 'retweets', *etc.*, which have been labeled *altmetrics* (alternative metrics) [22]. There is a wide scope of ongoing research exploring the role of social media and altmetrics in providing alternatives to the traditional research evaluation [3, 23, 24], primarily, exploring how much altmetrics data exist [25] and whether they can be used in evaluating academic impact [26]. For example, a recent study has found that earlier article [23] download metrics can be used for predicting the future impact of academic papers, and some researchers even suggest that academics should include altmetrics in their CVs [21] as an innovative indicator of academic importance.

In this study, our attention was drawn by Wikipedia, a web-based encyclopedia which allows any user to freely edit its content, create and discuss the articles - all in the absence of central authority or stable membership. This model of a decentralised bottom-up knowledge construction draws on the wisdom of the crowds rather than on professional writers and peer-reviewed material, which makes Wikipedia similar to a social media platform. Unlike other encyclopedias, Wikipedia is unrestricted in size and range of topics covered, and thereby holds the potential to become the most comprehensive repository of human knowledge. Although many studies have raised concerns about reliability and accuracy of Wikipedia content [27–29] for many people, not excluding scientists, Wikipedia is the first port of call for quick superficial information search: 29.6% of academics prefer Wikipedia to online library catalogues [30], and 52% of students are frequent Wikipedia users, even if the instructor advised against it [31]. In general, browsing Wikipedia is the third most popular online activity, after watching YouTube videos and engaging into social networking: it attracts 62% of Internet users under 30 [32]. The popularity of Wikipedia seems to be facilitated by the Google search engine itself. A recent study has found that in 96% of cases Wikipedia ranks within the top 5 UK Google search results [33], which means that Wikipedia content becomes (1) highly visible, taking a direct part in shaping public opinion on a variety of topics, and (2) virtually unavoidable, whether the user was searching for it or not.

In the present study, we wanted to investigate how the academia itself is represented on Wikipedia. Previous research suggests that editing Wikipedia can be an influential way of improving researchers' visibility or getting the message across, even in academic community [4]. Although there has not been sufficient research on exactly what it means if a scholar has a Wikipedia page, it is considered prestigious to have one. According to an online survey conducted by Nature, nearly 3% of scholars have edited their Wikipedia biographies, and about 25% check Wikipedia for references to themselves or their work [4]. The decisions on the inclusion/deletion of the articles in the encyclopedia are adopted through the consensus among the editors, rather than imposed by a controlling institution. The articles need to satisfy some notability criteria in order to be deemed worthy of inclusion, and in most cases are speedily deleted if the community of editors deems them irrelevant [34]. Previous research has demonstrated that the topical coverage of Wikipedia is driven by the interests of its users, and its comprehensiveness is likely to vary depending on the topic [29]. Moreover, the cultural preferences of the community of Wikipedia editors introduce additional subjectivity in the editorial process of the encyclopedia [35].

A few studies have examined Wikipedia coverage of academically related topics. Elvebakk compared Wikipedia coverage of 20th century philosophers with two peer-reviewed Web encyclopedias and concluded that through the inclusion of 'minor' and amateur philosophers, Wikipedia gives a messier, more dynamic picture of the field, which, however, is not fundamentally different from more traditional sources, but shows a slight tendency to a more 'popular' understanding of the discipline [36]. Another qualitative evaluation of Wikipedia was done by the experts in Communication studies who examined the encyclopaedia's articles on communication research and revealed that Wikipedia is missing the contemporary research and offers an incomplete and faulty impression on the current state of communication studies [37]. To the best of our knowledge, the only quantitative study that examined Wikipedia in academic context argues that among Computer Science related topics and authors, those ones mentioned in the encyclopedia are more likely to have higher academic and societal impact [38]. Yet, we see some fallacies in these results obtained by Jiang *et al.* Firstly, the reported Spearman correlation coefficient between academic and Wikipedia ranking of authors is close to zero, which implies very low tendency for one to predict the other. Secondly, their selection of authors is limited to those Computer Scientists mentioned in the ACM Digital Library papers, which makes generalising the findings to other fields and academia as a whole impossible. Lastly, the problem of name ambiguity was not addressed in the study.

Overall, the existing research is based on small samples limited to one discipline, and offers a fragmented view of Wikipedia coverage of academic topics. This does not allow drawing holistic conclusions about the role of the encyclopedia in both formal and informal academic communication. To further investigate this matter, we examined 400 biographical Wikipedia articles on living academics from the fields of (1) Biology, (2) Physics, (3) Computer Science, (4) Psychology and Psychiatry. The articles differed in comprehensiveness and structure of contents, but generally included researchers' short biography

Table 1 Average citation metrics of 4 x 100 researchers randomly sampled from the corresponding Wikipedia categories (bibliographical data are taken from Scopus)

Field	# Papers	Citations	Citation per Paper	*h*-index	# co-authors	Years active	Field ave. *h*-index	*h*-index above field ave.
Biol	166 (±24)	5,612 (±932)	33 (±4)	23 (±2)	92 (±6)	32 (±2)	22	36%
CoSi	92 (±9)	1,638 (±219)	19 (±2)	13 (±1)	75 (±5)	25 (±1)	15	31%
Phys	139 (±16)	3,512 (±447)	27 (±4)	19 (±2)	95 (±6)	31 (±1)	33	22%
Psyc	78 (±14)	3,081 (±623)	30 (±4)	15 (±2)	60 (±6)	40 (±11)	21	24%

The last column shows the proportion of researchers in the sample whose *h*-index was above the field average (field-specific averages of *h*-indexes were taken from previous research [10, 39]). The numbers in parentheses are the standard errors of the average.

and sections covering their personal and public life, research activities, scientific contributions, affiliation with institutions, awards, *etc.* We tested the correlation between such parameters of the Wikipedia articles as length, number of views, editors, edits, *etc.*, and citation indexes of the academics, such as total number of publications, total number of citations, *h*-index, *etc.* retrieved from the bibliographical database Scopus. The analysis of the data allowed us to identify whether the researchers featured on Wikipedia have high academic notability in their fields. To complete the picture, we also examined the Wikipedia coverage of scientists introduced as 'influential' by Thomson Reuters, a world leading expert in bibliometrics and citation analyses.

Results

Out of 400 randomly selected English Wikipedia articles on researchers (see Methods), 91% of scholars were academically active and had Scopus profiles (87 Biologists, 94 Computer Scientists, 98 Physicists, and 86 Psychologists and Psychiatrists). Of the remaining 9% with no Scopus record of publications, all had some relevant academic experience; namely, 34% changed occupation after completing their degrees; 31% contribute to popularising science in their fields; 29% are active academics, and 6% have retired. The field-specific average Scopus metrics are summarised in Table 1. On average, biologists in the sample are the most prolific authors, accumulating the highest number of citations per document, total citations, and *h*-indexes. Computer Scientists have the fewest average citations per document and demonstrate the lowest *h*-indexes in the sample. Psychologists and Psychiatrists scholars on average have longest careers and collaborate with fewer co-authors than researchers from other fields, generally producing the smallest number of documents.

We compared the *h*-indexes of researchers from the Wikipedia samples who have Scopus profiles with the overall average *h*-indexes by field established in previous research [10, 39]. The researchers, whose *h*-index was higher than the field average, were considered notable. Figure 1 demonstrates the histograms of *h*-indexes in the observed fields and their distribution in relation to the field-specific average *h*-indexes. The analysis has shown that only a small percentage of researchers mentioned on Wikipedia (36% of Biologists, 31% of Computer Scientists, 24% Psychologists and Psychiatrists, and 22% Physicists) are notable according to the traditional means of evaluation (citation indexes). Table 2 summarises the averages of Wikipedia articles metrics, and reveals field-specific differences in the appearance and popularity of the articles. The articles on Physicists have the most diverse coverage in other language editions of Wikipedia, are the longest in the sample, and

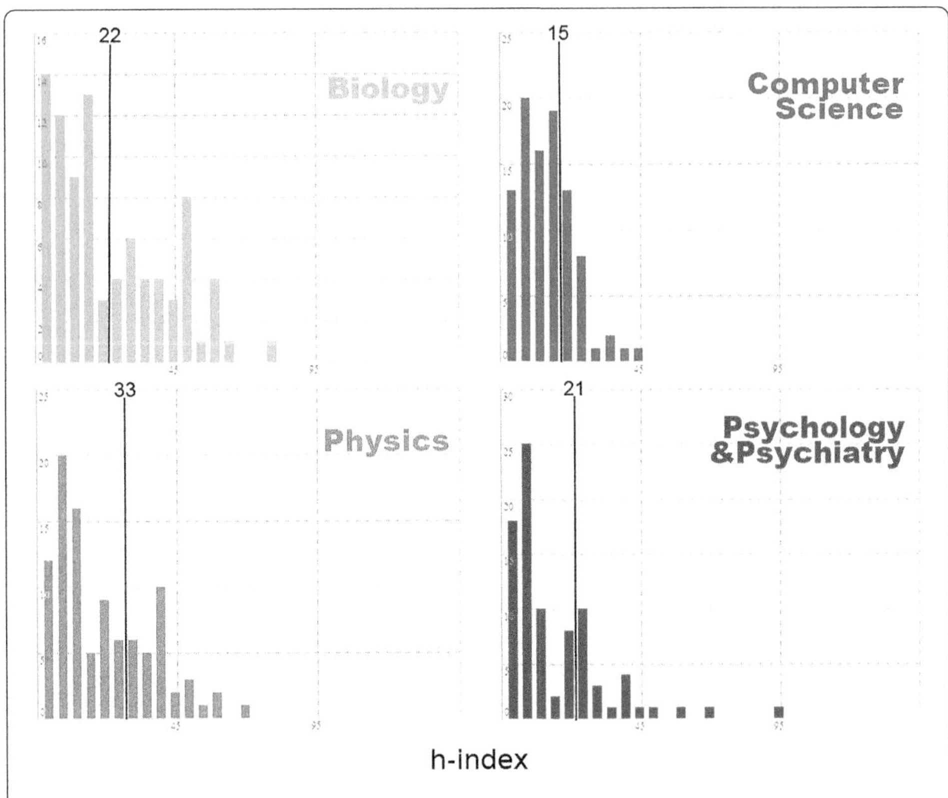

Figure 1 Histograms of the *h*-indexes of the authors in the Wikipedia samples. The black line indicates the average *h*-index in the field taken from the previous research [10, 39].

Table 2 Average metrics of Wikipedia articles on researchers from the selected fields

Field	Length (page)	Editors/excluding bots	Edits/excluding bots	In-degree	Daily views (2012)	Languages
Biol	2.2 (±0.2)	27/22 (±3/±3)	54/47 (±6/±6)	15 (±2)	11 (±2)	2 (±0.4)
CoSi	2.0 (±0.1)	34/28 (±4/±4)	59/51 (±6/±6)	30 (±6)	19 (±4)	2 (±0.5)
Phys	2.7 (±0.3)	37/30 (±5/±4)	87/77 (±20/±19)	24 (±5)	17 (±3)	3 (±0.7)
Psyc	2.5 (±0.2)	34/29 (±6/±6)	76/69 (±14/±14)	16 (±5)	23 (±6)	1 (±0.3)

The length of a page is taken as 2,638 characters (a standard A4 Word document, Arial 12, 1.5 spaced). Languages column includes the number of language editions of Wikipedia covering the same scholar (excluding English). The numbers in parentheses are the standard errors of the average.

on average attract the largest number of unique editors and edits, which suggests a heightened interest of Wikipedians in covering this topic. The articles on Computer Scientists, despite being the shortest, have the highest in-degree and thus, are most connected with other Wikipedia articles. The articles on Psychologists and Psychiatrists are on average the most viewed ones.

For all scholars with Scopus IDs, we examined 6×8 binary permutations of Scopus and Wikipedia metrics (presented in Tables 1 and 2), and performed regression analysis in logarithmic space. All the calculated correlation coefficients are presented in Additional file 1, Table A1. Although we tried to consider all the potentially correlated pairs of parameters, to make sure that we do not miss any aspect of relation, but we discovered no significant correlation between any of the pairs. The strongest positive correlation ($R^2 = 0.13$) in the dataset was found between in-degree (Wikipedia) and years active (Scopus) pair of vari-

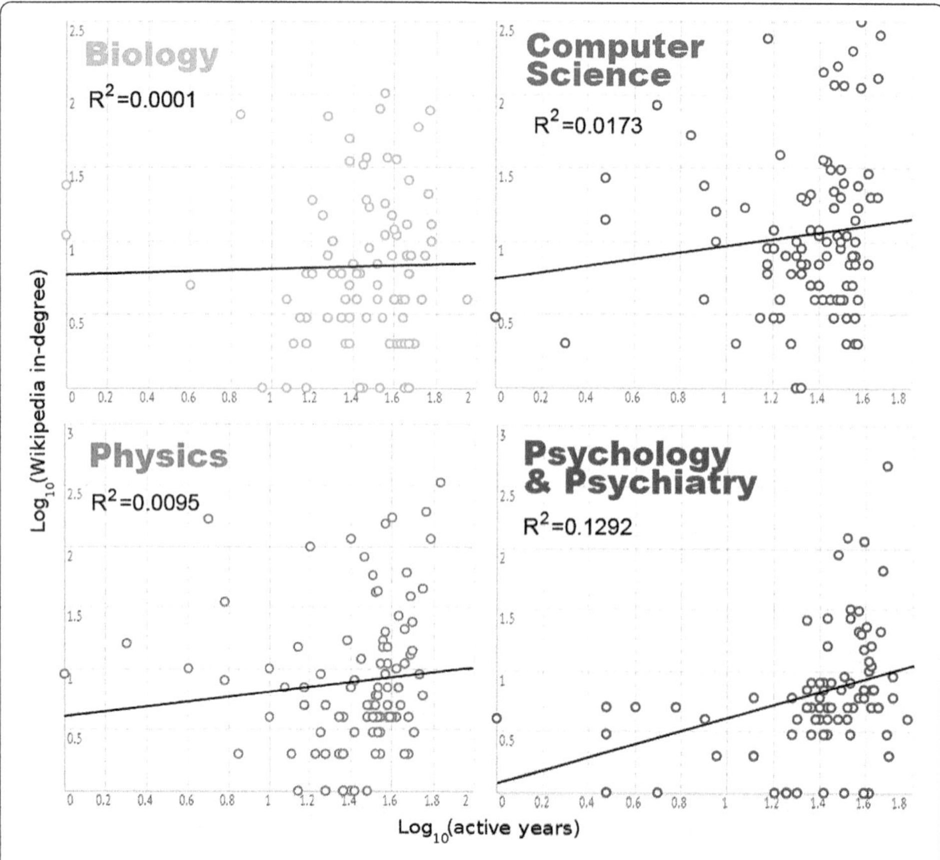

Figure 2 Scatterplots of the Wikipedia in-degree of the articles *vs.* the number of active years. The solid line shows the best linear fit (using the least squares algorithm) to the data in log-log scale. The strongest positive correlation is found in the Psychologists and Psychiatrists subset (R^2 = 0.1292).

ables in Psychologists and Psychiatrists subset (shown in Figure 2). The strongest positive correlations in other subsets included the following pairs: number of language editions (Wikipedia) *vs.* years active (Scopus) in Biologists (R^2 = 0.019), in-degree (Wikipedia) *vs.* mean citations (Scopus) in Computer Scientists (R^2 = 0.023), and number of languages editions (Wikipedia) *vs.* mean citations (Scopus) in Physics (R^2 = 0.035).

To investigate the coverage of the prominent researchers by Wikipedia, we also analysed a random sample of 219 academics selected from the Thomson Reuters list of 1317 people 'behind the world's most influential research' [40]. The results demonstrated that Wikipedia left out 52% of the most prominent Computer Scientists, 62% of the most influential Psychologists and Psychiatrists, as well as 67% of Biologists and Biochemists. The poorest coverage was observed in Physics: 78% were not found on Wikipedia. Importantly, the list of highly cited researchers was published in 2010, whereas our data describe the current state of Wikipedia, having left sufficient time to Wikipedia editors for a proper inclusion of the listed prominent scientists. Despite this, Wikipedia has no record of the majority of the examined scientists regardless of their field.

In order to measure the overall performance of Wikipedia in representing the notable scholars, we calculated the F-scores for each of the examined fields (Table 3). F-score is a measure of a classification accuracy based on the harmonic mean of precision (the proportion of retrieved instances that are relevant, in this case the ratio of researchers

Table 3 Overview of Wikipedia's accuracy in representing notable scholars

Wikipedia category	Precision	Recall	*F*-score	Total number of articles in category
Biologists	36%	33%	0.34	81631
Computer Scientists	31%	48%	0.37	13789
Physicists	22%	22%	0.22	4554
Psychologists and Psychiatrists	24%	38%	0.29	4777

Precision is the ratio of researchers on Wikipedia with h-index above field average and *recall* is the percentage of Highly Cited researchers covered by Wikipedia. F-score is the harmonic mean of these two.

on Wikipedia with h-index above field average) and recall (the proportion of relevant instances that are retrieved, in this case the percentage of Highly Cited researchers covered by Wikipedia); $F = 2 \times \frac{\text{precision} \times \text{recall}}{\text{precision}+\text{recall}}$.

F-score = 1 shows a perfect match between the model and the data, and a null model of random assignment leads to $F = 0.5$. Table 3 shows that in each of the four inspected fields, the F-scores were below the accuracy of a random assignment. In other words, Wikipedia failed in both of the examined dimensions: being on Wikipedia does not signify academic notability, and being notable does not guarantee Wikipedia coverage. Surprisingly, smaller categories sometimes demonstrated higher recall than the bigger categories, which indicates that the growth of categories in terms of the number of articles, does not necessarily lead to a more inclusive coverage.

Discussion

Wikipedia notability guidelines for academics suggest that the encyclopedia should only cover the researchers who have 'made significant impact in their disciplines', which 'in most cases' is associated with being 'an author of highly cited academic work' [41]. Consequently, in the eyes of a lay user, the mere presence of a scientist on Wikipedia is associated with their academic prestige and authority. However, we observed that, contrary to the expectations, the majority of the researchers' biographies on Wikipedia do not meet the primary notability criteria and thus, their inclusion in the encyclopedia can be deceiving. Previous qualitative examination of Wikipedia articles on certain academics [36] and fields [37] suggested that the selection of authors and topics by academic community differs from the one suggested by the community of Wikipedians. Our findings show that this claim can be extended to a wider scope of fields and authors, establishing that Wikipedia offers a very different image of researchers on the front end of the scientific progress.

Our findings suggest that the inspection of Wikipedia is not useful in finding highly cited researchers. Moreover, counter intuitively we observed that in some cases, the articles on authors without a Scopus track of scientific publications were longer and attracted more editors than the articles on the scientists with high citation indexes. This implies that the decisions of WP editors about covering certain scholars were motivated by the reasons other than the prominence of those scholars' bibliographic records. Moreover, Wikipedia metrics of the articles about the prominent researchers (with high h-indexes) were not statistically larger than the same metrics from the less cited subset (Welch's t-test did not reject the null hypothesis of identical distributions; the smallest p-value among all metrics and disciplines was 0.18). Consequently, we establish that for a non-professional reader who turns to Wikipedia with an exploratory purpose of finding some prominent researchers in a field, the encyclopedia might be misleading, as it provides no reliable visual cues that might be a proxy of academic notability. We conclude that the absence of correlation between Scopus and Wikipedia metrics suggests that they measure different phenomena. As such, unlike other social media like Twitter and Facebook [42], Wikipedia cannot be used as an early indicator of academic impact. That comes as a surprise, especially considering that previous research has shown that Wikipedia activity data is a better predictor of financial success of movies than Twitter [43]. Yet, openness, speed, diversity, and collaborative filtering offered by Wikipedia, can be applied to measure other aspects of scientific impact that are not captured by the traditional citation analysis, for example social impact [38] or public engagement of a scientist.

We also investigated which proportion of truly prominent scientists (according to the ISI Highly Cited Research list of most notable scientists) have Wikipedia presence, and discovered that the coverage is below 50% in each of the four examined fields. Since the list has been publically available since 2010, this observation cannot be due to time constraints. We know from previous research that Wikipedia topical coverage is uneven and driven purely by the interests of its editors community [29].

Our findings establish that academic prominence of researchers (measured by citation counts) is not among the factors facilitating the decisions on articles inclusion. Instead, the interest of Wikipedians might be driven by other factors like scientists' social impact, public outreach, attention from media, popularity of their research topic, *etc.* Interestingly, we observe that the academics with very low h-indexes and high Wikipedia visibility (measured in gained views) are all noted figures, book authors, and popularisers of science. This democratising effect of Wikipedia and Web 2.0 gives young and promising academics more chance to be seen and found. On the other hand, it introduces a subjective element into the hitherto structured and well-established system of peer-review-based academic evaluation. Despite Wikipedia's inconsistency with the traditional view of scientific impact, its content is highly visible and virtually unavoidable. The encyclopedia is making its way into society, playing a role in forming public image on a variety of issues, not excluding science; and this rise of Wikipedia is difficult to ignore. As the articles are being actively edited and viewed, individual scientists, their fields, and entire academic institutions, can be easily affected by the way they are represented in this important online medium.

One of the limitations of the present study relates to the inherent characteristics of bibliographical database Scopus. Its citation metrics are restricted to the pool of 12,850 reviewed journals and do not cover any publications before 1966 [44]. This study only scrutinises one aspect of scholarly notability - the citation metrics. Future studies might focus on testing whether other aspects - for example, prestigious academic awards, membership in highly selective scholarly societies, the impact of the work in the area of higher education and outside academia - raise the likelihood of being included into Wikipedia. It could be instructive to qualitatively study the talk pages of Wikipedia articles on academics in order to understand the motives for the inclusion/deletion of the articles, and examine how the editors perceive the notability of the scientists covered. Future work can also scrutinise if the presence on Wikipedia serves as a proxy to academics' social impact or public visibility. And more importantly: Who is writing Wikipedia articles on academics (lay users, academics, or the subjects of the article and their immediate social surroundings)? What motivates their selection choices? How do the readers perceive the articles on academics? More research is also needed to understand how the online image of scientists affects their reputation offline, as well as the decisions regarding funding, conference invitations, grant allocation, collaboration, and promotion. And specifically, what role does Wikipedia play in shaping this online image?

Methods

Data sources and collection

Wikipedia

We used English Wikipedia's internal category tree structure to retrieve the full lists of articles in the following categories: Biologists (81,631 articles), Physicists (4,554 articles), Computer Scientists (13,789 articles), Psychologists and Psychiatrists (4,777 articles). From each of the lists, we took a random sample of 300 entries and manually selected the first 100 articles that met the following criteria: (1) the researcher was alive at the moment of data collection; (2) the article page had no warning of a problem with Wikipedia notability guidelines for biographies; (3) the content of the article and the assigned category suggested the same field affiliation. This left us with a dataset of 400 articles. The article metrics were collected using SQL access to Wikimedia Toolserver database and included: page ID, number of unique editors and edits, number of editors and edits excluding those made by bots ('bot' is a piece of code that runs through Wikipedia to implement minor edits and other repetitive operations that help maintain the quality of Wikipedia articles [45]), length, in-degree (in this case, in-degree refers to the number of Wikipedia articles linking to the selected article), number of page views, and number of other language editions of Wikipedia in which the article was covered.

Scopus

We searched the academics from the 400 selected Wikipedia articles in Scopus bibliographical database, and in cases where they were available, collected the following citation metrics: author ID; number of documents, citations, co-authors, and years active; h-index, and mean citations per paper. The data were collected and verified manually in order to exclude the name ambiguity problem. In cases when the same researcher had two profiles, the citation data were taken from the profile with most citations.

The complete datasets are available online in Additional file 2, Dataset A1.

Prominent researchers

To identify the researchers behind the most fundamental contributions to the advancement of science, we used the data from the ISI Highly Cited Research study by Thomson Reuters [40]. The study is based on the top cited publications covered in Web of Science from 1981-2008, and is freely available online. We downloaded the list of the prominent researchers in each of the four relevant fields (sampling frames) from http://highlycited.com/ website. The entries were arranged alphabetically and consisted of researcher's name, surname, and organization. From each of the sampling frames, we extracted every sixth entry and obtained four systematic random samples: Biology and Biochemistry (49 researchers); Computer Science (63 researchers); Physics (54 researchers); Psychology and Psychiatry (53 researchers). Then each author was searched in Wikipedia to check whether there was a corresponding article. All data were collected in August 2013. The list of 'prominent researchers' is available online in Additional file 3, Dataset A2.

Data analysis

The data were imported into MATLAB to test the possible correlations between Wikipedia and Scopus statistics. Histograms of all variables were visually inspected for normality and the data were logarithmically transformed to compensate for the skewness of the data distribution. We built a linear regression model and calculated the coefficient of determination R^2 to measure the strength of association between all possible permutations of variables. The researchers with no Scopus IDs were examined as separate cases.

Additional material

Additional file 1: Table A1 contains R^2 values for all 6 × 8 binary permutations of Wikipedia and Scopus metrics by field.
Additional file 2: Dataset A1 contains the complete list of Wikipedia metrics and Scopus data for all four disciplines.
Additional file 3: Dataset A2 contains the random sample of prominent researchers by field taken from the "ISI Highly Cited Research" by Thomson Reuters.

Competing interests

The authors declare that they have no competing interests.

Authors' contributions

AS and TY conceived and designed the research; AS analysed the data and wrote the main manuscript text. All authors reviewed the manuscript.

Acknowledgements

We would like to thank Ralph Schroeder, Eric T. Meyer (University of Oxford), Jasleen Kaur, and Filippo Radicchi (Indiana University) for insightful discussions. We also thank Wikimedia Deutchland e.V. and Wikimedia Foundation for the live access to the Wikipedia data via Toolserver.

References

1. Kelly B (2013) Using social media to enhance your research activities. In: Social media in social research 2013 conference
2. Gruzd A, Goertzen M, Mai P (2012) Survey results highlights: trends in scholarly communication and knowledge Dissemination in the Age of Social Media. Halifax, NS, Canada
3. Bar-Ilan J, Haustein S, Peters I, Priem J, Shema H, Terliesner J (2012) Beyond citations: scholars' visibility on the social web. In: Proceedings of the 17th international conference on science and technology indicators, Montréal, Canada, pp 98-109
4. Reich ES (2011) Online reputations: best face forward. Nature 473:138-139
5. Bik HM, Goldstein MC (2013) An introduction to social media for scientists. PLoS Biol 11:1001535
6. Borgman CL (2007) Scholarship in the digital age: information, infrastructure, and the Internet. MIT Press, Cambridge
7. Nentwich M, König R (2012) Cyberscience 2.0: research in the age of digital social networks. Campus Verlag
8. Wouters P, Beaulieu A, Scharnhorst A, Wyatt S (2013) Virtual knowledge: experimenting in the humanities and the social sciences. MIT Press, Cambridge
9. Wouters P, Costas R (2012) Users, narcissism and control: tracking the impact of scholarly publications in the 21st century. SURF foundation
10. Kaur J, Radicchi F, Menczer F (2013) Universality of scholarly impact metrics. J Informetr (in press)
11. Hirsch JE (2005) An index to quantify an individual's scientific research output. Proc Natl Acad Sci USA 102(46):16569-16572
12. Egghe L (2006) Theory and practise of the *g*-index. Scientometrics 69(1):131-152
13. Meho LI (2006) The rise and rise of citation analysis. Physics World
14. Bornmann L, Daniel H-D (2006) Selecting scientific excellence through committee peer review - a citation analysis of publications previously published to approval or rejection of post-doctoral research fellowship applicants. Scientometrics 68(3):427-440
15. Bornmann L, Wallon G, Ledin A (2008) Does the committee peer review select the best applicants for funding? An investigation of the selection process for two European molecular biology organization programmes. PLoS ONE 3(10):3480
16. Penner O, Pan RK, Petersen AM, Kaski K, Fortunato S (2013) On the predictability of future impact in science. Scientific Reports 3(3052)
17. Pan RK, Kaski K, Fortunato S (2012) World citation and collaboration networks: uncovering the role of geography in science. Scientific Reports 2(902)
18. Jacsó P (2006) Deflated, inflated and phantom citation counts. Online Inf Rev 30(3):297-309
19. Meho LI, Yang K (2007) Impact of data sources on citation counts and rankings of lis faculty: Web of science versus scopus and google scholar. J Am Soc Inf Sci Technol 58(13):2105-2125

20. Jacsó P (2008) Testing the calculation of a realistic *h*-index in Google scholar, scopus, and web of science for f. w. lancaster. Libr Trends 56(4):784-815
21. Piwowar H, Priem J (2013) The power of altmetrics on a CV. Bull Am Soc Inf Sci Technol 39(4):10-13
22. Priem J, Taraborelli D, Groth P, Neylon C (2010) altmetrics: a manifesto. altmetrics.org. Retrieved July 5, 2013, from http://altmetrics.org/manifesto/
23. Priem J, Hemminger B (2010) Scientometrics 2.0: New metrics of scholarly impact on the social web. First Monday 15(7)
24. Torres-Salinas D, Cabezas-Clavijo A, Jimenez-Contreras E (2013) Altmetrics: New indicators for scientific communication in web 2.0. arXiv:1306.6595
25. Priem J, Costello KL (2010) How and why scholars cite on Twitter. In: Proceedings of the 73rd ASIS&T annual meeting on navigating streams in an information ecosystem. ASIS&T'10, vol 47. American Society for Information Science, Silver Springs, pp 75-1754
26. Priem J, Piwowar HA, Hemminger BM (2012) Altmetrics in the wild: using social media to explore scholarly impact. arXiv:1203.4745
27. Callahan ES, Herring SC (2011) Cultural bias in Wikipedia content on famous persons. J Am Soc Inf Sci Technol 62(10):1899-1915
28. Giles J (2005) Internet encyclopaedias go head to head. Nature 438(7070):900-901
29. Halavais A, Lackaff D (2008) An analysis of topical coverage of Wikipedia. J Comput-Mediat Commun 13(2):429-440
30. Weller K, Dornstädter R, Freimanis R, Klein RN, Perez M (2010) Social software in academia: three studies on users' acceptance of web 2.0 services. In: Proceedings web science conf, pp 26-27
31. Head A, Eisenberg M (2010) How today's college students use Wikipedia for course-related research. First Monday 15(3)
32. Zickuhr K, Rainie L (2011) Wikipedia, past and present. Retrieved July 8, 2013, from http://pewinternet.org/Reports/2011/Wikipedia.aspx
33. Silverwood-Cope S (2012) Wikipedia: Page one of Google UK for 99% of searches. Intelligent positioning. Retrieved July 8, 2013, from http://www.intelligentpositioning.com/blog/2012/02/wikipedia-page-one-of-google-uk-for-99-of-searches/
34. Gelley BS (2013) Investigating deletion in Wikipedia. arXiv:1305.5267
35. Yasseri T, Spoerri A, Graham M, Kertész J (2014) The most controversial topics in Wikipedia: a multilingual and geographical analysis. In: Fichman P, Hara N (eds) Global Wikipedia: international and cross-cultural issues in online collaboration. Scarecrow Press, Lanham
36. Elvebakk B (2008) Philosophy democratized? First Monday 13(2)
37. Rush EK, Tracy SJ (2010) Wikipedia as public scholarship: communicating our impact online. J Appl Commun Res 38(3):309-315
38. Shuai X, Jiang Z, Liu X, Bollen J (2013) A comparative study of academic and Wikipedia ranking. In: Proceedings of the 13th ACM/IEEE-CS joint conference on digital libraries. JCDL'13. ACM, New York, pp 25-28
39. Radicchi F, Castellano C (2013) Analysis of bibliometric indicators for individual scholars in a large data set. Scientometrics 97:627-637
40. Reuters T (2008) Highly cited research. Retrieved July 16, 2013, from http://highlycited.com/
41. Wikipedia (2013) Wikipedia: Notability (academics). Retrieved July 23, 2013, from http://en.wikipedia.org/wiki/Wikipedia:Notability_(academics)
42. Thelwall M, Haustein S, Larivière V, Sugimoto CR (2013) Do altmetrics work? Twitter and ten other social web services. PLoS ONE 8(5):64841
43. Mestyán M, Yasseri T, Kertész J (2013) Early prediction of movie box office success based on Wikipedia activity big data. PLoS ONE 8(8):71226
44. Falagas ME, Pitsouni EI, Malietzis GA, Pappas G (2008) Comparison of PubMed, scopus, web of science, and Google scholar: strengths and weaknesses. FASEB J 22(2):338-342
45. Wikipedia (2013) Wikipedia: Bots. Retrieved July 18, 2013, from http://en.wikipedia.org/wiki/Wikipedia:Bots

7

Dynamics and spatial distribution of global nighttime lights

Peter Cauwels*, Nicola Pestalozzi and Didier Sornette

*Correspondence: pcauwels@ethz.ch
Department of Management, Technology and Economics, ETH Zurich, Scheuchzerstrasse 7, Zurich, CH-8092, Switzerland

Abstract

Using open source data, we observe the fascinating dynamics of nighttime light. Following a global economic regime shift, the planetary center of light can be seen moving eastwards at a pace of about 60 km per year. Introducing spatial light Gini coefficients, we find a universal pattern of human settlements across different countries and see a global centralization of light. Observing 160 different countries we document the expansion of developing countries, the growth of new agglomerations, the regression in countries suffering from demographic decline and the success of light pollution abatement programs in western countries.

Keywords: DMSP; NGDC; NOAA; nighttime light; light emission; Gini coefficients

1 Introduction

In the mid-1960s, the U.S. Air Force started a research project called the Defense Meteorological Satellite Program (DMSP[a]). The main purpose of this enterprise was to provide the military with daily information on worldwide cloud coverage. After scrutinizing the first results, it was discovered that, besides the initial goal of measuring cloud coverage, nighttime light was also very well captured by the sensors. When the system was declassified in 1972, and the data made publicly available, this unexpected, but very convenient, side-effect, gradually gained more interest from the scientific community.

Light emission is a quantity that can be measured instantaneously, objectively and systematically. This is in stark contrast to many widely used economic and demographic indicators, which are often based on estimates and censuses, such as the gross domestic product, energy consumption, population levels, or the degree of poverty. In the standard approaches, biases, time lags and inaccuracies are unavoidable and the comparison between different countries is often problematic. In contrast, nighttime lights are remotely sensed from one single satellite, with the same resolution, at the same time-of-day, in a systematic way, covering the surface of the whole planet.

Since 1992, the images have been systematically digitized and are now freely downloadable from the web [1]. This has opened a treasure of data, available at no cost, to the scientific community. As a consequence, in the past decade, a new research field has prospered using these observations of nighttime light and its dynamics in space and in time, aimed at studying economic activity, demographics, energy consumption, poverty and development, conflicts, urbanism and the environment.

We will discuss the data, the different products that are freely available on the web and our additional processing and enhancement tools in Section 2. In Section 3, we will review the existing research and academic literature. From our synthesis of the wide range of papers using nighttime images, a best-practice approach will be proposed.

This paper will further contribute to the existing research and literature with the following unique results. Firstly, in Section 4.1, we will calculate the dynamics of our planet's mean center of light. It will be shown that, over the past two decades, this center of light has gradually shifted eastwards over a distance of roughly 1,000 km. This result will be compared with a recent study of the McKinsey Global Institute [2], which calculated the dynamics of the global economic center of gravity based on GDP figures.

Next, in Section 4.2, a spatial light Gini coefficient will be introduced. This will make a comparison possible of how evenly light is distributed in different countries. We will come to the fascinating conclusion that, if only relatively dense urbanized areas are considered, the Lorenz curves and Gini coefficients of light are almost identical in every country, even though the considered area can differ up to two orders of magnitude. Additionally, it will be shown that the Gini coefficients follow a slightly increasing trend over the past two decades. This is evidence of a continuous centralization of light, or, the gradual increase in the inequality of the spatial distribution of light.

Global light is centralizing. In Section 4.3, we will dig deeper into this observation, analyzing the dynamics of bright versus dimly lit areas. It will be shown that dimly lit areas have increased proportionally more than bright areas, with a 49% compared to a 19% growth rate over the past 17 years. From this, it can be concluded that the area of dimly lit settlements has increased proportionally more than the area of the bright cities. Maybe counter-intuitively, this appears to be the major driver behind the observed increase in spatial light Gini coefficients over that period. Further, in this section, we will compare the nighttime light dynamics of economic tigers like China, India and Brazil, with countries that have seen a sensitive reduction in the urban population like Russia (excluding Moscow), Ukraine and Moldova. Additionally, it will be shown that, in some developed countries like Canada or the U.K., the size of the largest light agglomerations is slightly diminishing. This demonstrates the relative success of light pollution abatement programs launched in different countries around the world. Finally, the notion of a country will be dropped and the concept of light-defined agglomerations will be introduced. Tables and graphs will be given of the 20 largest light agglomerations worldwide in 1992 compared with 2009. This will demonstrate quantitatively how dramatically fast-growing megalopolis are changing in some developing countries like China and Egypt.

In this paper, we will look at the dynamics of global light growth covering almost two decades of available data. A review of the literature reveals that the majority of existing studies makes use only of single one-year snapshots and does not study time evolutionary processes. One of the reasons for this is the complex data handling and inter-calibration between the different satellite sensors. We therefore explain in details how we have addressed this problem.

2 Data and methods

2.1 The satellites

In the DMSP program, typically two satellites are orbiting simultaneously, in a sun-synchronous low earth orbit, at an 833 km altitude. The satellites, which have a lifespan of about 6 to 8 years, pass over any given point on Earth between 8.30 pm and 9.30 pm, local time [3]. They are equipped with a so-called Operational Line-scan System (OLS).[b]

Table 1 The available composites

Year	Satellites					
1992	F10					
1993						
1994		F12				
1995						
1996						
1997			F14			
1998						
1999						
2000				F15		
2001						
2002						
2003						
2004					F16	
2005						
2006						
2007						
2008						
2009						
2010						F18

For most of the time, two satellites were orbiting simultaneously.

This consists of two sensors, one operating in the visible, near-infrared (400 to 1,100 nm) spectrum and the other operating in the thermal infrared (10.5 to 12.6 μm) domain. Each detector has a field of view of 3,000 km and captures images at a resolution of approximately 0.56 km.

2.2 The stable lights product

Creating good-quality scientific products from the raw data of the satellites is an undertaking of monumental difficulty and requires a huge processing effort. The National Geophysical Data Center (NGDC) of the National Oceanic and Atmospheric Administration (NOAA) has a research project dedicated exclusively to this task.

Firstly, the usable area of each image must be selected taking into account daylight scattering. Further, the parts with a scan angle greater than a certain threshold have to be excluded because these suffer from background noise and give a poor accuracy on the geolocation [4]. Then, the images are re-projected into 30 arc-second grids; this represents an area of about 0.86 square kilometers at the equator. A geo-location is assigned to each pixel of the usable area, based on different variables such as scan angles, satellite altitude and azimuth. In order to obtain a composite that covers the whole globe, all the selected satellite images are entwined. In the end, each composite represents a one-year average nighttime light image of the world, covering an area between 180 and −180 degrees longitude and −65 and 75 degrees latitude. Some parts of Greenland, Alaska, Canada, Scandinavia and Antarctica are missing. However, it has been estimated that only about 10,000 people or a mere 0.0002% of the world population lives there [5]. Since many observations were disturbed by clouds, moonlight, sun glare and other factors, it is estimated that each pixel is the result of 20 to 100 clear observations [6].

Table 1 shows the list of available composites. When two satellites were orbiting at the same time, two different composites were produced. This creates a redundancy that can be used to inter-calibrate the images. We will come back to this in the following section. At the time of writing, there are 31 composite images available covering a time-span of 18 years. For each of these composites, a product called Stable Lights is available. In this product, fires and other ephemeral lights are removed, based on their high brightness and short duration. In the final result, each pixel quantizes the one-year average of stable light in a 6-bit data format. The pixel values, which we will call Digital Number (DN) in the following part of this paper, are integers ranging from 0 to 63. A comprehensive description of the methodology is given in [4]. It should be mentioned here that there are some artifacts in this final product, which have also been discussed by Henderson *et al.* [5]. As a result of the noise and unstable light removal, the number of dim pixels, with a DN below 5, is unreasonably low, *e.g.* in the year 2000 composite of satellite F14 (see Table 1 for an overview), there are no pixels with a Digital Number equal to 1. A second artifact is the occurrence of a saturation, which can be seen in the higher end of the spectrum for pixels with a DN of 60 and above. We have carefully considered these matters during the measurements and data analyses presented in this paper and will discuss them when relevant in our analyses presented below.

Following an attentive study of the literature and a consultation with the authors of the dataset, we decided that the Stable Lights product is the most suitable for our research. All the described methods and analyses from here onward refer therefore to the Stable Lights dataset, version 4 [1].

2.3 Data processing

2.3.1 Tools

Dealing with geographical images of up to 3 Gigabytes in size is not trivial. Therefore, all the preliminary data processing is done using the ArcGIS[c] software package; this is the Geographic Information System from ESRI.[d] The country boundaries used in this research were downloaded as a polygonal shapefile from CShapes [7]. All countries that ceased to exist (*e.g.* Yugoslavia, USSR) were removed, such that a total of 194 non-overlapping countries remained in the dataset. For the geo-location of big cities, the point-based shapefile from [8] was used. It features the center of the 589 cities with a population larger than 750,000 in 2010. Additional analysis of the data was done using MATLAB.[e]

2.3.2 Gas flares removal

Gas flares are combustion devices used mainly in oil wells and big offshore platforms to burn flammable gas (mostly methane) released during the operations of oil extraction. They are a continuous phenomenon. Consequently, they are not filtered from the Stable Lights product. As the goal of this research is to study human settlements, they should be removed in order to avoid their misinterpretation as small cities. Gas flares have a characteristic circular shape of saturated pixels with glowing surroundings. These features make it possible to map their location [6]. The shapefiles, containing the gas flares' geo-location, one per country, were downloaded from the NGDC[f] website and then merged within the ArcGIS system. The obtained mask was then converted into a binary raster so that the gas flares' locations were given value zero, whereas all others pixels had a value of one. Every Stable Light composite was then multiplied with this raster to obtain images free of gas flares. Unfortunately, the polygons that encircle the gas flares are relatively large. Thus, it is unavoidable that certain areas of human-made lighting are improperly canceled out in this procedure. According to Henderson, [5], only 0.9% of the world land area and 0.3% of the world population in 2000, fell into the excluded polygons. Only a fraction of this is improperly excluded from the dataset. It is, however, not possible to quantify this error, but it must be a very small amount, given the meticulous selection procedure [6]. The small drawback of excluding this tiny fraction of data, however, does not outweigh keeping the whole set of gas flares in the composites.

2.3.3 Inter-calibration

In this paper, we research the dynamics and the evolution in time of global nightlight, covering two decades of available data. The comparison between different image-years must be done with great care. Different satellites have different sensor settings. Also for the same satellite, the captured images are subject to a natural deterioration of the sensor over time and of undocumented gain adjustments.

To correct for these effects, we decided to apply the method of Elvidge [6], because it is fully documented, complete and has been used as an academic standard in different previous studies (*e.g.* [9–12] and [13]). Three calibrating parameters, C_0, C_1 and C_2, are calculated for each year and satellite. In this way, the new, inter-calibrated, Digital Numbers (DN) can be calculated directly from the old numbers, for each image, using the following equation:

$$\mathrm{DN}_{\mathrm{new}} = C_0 + C_1^* \mathrm{DN}_{\mathrm{old}} + C_2^* \mathrm{DN}_{\mathrm{old}}^2. \quad (1)$$

The inter-calibration coefficients that are provided in the referenced publication only cover the years 1994 until 2008. However, additional calibration coefficients were found, for the year 2009, in a not yet published paper by the same authors [13]. In the end, only the 2010 image of the satellite F18 had to be removed from the analysis because no calibration coefficients were obtainable.

An indicator of the goodness of the calibration is that the Sum of Lights (SOL), *i.e.* the sum of all pixel values for a certain region, matches between two composites of the same year coming from different satellites. Figure 1 gives the example of China. It can be clearly seen that the overlaps between the different satellites is much smoother after calibration.

2.3.4 Re-projection

The 30 arc-seconds grid, used in the composite, does not correspond to an equal area at the surface of the earth. For example, in Quito (on the Equator), one pixel tallies a 0.86 square kilometer surface, whereas in Reykjavik (at 64°N latitude), it fits a surface less than half this size, or 0.41 square kilometer. Since we want to analyze spatial dynamics of nightlight, a re-projection is needed so that each new pixel or cell in the satellite image corresponds to an equal area at the planet's surface. For this purpose, the Mollweide projection was applied. This is a pseudo-cylindrical map projection where the accurate representation of areas takes precedence over the shape.

3 Literature review

The availability of the digitized and freely downloadable nighttime light images from the NGDC website is a treasure of data that has instigated new research in economics, social sciences and environmental studies. Nighttime lights can be remotely sensed, objectively, at the same time-of-day, in a systematic way, covering the surface of the whole planet. This is in stark contrast to many widely used economic and demographic indicators, which are often based on estimates and censuses, where biases, time lags and inaccuracies are unavoidable and the comparison between different countries is problematic.

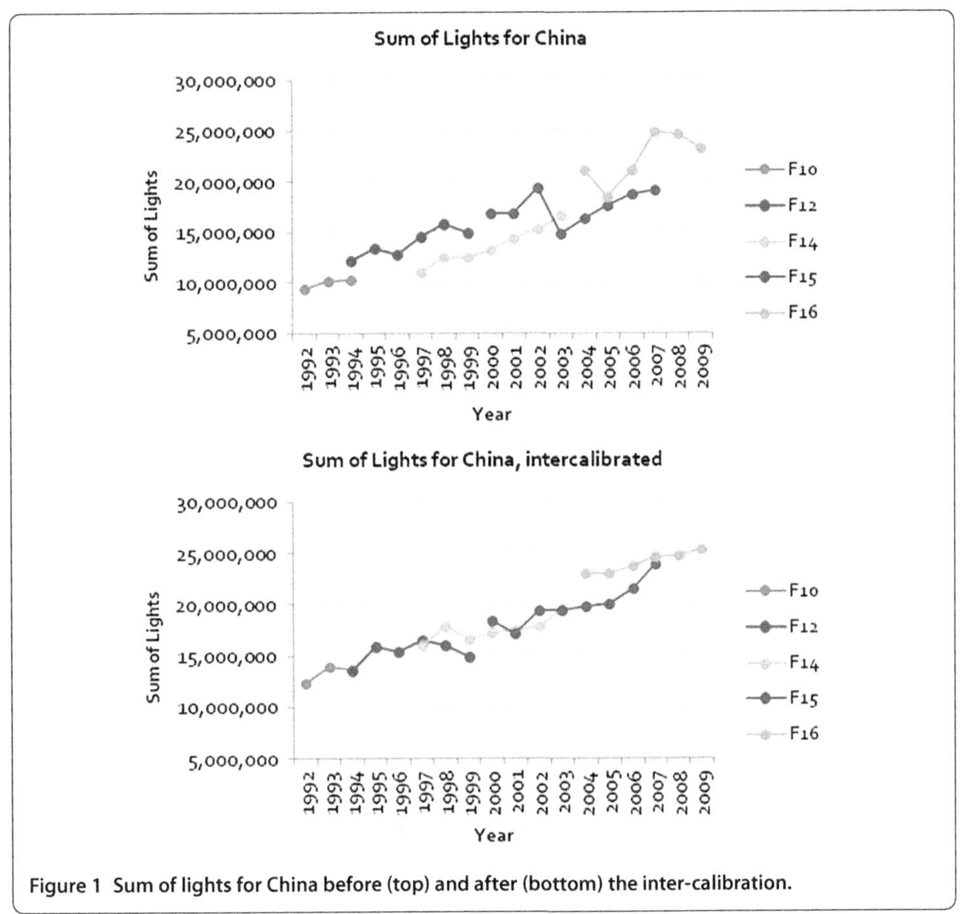

Figure 1 Sum of lights for China before (top) and after (bottom) the inter-calibration.

3.1 Economics

Nighttime lights provide an appealing innovative instrument to measure economic activity. However, the relationship between economics and light is not entirely trivial, which makes it difficult to construct reliable estimators. Nevertheless, especially for countries with poor data quality, the approach can add significant value to existing statistics.

In one of the first economic studies applying nighttime light data, Doll *et al.* [14] used the 1996 night images of 11 European countries. They found a very strong linear relationship (with an R^2 value of 0.98) between the night light energy emission of these countries and their nominal GDP. This result was further confirmed by Sutton *et al.* [15]. Using the Stable Light product for the year 2000 of the U.S., India, China and Turkey, they found a log-linear relationship between the night light energy emission and the nominal GDP (with an R^2 value of 0.74). Similar studies were conducted for China [9], India [16] and Mexico [17], always using a one-year snapshot only.

In more recent work, Chen and Nordhaus [12] and Kulkarni *et al.* [18] link the time evolution of nighttime light to economic activity. They do not limit their research to one specific year only, but make use of all of the available data. They conclude that light can be used as a proxy for nominal GDP, but that this approach only adds value to the official statistics for countries with poor reporting standards and low data quality. This was further confirmed for GDP growth by Henderson *et al.* [5], who found that growth estimates, based on nighttime light images, differ substantially from the official statistics for countries with low data quality. A case in point is Myanmar. According to the World Development Indicator of the World Bank (WDI), the average annual growth rate, between 1992 and 2006, was 10%. This is to be compared with a 3.3% estimate based on the nighttime light images. For Burundi, on the other hand, the WDI predicted a GDP decline of −0.3%, whereas satellite data implied a growth of 2.9% annually, over that same period.

3.2 Demographics and politics

Persistent light is a clear indicator of the presence of human settlements. An early attempt to estimate population densities with nighttime light images was done by Sutton [19]. He compared data from the 1990 U.S. census with a binary image containing only the saturated pixels. It was found that these images could only explain 25% of the variation in the population density of the urban areas in the continental U.S. In a later study, the same author and collaborators estimated the global human population for the year 1997. He came up with a figure of 6.3 billion people compared to 5.9 billion, which was the generally accepted estimate for that year [20]. Similar studies were done at the national levels, *e.g.* for China [21, 22] and Brazil [23]. Light alone may not be a perfect proxy to measure populations but, combined with other sources, it can substantially add value. It is worth noting that the Gridded Population of the World (GPW),[g] which is one of the most widespread databases of the global population density, uses nighttime lights as one of its many inputs.

Also using nighttime light images, Elvidge *et al.* [24] constructed a global Poverty Index (PI) by dividing population numbers by the average light. This shows the regions where people are living without satellite detectable stable light, which is, according to the authors, an indicator for poverty. After calibrating the index with official statistics on poverty, it was estimated that 2.2 billion people live with an income below $2 a day. This is to be compared with the 2.6 billion estimated by the World Bank.

Another application of nighttime light images is the mapping and measurement of urban boundaries. This was done by Imhoff *et al.* [25] for urban land areas in the U.S. and later by Henderson *et al.* [26] for three distinct cities: Lhasa, San Francisco and Beijing. In that same field, Small *et al.* [27] came up with the very interesting result that conurbations, with a diameter larger than 80 km, account for less than 1% of all settlements but for about half the total lighted area worldwide. Other detailed studies on the level of urbanization in China can be found in [28–30].

Some authors suggested that conflict related events also could have an impact on the light emission of a region and may, as such, be studied by means of nighttime images. One such study evaluates the U.S. military surge in Iraq in 2007 [31], which was aimed to stabilize and rebuild the cities after the war. The authors expected an increase in luminosity over time, because of the restoration of the electrical infrastructure. However, no observable effect could be found. Another study looked for effects of the wars in the Caucasus regions of Russia and Georgia [32]. The authors claim to be able to detect oil fires and large refugee outflows, as well as settlement (re)construction. In summary, the one-year time resolution of the images may be too coarse to detect the actual impact of wars, but for large conflicts with a longer duration, light can be used to study the impact of damages and the dynamics of reconstruction.

The politics of electricity distribution in certain regions of India was studied by Min [33]. Although there is a relatively reliable network infrastructure, the actual power supply is by far not sufficient to meet the demand. The decisional power of giving energy to a certain municipality, district or county is quite centralized and involves political control.

However, only a weak correlation could be found between the availability of energy in the municipalities and the political party that won the elections.

3.3 Environmental studies

One obvious application of the night light data is to measure and estimate energy consumption. In an early study, Elvidge *et al.* [34] showed a very strong log-log relationship (with an R^2 value of 0.96) between the lighted area and the energy consumption at a country level. Further similar studies were conducted at the national level for India [35], Brazil [36] and Japan [37].

As mentioned earlier in Section 2.3, other, probably less known, features recorded in the light maps are the so-called gas flares. These are combustion devices to burn flammable gas released during the operations of oil extraction. The gas is burned only for convenience, or for lack of infrastructure, so that the energy is wasted and huge amounts of CO_2 are released in the atmosphere. The monitoring of this harmful and quite uncontrolled activity is motivated by environmental and health concerns, besides energy efficiency reasons. Most gas flares burn uninterruptedly. Consequently, this phenomenon is still observable in the Stable Lights products. Using night light images, Elvidge *et al.* [6] estimated that, in 2008, approximately 139 billion cubic meters gas were wasted on a global scale. This is equivalent to 21% of the total natural gas consumption of the U.S. and has a retail market value of $68 billion and an impact on the atmosphere of 278 million metric tons of CO_2 equivalent.

Large forest fires (natural and human made) can also be visible from space. Studies were done to monitor the surface of forests affected by fires in India [38], Indonesia [39] and Brazil [40].

Even some fishing activities can be seen from outer space. This is the case for a specific technique where bright lights are mounted on the boats to attract squid. The illumination can be so intense and persistent that it remains visible after the filtering procedure in the Stable Lights images. Particular studies on this subject were made for Japan [41], where the spatial and temporal variability of night fishing were analyzed to better understand the migration of squid. The impact on ecological systems around coral reefs, where the illumination is seen as a stressor and a threat, was studied by Aubrecht *et al.* [42].

There are many reasons why light pollution can have negative consequences: firstly, astronomical light pollution reduces the number of visible stars and disturbs the scientific observation of the sky. Secondly, the ecological light pollution represents a threat to entire ecosystems, substantially altering the behavioral patterns of the animal population (orientation, foraging, reproduction, migration, communication and so on). And finally, wasted light means also wasted energy. Some human health disorders were also found to be correlated with prolonged exposure to light during night. Studies on light pollution, using the nighttime light images, have been done for Europe [43, 44] and Iran [45].

3.4 Discussion

Making the nighttime light images available for the scientific community has instigated a lot of research covering a broad range of disciplines. Table 6 in Appendix A.1 summarizes all the publications that were cited in the preceding literature review. This table makes it possible to do a comparative and a qualitative analysis between the different studies and may be helpful in setting up a best-practice in using the night images for different research purposes.

It can be seen that most of the studies used a single one-year snapshot only, although the images are available for 18 satellite-years. More surprisingly, however, is the fact that quite a few of the analyses that cover multiple years of data did not perform an inter-calibration of the images. It is known and documented [6], however, that the sensors have different sensitivities (for example, F14 produced substantially dimmer images [46]), and even for the same satellite, in addition to the natural deterioration of the sensor over time, undocumented gain adjustments were made during its lifetime, so that the comparison between different image-years is really delicate.

For most of the studies that were subject to this review, the gas flares are not relevant; they should be removed before performing any analysis. However, this operation was hardly ever done, or else, it was not mentioned explicitly in the publication. This phenomenon is present in at least 20 countries, notably Russia, Nigeria, Iran, Iraq and Algeria, and, especially for small countries (such as Qatar, Kuwait) it could lead to a misinterpretation of the results, since gas flares can be easily confused with small cities. It was calculated for the year 2000, that gas flares represented 3.2 percent of the worldwide light emanation, and in some regions, such as sub-Saharan Africa (*e.g.* Nigeria) they accounted for even 30% of the total illumination [5].

Another very important preprocessing operation is the re-projection of the images with an equal-area method. This is always needed when analyzing spatial extent, because, as we explained in Section 2.3.4, the pixels in the 30 arc-seconds grid represent different land areas depending on the latitude. Nevertheless, as can be seen in Table 6 in the Appendix, this process seems to be often neglected, or, not specifically mentioned in the publication.

Finally, the different products are also available in different versions, depending on the algorithm that was used for creating the Stable Lights image. It can be seen in Table 6 that most publications fail to mention explicitly the specific version. This may complicate the reproduction and comparison of different studies.

In this research, we tried to follow a best-practice by inter-calibrating and re-projecting the different images and removing the gas flares. The Stable Lights dataset version 4 [1] was used.

4 Results

4.1 The planet's mean center of light

In a recent study by the McKinsey Global Institute [2], called 'Urban World: Cities and the rise of the consuming class', a method is presented to calculate the economic center of gravity of the world. The research uses data and approximations from the year 1 CE until 2010. Additionally, projections are given until 2025. The result shows that, propelled by the industrialization and urbanization of Europe and the U.S., the economic center of gravity (located near Kabul at year 1) has been gradually shifting towards the northwest (up to the vicinity of Reykjavik) until around 1950. After that, driven by the rise of Japan, the regime shifted and the dynamic reversed. Since then, in the last 60 years, the economic center of gravity has been moving back eastwards rapidly. The most recent decade, between 2000 and 2010, has seen the fastest rate of change, in global economic balance, in history. During this period, the world's economic center of gravity has shifted by about 140 kilometers per annum. Figure 2 graphically demonstrates the result of this study.

The inter-calibrated nighttime light images that are at our disposal cover the period between 1992 and 2009. This includes exactly the period of the dramatic regime shift that

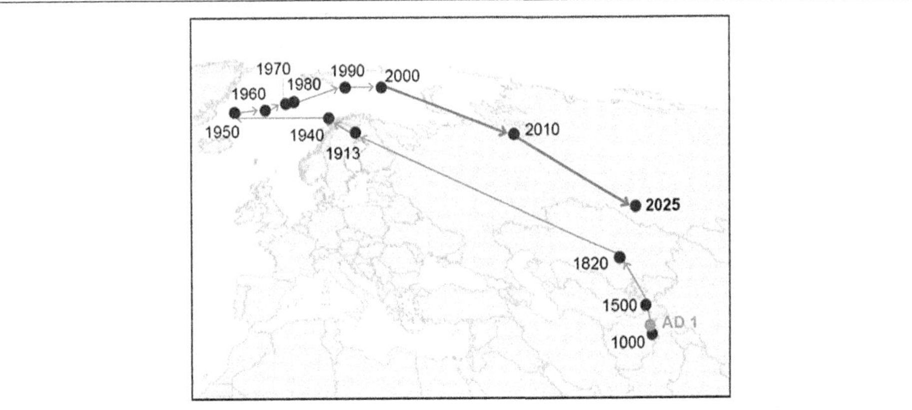

Figure 2 The dynamic of the global center of gravity (GDP based) from year 1 to 2010, and the projection for 2025. Source: [2]

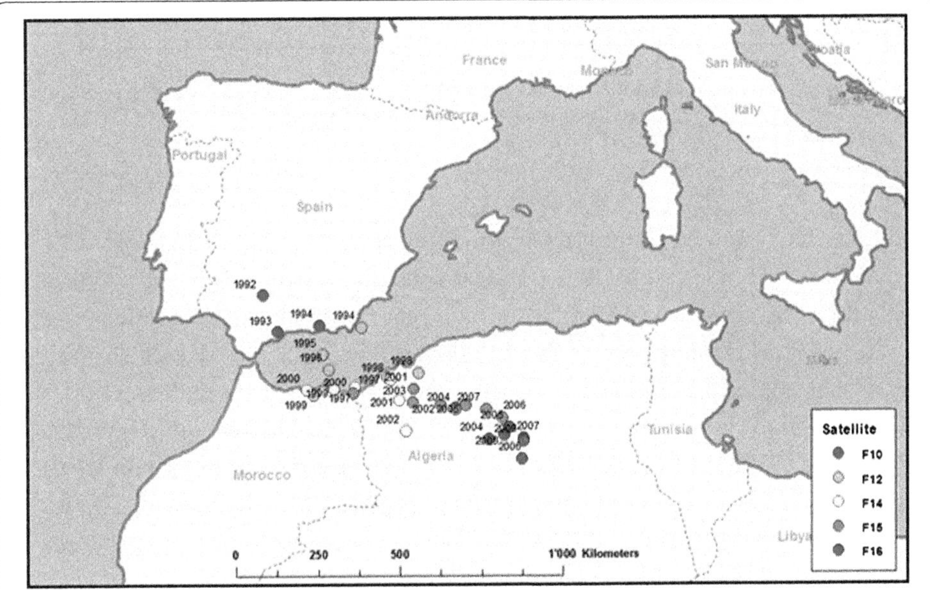

Figure 3 The dynamic of the light mean center for the different satellites and years. Note the strong shift eastwards. The amplitude of the movement, between 1992 and 2009, is about 1,000 km; this is roughly half the estimate of MGI.

can be seen in the MGI study. Therefore, we decided to challenge this fascinating study and compare the dynamics of the economic center of gravity with the center of gravity of nighttime light emissions. This was calculated as follows: First, the Digital Numbers of all pixels for one specific satellite and one specific year were added up for each country individually. This resulted in one DN-sum positioned at the centroid of each country. The position of the mean center is the average x and y co-ordinate of these centroids using the DN-sums as weights. Because we have different yearly observations for each satellite image, we can observe the dynamics of this light mean center.

Figure 3 gives the results per satellite and year; Figure 4 shows the result per satellite over the years of its operation. The first fact is that the location of the light center deviates substantially from the economic center. Although the distinction could be partly explained by the use of different projection methods,[h] this demonstrates that the com-

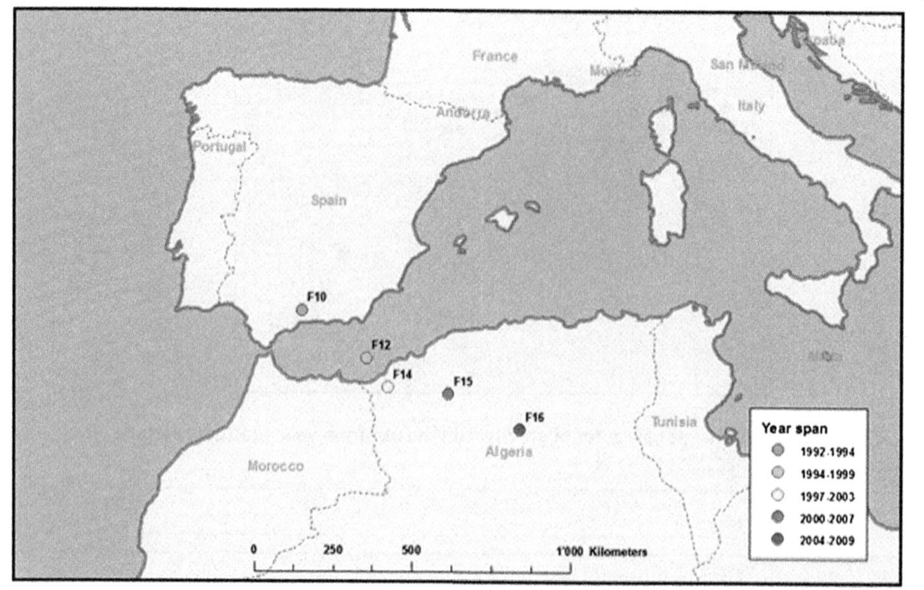

Figure 4 The dynamic of the light mean center for the different satellites. Here, the centroids are calculated on the average sum of lights per satellite (labeled), in order to emphasize the direction of the shift. Each satellite covers the year span indicated in the legend.

parison of light and economic indicators is non-trivial. The direction of the movement, however, appears to be consistent: there is a clear and strong southeastern shift, though the speed of this move is much smaller for the light center than for the economic center. The amplitude of the light movement is about 1,000 km between 1992 and 2009; this corresponds to about 60 km per year, which is less than half of the 140 km from the McKinsey study. Even though there are some quantitative differences with the economic approach that was followed by the McKinsey Global Institute [2], which comes from the non-trivial relationship between economics and light, as we discussed in the review Section 3.1, this result strongly demonstrates that nighttime light satellite images provide a powerful tool to monitor the global rebalancing of economic power.

4.2 The spatial light Gini coefficient

In this section, we analyze the distribution of nighttime light for different countries. More specifically, we want to understand the level of 'centralization' of light. For this purpose, we will calculate spatial light Gini coefficients. These measure, in one single number, how the light is distributed over the area of a country. The lowest value of 0 corresponds to a complete equality, whereas the highest value of 1 is indicative for a total inequality; the higher the value, the more centralized the spatial distribution of light is. In our understanding, there are three distinct reasons why a country A would have a higher spatial light Gini coefficient than a country B, or, why the spatial light distribution in country A is more centralized:

- In country A, the small settlements occupy a larger fraction of the surface than the bright cities; the country area with low pixel values is relatively higher than the area with high pixel values;
- In country A, the light emission of the cities is brighter; this is difficult to measure, however, because of the saturation effect of the satellite sensors;

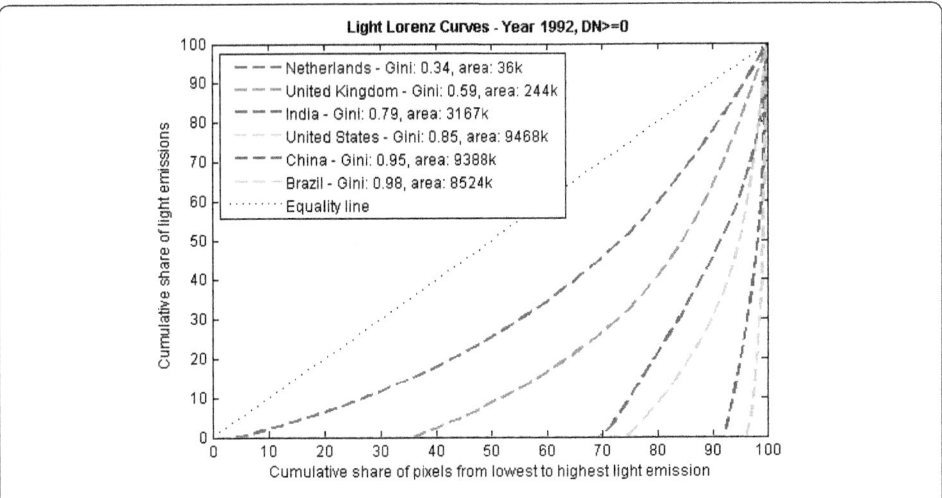

Figure 5 The Lorenz curves and Gini coefficients for selected countries in 1992. The variable 'area' indicates the amount of square kilometers (in thousands) in the country corresponding with pixels that have a DN higher than the lower cutoff value (in this case DN $\geq$ 0).

- In country A, there is a lower light emission in the small settlements.

Often, in reality, the reason may as well be a combination of these three.

Figure 5 gives the Lorenz curves and the Gini coefficients for a selected group of countries. It can be seen that the coefficients cover a wide range from a value of 0.34 for the Netherlands to 0.98 for Brazil. In these calculations, the full range of pixel values in the images was used, including the ones with a Digital Number (DN) equal to zero, which correspond to areas where there is no light emission. However, in most cases, this means that these calculations also take into account the portion of land that is inhabitable. Consequently, the huge difference between the Netherlands and Brazil has mainly a geographical explanation: a large portion of Brazil is covered by the Amazonian rainforest whereas most of the Netherlands is habitable.

In Figure 6, we corrected for this by excluding the zero-pixels from the calculations. Thus, the Gini coefficients are calculated for land area that has a DN greater than, or equal to, 1. As such, we have removed all the unlit land from the analysis. The results are much different now, and the gap between the countries has, to a large extent, disappeared with coefficients ranging from 0.29 to 0.40. This is quite astonishing, especially if we compare the areas: the U.S. has a lit area more than 70 times that of the Netherlands, yet, their Lorenz curves and the Gini coefficients are very similar. We take this approach a step further and gradually increase the lower cutoff of the Digital Numbers. The result is presented in Figures 7 and 8. It can be seen that the Lorenz curves and the Gini coefficients quickly converge for every country. This result suggests that the spatial configuration of the settlements follows a universal pattern across these different countries, even though the considered area can differ up to two orders of magnitude.

This part of the analysis has mainly focused on a one-year snapshot. Let us now take a look at the historical evolution of the spatial light Gini coefficients for the selected countries. The left graph in Figure 9 gives the result without using any pixel value threshold. The graphs are basically flat, suggesting that no dynamical change in the distribution of nighttime light occurred. This is not a surprise because the result is dominated by the

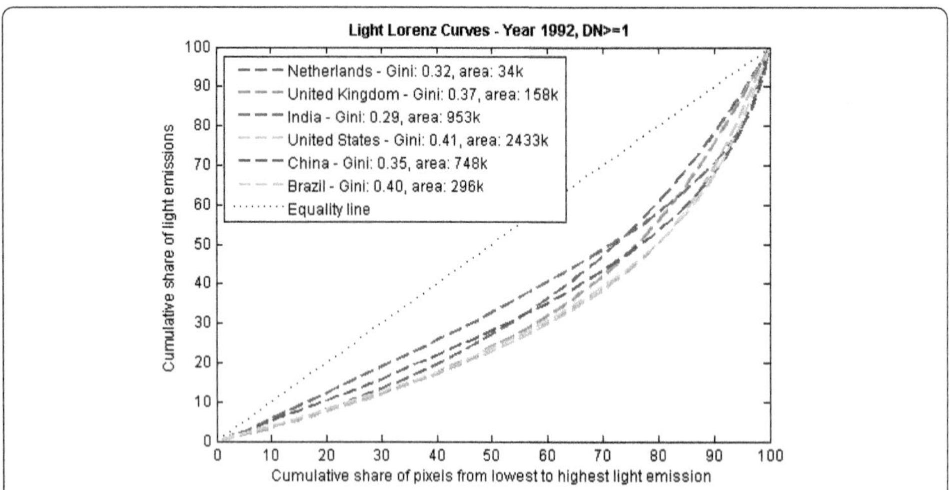

Figure 6 The Lorenz curves and Gini coefficients for selected countries in 1992, with a threshold pixel value greater than or equal to 1. The variable 'area' indicates the amount of square kilometers (in thousands) in the country corresponding with pixels that have a DN higher than the lower cutoff value.

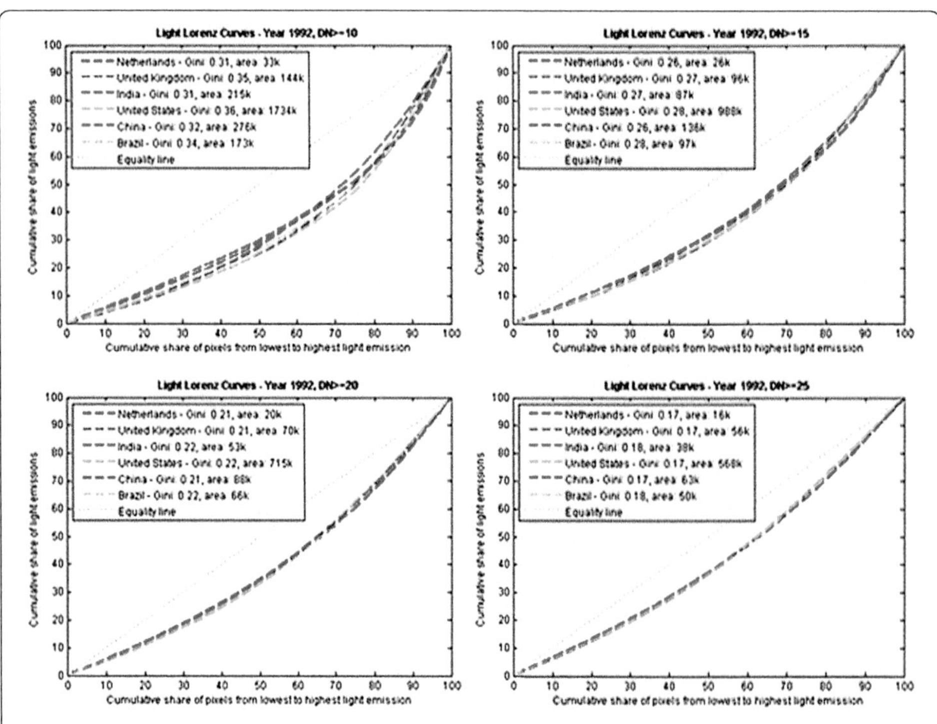

Figure 7 The Lorenz curves and Gini coefficients for selected countries in 1992, with increasing thresholds. Note how the Lorenz curves and the Gini coefficients converge. At the threshold of DN $\geq$ 25, *i.e.* still far below the middle of the spectrum, the Netherlands and United States have the same Gini coefficient, although the considered lit area differs by a factor of 35.

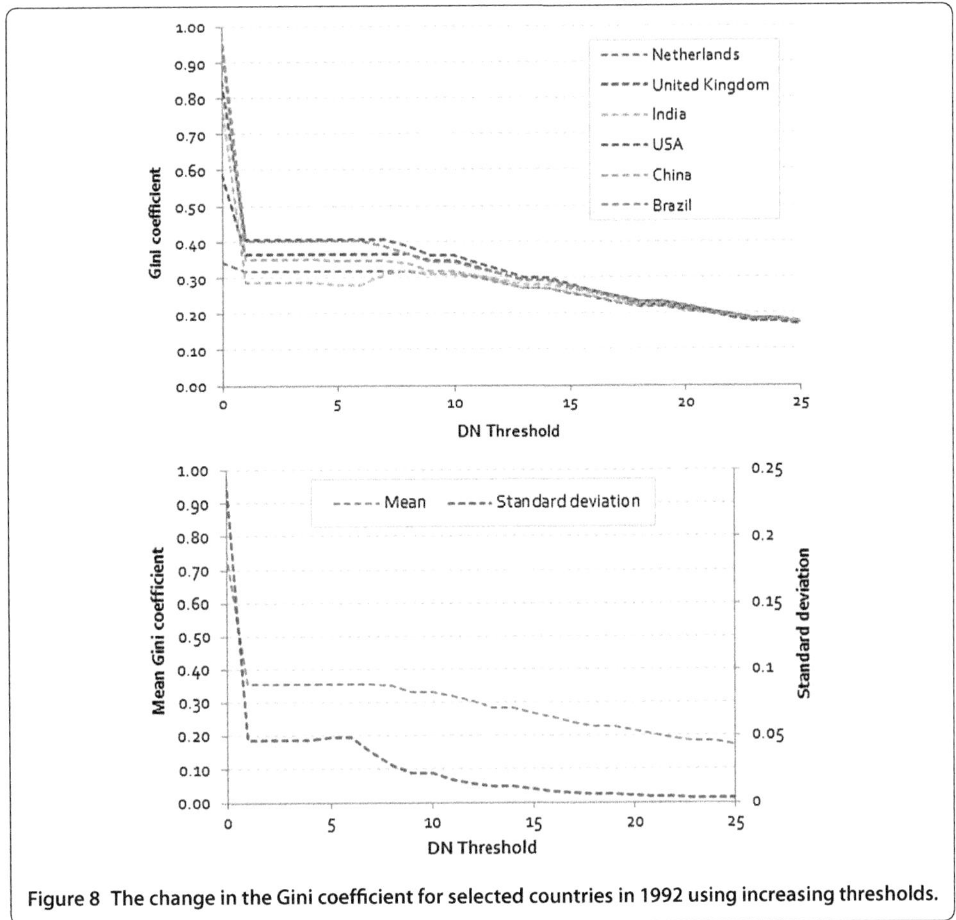

Figure 8 The change in the Gini coefficient for selected countries in 1992 using increasing thresholds.

non-habitable land in the analysis. When we filter the images, however, and only take those pixels into account which have a DN higher than 4, the result is quite different. Now, a clear rise can be seen for all countries. This is presented in the right graph of Figure 9.

This suggests that spatial light has gradually centralized over the past 17 years. This can be explained as follows:

- The dimly lit area increased proportionally more than the brighter area. This suggests that villages and small settlements have been built (respectively electrified) over a surface greater than the one occupied by the city growth;
- The brightness of the cities increased proportionally more than the brightness of the small settlements. Assuming, for example, that the illuminated area did not change, in order for the Gini coefficient to rise, the brighter pixels have to increase their DN proportionally more than the dimmer ones;
- The overall brightness of the small settlements decreased, so that the relative share of luminosity taken by the bright lit agglomerations increased, driving the Gini coefficient up.

4.3 Bright versus dimly lit areas

We have come to the conclusion that spatial light Gini coefficients have gradually increased over the timeline of our observations, which is the past 17 years. Now, we will further analyze the process behind this observation. It is important to mention that, be-

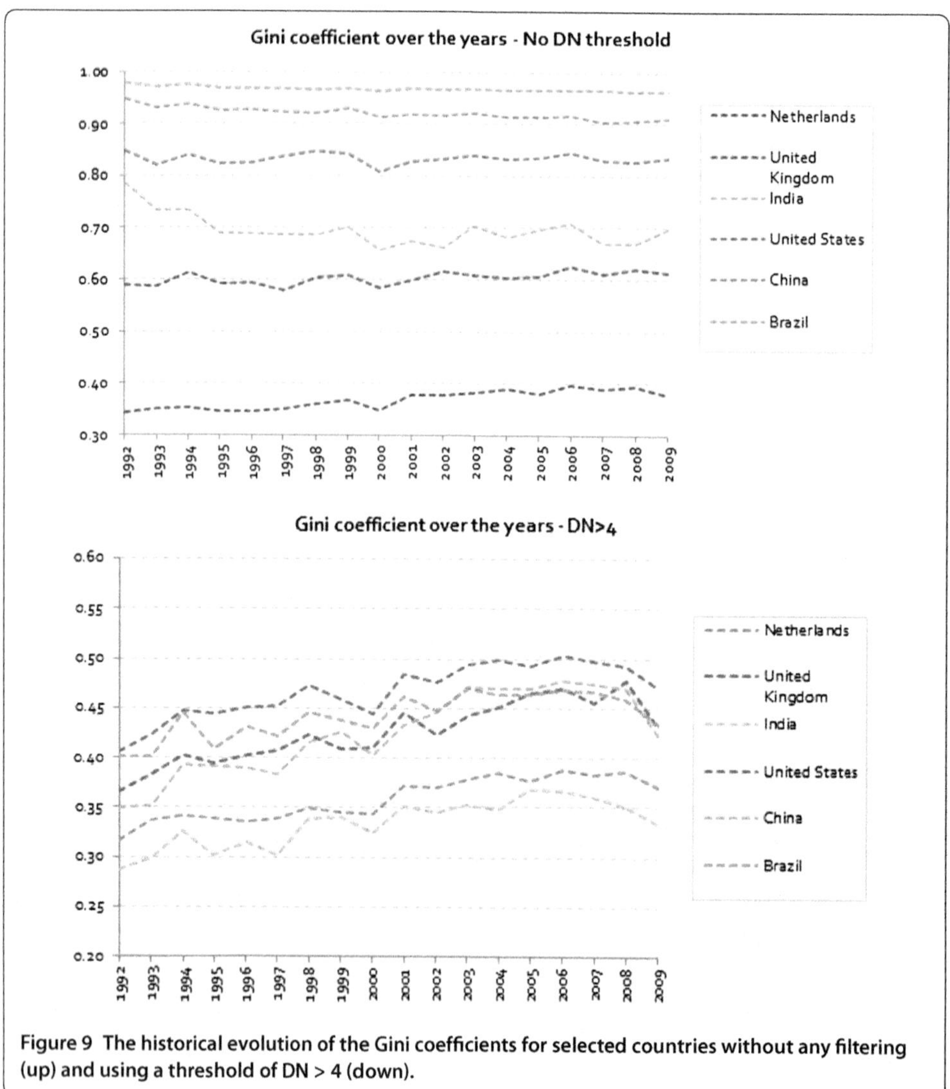

Figure 9 The historical evolution of the Gini coefficients for selected countries without any filtering (up) and using a threshold of DN > 4 (down).

cause of the pixel saturation in bright areas, it is not possible to use the nighttime light images to study changes in brightness. Thus, given the limitation of the tools at our disposal, we will have to focus on the change and evolution in the surface size of bright versus dimly lit areas.

In order to separate bright from dimly lit areas, binary images were produced using a threshold technique. Any pixel with a Digital Number higher than 1 and less than or equal to 30 was classified as dim; any pixel with a DN higher than 30 was classified as bright. This was done for the global image of the two individual years 1992 and 2009. The result of this exercise, for a total of 160 countries,[i] is given in an extensive Table 7 in the Appendix. A small extract from this table, showing the results for the BRIC countries, the U.S. and the World is summarized in Table 2. It can be seen that between 1992 and 2009, the worldwide dimly lit surface grew 49%, whereas the bright area expanded 19%. From the table, it becomes clear that the area of dimly lit settlements has, both in relative as in absolute terms, increased more than the area of the bright cities. It may be counter-intuitive, but this is the major driver behind the observed increase in spatial light Gini coefficients over that period.

Table 2 Change in the lit area in the world and in selected countries between 1992 and 2009

	Change of dimly lit area		Change of bright area	
	Absolute (km^2)	Percent	Absolute (km^2)	Percent
China	+574,609	+81.41%	+95,394	+225.76%
India	+448,852	+48.41%	+21,380	+80.95%
Brazil	+243,648	+94.19%	+21,232	+57.86
Russia	+261,858	+36.33%	−25,231	−24.85%
USA	+511,651	+81.41%	−6,316	−1.44%
World	+4,543,889	+48.92%	+261,530	+19.43%

A pixel threshold of 30 is applied to classify dim *versus* bright pixels.

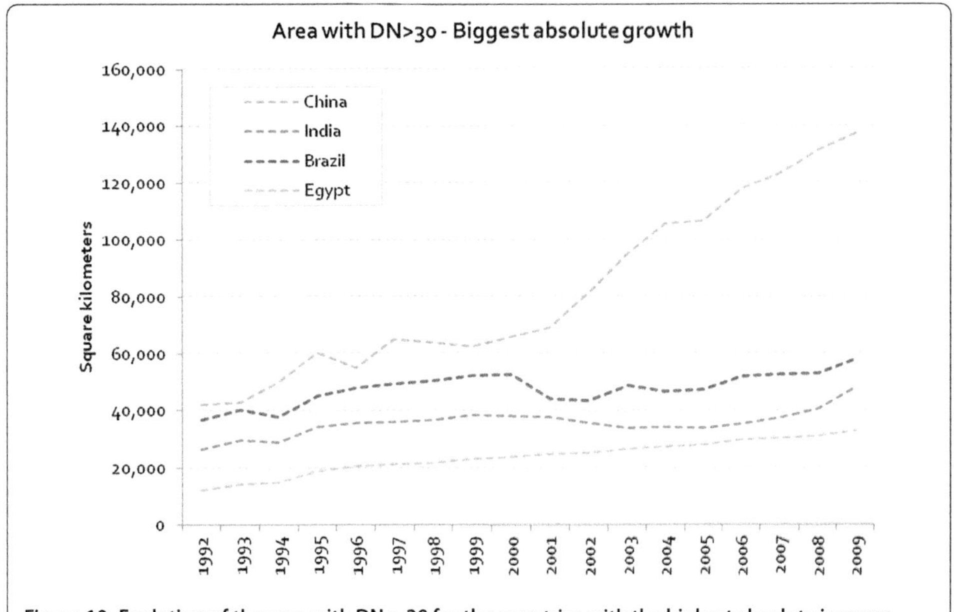

Figure 10 Evolution of the area with DN > 30 for the countries with the highest absolute increase between 1992 and 2009.

To give a more dynamical view of the process observed in the table, Figure 10 shows the evolution of the total bright area, in square kilometers, for the four countries with the largest increase between 1992 and 2009. Three of the four BRIC countries are dominating the ranking, China outclassing the other two with an impressive absolute (95,394 km^2) and relative (225%) growth. A clear concentration in the area around Shanghai and Shenzhen-Guangzhou could be seen. To show this, we generated images, which can be found in the Appendix A.3. The high ranking of Egypt may come as a surprise. This is, however, the result of the remarkable development of the delta and the coast along the Nile. For the images, demonstrating these assertions, we refer to the Figures 13-15 in the Appendix. It is also worthwhile mentioning that the evolutions of India and Brazil have been more diffuse. No clearly defined hot spots could be observed during the analysis, as was the case for China and Egypt.

Not all countries have seen an increase in bright area. A different dynamic is demonstrated in Figure 11. The graph shows the four countries with the largest absolute decrease. We can see two different processes at work here. For Russia and the Ukraine, the absolute decrease in the bright area goes hand in hand with a decrease in the urban population. This is further demonstrated in the table in Table 3, which gives an overview of the countries where the decrease of bright areas coincided with a considerable reduction of the

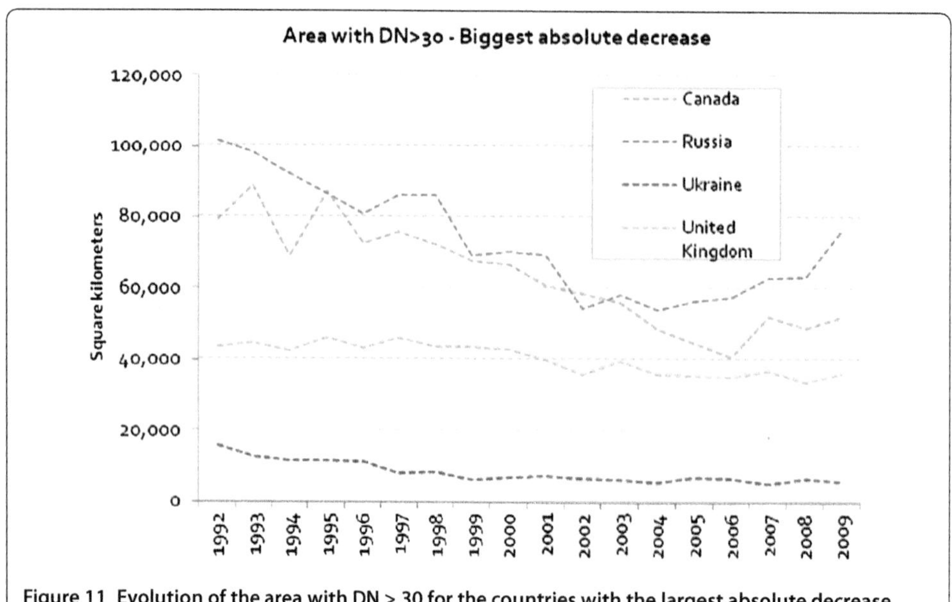

Figure 11 Evolution of the area with DN > 30 for the countries with the largest absolute decrease between 1992 and 2009.

Table 3 List of countries where the decrease of bright areas between 1992 and 2009 coincided with a considerable reduction of the urban population

	Bright area change		Urban population change	
	Absolute (km^2)	%	Absolute (people)	%
Russia	−25,231	−24.85%	−5,842,556	−5.35%
Ukraine	−9,899	−62.87%	−3,543,432	−10.16%
Moldova	−610	−77.81%	−249,382	−14.43%
Lithuania	−84	−10.41%	−256,730	−10.28%
Latvia	−17	−3.14%	−269,613	−14.92%
Georgia	−11	−2.30%	−332,121	−12.48%

The urban population figures are estimates from the World Bank [49].

urban population. In Canada and the United Kingdom, on the other hand, another process is at work. For those countries, we conjecture that the decrease is the result of the Light Pollution abatement programs. In Canada, various programs were introduced after 1991 to actively reduce the artificial sky brightness, notably from street and public lighting [47]. The worldwide reference for such programs is the International Dark-Sky association [48].

4.4 Dynamics of agglomerations

In this final section presenting our results, we will analyze agglomerations instead of countries. The goal is to identify the largest and respectively the most rapidly growing conurbations. We decided, however, not to use the administrative boundaries but to define agglomerations using a threshold method combined with a segmentation function to identify the size of each contiguous cluster. Like in the previous analysis of countries, a binary version of each image is made. All pixels with a digital number above the threshold are given a value of 1, the others, a value of 0. Next, using the 4-pixel Von Neumann neighborhood connectivity, the clusters' sizes are calculated and the name of the biggest and closest city is assigned by visual inspection. The results for different threshold are presented in Figure 12 and Tables 4 and 5. The regions were named after the included city

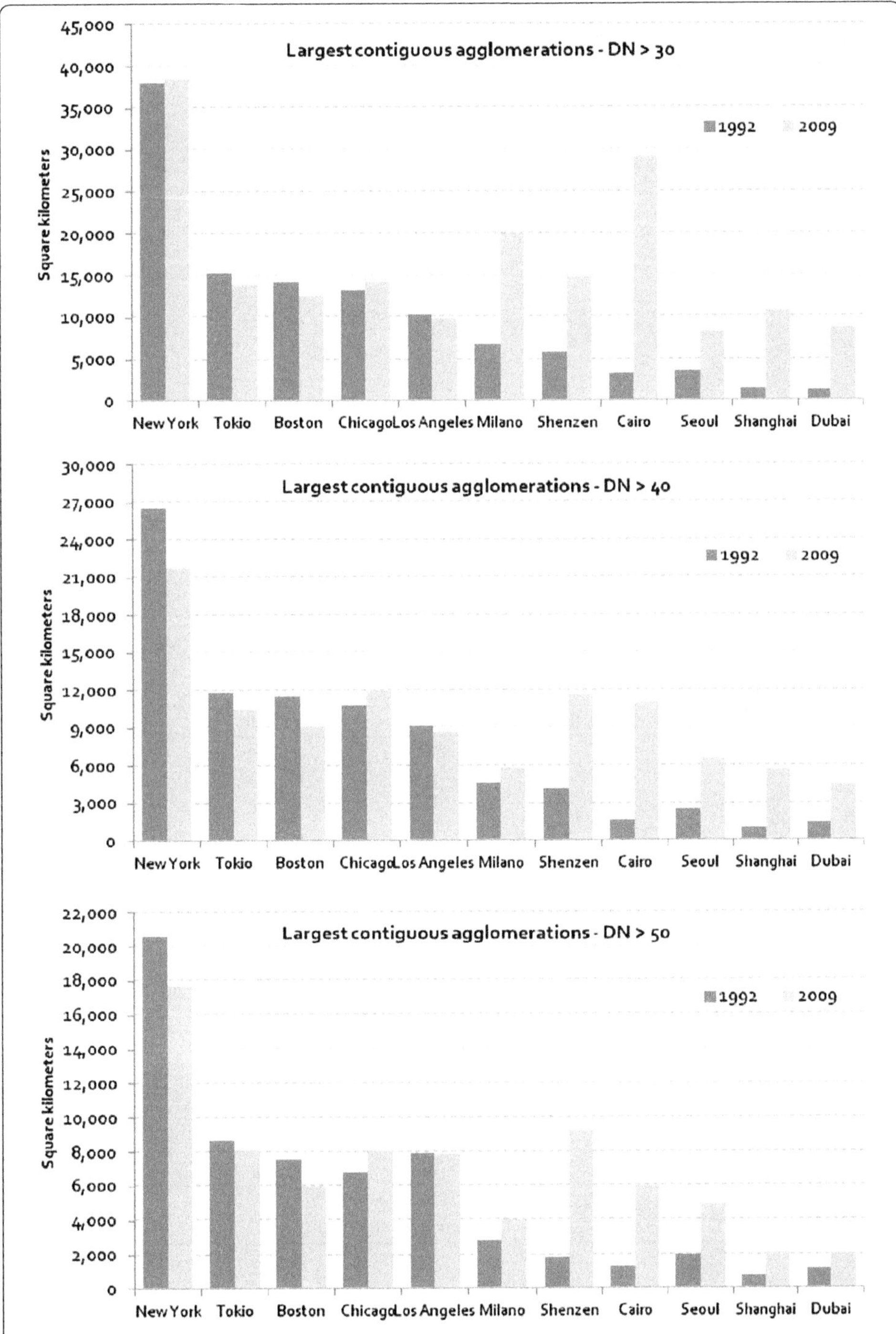

Figure 12 Largest contiguous light agglomerations detected with increasing thresholds: 30 (upper), 40 (middle) and 50 (bottom). The Western cities, in the left part of the graph, show a stable or slightly decreasing trend, whereas the other half experienced an incredible growth. Note how the trends are independent of the chosen threshold. Interesting are the remarkable growth of Cairo, due to the extraordinary development of the Nile Delta, and the agglomeration of Milano, resulting from the coalescence with the surrounding Monza, Bergamo and Brescia.

Table 4 The 20 largest contiguous light agglomerations in 1992, with different DN thresholds

DN > 30		DN > 40		DN > 50	
Area (km^2)	City	Area (km^2)	City	Area (km^2)	City
37,940	New York	26,533	New York	20,584	New York
18,263	Brussels	11,753	Tokyo	8,640	Tokyo
15,310	Tokyo	11,495	Boston	7,895	Los Angeles
14,101	Boston	10,812	Chicago	7,514	Boston
13,791	Liverpool	10,738	Brussels	6,761	Chicago
13,069	Chicago	9,159	Toronto	5,599	Washington
11,691	Toronto	7,452	Washington	4,588	Nagoya
10,249	Los Angeles	6,895	London	4,513	Dallas
8,568	Washington	6,231	Nagoya	4,419	London
8,541	London	5,834	Dallas	4,266	Houston
7,680	Nagoya	5,455	Houston	3,990	Osaka
6,999	Montreal	5,366	Osaka	3,882	Detroit
6,755	Osaka	5,219	Köln	3,716	Toronto
6,639	Milano	4,963	Montreal	3,700	Miami
6,473	Köln	4,860	Detroit	3,587	Cleveland
6,321	Dallas	4,745	Cleveland	3,500	San Francisco
6,098	Huston	4,533	Milano	3,464	Atlanta
6,083	Detroit	4,330	San Francisco	3,232	Montreal
5,796	Shenzhen	4,303	Tampa	3,067	Köln
5,723	Cleveland	4,238	Miami	2,920	Paris

Table 5 The 20 largest contiguous light agglomerations in 2009, with different DN thresholds

DN > 30		DN > 40		DN > 50	
Area (km^2)	City	Area (km^2)	City	Area (km^2)	City
38,418	New York	21,750	New York	17,649	New York
29,171	Cairo	11,889	Chicago	9,143	Shenzhen
19,970	Milano	11,607	Shenzhen	8,113	Tokyo
15,496	Brussels	11,016	Cairo	8,049	Chicago
14,836	Shenzhen	10,468	Tokyo	7,798	Los Angeles
14,146	Chicago	9,119	Boston	5,957	Cairo
13,810	Tokyo	8,672	Los Angeles	5,952	Boston
12,441	Boston	7,503	Tampa	5,526	Dallas
10,713	Shanghai	7,149	Brussels	5,343	Atlanta
10,225	Orlando	6,555	Seoul	5,046	Washington
9,732	Los Angeles	6,316	Washington	4,998	Houston
8,613	Dubai	6,300	Atlanta	4,912	Seoul
8,213	Seoul	6,261	Dallas	4,142	Detroit
7,978	Atlanta	5,826	Huston	4,088	Osaka
7,623	Toronto	5,799	Milano	4,004	Milano
7,415	Tel Aviv	5,709	Shanghai	3,914	Sao Paulo
7,372	Dallas	5,440	Nagoya	3,900	Nagoya
7,256	Moscow	5,201	Luxor	3,836	London
7,041	London	5,185	Detroit	3,753	Miami
6,825	Huston	5,176	London	3,518	Luxor

with the largest population, but often embrace also other cities. For example, whatever the threshold value, the New York light region also includes Philadelphia, Bridgeport and Hartford. Note in particular the newcomers in 2009 from China (Shenzhen, Shanghai), Korea (Seoul), Egypt (Cairo), and Brazil (Sao Paulo). Clearly, a diverging dynamic is observable between agglomerations in developing countries, which have seen an extraordinary growth, and agglomerations in developed countries, which have seen stagnation and even a decrease in size.

5 Conclusions

In this research paper, we have analyzed the dynamics, and the spatial distribution of nightlight. We started with an extensive literature review, which made it possible to do a comparative and a qualitative analysis of the broad range of preceding studies. This allowed us to set up a best-practice for the use of nighttime light images in different research projects. Firstly, when covering multiple years of data, we recommend that an inter-calibration of the images should be performed. Then, if not relevant for the study, the gas flares should be removed. Next, a re-projection of the images with an equal-area method should be carried out. And finally, to make reproduction and comparison of different studies possible, each analysis should explicitly mention the version of the Stable Lights product being used.

Using an ArcGIS software package, we first calculated the dynamics of our planet's mean center of light. It was found that, over the past 17 years, this has been gradually shifting eastwards over a distance of roughly 1,000 km, at a pace of about 60 km per year. This is less than half of the 140 km per year based on GDP as has been calculated by the McKinsey Global Institute [2].

Then, we introduced the new concept of spatial light Gini coefficients. When removing non-habitable land from the calculations, we came up with the astonishing result that the Lorenz curves and the Gini coefficients converge for all the countries in our analysis. This result suggests that the spatial configuration of settlements follows a universal pattern across different countries, even though the considered areas can differ by up to two orders of magnitude.

When looking at the historical evolution of the spatial light Gini coefficients, we saw a gradual increase over the time span of our observations, which is the past 17 years. This is indicative of a centralization of light. A detailed analysis revealed that, between 1992 and 2009, the worldwide dimly lit surface grew 49%, whereas the bright area expanded 19%. The total area of dimly lit settlements has, both in relative as in absolute terms, increased more than the area of the bright cities. It may be counter-intuitive, but this is the major driver behind the observed increase in spatial light Gini coefficients over that period.

This research was further completed with a detailed analysis of bright light (city) growth covering 160 different countries. The results showed that nighttime light images provide the perfect tool to monitor the expansion of developing countries (like India and Brazil), the growth of new agglomeration sizes (like Shanghai in China or the Nile delta in Egypt), the regression in countries suffering from demographic decline and a reduction in urban population (like Russia and the Ukraine) and the success of light pollution abatement programs in western countries like Canada and the United Kingdom.

Appendix

A.1 Evaluation table: literature review

Table 6 Evaluation of data and methods used in the selected publications

Application	Publication	Dataset version specified	Single year	Multiple years	Intercalibration	Gas flares removed	Equal-area reprojection
Economic activity	[14]		X				X
	[15]			X			
	[9]	2		X	X		X
	[16]		X		X	X	
	[17]		X				X
	[12]	4		X	X		
	[18]			X			
	[5]	4		X		X	
Demographics/politics	[19]		X				
	[20]		X				X
	[21]		X				X
	[22]	2	X				X
	[23]			X			
	[6]		X				
	[25]		X				X
	[26]		X				
	[27]			X			
	[28]		X			X	X
	[29]		X				X
	[30]	4		X	X		
	[31]	1		X			X
	[32]	4		X	X		
	[33]			X			
Environmental	[34]		X				X
	[38]		X				
	[36]		X				
	[37]		X				X
	[38]			X			
	[39]		X				
	[40]			X			
	[41]			X			
	[42]		X				
	[43]		X				X
	[44]		X				X
	[45]			X			
TOTAL	35	7	20	15	5	3	14

Only a minority of the publications performed an accurate preprocessing of the database. The cells were left blank if the operation was not explicitly mentioned in the study.

A.2 Change in bright areas

Table 7 Change in bright areas for all the countries that have been analyzed, in decreasing order from the largest absolute increase

Country	1992	2009	Diff	%
China	42,255	137,649	+95,394	+226%
India	26,411	47,791	+21,380	+81%
Brazil	36,694	57,926	+21,232	+58%
Egypt	12,231	32,973	+20,742	+170%
Italy	41,167	57,662	+16,495	+40%
Iran	16,085	30,700	+14,615	+91%
Spain	25,768	40,191	+14,423	+56%
Saudi Arabia	20,230	31,901	+11,671	+58%
South Korea	9,173	20,389	+11,216	+122%
Mexico	25,726	34,750	+9,024	+35%
Argentina	11,607	19,906	+8,299	+71%
Thailand	5,320	12,682	+7,362	+138%
Malaysia	3,120	10,422	+7,302	+234%
Portugal	4,208	10,709	+6,501	+154%
France	35,514	41,569	+6,055	+17%
Poland	9,978	15,713	+5,735	+57%
United Arab Emirates	4,767	9,657	+4,890	+103%
Turkey	6,896	11,617	+4,721	+68%
Vietnam	417	4,784	+4,367	+1,047%
Indonesia	5,214	9,152	+3,938	+76%
Libya	2,748	6,272	+3,524	+128%
Israel	4,971	8,026	+3,055	+61%
Oman	1,757	4,548	+2,791	+159%
Algeria	4,296	6,934	+2,638	+61%
Chile	2,664	5,128	+2,464	+92%
Greece	2,836	5,215	+2,379	+84%
Taiwan	6,749	8,802	+2,053	+30%
Romania	1,334	3,287	+1,953	+146%
Croatia	651	2,420	+1,769	+272%
Morocco	2,350	4,113	+1,763	+75%
Jordan	1,126	2,867	+1,741	+155%
Ecuador	1,606	3,230	+1,624	+101%
Peru	1,823	3,436	+1,613	+88%
Colombia	5,769	7,303	+1,534	+27%
Pakistan	8,411	9,825	+1,414	+17%
Australia	12,303	13,696	+1,393	+11%
Switzerland	4,121	5,468	+1,347	+33%
Kuwait	1,180	2,411	+1,231	+104%
Syria	2,241	3,389	+1,148	+51%
Austria	2,439	3,568	+1,129	+46%
Serbia	1,268	2,373	+1,105	+87%
Qatar	928	2,005	+1,077	+116%
Venezuela	10,770	11,800	+1,030	+10%
Philippines	1,464	2,480	+1,016	+69%
Angola	228	1,211	+983	+431%
Trinidad and Tobago	639	1,620	+981	+154%
Yemen	577	1,483	+906	+157%
Finland	11,059	11,937	+878	+8%
Ireland	1,706	2,493	+787	+46%
Tunisia	1,918	2,613	+695	+36%
Bolivia	861	1,547	+686	+80%
Lebanon	530	1,203	+673	+127%
Bosnia	11	639	+628	+5,709%
Paraguay	759	1,379	+620	+82%
Sudan	920	1,508	+588	+64%
Cuba	510	1,060	+550	+108%
South Africa	13,297	13,834	+537	+4%
Hungary	2,092	2,610	+518	+25%
Slovenia	387	893	+506	+131%
Uruguay	957	1,438	+481	+50%
Guatemala	553	1,014	+461	+83%
Cyprus	634	1,094	+460	+73%
Czech Republic	4,827	5,249	+422	+9%
Turkmenistan	1,091	1,498	+407	+37%
Myanmar	268	673	+405	+151%
Honduras	396	792	+396	+100%
Estonia	687	1,073	+386	+56%
Ghana	688	1,072	+384	+56%
Mozambique	170	532	+362	+213%
Dominican Republic	796	1,151	+355	+45%
Afghanistan	189	499	+310	+164%
Brunei	236	546	+310	+131%
Albania	16	291	+275	+1,719%
Panama	520	788	+268	+52%
Sri Lanka	517	758	+241	+47%
Norway	7,671	7,903	+232	+3%
Senegal	186	396	+210	+113%
Cote d,lvoire	400	605	+205	+51%
El Salvador	427	632	+205	+48%
Cambodia	33	209	+176	+533%
Nigeria	2,978	3,173	+195	+7%
Laos	60	239	+179	+298%
Macedonia	250	422	+172	+69%
Ethiopia	151	301	+150	+99%
Iraq	4,531	4,680	+149	+3%
Nicaragua	295	441	+146	+49%
Burkina Faso	118	256	+138	+117%
Botswana	158	295	+137	+87%
Armenia	204	338	+134	+66%
Mali	121	254	+133	+110%
Bulgaria	1,213	1,339	+126	+10%
Benin	86	194	+108	+126%
Costa Rica	923	1,027	+104	+11%
Kosovo	90	194	+104	+116%
Zambia	592	695	+103	+17%
Malawi	186	285	+99	+53%
Montenegro	87	180	+93	+107%
Mauritania	60	150	+90	+150%
Suriname	112	196	+84	+75%
Uganda	97	178	+81	+84%
Swaziland	67	142	+75	+112%
Mongolia	245	311	+66	+27%
Lesotho	34	92	+58	+171%
Namibia	235	287	+52	+22%
Guinea	54	104	+50	+93%
Tanzania	297	345	+48	+16%
Cameroon	291	337	+46	+16%
Gabon	169	215	+46	+27%
The Gambia	21	63	+42	+200%
Bahamas	221	262	+41	+19%
Belize	32	70	+38	+119%
Haiti	68	97	+29	+43%
Madagascar	72	98	+26	+36%
Chad	39	63	+24	+62%
Togo	118	138	+20	+17%
Djibouti	14	32	+18	+129%
Sierra Leone	10	25	+15	+150%
Guyana	34	47	+13	+38%
Timor Leste	3	16	+13	+433%
Niger	106	118	+12	+11%
Eritrea	33	41	+8	+24%
Vanuatu	9	14	+5	+56%
Congo	247	249	+2	+1%
Fiji	26	24	-2	-8%
Guinea-Bissau	7	0	-7	-100%
New Zealand	1,975	1,966	-9	-1%
Rwanda	70	61	-9	-13%
Burundi	44	34	-10	-23%
Georgia	478	467	-11	-2%
Latvia	542	525	-17	-3%
Central African	33	14	-19	-58%
Nepal	146	126	-20	-14%
North Korea	95	66	-29	-31%
Kenya	467	437	-30	-6%
Jamaica	564	518	-46	-8%
Papua New	183	123	-60	-33%
Congo, DRC	557	479	-78	-14%
Lithuania	807	723	-84	-10%
Kyrgyzstan	559	419	-140	-25%
Netherlands	11,250	11,046	-204	-2%
Iceland	616	397	-219	-36%
Bangladesh	1,254	1,012	-242	-19%
Azerbaijan	1,306	1,009	-297	-23%
Zimbabwe	868	494	-374	-43%
Tajikistan	634	149	-485	-76%
Belarus	3,052	2,541	-511	-17%
Moldova	784	174	-610	-78%
Germany	34,373	33,505	-868	-3%
Denmark	3,170	1,901	-1,269	-40%
Slovakia	2,684	1,256	-1,428	-53%
Kazakhstan	6,811	5,366	-1,445	-21%
Japan	59,241	57,409	-1,832	-3%
Belgium	14,195	12,166	-2,029	-14%
Uzbekistan	5,603	2,606	-2,997	-53%
Sweden	14,654	9,020	-5,634	-38%
United States	438,324	432,008	-6,316	-1%
United Kingdom	43,746	36,220	-7,526	-17%
Ukraine	15,745	5,846	-9,899	-63%
Russia	101,529	76,298	-25,231	-25%
Canada	79,571	52,176	-27,395	-34%

A bright lit area has pixels with a DN > 30.

A.3 The Nile delta, Shanghai and Shenzhen-Guangzhou

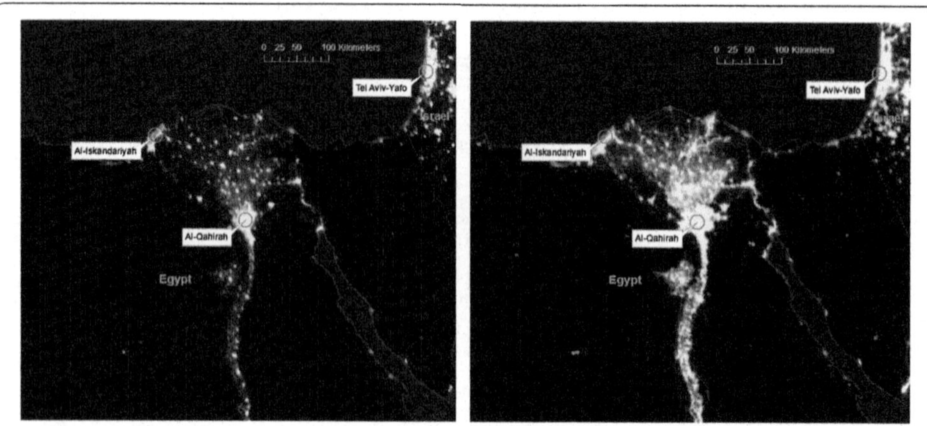

Figure 13 Nile delta in 1992 (left) and 2009 (right). Nearly the totality of light emission of Egypt comes from this area and the coast of the Nile. Note the consolidations along the interconnections between the settlements.

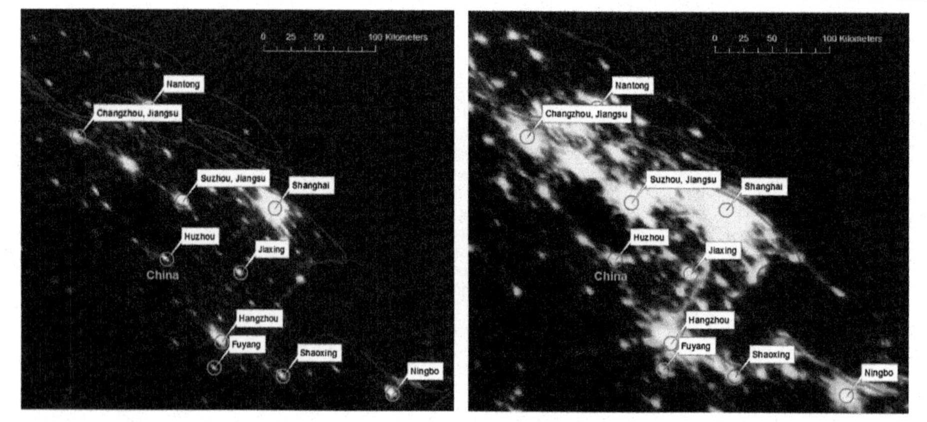

Figure 14 Impressive growth of lights in China around Shanghai from 1992 (left) to 2009 (right).

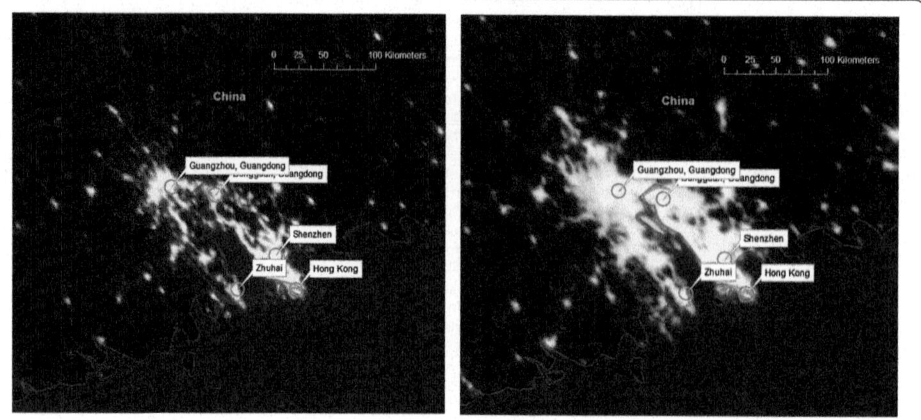

Figure 15 Lights growth for the agglomeration of Shenzhen-Guangzhou from 1992 (left) to 2009 (right).

Abbreviations

BRIC, Brazil, Russia, India and China; CE, Common Era, Current Era or Christian Era; CO_2, Carbon Dioxide; DMSP, Defense Meteorological Satellite Program; DN, Digital Number; ESRI, Environmental Systems Institute; GDP, Gross Domestic Product; GIS, Geographic Information System; GPW, Gridded Population of the World; MGI, McKinsey Global Institute; NGDC, National Geophysical Data Center; NOAA, National Oceanic and Atmospheric Administration; SOL, Sum Of Lights; OLS, Operational Linescan System; U.K., United Kingdom; U.S., United States; WDI, World Development Indicator.

Competing interests

The authors declare that they have no competing interests.

Authors' contributions

This paper stems from the master thesis of NP carried out at the Chair of Entrepreneurial Risks in the Department of Management, Technology and Economics of the ETH in Zurich under the supervision of DS and PC. NP carried out the analytical work and created the figures and the tables, PC drafted the manuscript and DS critically revised the document and gave final approval for publication.

Authors' information

Professor Dr. Didier Sornette studies the predictability and control of crises and extreme events in complex systems, with applications to financial bubbles and crashes, earthquake physics and geophysics, the dynamics of success on social networks and the complex system approach to medicine towards the diagnostic of systemic instabilities. He is the author of 500+ research papers and 7 books. Dr. Peter Cauwels is a senior researcher studying systemic instabilities in financial markets. Before joining the Chair of Entrepreneurial Risks, he worked for 10 years in the banking industry specializing in risk, portfolio management and quantitative research. He holds a PhD in physics from Ghent University in Belgium. Nicola Pestalozzi has a Bachelor degree in Computer Science and a Master degree in Management, Technology and Economics from the ETH in Zurich. He currently works as a consultant in the financial industry.

Acknowledgements

This paper is an outgrowth of the master thesis completed in Nov. 2012 by Nicola Pestalozzi entitled 'Earth Nighttime Lights to study economic and urban growth', performed under the supervision of the other authors. Additional material, including images and videos that were made for the master thesis project, can be found on www.worldatnight.ethz.ch. The thesis is available online at http://www.worldatnight.ethz.ch/content/doc/Nicola_Pestalozzi_Master_Thesis.pdf. We wish to heartily thank the whole Land Use Engineering Research Group (LUE) of Professor Hans Rudolf Heinimann. We would like to mention Daniel Trüssel and Monika Niederhuber in particular for sharing their expertise on ArcGIS. Thanks also to Luc Girardin and Sebastian Schutte from the International Conflict Research Group (ICR) of Professor Lars-Erik Cedermann for their help, especially in the initial phase of the work. This work exemplifies the collaborative and collegial atmosphere within the Risk Center at ETH Zurich (www.riskcenter.ethz.ch), which includes the three chairs of Prof. Heiniman, Prof. Cederman and Prof. Sornette.

Endnotes

[a] http://www.ngdc.noaa.gov/dmsp/dmsp.html (Accessed Feb 2013).

[b] http://www.ngdc.noaa.gov/dmsp/sensors/ols.html (Accessed Feb 2013).

[c] ArcGIS Desktop 10.0, Service Pack 5.

[d] Environmental Systems Institute - http://www.esri.com (Accessed Feb 2013).

[e] Matlab 7.12.0.

[f] http://www.ngdc.noaa.gov/dmsp/interest/gas_flares_countries_shapefiles.html (Accessed Feb 2013).

[g] http://sedac.ciesin.columbia.edu/data/collection/gpw-v3 (Accessed Feb 2013).

[h] In this study, the 'Mean Center' function of ArcGIS is used on the maps, after the Mollweide projection was applied. More details on the McKinsey Global Institute's approach can be found in their publication [2].

[i] Countries with an area of less than 5,000 square kilometres (mainly islands) were excluded because of misleading results in the percentages. A total of 160 countries remained in the database.

References

1. NGDC (2012) NOAA national geophysical data center, version 4 DMSP-OLS nighttime lights time series. http://www.ngdc.noaa.gov/dmsp/downloadV4composites.html. Accessed Feb 2013
2. MGI (2012) Urban world: cities and the rise of the consuming class. s.l.: McKinsey&Company. Accessed Feb 2013
3. Elvidge C et al (2001) Nighttime lights of the world: 1994-1995. ISPRS J Photogramm Remote Sens 56:81-99
4. Baugh K, Elvidge C, Ghosh T, Ziskin D (2010) Development of a 2009 stable lights products using DMSP-OLS data. Hanoi, Asia-Pacific advanced network
5. Henderson V, Storeygard A, Weil D (2012) Measuring economic growth from outer space. Am Econ Rev 102(2):994-1028
6. Elvidge C et al (2009) A fifteen year record of global natural gas flaring derived from satellite data. Energies 2:595-622
7. Weidmann N, Kuse D, Skrede Gleditsch K (2010) The geography of the international system: the CShapes dataset. Int. Interact. 36(1):86-106
8. Nordpil (2009) World database of large urban areas. http://nordpil.com/go/resources/world-database-of-large-cities/. Accessed Feb 2013
9. Zhao N, Currit N, Samson E (2010) Net primary production and gross domestic product in China derived from satellite imagery. Ecol Econ 70(2011):921-928
10. Small C, Elvidge C, Balk D, Montgomery M (2010) Spatial scaling of stable night lights. Remote Sens Environ 115(2011):269-280

11. Small C, Elvidge C (2012). Night on earth: mapping decadal changes of anthropogenic night light in Asia. Int. J Appl. Earth Obs. Geoinf. (in press)
12. Chen X, Nordhaus W (2011) Using Luminosity data as proxy for economic statistics. Proc Natl Acad Sci USA 108(21):8589-8594
13. Elvidge C et al. (2011) National trends in satellite observed lighting: 1992-2009. Remote Sens. 3 (submitted for publication)
14. Doll C, Muller J-P, Morley J (2005) Mapping regional economic activity from night-time light satellite imagery. Ecol Econ 57:75-92
15. Sutton P, Elvidge C, Ghosh T (2007) Estimation of gross domestic product at sub-national scales using nighttime satellite imagery. Int J Ecol Econ Stat 8:5-21
16. Bhandari L, Roychowdhury K (2011) Night lights and economic activity in India: a study using DMSP-OLS night time images. Hanoi, Asia-Pacific advanced network
17. Ghosh T et al (2009) Estimation of Mexico's informal economy and remittances using nighttime imagery. Remote Sens. 1:418-444
18. Kulkarni R, Haynes K, Stough R, Riggle J (2011) Revisiting night lights as proxy for economic growth: a multi-year light based growth indicator (LGBI) for China, India and the U.S. GMU School of Public Policy, Research Paper
19. Sutton P (1997) Modeling population density with night-time satellite imagery and GIS. Comput Environ Urban Syst 21(3/4):227-244
20. Sutton P, Roberts D, Elvidge C, Baugh K (2001) Census from Heaven: an estimate of the global human population using night-time satellite imagery. Int J Remote Sens 22(16):3061-3076
21. Lo C (2001) Modeling the population of China using DMSP operational linescan system nighttime data. Photogramm Eng Remote Sens 67(9):1037-1047
22. Zhuo L et al (2009) Modelling the population density of China at the pixel level based on DMSP/OLS non-radiance-calibrated night-time light images. Int J Remote Sens 30(4):1003-1018
23. Amaral S, Monteiro V, Camara G, Quintanilha JA (2006) DMSP/OLS night-time light imagery for urban population estimates in the Brazilian Amazon. Int J Remote Sens 27(5):855-870
24. Elvidge C et al (2009) A global poverty map derived from satellite data. Comput Geosci 35:1652-1660
25. Imhoff M et al (1997) Using nighttime DMSP/OLS images of city lights to estimate the impact of urban land use on soil resources in the United States. Remote Sens Environ 59:105-117
26. Henderson M, Yeh E, Gong P, Elvidge C (2003) Validation of urban boundaries derived from global night-time satellite imagery. Int J Remote Sens 24(3):595-609
27. Small C, Pozzi F, Elvidge C (2005) Spatial analysis of global urban extent from DMSP-OLS night lights. Remote Sens Environ 96:277-291
28. Elvidge C et al (2007) Global distribution and density of constructed impervious surfaces. Sensors 7:1962-1979
29. Lo C (2002) Urban indicators of China from radiance-calibrated digital DMSP-OLS nighttime images. Ann Assoc Am Geogr 92(2):225-240
30. Ma T et al (2012) Quantitative estimation of urbanization dynamics using time series of DMSP/OLS nighttime light data: a comparative case study from China's cities. Remote Sens Environ 124:99-107
31. Agnew J, Gillespie T, Gonzales J, Min B (2008) Baghdad nights: evaluating the US military 'surge' using nighttime light signatures. Environ Plan 40:2285-2295
32. Witmer F, Loughlin J (2011) Detecting the effects of wars in the Caucasus regions of Russia and Georgia using radiometrically normalized DMSP-OLS nighttime lights imagery. GISci. Remote Sens. 4:478-500
33. Min B (2009) Distributing power: public service provision to the poor in India. Toronto, American political science association meeting
34. Elvidge C et al (1997) Relation between satellite observed visible-near infrared emissions, population, economic activity and electric power consumption. Int J Remote Sens 18(6):1373-1379
35. Kiran Chand T, Badarinath KVS, Elvidge C, Tuttle B (2009) Spatial characterization of electrical power consumption patterns over India using temporal DMSP-OLS night-time satellite data. Int J Remote Sens 30(3):647-661
36. Amaral S et al (2005) Estimating population and energy consumption in Brazilian Amazonia using DMSP night-time satellite data. Comput Environ Urban Syst 29:179-195
37. Letu H et al (2010) Estimating energy consumption from night-time DMSP/OLS imagery after correction for saturation effects. Int J Remote Sens 31(16):4443-4458
38. Kiran Chand T et al (2007) Active forest fire monitoring in Uttaranchal State, India using multi-temporal DMSP-OLS and MODIS data. Int J Remote Sens 28(10):2123-2132
39. Fuller D, Fulk M (2010) Comparison of NOAAAVHRR and DMSP-OLS foroperational fire monitoring in Kalimantan, Indonesia. Int J Remote Sens 21(1):181-187
40. Elvidge C et al (2010) DMSP-OLS estimation of tropical forest area impacted by surface fires in Roraima Brazil: 1995 versus 1998. Int J Remote Sens 22(14):2661-2673
41. Kiyofuji H, Saitoh S-I (2004) Use of nighttime visible images to detect Japanese common squid Todarodes pacificus fishing areas and potential migration routes in the Sea of Japan. Mar Ecol Prog Ser 276:173-186
42. Aubrecht C et al (2008) A global inventory of coral reef stressors based on satellite observed nighttime lights. Geocarto Int. 23(6):467-479
43. Cinzano P, Falchi F, Elvidge C, Baugh K (2000) The artificial night sky brightness mapped from DMSP satellite operational linescan system measurements. Mon Not R Astron Soc 318:641-657
44. Cinzano P, Elvidge C (2004) Night sky brightness at sites from DMSP-OLS satellite measurements. Mon Not R Astron Soc 353:1107-1116
45. Tavoosi H, Darvishzadeh R, Shakiba A, Mirbagheri B (2009) Modelling light pollution in suburbs using remote sensing and GIS. Yokohama, The seventh International Conference on Urban Climate
46. Doll C (2008) CIESIN thematic guide to night-time lights remote sensing and its applications. The Trustees of Columbia University, New York
47. Royal Astronomical Society of Canada (2011) Light-pollution abatement. http://rasc.ca/lpa. Accessed Feb 2013
48. International Dark-Sky Association (2012) International Dark-Sky Association. http://www.darksky.org/resources. Accessed Feb 2013

49. World Bank Group (2012) The World Bank - working for a world free of poverty. www.worldbank.org. Accessed Feb 2013

8

The role of hidden influentials in the diffusion of online information cascades

Raquel A Baños[1], Javier Borge-Holthoefer[1] and Yamir Moreno[1,2*]

*Correspondence: yamir.moreno@gmail.com
[1] Institute for Biocomputation and Physics of Complex Systems (BIFI), University of Zaragoza, Zaragoza, 50018, Spain
[2] Department of Theoretical Physics, Faculty of Sciences, University of Zaragoza, Zaragoza, 50009, Spain

Abstract

In a diversified context with multiple social networking sites, heterogeneous activity patterns and different user-user relations, the concept of 'information cascade' is all but univocal. Despite the fact that such information cascades can be defined in different ways, it is important to check whether some of the observed patterns are common to diverse contagion processes that take place on modern social media. Here, we explore one type of information cascades, namely, those that are time-constrained, related to two kinds of socially-rooted topics on Twitter. Specifically, we show that in both cases cascades sizes distribute following a fat-tailed distribution and that whether or not a cascade reaches system-wide proportions is mainly given by the presence of so-called hidden influentials. These latter nodes are not the hubs, which on the contrary, often act as firewalls for information spreading. Our results contribute to a better understanding of the dynamics of complex contagion and, from a practical side, for the identification of efficient spreaders in viral phenomena.

1 Introduction

Population-wide information cascades are rare events, initially triggered by a single seed or a small number of initiators, in which rumors, fads or political positions are adopted by a large fraction of an informed community. In recent years, some theoretical approaches have explored the topological conditions under which system-wide avalanches are possible [1–5]; whereas others have proposed threshold [6], rumor- [7] or epidemic-like [8] dynamics to model such phenomena. Beyond these efforts, digitally-mediated communication in the era of the Web 2.0 has enabled researchers to peek into actual information cascades arising in a variety of platforms - blogs and Online Social Networks (OSNs) mainly, but not exclusively [9, 10].

Notably, these latter empirical works deal with a wide variety of situations. First, the online platforms under analyses are not the same. Indeed, we find research focused on distinct social networks such as Facebook [11], Twitter [12, 13], Flickr [14], Digg [15] or the blogospehere [8, 16, 17] - which build in several types of user-user interactions to satisfy the need for different levels of engagement between users. As a consequence, although scholars make use of a mostly common terminology ('seed', 'diffusion tree', 'adopter', *etc.*) and most analyses are based on similar descriptors (size distributions, identification of influential nodes, *etc.*), their operationalization of a cascade - *i.e.*, how a cascade is defined - largely varies. This fact is perfectly coherent, because how information flows differs from one context to another. Furthermore, even *within* the same OSN different definitions may be found (compare for instance [12] and [13]). Such myriad of possibilities is not necessarily controversial: it merely reflects a rich, complex phenomenology. And yet it places weighty constraints when it comes to generalizing certain results. The study of information cascades easily evokes that of influence diffusion patterns, which in turn has obvious practical relevance in terms of enhancing the reach of a message (*i.e.* marketing) or for prevention and preparedness. In these applications a unique definition would be highly desirable, as proposed in classical communication theory [18]. On the other hand, the profusion of descriptions and the plurality of collective attention patterns [19] hinder some further work aimed to confirm, extend and seek commonalities among previous findings.

In this work we capitalize on a type of cascade definition which pivots on time constraints rather than 'content chains'. Despite the aforementioned heterogeneity, all but one [11] empirical works on cascades revolve exclusively around information forwarding: the basic criterion to include a node i in a diffusion tree is to guarantee that (a) the node i sends out a piece of information at time t_1; (b) such piece of information was received from a friend j who had previously sent it out, at time t_2; and finally (c) i and j became friends at t_3, before i received the piece of information (the notion of 'friend' changes from OSN to OSN, and must be understood broadly here). Note that no strict time restriction exists besides the fact that $t_1 > t_2 > t_3$, the emphasis is placed on whether the *same* content is flowing. This work instead turns to topic-specific data in which it is safely assumed that content is similar, and the inclusion in a cascade depends not on the retransmission of a message but rather on the engagement in a 'conversation' about a matter.

Beyond our conceptualization of a cascade, this work seeks first to test the robustness of previous findings in different social contexts [20, 21], and then moves on towards a better understanding of how deep and fast do cascades grow. The former implies reproducing some general outcomes regarding cascade size distributions, and how such cascades scale as a function of the initial node's position in the network. The latter aims at digging into cascades, to obtain information about their temporal and topological hidden patterns. This effort includes questions such as the duration and depth of cascades, or the relation between community structure and cascade's outreach. Our methodology allows to prove the existence of an evasive class of reputed nodes, which we identify as 'hidden influentials' after [22], who have a major role when it comes to spawn system-wide phenomena.

2 Data

Our data comprise a set of messages publicly exchanged through www.twitter.com from the 1st of March, 2011, to the 31st of March, 2012. The whole sample of messages was filtered by the Spanish start-up company *Cierzo development*, restricting them to those that contained at least one of 20 preselected hashtags (see Table 1). *Cierzo development* exploits its own private SMMART (Social Media Marketing Analysis and Reporting Tool) platform, thus no details can be disclosed. The SMMART platform collects 1/3 of the total Twitter traffic, according to previous reports. The filtered hashtags correspond to distinct topics, thus we obtained different subsets to which we assign a generic tag.

We present the results for two of these subsets. One sample consists of 1,188,946 tweets and is related to the Spanish grassroots movement popularly known as '15M', after the events on the 15th of May, 2011. This movement has however endured over time, and in this work we will refer to it as *grassroots*. Messages were generated by 115,459 unique users. It is worth stressing that some hashtags that might appear to be disconnected from

Table 1 Filtered hashtags and keywords

Keyword	Topic	Hashtags	Mentions	Words
15m	grassroots	389,818	3,475	132,049
acampada	grassroots	13,732	3,423	76,689
acampadasol	grassroots	251,344	90,737	3,866
anonymous	grassroots	70,037	4,188	112,859
democraciarealya	grassroots	81,256	1,893	8,798
indignados	grassroots	23,371	348	185,615
nonosvamos	grassroots	63,490	124	245
notenemosmiedo	grassroots	35,249	106	55
occupy	grassroots	18,223	1,467	39,037
perroflauta	grassroots	1,394	20	26,325
spanishrevolution	grassroots	242,426	926	3,123
20n	elections	180,323	227	71,440
25m	elections	59,812	40	11,887
elecciones	elections	30,935	269	593,046
hondt	elections	5	0	3,713
iu	elections	2,726	1,127	33,168
nolesvotes	elections	156,133	2,984	4,621
pp	elections	20,412	3,106	201,136
psoe	elections	14,896	22,681	122,222
vota	elections	11,464	297	246,764

Both 'grassroots' and 'elections' data sets were collected filtering Twitter traffic according to related keywords, which are listed in this table. For each keyword we display the number of hashtags found (keywords preceded by '#'), the number of mentions (keywords preceded by '@') and the number of words (keywords with no preceding symbol).

the 15M movement were included either for technical or for sociological reasons. For instance, 'anonymous' spontaneously arises from a previous '15M' dataset, which comprised messages exchanged from the 25th of April to the 26th of May, 2011. During the gathering of data used in this work, this hashtag appeared with a relatively high frequency (313 filtered tweets during the period under consideration) and therefore it was included in the filtering of messages. As far as 'occupy' is concerned, the movement at the origin of the hashtag (the Occupy Wall Street Movement) began long after the 15M grassroots appeared. However, one can find a clear correlation between both movements suggesting that 15M users were also involved in 'occupy'. Indeed, it is well documented that the original call for mobilizations around Occupy Wall Street was inspired by both Egyptian uprising and the Spanish 'indignados' [23, 24].

The second dataset includes 606,645 filtered tweets that refer to the topic 'Spanish elections', which were celebrated on the third week of November, 2011. This sample was generated by 84,386 unique users.

Using the Twitter API we queried for the list of followers for each of the users, discarding those who did not show outgoing activity during the period under consideration. In this way, for each data set, we obtain an unweighted directed network in which each node represents an active user (regarding a particular topic). A link from user i to user j is established if j follows i. Therefore, out-degree (k_{out}) represents the number of followers a node has, whereas in-degree (k_{in}) stands for its number of friends, *i.e.*, the number of users it follows. The link direction reflects the fact that a tweet posted by i is (instantaneously) received by j, indicating the direction in which information flows. Although the set of links may vary in the scale of months we take the network structure as completely static, considering the topology at the moment of the scrap.

3 Methods

3.1 Time-constrained information cascades

Twitter is most often *exclusively* defined as a microblogging service, emphasizing its broadcasting nature. Such definition overlooks however other facets, such as the use of Twitter to interact with others, in terms of *conversations* [25] or *collaboration*, for instance connecting groups of people in critical situations [26, 27]. *Addressivity* accentuates these alternative features [12, 25]. Moreover, observed patterns of link (follower relation) reciprocity [28] (see Table 2) hint further the use of Twitter as an instant messaging system, in which different pieces of information around a topic may be circulating (typically over short time spans) in many-to-many interactions, along direct or indirect information pathways [29].

It is precisely for this type of interactions where the definition of a time-constrained cascade is a useful tool to uncover how - and how often - users get involved in sequential message interchange, in which the strict repetition of contents is not necessary (possibly not even frequent). A time-constrained cascade, starting at a *seed* at time t_0, occurs whenever some of those who 'hear' the piece of information react to it - including replying or forwarding it - within a prescribed time frame $(t_0, t_0 + \Delta\tau]$, thereby becoming *spreaders*. The cascade can live further if, in turn, reactions show up in $t_0 + 2\Delta\tau$, $t_0 + 3\Delta\tau$, and so on. Thus, neighbors of a user that emits a message are considered part of the same cascade if they react to the message within a time window $\Delta\tau$. Moreover, since messages in Twitter are instantly broadcasted to the set of users following the source, we define listener cascades as those including both active (spreader) and passive participants. In considering so we account for the upper bound of awareness over a certain conversation in the whole

Table 2 Network properties summary

	grassroots	elections
Network descriptor		
N_V	115,459	84,386
N_e	10,191,105	7,427,825
WCC	113,671	83,331
SCC	102,750	76,941
$\max(k_{in} + k_{out})$	38,028	32,073
$\max(k_{in})$	8,262	7,924
$\max(k_{out})$	37,810	31,402
$\max(k_c)$ (undirected)	228	210
L	3.175	3.092
D	10	9
r	−0.116	−0.124
ρ	0.455	0.489
Mesoscale characterization		
Q	0.413	0.448
N_{com}	5,838	4,665
S_{max}/N	0.196	0.110

N_V number of vertices, and N_e number of edges. WCC stands for the size of the weakly connected component; SCC is the size of the strongly connected component. Next we report the maximum degree and core values considering both in- and out-connectivity ($k_{in} + k_{out}$), the network of friends (k_{in}), and the network of followers (k_{out}). Average shortest path L and diameter D (the largest shortest path in the network) provide some hints about how deep in the structure can a cascade travel. r stands for the degree-degree correlation index (assortativity). Remarkably, $r < 0$ (in accordance with other reported assortativity values for OSNs, but clearly in contrast with other types of social networks [30]). Reciprocity ρ is a type of correlation expressing the tendency of vertex pairs to form mutual connections. Notably, results for the datasets in this works are higher than those for social networks in [28], and are actually comparable to reciprocity in neural networks. In our context, it reinforces the idea that Twitter may be used *both* as a microblogging system and a message interchange service. Finally, we report on some quantities regarding the Walktrap community detection outcome. Q stands for the best modularity value attained by the heuristics; N_{com} expresses the number of modules in the Q-optimal partition. The quotient of the largest community's size and the network size, S^{max}/N, is also shown.

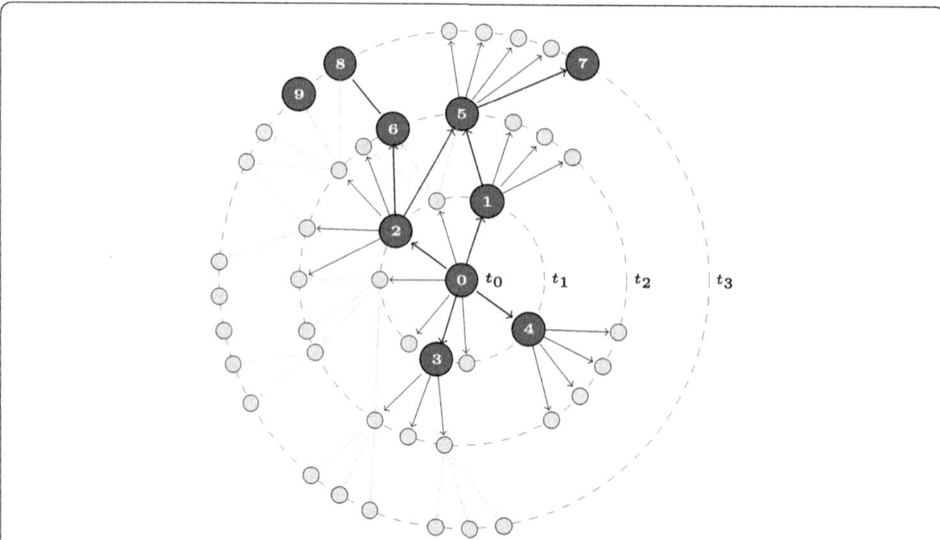

Figure 1 Time-constrained information cascade. Time-constrained cascades: nodes are disposed in concentric circles indicating the time when they received a specific tweet. Links between them represent the follower/friend relationship: an arrow from *i* to *j* indicates that *j* follows *i*, as any tweet posted by *i* is automatically received by *j*. Red nodes are those who posted a new message at the corresponding time, whereas gray nodes only *listened* to their friends. In this particular example, user 0 acts as the initial seed, emitting a message at time t_0 which is instantaneously sent to its nearest neighbors, laying on the first dashed circle, who are counted as part of the cascade. Some of them (nodes 1, 2, 3 and 4) decide to participate at the following time step, $t_1 = t_0 + \Delta\tau$, posting a new message and becoming intermediate spreaders of the cascade. If any of their followers show activity at $t_2 = t_0 + 2\Delta\tau$ the process continues and the cascade grows in size as new users listen to the message. The process finally ends when no additional users showed activity (as it happens in the cases of users 3 and 4), or when an intermediate spreader does not have any followers (users 7, 8 and 9).

population (see Figure 1 for illustration). Admittedly, our conceptualization does not control for exogenous factors which may be occurring at the onset of and during cascades.

We apply the latter definition [20, 21] to explore the occurrence of listener cascades in the 'grassroots' and 'elections' data. In practice, we take a seed message posted by s at time t_0 and include all of s followers in the diffusion tree hanging from s. We then check whether any of these listeners showed some activity at time $t_0 + \Delta\tau$, increasing the depth of the tree. This is done recursively, the tree's growth ends when no other follower shows activity. Passive listeners constitute the set of leaves in the tree. In our scheme, a node can only belong to one cascade (but could participate in it multiple times); the mentioned restriction may introduce measurement biases. Namely, two nodes sharing a follower may show simultaneous activity, but their follower can only be counted in one or the other cascade (with possible consequences regarding cascade size distributions or depth in the diffusion tree). To minimize this degeneration, we perform calculations for many possible cascade configurations, randomizing the way we process data.

In the next sections we report some results for the aforementioned data subsets ('grassroots', 'elections') considering all their time span (over one year). Our results have been obtained for $\Delta\tau = 24$ hours. Previous works [20, 21] showed the robustness of cascade statistics for $2 \leq \Delta\tau \leq 24$; also, a 24-hour window may be regarded as an inclusive bound of the popularity of a piece of information over time on different OSNs, including Twitter [8, 11, 14, 15]. Finally, the chosen window excludes eventual correlations due to the effect of circadian activity in human online behavior or the time differences due to individuals belonging to different geographical areas.

3.2 Community analyses

The identification of modules in complex networks has attracted much attention of the scientific community in the last years, and social networks constitute a prominent example. A modular view of a network offers a coarse-grained perspective in which nodes are classified in subsets on the basis of their topological position and, in particular, the density of connections between and within groups. In OSNs, this classification usually overlaps with node attribute data, like gender, geographical proximity or ideology [31, 32].

To detect statistically significant clusters we rely on the concept of modularity Q [33]:

$$Q = \frac{1}{2N_e} \sum_i \sum_j \left(a_{ij} - \frac{k_i k_j}{2N_e} \right) \delta(C_i, C_j), \tag{1}$$

where N_e is the number of links in the network; a_{ij} is 1 if there is a link from node i to j and 0 otherwise; k_i is the connectivity (degree) of node i; and finally the Kronecker delta function $\delta(C_i, C_j)$ equals 1 if nodes i and j are classified in the same community and 0 otherwise. Summarizing, Q quantifies how far a certain partition is from a random counterpart (null model).

From the definition of Q, algorithms and heuristics to optimize modularity have appeared ever faster and with an increased degree of accuracy [34]. All these efforts have led to a considerable success regarding the quality of detected community structure in networks, and thus a more complete topological knowledge at this level has been attained. In this work we present results for communities detected using the Walktrap method [35] in which a fair balance between accuracy and efficiency is sought. The algorithm exploits random walk dynamics. The basic idea is that a random walker tends to get trapped in densely connected parts of the graph, which correspond to communities. Pons and Latapy's proposal is particularly efficient because, as Q is increasingly optimized, vertices are merged into a coarse-grained structure, reducing the computational cost of the dynamics. The resulting clusters at each stage of the algorithm are aggregated, and the process is repeated iteratively. Although results in the following section refer to a partition extracted through Walktrap, other methods (Louvain [36] and Infomap [37]) have been tested with similar results.

A community analysis is useful because it provides a deeper understanding of the position of a node [38] at an intermediate (*i.e.*, mesoscale) topological level. In terms of information diffusion - and much like in [39] - we explore whether community structure (and in particular, the relation of a seed node with the module it belongs to) has an impact on the success of a cascade. To do so we adopt the node descriptors proposed by Guimerà *et al.* in [40]: the z-score of the internal degree of each node in its module, and the participation coefficient of a node i (P_i) defined as how the node is positioned in its own module and with respect to other modules.

The *within-module degree* and the *participation coefficient* are easily computed once the modules of a network are known. If κ_i is the number of links of node i to other nodes in its module C_i, $\overline{\kappa}_{C_i}$ is the average of κ over all the nodes in C_i, and $\sigma_{\kappa_{C_i}}$ is the standard

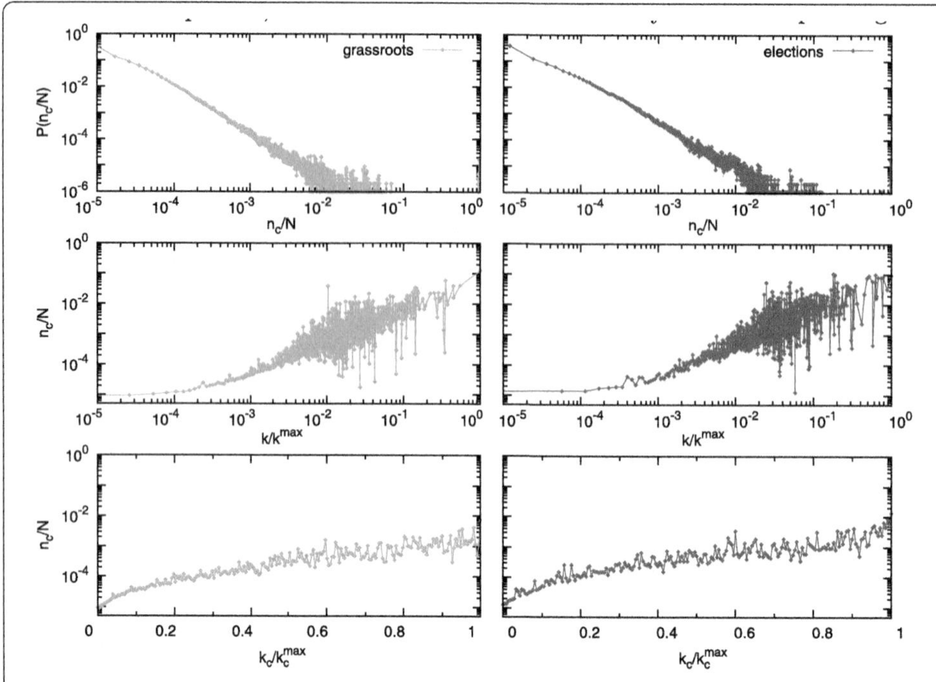

Figure 2 Cascade size distributions and seed attributes. Upper panels: cascade size distributions for the topics under consideration (left: 'grassroots'; right: 'elections'). Middle panels: average spreading capability (rescaled by the system size) grouped by the connectivity of the initial seed, *k*. Lower panels: spreading capability grouped by the *k*-core of the initial spreader. For the sake of comparison, *k* and *k*-core have been rescaled by their corresponding maxima.

deviation of κ in C_i, then

$$z_i = \frac{\kappa_i - \overline{\kappa}_{C_i}}{\sigma_{\kappa_{C_i}}} \tag{2}$$

is the so-called *z*-score.

The participation coefficient P_i of node i is defined as:

$$P_i = 1 - \sum_{C=1}^{N_M} \left(\frac{\kappa_{iC}}{k_i} \right)^2, \tag{3}$$

where κ_{iC} is the number of links of node i to nodes in module C, and k_i is the total degree of node i. Note that the participation coefficient P_i has a maximum at $P_i = 1 - \frac{1}{N_M}$, when the i's links are uniformly distributed among all the modules (N_M), while it is 0 if all its links belong to its own module. Those nodes that deviate largely from average internal connectivity are local hubs, whereas large values of P_i stands for connector nodes bridging different modules together.

4 Results

4.1 Cascade size distributions

As a starting point, we test the robustness of the results partially presented in [20], and further explored in [21]. Results shown in Figure 2 confirm these findings. The upper panels show that the size of time-constrained cascades is distributed in a highly heterogeneous manner, with only a small fraction of all cascades reaching system-wide proportions. This is also in good agreement with most preceding works, that have also found that large cascades occur only rarely. On the other hand, when cascades are grouped together such that the reported size corresponds to an average over topological classes, we find that both the degree k (middle panels) and coreness (k-core, lower panels) of nodes correlate positively with cascades' sizes. Some theoretical approaches predict similar behavior [41, 42].

4.2 Cascades' temporal and topological penetration

Next, we characterize how deep - both temporally and structurally - a cascade unfolds. We define the *topological penetration*, Δr of a cascade as the shortest path between the seed of the cascade and the farthest node involved in the cascade. The results shown in Figure 3 (upper panels) give quantitative support to a well-known fact: over 95% of cascades actually die with one single spreader (instantaneous cascades), which corresponds to a shallow tree - though it may be quite wide [8, 12, 13]. In this most frequent case, the cascade of listeners simply accounts for the out-degree k_{out} of the seed node (or a subset of it, if any of its neighbors is already counted in another cascade). Additionally, the bulk of non-instantaneous cascades penetrates up to $\Delta r = 3$ or $\Delta r = 4$ (see middle panels in Figure 3), both for 'grassroots' and 'elections', which is in the range of the average path length, but fairly below the upper bound, which is set by the network's diameter (10 and 9 respectively; see Table 2). Interestingly, as shown in the figure, when a cascade moves beyond the average path length between the initial node and any node on the network,

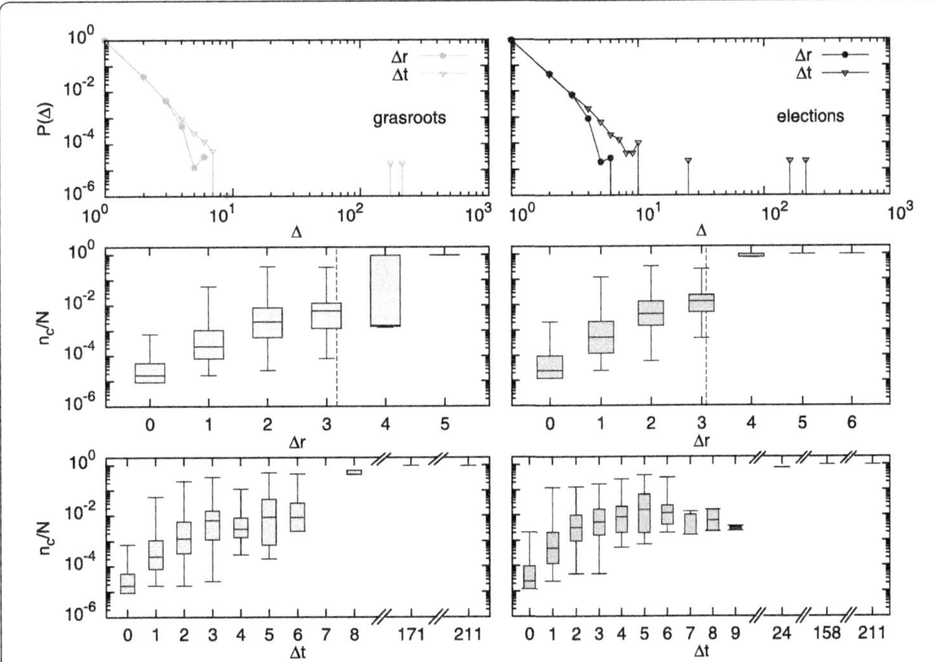

Figure 3 Topological and temporal penetration. Upper panels: distributions of topological and temporal penetrations for the topics under consideration (left: 'grassroots'; right: 'elections'). Δr is the largest shortest path length between the initial seed and any node involved in the same cascade, where as Δt refers to a cascade's lifetime. Middle panels: box-plots for topological penetration. Note that large cascades occur mainly for Δr close to the average path length (dashed vertical line). Lower panels: box-plots for temporal penetration. Cascades' spreading success grows with time, and some exceptional conversations can last for months (note the broken axis).

namely, to nodes distant $\Delta r > 3$, a large fraction of the population will likely be engaged in a cascade that will reach system-wide sizes with high probability.

Temporal patterns, as given by the lifetime Δt of a cascade, follow a similar trend: most cascades die out after 24 hours, which closely resembles previously reported results [8]. However, in Figure 3 (upper panels) we observe a richer distribution (compared to topological penetration Δr) such that cascades may last over 100 days, suggesting that the survival of a conversation does not exhibit an obvious pattern. Again, this result confirms - from a different point of view - empirical results published elsewhere [11, 19]. Finally, the duration of cascades takes into account the fact that a node may participate multiple times in a single cascade - although it is counted just once. This is implicit in the definition of a time-constrained cascade, which comprehends self-sustained activity. In any case, Figure 3 (lower panels) illustrates that survival can not guarantee system-wide cascades, although an increasing pattern is observed as survival time grows.

4.3 Identification and role of hidden influentials

Up to now we have related a cascade's size to certain features of the seed node. Although we observe a clear positively correlated pattern (the larger the seed's descriptor, the larger the resulting cascade), one might fairly argue that in a wide range of values below the maximum, a similar outcome is obtained. So, for instance, seeds in the range $10^{-2} \leq k/k^{\max} \leq 10^{-1}$ (Figure 2) can sometimes trigger large cascades; the same can be said for $k_c/k_c^{\max} \geq 0.6$. This finding prompts us to hypothesize that the success of an activity cascade might greatly depend on intermediate spreaders characteristics, and not only on the properties of the seed nodes. That being so, a large seed k_{out} (*i.e.* its follower set) may be a sufficient but not a necessary condition for the generation of large-scale cascades. In this section we explore how some topological features of the train of spreaders involved in a cascade affects its final size.

To study the role of intermediate spreaders we split our results, distinguishing instantaneous cascades (those with a unique spreader) from those with multiple spreaders. The former merely underlines the fact that the seed's k_{out} suffices to observe large cascades. Interestingly, the latter unveils a new character in the play: *hidden influentials*, *i.e.*, relatively smaller (in terms of connectivity and centrality) nodes which, on the aggregate, can make chain reactions turn into global cascades. Figure 4, which confronts relative cascade sizes n_c/N with the average degree of intermediate spreaders $\langle k_{\text{sp}} \rangle$ (that is, excluding the initial seed), reveals these special users: note that larger effects are obtained for those spreaders who, on average, have 10^2 to 10^3 neighbors (both for 'grassroots' and 'elections'). These nodes do not occupy key topological positions that would *a priori* identify them as influential, and yet they play a major role promoting system-wide events [22, 43]. Therefore, getting these nodes involved has a multiplicative impact on the size of the cascades.

To quantify such effect, we introduce the *multiplicative number* of a given node i, Δl (in analogy with the basic reproductive number in disease spreading), which is the quotient of the number of listeners reached one time step after i showed activity, $l(t + \Delta\tau)$, and the number of i's nearest listeners, *i.e.*, those who instantaneously received its message, $l(t)$ (which is given by the number of followers of i that are involved in the cascade). Thus, the ratio Δl measures the multiplicative capacity of a node: $\Delta l > 1$ indicates that a user has been able to increase the number of listeners who received the message beyond its immediate followers.

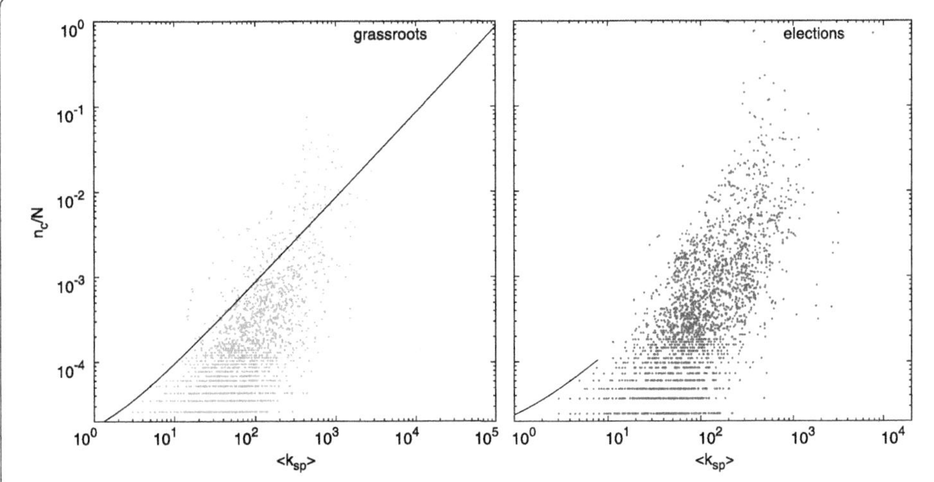

Figure 4 Intermediate spreaders connectivity. Cascade size vs. average connectivity of intermediate spreaders $\langle k_{sp} \rangle$ (left: 'grassroots'; right: 'elections'). Non-instantaneous cascades are displayed, where the initial seed and its inactive listeners have been removed in order to dismiss the effect of the initial seed on the cascade size. There is a clear correlation between both magnitudes, although some unexpected behavior shows up: the existence of cascades containing 'hidden spreaders', users who are capable of generating large cascades despite not having hub-like connectivity. In both panels the function $y = (x + 1)/N$ is drawn as a reference.

Figure 5 shows how Δl is distributed as a function of k_{out}. Top panels represent the proportion of nodes with $\Delta l > 1$ and $\Delta l \leq 1$ per degree class. In this case, normalization takes into account all possible k_{out} and all Δl (above and below 1) counts, so as to evidence that in most cases cascades progressively shrink as they advance. The fact that the area corresponding to the region $\Delta l > 1$ is much smaller than that for $\Delta l \leq 1$ tells us that most cascades are small, which is consistent with the reported cascades' size distribution. On the other hand, bottom panels in Figure 5 focus on the same quantity, but in this case we represent the probability $P(k_{out}, \Delta l > 1)$ ($P(k_{out}, \Delta l \leq 1)$) that a node of out-degree k_{out} has (does not have) a multiplicative effect. As before, the results indicate that, in both datasets, the most-efficient spreaders (those with a multiplicative number larger than one) can be found most often in the degree classes ranging from $k_{out} = 10^2$ to $k_{out} = 10^3$, *i.e.*, significantly below k_{max} (see Table 2). These nodes are the actual responsible that cascades go global and must be engaged if one would like to increase the likelihood of generating system-wide cascades.

The previous features of hidden influentials poses some doubts about what is the actual role of hubs in cascades that are not initiated by them. Interestingly, we next provide quantitative evidence that, in contrast to what is commonly assumed, hubs often act as cascade firewalls rather than spawners. To this end we have measured $\langle k_{nn} \rangle$ (average nearest neighbors degree) with respect to seed nodes. Each point in Figure 6 represents the relationship between the size of cascades and $\langle k_{nn} \rangle$. The initial trend is clear and expected: the larger the average degree of the seed's neighbors is, the deeper the tree grows. However, at some point this pattern changes, indicating that cascades may die out when they encounter a hub, more often than not. If this were not the case, one would observe a monotonically increasing dependence with $\langle k_{nn} \rangle$. This counterintuitive hub-effect is mirrored in classical rumor dynamics [7] and can be explained scrutinizing the typically-low activity patterns of these (topologically) special nodes [27, 44].

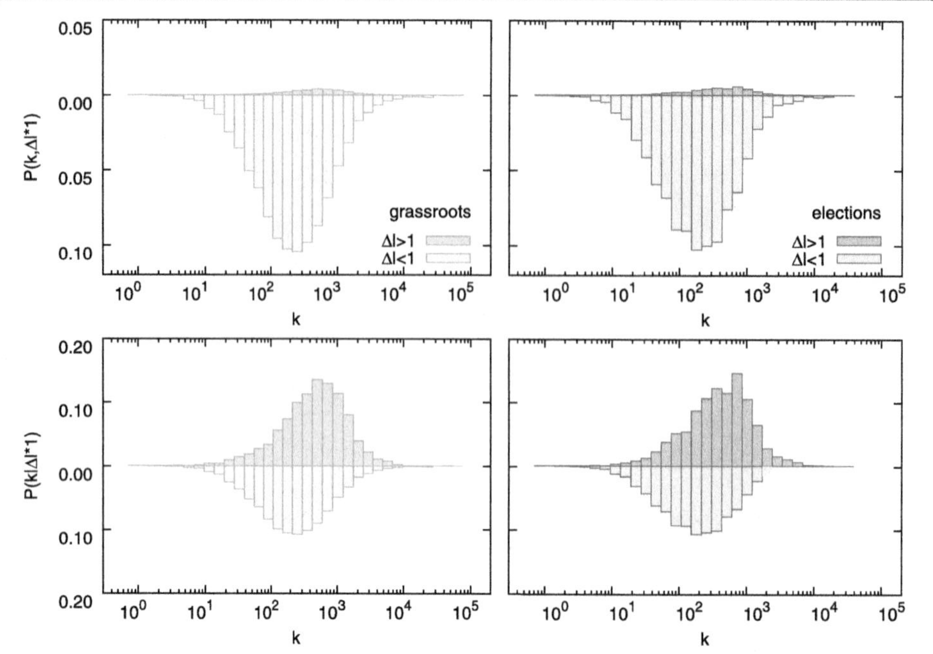

Figure 5 Quantifying the multiplicative effect. Top panels represent the distribution of the multiplicative number, ΔI for both datasets as indicated. In most cases $\Delta I \leq 1$, which reflects the rare occurrence of large cascades. The bottom panels, instead, represent the probabilities $P(k_{\text{out}}, \Delta I > 1)$ (above 0 baseline) and $P(k_{\text{out}}, \Delta I \leq 1)$ (below it) that a node of out-degree k_{out} has or has not a multiplicative effect, respectively. Both low- and high-connectivity nodes do not exhibit $\Delta I > 1$.

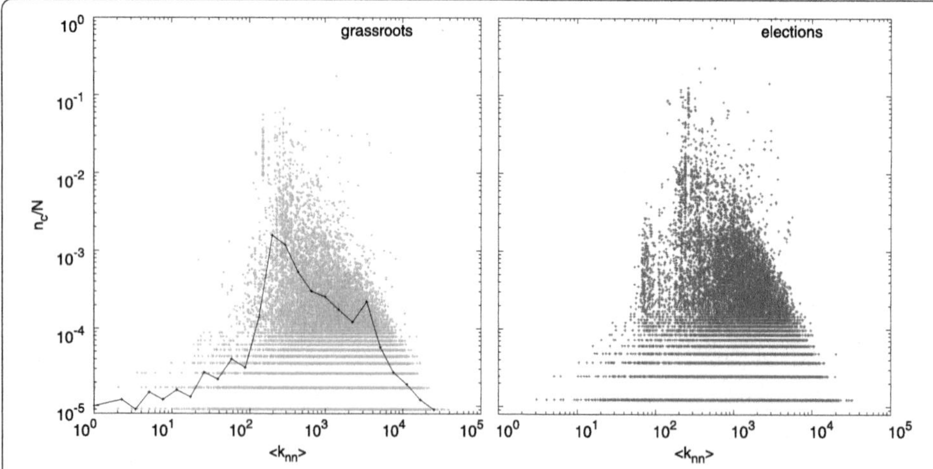

Figure 6 Nearest neighbors average degree. Cascades' outreach as a function of seed's average nearest neighbors degree $\langle k_{\text{nn}} \rangle$: remarkably, nodes with the highest connectivity do not enhance, but rather diminish, cascades growth. As in the previous figure, largest cascades are obtained when second spreaders (the seed's neighbors) have, on average, $10^2 < k_{\text{out}} < 10^3$ for the (left: 'grassroots'; right: 'elections').

4.4 The role of community structure in information diffusion

It is generally accepted that cohesive sub-structures play an important role for the functioning of complex systems, because topologically dense clusters impose restrictions to dynamical processes running on top of the structure [45, 46]. For example, in the context of OSNs, detected communities in *@mention* Twitter networks were found to encode both geographical and political information [44], suggesting that a large fraction of interactions take place locally, but many of them also correspond to global modules - for instance, users rely on mass media accounts to amplify their opinion. Focusing on information diffusion, inter- and intra-modular connections in OSNs have already been explored [39] regarding the nature of user-user ties. We instead investigate other questions, such as: (i) are modules actual bottlenecks for information diffusion?; (ii) is the spreading of information more successful for 'kinless' nodes (those who have links in many communities besides their own one)? Or (iii) do local hubs - those with larger-than-expected intra-modular connectivity - have higher chances to trigger system-wide cascades?

We apply the community analysis described in Section 3.2 and obtain a network partition in $S = 5{,}838$ and $S = 4{,}665$ modules, for the 'grassroots' and 'elections' data sets respectively, with optimized Q values and maximum module size $S_{\max}$ given in Table 2 (note that we report only on results for the Walktrap algorithm). Next, for each cascade we compute how many nodes in the resulting diffusion tree belong to the same cluster of the seed (n_{int}). This allows us to know, as shown in Figure 7, how often a cascade spills over the module where it began. Interestingly, small to medium-sized cascades ($\sim 10^3$) mainly diffuse within the same community where they were initiated, which suggests that influence occurs within friendship circles or specialized topics [27]. Note however that our approach to community analysis is blind to contents or user metadata (age, name, hobbies, *etc.*), and relies solely on the underlying topology. Thus we can only make an educated guess regarding whether modules cluster users around a certain topic or personal acquaintance (*i.e.* assuming *homophily* [47, 48]). Remarkably, our results match - qualitatively at least - the predicted behavior in [2, 4] regarding cascades in modular networks, in the sense that inter-modular boundaries place actual constraints on information flow.

Turning to the individual level, the results depicted in the z-P plane of Figure 8 confirm the importance of connectivity - in this case, within-module leadership - to succeed when

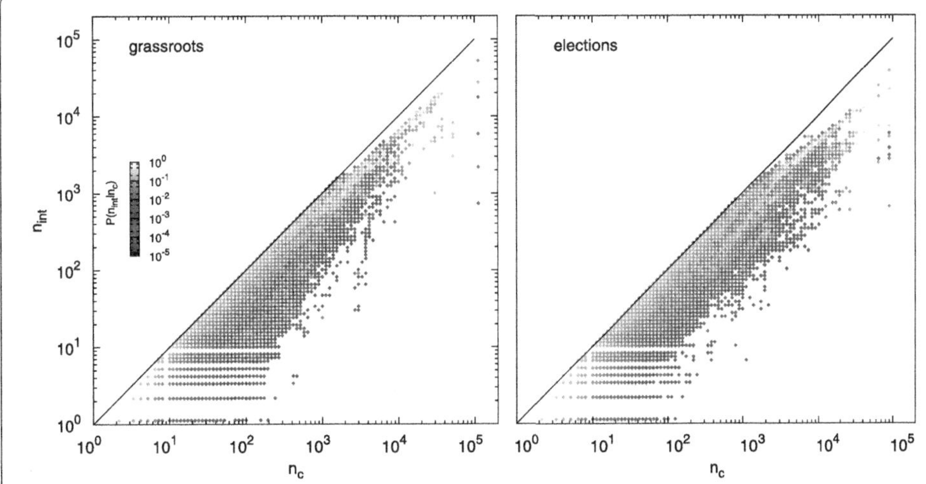

Figure 7 Inter- and intra-modular cascading events. Inter- and intra-modular cascading events for the topics under consideration (left: 'grassroots'; right: 'elections'). Binned representation of the relationship between the number of nodes in a cascade that unfolds in the same community of the initial seed (n_{int}) and the size of the cascade itself (n_c). Proportions have been normalized column-wise, *i.e.* by the total number of cascades with same size. Note that cascades affecting up to 10^3 nodes mostly lie close to the diagonal, *i.e.* a vast majority of the cascade occurs within the community where it began. At a certain point (beyond $n_c \approx 10^3$) cascades spill over the module where they began.

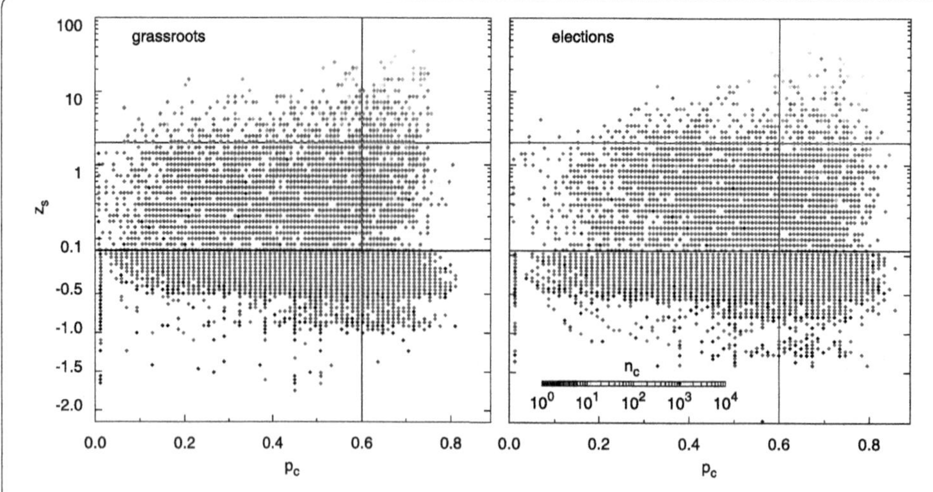

Figure 8 Relation between seeds' position in the mesoscale and final cascade size. Color-coded z-P planes to assess whether the modular structure of the following/friend network places dynamical constraints in the growth of cascades (left: 'grassroots'; right: 'elections'). A first clear result is that when local leaders ($z > 2$) precipitate information cascades, these tend to be more successful. More interestingly, connector nodes ($P_i > 0.6$) also succeed quite often, suggesting that a node's position in the mesoscale can sometimes play a more important role than a rich connectivity.

a cascade is triggered. Indeed, most nodes for which $z > 1$ elicit large cascades in both samples. However, and most interestingly, it suggests that connector or kinless ($P_i > 0.6$) nodes [40] can perform better than expected at precipitating system-wide cascades if only internal connectivity is attended. As shown in the figure, nodes with a z-score between 0 and 1 acting as connectors are still able to generate system-wide cascades because they compensate their relative lack of connectivity by bridging different modules. This feature is specially noticeable in the case of the 'election' dataset (right panel). Altogether, our results establish that topological modules indeed represent dynamical bottlenecks, which need to be bypassed - through high but also low connectivity users - to let a cascade go global.

5 Discussion

In just one decade social networking sites have revolutionized human communication routines, placing solid foundations to the advent of the Web 2.0. The academia has not ignored such eruption, some researchers foreseeing a myriad of applications ranging from e-commerce to cooperative platforms; while others soon realized that OSNs could represent a unique opportunity to bring empirical evidence at large into open sociological problems. Information cascades fall somewhere in between, both attracting the interest of viral marketing experts - who worry about optimal outreach and costs - and collective social action and political scientists - concerned about grassroots movements, opinion contagion, *etc.*

However, the diversity of OSNs - which constrains the format and the way information flows between users - and the complexity of human communication patterns - heterogeneous activity, different classes of collective attention - have resulted in a multiplicity of empirical approaches to cascading phenomena - let alone theoretical works. While all of them highlight different interesting aspects of information dissemination, little has been done to confirm results testing its robustness across different social platforms and social contexts.

In this regard, the present work capitalizes on previous research to collect, in new large datasets, the statistics of time-constrained information cascades. Message chains are reconstructed assuming that conversation-like activity is contagious if it takes place in relatively short time windows. The main preceding observed trends are here reproduced successfully. Furthermore, we extend the study to uncover other internal facets of these cascades. First, we have discussed how long in time and how deep in the topology cascades go, to realize that, as in neuronal activity, time-constrained cascades can exhibit self-sustained activity. We have then paid attention not only to the nodes that trigger a cascade, but also to those that actively participate in and sustain a cascade beyond its onset.

Our main results point at two counterintuitive facts, by which hubs can short-circuit information pathways and close-to-average users - hidden influentials - fuel system-wide events. We have found that for a cascade to be successful in terms of the number of users involved in it, key nodes should be engaged. These nodes are not the hubs, which more than often behave as firewalls, but belong to a middle class that either has a high multiplicative capacity or bridges the modules that make up the system. Presumably, modular topologies - abundant in the real world - entail the presence of information bottlenecks (poor inter-modular connectivity) which place constraints to efficient diffusion dynamics. Indeed, we find that medium-sized and small cascades (the most frequent ones) happen mainly within the community where a cascade originated. Furthermore, those seed nodes which happen to be poorly classified (they participate in many modules besides their own) are more successful at triggering large cascades.

A better understanding of time-constrained cascading behavior in complex systems leads to new questions. First, it seems clear that the bulk of theoretical work devoted to information spreading is not meant to model this conversation-type dynamics - it is rather focused on rumor and epidemic models. Other approaches need to be sought to fill this gap. Also, time-constrained cascades have always been studied in the context of political discussion and mobilization. As such, this is a fairly limited view of what happens in a service with (as of late 2012) over 200 million active users. Results like the ones obtained here will anyhow provide new hints for a better understanding of social phenomena that are mediated by new communication platforms and for the development of novel manmade algorithms for effective and costless dissemination (viral) dynamics.

Competing interests
The authors declare that they have no competing interests.

Authors' contributions
RAB, JBH and YM conceived the experiments. RAB and JBH performed the analysis. All authors wrote and approved the final version of the manuscript.

Acknowledgements
We thank A Rivero for helping us to collect and process the data used in this paper. We are also indebted to S González-Bailón and JP Gleeson for their useful comments on the manuscript. This work has been partially supported by MINECO through Grant FIS2011-25167; Comunidad de Aragón (Spain) through a grant to the group FENOL and by the EC FET-Proactive Project PLEXMATH (grant 317614). RAB acknowledges support from the FPI program of the Government of Aragón, Spain.

References

1. Watts D (2002) A simple model of global cascades on random networks. Proc Natl Acad Sci USA 99(9):5766-5771
2. Galstyan A, Cohen P (2007) Cascading dynamics in modular networks. Phys Rev E 75(3):036109
3. Gleeson J, Cahalane D (2007) Seed size strongly affects cascades on random networks. Phys Rev E 75(5):056103
4. Gleeson J (2008) Cascades on correlated and modular random networks. Phys Rev E 77(4):046117
5. Hackett A, Melnik S, Gleeson J (2011) Cascades on a class of clustered random networks. Phys Rev E 83(5):056107
6. Centola D, Eguíluz V, Macy M (2007) Cascade dynamics of complex propagation. Phys A, Stat Mech Appl 374:449-456
7. Borge-Holthoefer J, Moreno Y (2012) Absence of influential spreaders in rumor dynamics. Phys Rev E 85:026116
8. Leskovec J, McGlohon M, Faloutsos CG, Hurst M (2007) Cascading behavior in large blog graphs. In: Proc. 7th SIAM int. conf. on data mining (SDM), pp 29406-29413
9. Liben-Nowell D, Kleinberg J (2008) Tracing information flow on a global scale using Internet chain-letter data. Proc Natl Acad Sci USA 105(12):4633-4638
10. Miritello G, Moro E, Lara R (2011) Dynamical strength of social ties in information spreading. Phys Rev E 83(4):045102
11. Sun E, Rosenn I, Marlow C, Lento T (2009) Gesundheit! Modeling contagion through Facebook news feed. In: Proc. ICWSM
12. Kwak H, Lee C, Park H, Moon S (2010) What is Twitter, a social network or a news media. In: Proceedings of the 19th international conference on World Wide Web. ACM, New York, pp 591-600
13. Bakshy E, Hofman J, Mason W, Watts D (2011) Everyone's an influencer: quantifying influence on Twitter. In: Proceedings of the fourth ACM international conference on web search and data mining. ACM, New York, pp 65-74
14. Cha M, Mislove A, Gummadi K (2009) A measurement-driven analysis of information propagation in the Flickr social network. In: Proceedings of the 18th international conference on World Wide Web. ACM, New York, pp 721-730
15. Lerman K, Ghosh R (2010) Information contagion: an empirical study of the spread of news on Digg and Twitter social networks. In: Proceedings of 4th international conference on weblogs and social media (ICWSM)
16. Gruhl D, Guha R, Liben-Nowell D, Tomkins A (2004) Information diffusion through blogspace. In: Proceedings of the 13th international conference on World Wide Web. ACM, New York, pp 491-501
17. Adar E, Adamic L (2005) Tracking information epidemics in blogspace. In: Web intelligence, 2005. Proceedings. The 2005 IEEE/WIC/ACM international conference on. IEEE Press, New York, pp 207-214
18. Rogers E (1962) Diffusion of innovations. Free Press, New York
19. Lehmann J, Gonçalves B, Ramasco JJ, Cattuto C (2012) Dynamical classes of collective attention in Twitter. In: Proceedings of the 21st international conference on World Wide Web. ACM, New York, pp 251-260
20. González-Bailón S, Borge-Holthoefer J, Rivero A, Moreno Y (2011) The dynamics of protest recruitment through an online network. Sci Rep 1:197
21. Borge-Holthoefer J, Rivero A, Moreno Y (2012) Locating privileged spreaders on an online social network. Phys Rev E 85:066123
22. González-Bailón S, Borge-Holthoefer J, Moreno Y (2013) Broadcasters and hidden influentials in online protest diffusion. Am Behav Sci (in press). doi:10.1177/0002764213479371
23. Adbusters (2011) https://www.adbusters.org/blogs/adbusters-blog/occupywallstreet.html
24. Gerbaudo P (2012) Tweets and the streets: social media and contemporary activism. Pluto Books, London
25. Honey C, Herring SC (2009) Beyond microblogging: conversation and collaboration via Twitter. In: System sciences, 2009. HICSS'09. 42nd Hawaii international conference on, IEEE Press, New York, pp 1-10
26. Mungiu-Pippidi A, Munteanu I (2009) Moldova's 'Twitter revolution'. J Democr 20(3):136-142
27. Cha M, Haddadi H, Benevenuto F, Gummadi K (2010) Measuring user influence in twitter: the million follower fallacy. In: 4th international AAAI conference on weblogs and social media (ICWSM)
28. Garlaschelli D, Loffredo MI (2004) Patterns of link reciprocity in directed networks. Phys Rev Lett 93(26):268701
29. Kossinets G, Kleinberg J, Watts D (2008) The structure of information pathways in a social communication network. In: Proceeding of the 14th ACM SIGKDD international conference on knowledge discovery and data mining. ACM, New York, pp 435-443
30. Newman M (2003) Mixing patterns in networks. Phys Rev E 67(2):26126
31. Conover M, Ratkiewicz J, Francisco M, Gonçalves B, Flammini A, Menczer F (2011) Political polarization on Twitter. In: Proc. 5th intl. conference on weblogs and social media
32. Conover M, Gonçalves B, Flammini A, Menczer F (2012) Partisan asymmetries in online political activity. EPJ Data Sci 1:6
33. Newman MEJ, Girvan M (2004) Finding and evaluating community structure in networks. Phys Rev E 69:026113
34. Fortunato S (2010) Community detection in graphs. Phys Rep 486(3-5):75-174
35. Pons P, Latapy M (2005) Computing communities in large networks using random walks. In: Computer and information sciences. Lecture notes in computer science, vol 3733, p 284
36. Blondel V, Guillaume J, Lambiotte R, Lefebvre E (2008) Fast unfolding of communities in large networks. J Stat Mech Theory Exp 2008:P10008
37. Rosvall M, Bergstrom C (2008) Maps of random walks on complex networks reveal community structure. Proc Natl Acad Sci USA 105(4):1118
38. Arenas A, Borge-Holthoefer J, Gomez S, Zamora-Lopez G (2010) Optimal map of the modular structure of complex networks. New J Phys 12:053009
39. Grabowicz PA, Ramasco JJ, Moro E, Pujol JM, Eguiluz VM (2012) Social features of online networks: the strength of intermediary ties in online social media. PLoS ONE 7:e29358
40. Guimerà R, Amaral LAN (2005) Functional cartography of complex metabolic networks. Nature 433:895-900
41. Kitsak M, Gallos L, Havlin S, Liljeros F, Muchnik L, Stanley H, Makse H (2010) Identification of influential spreaders in complex networks. Nat Phys 6:888-893
42. Borge-Holthoefer J, Meloni S, Gonçalves B, Moreno Y (2012) Emergence of influential spreaders in modified rumor models. J Stat Phys 148(6):1-11
43. Watts D, Dodds P (2007) Influentials, networks, and public opinion formation. J Consum Res 34:441
44. Borge-Holthoefer J, Rivero A, García I, Cauhé E, Ferrer A, Ferrer D, Francos D, Iñiguez D, Pérez M, Ruiz G et al (2011) Structural and dynamical patterns on online social networks: the Spanish May 15th movement as a case study. PLoS ONE 6(8):e23883

45. Arenas A, Díaz-Guilera A, Pérez-Vicente C (2006) Synchronization reveals topological scales in complex networks. Phys Rev Lett 96(11):114102
46. Danon L, Arenas A, Díaz-Guilera A (2008) Impact of community structure on information transfer. Phys Rev E 77(3):36103
47. McPherson M, Smith-Lovin L, Cook JM (2001) Birds of a feather: homophily in social networks. Annu Rev Sociol 27:415-444
48. Centola D, Gonzalez-Avella JC, Eguiluz VM, San Miguel M (2007) Homophily, cultural drift, and the co-evolution of cultural groups. J Confl Resolut 51(6):905-929

The network positions of methicillin resistant *Staphylococcus aureus* affected units in a regional healthcare system

Jan Ohst[1], Fredrik Liljeros[2,3], Mikael Stenhem[4,5] and Petter Holme[3,6,7*]

*Correspondence:
petter.holme@physics.umu.se
[3]Institute for Future Studies, Stockholm, 10131, Sweden
[6]Department of Energy Science, Sungkyunkwan University, Suwon, 440-746, Korea
[7]IceLab, Department of Physics, Umeå University, Umeå, 90187, Sweden
Full list of author information is available at the end of the article

Abstract

We studied a dataset of care episodes in a regional Swedish hospital system. We followed how 2,314,477 patients moved between 8,507 units (hospital wards and outpatient clinics) over seven years. The data also included information on the date when patients tested positive with methicillin resistant *Staphylococcus aureus*. To simplify the complex flow of patients, we represented it as a network of units, where two units were connected if a patient moved from one unit to another, without visiting a third unit in between. From this network, we characterized the typical network position of units with a high prevalence of methicillin resistant *Staphylococcus aureus*, and how the patient's location in the network changed upon testing positive. On average, units with medium values of the analyzed centrality measures had the highest average prevalence. We saw a weak effect of the hospital system's response to the patient testing positive - after a positive test, the patient moved to units with a lower centrality measured as degree (i.e. number of links to other units) and in addition, the average duration of the care episodes became longer. The network of units was too random to be a strong predictor of the presence of methicillin resistant *Staphylococcus aureus* - would it be more regular, one could probably both identify and control outbreaks better. The migration of the positive patients with within the healthcare system, however, helps decreasing the outbreak sizes.

Keywords: network epidemiology; methicillin resistant *Staphylococcus aureus*; hospital system; healthcare associated infections

1 Background

It has long been observed that interpersonal contacts with an ability to transmit a disease are not random as assumed by simple models of infectious disease spreading. If it is possible to estimate the characteristics of such a non-random network of contacts between individuals, we could improve the predictive and explanatory power of epidemic models. There are not so many pathogens, however, that spread over pathways where the network structure can be estimated. For this to be possible, contacts with the capacity to transmit the disease need to be discernable among all different types of inter-individual contacts, so that a network of effective contacts can be faithfully constructed. This is the case for e.g. sexually transmitted infections [1] and - the topic of this paper - healthcare associated infections (HAI) [2].

The first network-epidemiological study of the spread of disease in healthcare systems is, to our knowledge, Meyers *et al.* [3]. In this work, the authors model contagion between units populated by immobile patients. The model assumes the disease to spread between units by medical staff acting as vectors [4, 5] and is used to argue for the key-role of the staff in the spreading dynamics. Karkada *et al.* [6] and Lee *et al.* [7] make similar simulation-based studies concluding that patient transfer in critical care and nursing homes, respectively, are important factors in the dynamics of HAIs. Liljeros *et al.* [8] investigated a subset of the dataset we use in this paper. This smaller dataset recorded 295,108 inpatients from the Stockholm area of Sweden over two years. Liljeros *et al.* focused mostly on methodological questions, such as how to represent this dataset as a network of patients that is as relevant for investigating disease spreading as possible. The authors argue that different diseases need different network representations depending on their route of transmission. Ueno and Masuda [9] investigate a dataset from Tokyo community hospital sampling 388 patients and 217 doctors and nurses. They simulate disease transmission in this data and evaluate different strategies for controlling epidemics. Vanhems *et al.* [10] use a data set of similar size acquired from wearable sensors (detecting when patients or health-care workers are within a range of 1–1.5 m). They find a very heterogeneous contact structure where some health-care workers are much more central in the contact network than others. Hornbeck *et al.* [11] use a very similar data set to reach very similar conclusions. Donker *et al.* [12, 13] study a large dataset of patient flow between hospitals within the Netherlands. Their data is aggregated on a coarser level than ours - a node in the network is a hospital - but it does cover an entire nation. Donker *et al.* find a directionality of the flow towards larger, academic hospitals. This could, they argue, be exploited to control the transmission of healthcare associated pathogens (in Ref. [14] they make this point stronger by simulations and argue that just reversing the patient flow would reduce the HAI prevalence dramatically). The final network-epidemiological study of HAI we are aware of is Walker *et al.*'s study of *Clostridium difficile* in inpatients of the Oxfordshire region of the United Kingdom [15]. In this paper, the authors retrace possible transmission trees among 1,282 positive cases. They find that about 25% of the cases can be explained by an infection within the hospital system.

Currently researchers have, as seen above, either studied smaller, high precision data recorded by electronic sensors or large-scale patient referral data. These two types of data have their pros and cons - with high precision data could perhaps identify singular infection events, on the other hand, an epidemic outbreak is a large-scale phenomenon that is affected by the large-scale contact structure that at present can only be studied by patient referral data. The present paper investigated a dataset of the large-scale category.[a] We use a record of all care episodes in the Stockholm region, making it possible to map the patient flow between units (that could be either a hospital ward or an outpatient clinic), we also knew who tested positive with methicillin-resistant *Staphylococcus aureus* (MRSA) - an important nosocomial pathogen - and when they tested positive. However, we did not (like Ueno and Masuda [9]) have records of the movement of the medical staff. We had to assume that the transmission of MRSA could take place outside the dataset (i.e. a patient could be infected in the community outside the healthcare system). One interesting question is how to infer these missing chains, which implicitly would mean how one can predict the false negative patients within the records of the regional healthcare system. For our data, and the methods we can envision, this would give too uncertain results at an individual level. We would have to aggregate the results to make meaningful observations. In this work, we do not take such an individual-level approach and integrate the results. Rather, we study the system at an intermediate level - the level of health-care units. We represented the hospital system as network of units. Briefly stated, we linked two units A and B if a patient had care episodes in both units without having been admitted in any other unit in between. The links between units thus capture the possibility of infection spreading from one unit to another (or in terms of newly infected patients the link, or course, represents certainty). Just like the topology of the contact network can help us to better understand how the contact patterns between individuals affect disease transmission (which individuals that are most influential, how influential they are relative to the average, how a disease can most efficiently be mitigated, etc.) [1, 16, 17], a network of units can teach us about how the organization of the hospital system affects disease spreading. There has recently been a debate in the literature of the of the benefits of screening patients for MRSA (see Refs. [18, 19] and further references therein). A more cost effective alternative to screening all patients would be to, guided by analyses like the ones in this paper, focus on high-risk units.

2 Methods

2.1 The network of units

As in many countries, the Swedish public healthcare system is organized hierarchically into hospitals that are divided into departments that are divided into wards. In this work, we focus on at the lowest level - hospital wards and outpatient clinics - and consider the network of such units connected if at least one patient has been transferred from one unit to another. In total we study 8,507 units and 66,527,638 care episodes involving 2,314,477 individuals observed for 3,059 days. We represent this system as a network by considering a unit as a node and connecting two nodes if they, at some point in the data, had a patient transferred between each other. The links can be weighted by the number of patients transferred along it, or directed, indicating the net flow - unless otherwise stated we use the simplest representation where a link indicates the presence or absence of any patient transfer.

It is not completely trivial how to define such a transfer, especially for patients that go out of the healthcare system and then come back. The simplest solutions to this problem are either to omit the stay outside the healthcare system (and put a link between the unit that the patient is discharged from, to the first unit where the patient reenters the healthcare system), or to not add such a link at all. Since MRSA colonization can have happened before the testing, we use the first approach. The drawback is that the links no longer represent a direct referral between two units, and thus is more indirectly related to the patient flow. Another alternative approach would be to add the outside as a node, but then that node would not be easily comparable with the other nodes. For example, the real risk of transmission between individuals in that outside node would be much lower, since the probability that two persons might meet on a given day outside the healthcare system is very low.

A slight complication in our data set is that patients can be registered at different units simultaneously. It is a rather rare event (happening for about 2.7% of the patients). We represent the event that one patient is at two units a certain day by adding one unit in both directions to the weight between these units. Another feature that could affect some

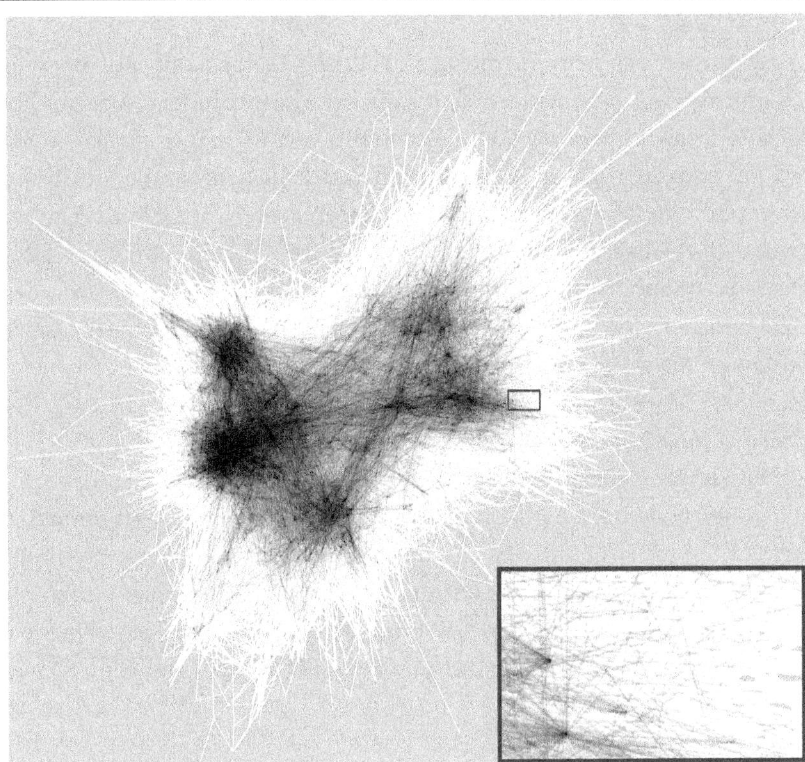

Figure 1 Ridiculogram of the patient flow. This is a visualization of the entire patient flow in the hospital system of the 8,507 units that at some point has an MRSA infected patient. It is created by a spring-embedding algorithm that forces nodes (units) exchanging many patients to be close. In this visualization, the nodes are not directly visible, only the links. The darker colors represent stronger overlap. We can see that the system is strongly connected and the hierarchical administrative organizations are not very clearly reflected in the patient flow. At the same time, there is more structure than in a purely random network which would look uniform in this type of plot - the dark blobs corresponds more or less to the major hospitals (we do not have information about what larger unit that a unit belongs to). This type of visualization should not be overinterpreted (which is often the case, hence the sobriquet "ridiculogram"). To understand the structure of the unit network, we need network metrics, which is the topic of the paper.

results is that the id number if some units (the outpatient clinics) change without the system being reorganized *per se*. Rather than cleaning the data from such short-lived nodes, we keep their presence in mind when discussing the results.

In Figure 1, we show a plot of the unit network as displayed by a spring-embedding algorithm. In this case, and unless otherwise stated, the network is aggregated over the entire sampling time. The picture that the unit network is more randomly organized than the hierarchical organization of hospital systems still holds if one plots the graph in other ways with other layout programs. Still, there are visible clusters, presumably corresponding to hospitals. In other words, the unit network has some structure that can affect MRSA transmission.

2.2 Network structural measures

We related the average prevalence of MRSA, over the study period, at unit level to different measures of network centrality. In network analysis centrality is an umbrella for a number of measures quantifying different aspects of how central a node or link is in the network [16, 17]. The following centrality measures were used:

2.2.1 Degree centralities

The simplest measures of centrality are the *in-* and *out-degree*, the number of other units that the focal unit receives patients from and transfers patients to, respectively. These measures are both local, in the sense that the centrality of a node is only affected by its neighborhood (the nodes to which it has a link). Potentially, many-step processes, where a patient is transferred through a chain of units, could be important. However, such events do not contribute to the degree centralities, which motivate the use of more elaborate metrics. If degree centrality has a capacity to explain MRSA prevalence comparable to other centrality measures, then it may even be the preferable centrality measure, since it is simple both conceptually and computationally.

2.2.2 Weighted and unweighted betweenness centrality

Another centrality concept comes from thinking about the traffic through a node. If we assume traffic originate between pairs of nodes with equal rate, and travel through the network along shortest paths, the amount of traffic through a node would then be proportional to its betweenness centrality. More technically, let $\sigma(i,j)$ be the number of shortest paths between i and j (a shortest path does not have to be unique) and let $\sigma_l(i,j)$ be the number of shortest paths between i and j that pass l, then l's betweenness centrality is

$$C_B(l) = \sum_j \sum_{i \neq j} \frac{\sigma_l(i,j)}{\sigma(i,j)}. \quad (1)$$

This definition holds for both weighted and unweighted networks (although for weighted networks the shortest path is often unique and so the denominator is strictly one).

2.2.3 PageRank

Proposed as a measure to rank web pages, PageRank takes inspiration from a Web surfer's behavior. If people would follow hyperlinks randomly except occasionally when they go to a random page, then the popularity of a page would be proportional to its PageRank. Algorithmically, PageRank is easiest to describe as an iterative process. Let $C_P^t(i)$ be the PageRank centrality of node i at iteration t, then

$$C_P^{t+1}(i) = \frac{1-d}{N} + d \sum_{j \in \Gamma_i^{\text{in}}} \frac{C_P^t(j)}{k_j^{\text{out}}}, \quad (2)$$

where Γ_i^{in} is the set of nodes with a link pointing to i and k_j^{out} is the out-degree of j. d is a parameter that sets the balance between when the surfer follows a link and move to a random node. In this paper, we use the standard value $d = 0.85$. PageRank belongs to a class of centrality measures (including eigenvector centrality and Katz' centrality) that imagine a flow of centrality along the edges, and the actual centrality values as the steady state distribution of this flow [10].

2.2.4 Overturn

In addition to the static network measures, we also measured the overturn of patients of a unit, defined as the average number of patients entering the unit per day.

2.3 Constructing the control set

In some of our analyses, we need to compare our statistics for the MRSA-positive patients with the results for a random control set of patients that are not tested for MRSA. We generate the control set by, for every MRSA-case, finding one person from the set of non-tested patients that stays about as long time in the health care system (within 904 days) as the MRSA case. Furthermore, to get patients with similar clinical conditions, we restricted the control cases to those entering the healthcare system at the same unit as the specific patient. To make the dataset complete, we also needed to assign a test date. We choose this as the test date of the original infected person.

2.4 Prevalence

As a measure of the (relative) prevalence of MRSA at a unit, we calculate

$$P(i) = \frac{D_I(i)}{D(i)}, \tag{3}$$

where $D_I(i)$ is the total number of days a patient that has tested positive spends at unit i. $D(i)$ is the accumulated patient-days of i. A case of MRSA can be prevalent in a unit for one of two reasons. Either the case through transmission became a new case of MRSA while staying in that unit, or the case was admitted to the unit with an earlier diagnose of MRSA.

2.5 Response to infected patients

When a patient tests positive with MRSA, the healthcare system might move the patient to particular units as a precautionary measure after the diagnosis. Such units could have differing network characteristics (such as being smaller and less central). We addressed this issue by measuring network structure of the units as a function of the time when the patient was there, relative to the date of the positive test.

3 Results

3.1 Basic structure of the network of units

The unit network had 8,507 units and 3,185,710 links giving a mean number of neighbors of 749. In Figure 2A, we study the growth of the number of units mentioned (in the context of a patient being admitted to or discharged from a unit) over windows of constant size, from random starting points. This number grew first rapidly, later following a linear increase (see Figure 2A). The rapid initial growth comes from the units present in the beginning of the dataset being mentioned (through a patient being admitted or recharged at the unit) for the first time. The later linear increase comes from reorganization and re-registration of primarily private units. The number of links between units showed a sublinear growth (Figure 2B), reflecting that the distribution of the frequency of patient transfer was broadly distributed (not shown).

Next, we tried to get a more detailed view of the network structure of the aggregated unit network. In Figure 3A, we plot its in-degree distribution - the probability mass function of the number of units that ever sent a patient to a particular unit. This distribution roughly follows power-law with an exponential cutoff. This is interesting since even broader degree distributions, like power-law distributions, make the spreading faster and epidemic thresholds lower [20]. The in- and out-degrees of units are very similar, especially in the

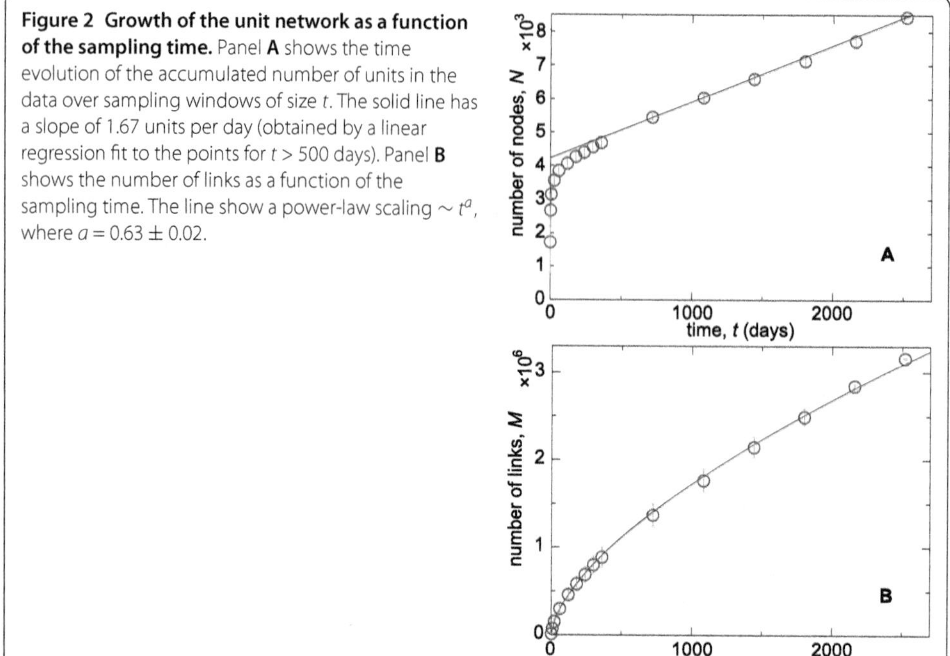

Figure 2 Growth of the unit network as a function of the sampling time. Panel **A** shows the time evolution of the accumulated number of units in the data over sampling windows of size t. The solid line has a slope of 1.67 units per day (obtained by a linear regression fit to the points for $t > 500$ days). Panel **B** shows the number of links as a function of the sampling time. The line show a power-law scaling $\sim t^a$, where $a = 0.63 \pm 0.02$.

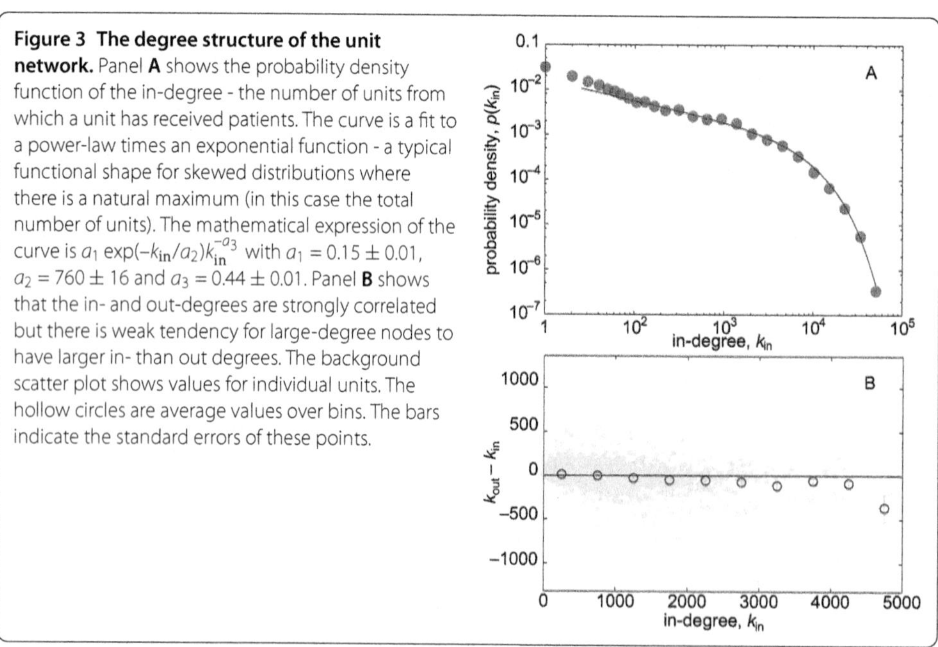

Figure 3 The degree structure of the unit network. Panel **A** shows the probability density function of the in-degree - the number of units from which a unit has received patients. The curve is a fit to a power-law times an exponential function - a typical functional shape for skewed distributions where there is a natural maximum (in this case the total number of units). The mathematical expression of the curve is $a_1 \exp(-k_{in}/a_2)k_{in}^{-a_3}$ with $a_1 = 0.15 \pm 0.01$, $a_2 = 760 \pm 16$ and $a_3 = 0.44 \pm 0.01$. Panel **B** shows that the in- and out-degrees are strongly correlated but there is weak tendency for large-degree nodes to have larger in- than out degrees. The background scatter plot shows values for individual units. The hollow circles are average values over bins. The bars indicate the standard errors of these points.

sense that none of the nodes with very high in-degree have a low out-degree, and vice versa (Figure 3B). This figure shows that there is a small tendency that the difference between in- and out-degree decrease with the in-degree, but the main result is that this correlation is weak. There are mechanisms that can explain both the decreasing tendency of $k_{out} - k_{in}$ and the fact that it is rather small. In the case that a patient is referred to another unit, and then returns shortly afterwards to the original unit - a common series of events - there will be a flow in both directions, the link will be bidirectional and thus contribute equally to k_{in} and k_{out}. On the other hand, if we assume some units are more in demand than oth-

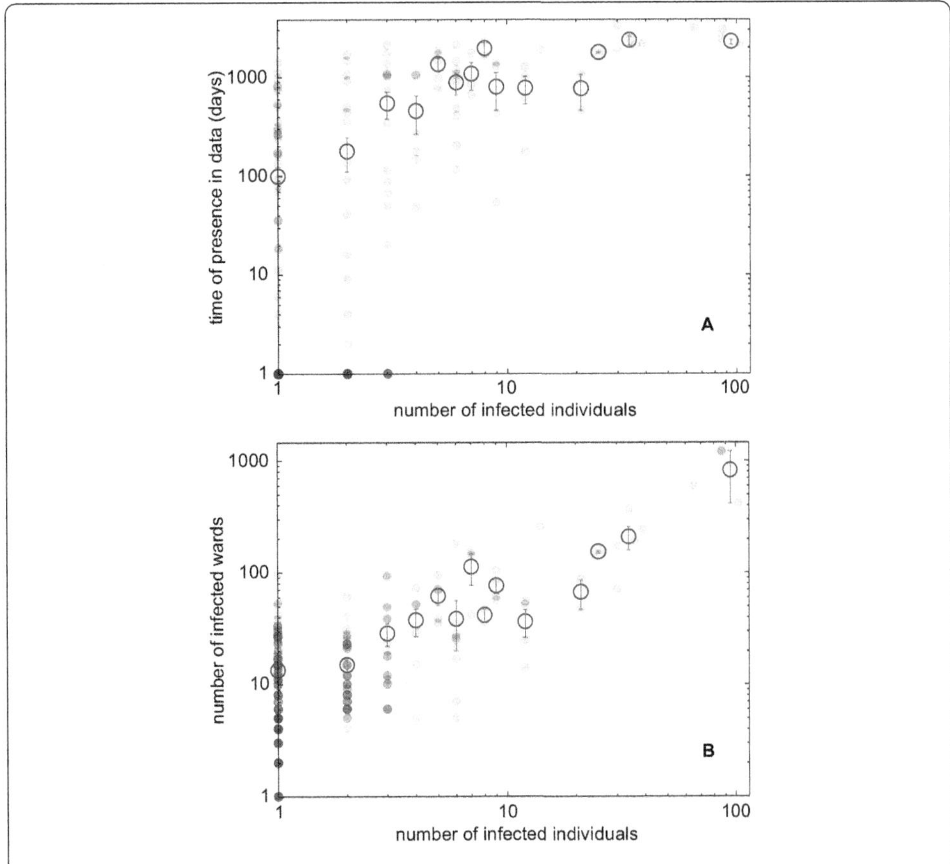

Figure 4 Network statistics for different MRSA clones. Each point in the background scatterplots corresponds to one clone of MRSA. Panel A shows the duration of the infection - from the first to the last day someone who has tested positive with a strain is present in the data - as a function of the total number of cases of the clone. In panel B, we see the number of units ever visited by a patient infected with the clone in question, as a function of the total number of cases. The circles represent average values in bins of exponentially increasing sizes (logarithmic binning). Bars indicate standard errors.

ers, while at the same time not requiring more service than usual, then that would give a decreasing trend in a $k_{out} - k_{in}$ vs k_{out} plot. If there is such a celebrity effect in this data, however, we deem it too small to mention.

In summary, the unit network had a skewed degree distribution - which in principle would speed up disease spreading - but not as skewed as scale-free networks [16, 17], that has been argued to model many types of contact patterns. The network was also symmetric in the sense that the in- and out-degrees were similar between units.

3.2 Statistics for different genotypes

As mentioned, the MRSA isolates were genotyped (multi-locus sequence typing by pulsed-field gel electrophoresis [21]), which offers the possibility to tell whether MRSA transmission could have occurred between two MRSA cases that had been admitted to the same unit simultaneously when one of the cases was already diagnosed with the disease and the other case still MRSA negative. In Figure 4, we show some quantities describing the outbreak statistics of different epidemiologic types. We note from panel A that the size of the outbreaks for the different types are broadly distributed with a few types having infected around a hundred patients while the majority of clones only infected a few.

Walker *et al.* made a similar observation studying data from the Oxford region of United Kingdom [15]. Probably the more common clones are associated with infections within the health care, while the more rare ones are primarily community acquired. The duration of the presence of a clone in the data - the time between the test-dates of the first and last infected patient - varies much. The most long-lived clones are present in the data throughout the sampling period. Figure 4A shows the time of presence as a function of the total number of infected individuals of that particular clone. It is an increasing function for smaller outbreaks and seems to stabilize for longer outbreak sizes. That the points seem to converge is most likely a cut-off effect from the limited sampling time. In Figure 4B, we show the number of infected units as a function of the total size of the outbreak for all the clones. The average number of infected units scale linearly with the number of infected patients. This tells us what one would assume from the beginning - there is no difference between common and rare types in their distribution in the unit network with respect to the network position.

3.3 Network-structural determinants of MRSA prevalence

The most natural candidates for units that play an important role in the spreading of HAIs are the ones at the center of the network. As mentioned, there are different ways of measuring centrality, all capturing different aspects of the concept. Instead of reasoning about which one that is most appropriate in our case, we tested several of the most common centrality metrics. In Figure 5, we show the dependence of the MRSA prevalence as a function of the total number of patient days at the unit. There was a weak tendency for units of intermediate in-degree to have higher MRSA prevalence, but the chance to find a MRSA positive patient in a high-degree unit was almost as high. The low-degree units with zero prevalence are so few that, by stochastic fluctuations, they just happen to be zero. This is not remarkable - these units not only have low-degree, they had few patients too, and in the entire dataset there are only about 0.4% positive cases.

In Figure 6, we separated units with zero and non-zero prevalence and plot prevalence in the non-zero units as a function of the four centrality measures - in-degree (which according to the results shown in Figure 2 amounts to the same figure as out-degree), PageRank, betweenness and weighted betweenness. The relationship between MRSA-prevalence and the four measures of centrality was similar, as is evident from Figure 6. First, the fraction of units with at least one MRSA cases increased with a sigmoidal dependence of the logarithm of all the centrality measures. Second, of the units which ever cared for MRSA-cases, there was a negative correlation with centrality. In other words, out of the units that

Figure 5 Average MRSA prevalence as a function of in-degree. The prevalence values are averaged for all units of a certain in-degree. Prevalence is defined as the ration of patient hours of MRSA infected patients and all patients. The bars indicate standard errors. The data is logarithmically binned.

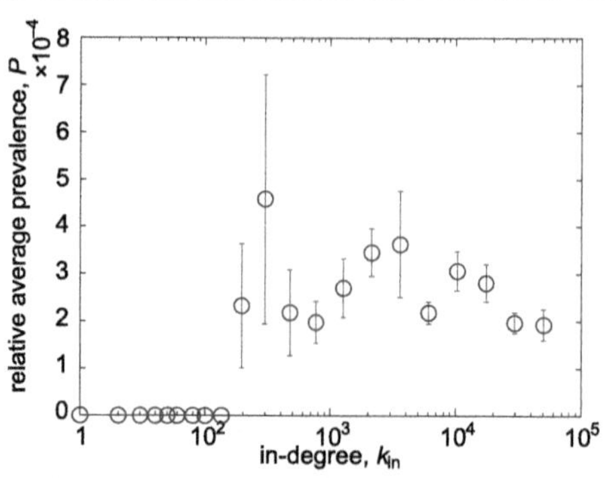

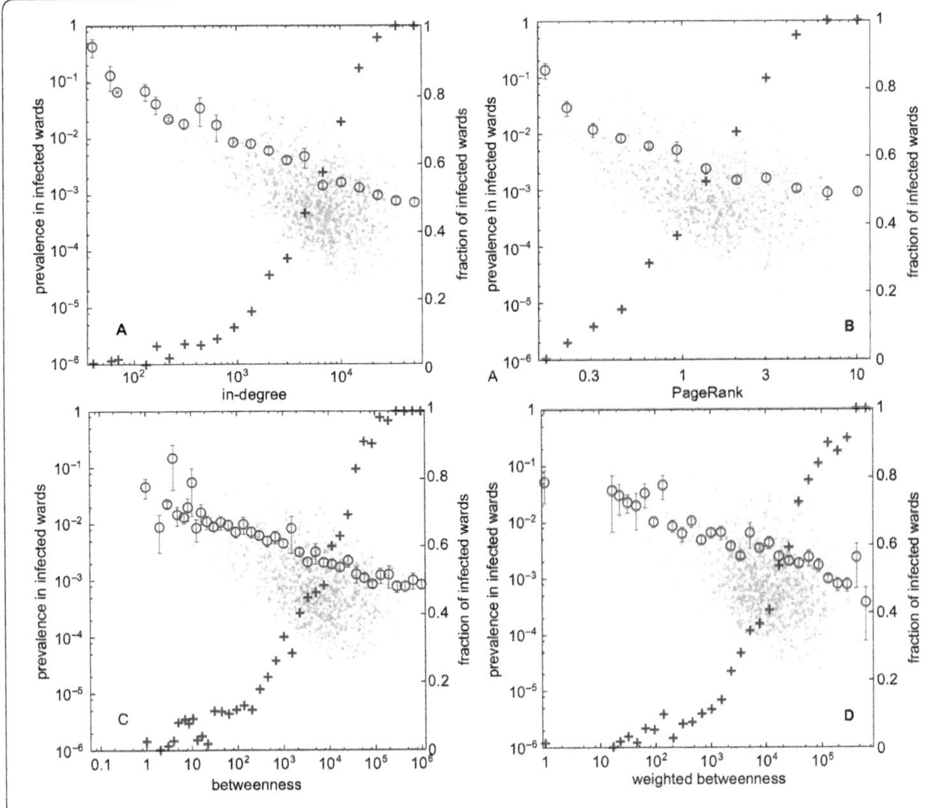

Figure 6 Correlation between prevalence indicators and network metrics. The plus symbols (corresponding to the right-hand abscissae) show the fraction of units with non-zero prevalence (i.e., where there has been at least one MRSA patient). The open circles represent the average prevalence (measured by the fraction of hospital days of infected patients out of the total patient days at the unit) in the units with non-zero prevalence. The point cloud shows the prevalence for individual units.

had any MPSA patient the peripheral ones (those low centrality) had a higher average load. These two factors combined did almost, but not completely, cancel out, so that the average prevalence has a weak peak for intermediate centrality values (cf. Figure 4). In summary, the MRSA prevalence has a weak dependence on centrality measures, probably too weak to be of practical use in the control of MRSA. Of course, it is often neither convenient nor feasible to impose a strict control of the patient flow, but if it followed the hierarchical, administrative organization of the healthcare systems, then the network structure would probably be more useful for controlling the disease spreading. Since that would compartmentalize the patient flow, it would also slow down the spreading - one outbreak could be effectively confined to one unit, e.g. hospital, of the healthcare system. To some extent, this is an ongoing effort within the administration of the healthcare system.

3.4 The trajectory of patients in the healthcare system

In Figure 7, we plotted the fraction of patients that were hospitalized as a function of when they tested positive t. We notice that both the increase before the test date, and decay after, is exponential. This reflects an exponential distribution of hospitalization times. It is common that patients undergo a thorough examination, including MRSA testing, on the day they become hospitalized. This explains the most asymmetric feature between the curves before and after t - the jump as t approaches zero from below.

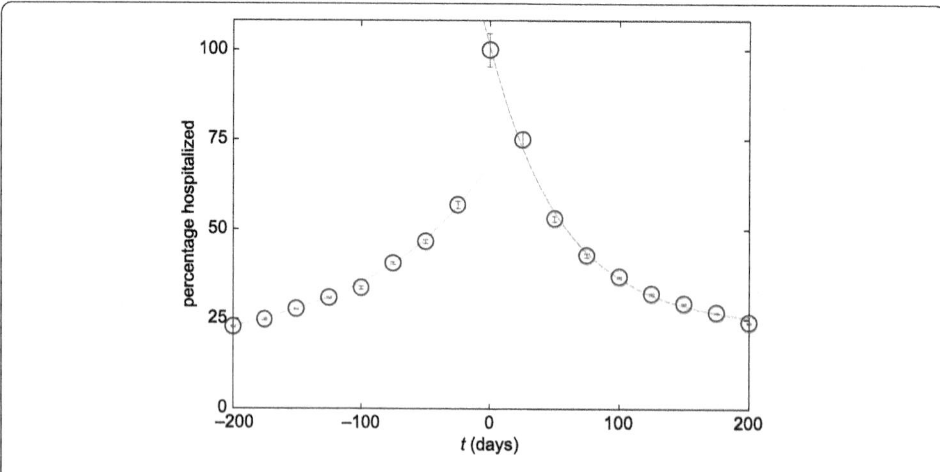

Figure 7 The probability that a patient is hospitalized a time *t* from the date of a positive test. The curves are fits to an exponential form $a_0 + a_1 \exp(-t/a_2)$ with $a_0 = 875 \pm 47$, $a_1 = 2{,}939 \pm 60$ and $a_2 = 56 \pm 3$ days before $t = 0$, and $a_0 = 624 \pm 89$, $a_1 = 1{,}985 \pm 100$ and $a_2 = -97 \pm 14$ days. Our control set would have a time independent level around 20%.

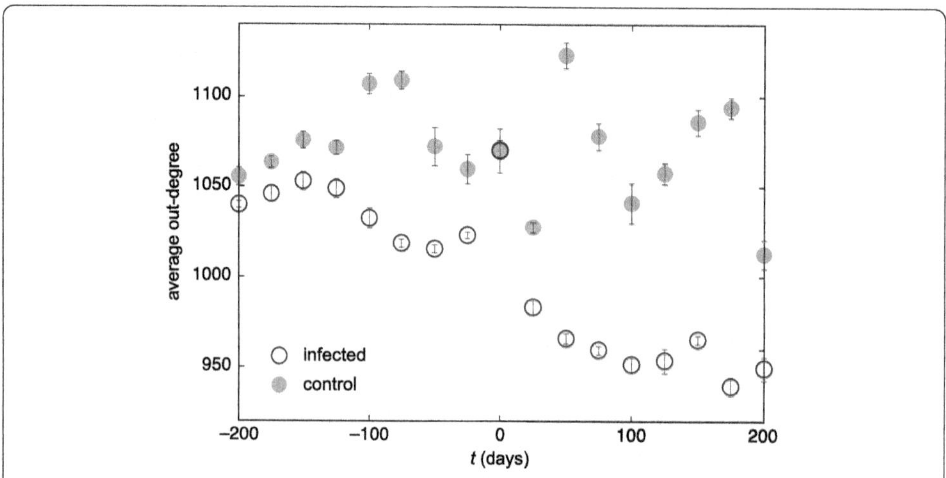

Figure 8 Average out-degree of the unit of an MRSA-positive relative to when the patient tested positive. The ordinate shows the average out-degree of the units where the patients in the case and control groups were at the time Δt relative to the date the person tested positive. The bars represent standard errors. The control group consists of patients with similar hospital history as the MRSA cases (for details see the text).

In Figure 8, we show the centrality of the unit as a function of the time relative to the date for testing positive with MRSA. The control case curve is, as predicted, quite constant. This is not true for the MRSA positives, whose units decrease in centrality with time. There can be two explanations for this phenomenon. First, this observation may reflect the response of the hospital system; i.e. to send the patients to more specialized (perhaps deliberately isolated) units. Second, it could be that the disease itself (i.e. the condition of the patient), leads the patient to units of lower centrality. From the data we have, these two scenarios are indistinguishable. This figure hints that there are more regularities to be discovered if we change from a unit to an individual perspective, something we plan for future work.

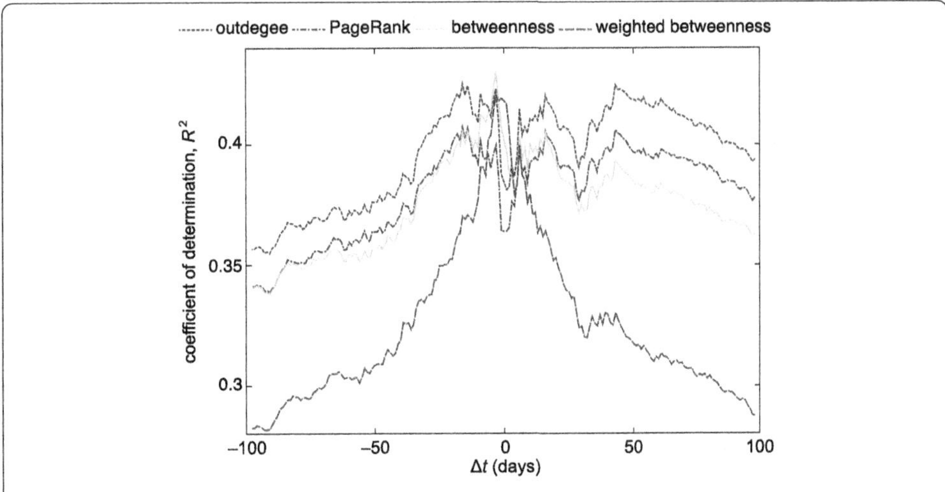

Figure 9 Strength of correlation (measured by R^2) between prevalence and static network measures as a function of the time when a patient tests positive. For this plot, we start from scatter plots between centrality measures and prevalence - like the ones in Figure 6 - and make a linear regression on these to calculate R^2, but we restrict the data to periods between the time the patient tests positive and Δt.

3.5 Correlations between simulated outbreak sizes and centrality

One explanation of the divergence of Figure 8 could be that the health care system was required to take precautionary measures if one treats an MRSA-positive patient. To investigate this further, we simulated disease transmission originating from one focal patient that we assumed was infective from a time $-t$ before the test date (i.e. we use the minus sign to indicate the infective period starts before the test date) to the test occasion. We used the SIR model for the disease dynamics as detailed above. In general, nodes that are more central give larger outbreak sizes. We quantify this trend by the coefficient of determination R^2 between the average outbreak size in the simulation and various measures of the centrality of the unit where the patient tested positive. R^2 can also be interpreted as a measure of the strength of the descriptive or predictive power of the centrality measure. We diagram both positive and negative t values to test the scenario that proactive measures are ineffective, or have a delayed effect. The results, plotted in Figure 9, show that the out-degree has the strongest predictive power for almost all t values (the in-degree gives a very similar curve and is thus not shown). This means that degree is the best static measure to identify risk units. The fact that degree, as a measure of centrality, discards secondary transmission events (the network two steps away from a node does not matter) suggests that only the local surroundings of the units matter in the outbreak dynamics. If one looks at the turnover of patients in the unit instead of the degree, or any other static network measure, the predictability increases much (Figure 10), which suggest that the turnover of patients is more important than the topology of the static unit network. The general, peaked shape of the R^2 vs t curves reflects that the more one includes of the patients history far from (before or after) the location at the test date, the less is the outbreak size correlated with the network structure of the unit where the patient is at the test date. This is natural, of course, but it does show that the structure of the unit network is not completely random - there is structure enough to affect the prevalence of MRSA.

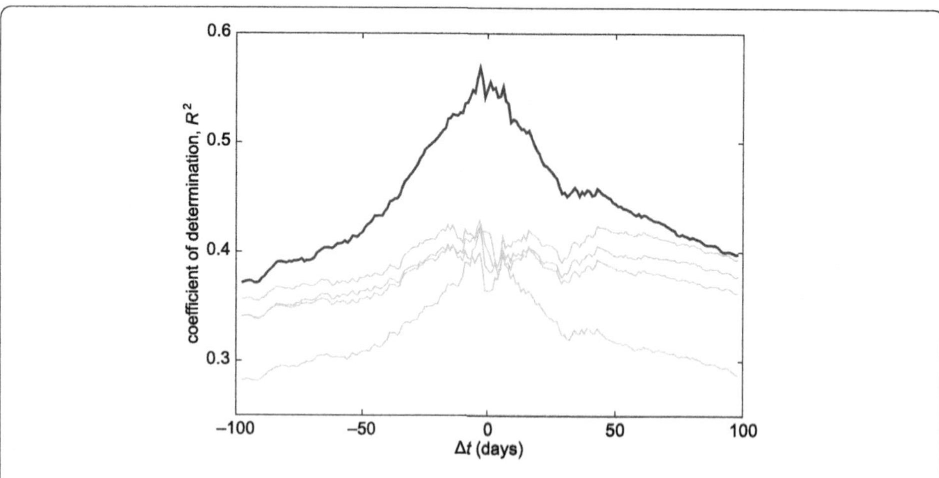

Figure 10 Strength of correlation (measured by R^2) between prevalence and overturn of patients as a function of the time when a patient tests positive. This curve is of the same type as the curves in Figure 9 but for a dynamic measure (the turnover of patients) rather than static network measures (for comparison, the curves of Figure 9 are shown, but greyed out).

4 Discussion

Since it is possible to estimate the contact structure, in terms of both time and network topology, behind the transmission of hospital-acquired disease, such diseases are well suited for studying with network theory. In this work, we analyzed a large dataset of patient flow over seven years in a healthcare system. This is such a large dataset that unless one wants to be restricted to the fastest quantities to calculate, one needs to reduce it further. One natural such reduction, the one we are investigating in this work, is to investigate the unit network (where two units are connected if a patient has transferred from one unit to another).

Just like the network of patients in close enough proximity for MRSA transmission, the unit network is not static. Indeed, private clinics can change their id numbers in the data. This phenomenon gives, effectively speaking noise to our measurements. With more consistent information about which units that split and merge, or change id number, we could model the system more accurately. Our results do still give a lower bound of the structural effects of the patient flow. Another option would be to break the network into shorter time segments during which the set of units is more stable (cf. Ref. [22]), but those segments cannot be too short - then they would not cover the infrequent links that could be very important for the size of an outbreak [23]. The network structure of the unit network is characterized by a skewed distribution of in- and out-degrees, but far from as broad distributions as power-laws (that are known to have low epidemic thresholds [16, 17]). The in- and out-degrees are strikingly symmetric, mostly because of a large fraction of reciprocal links.

Measuring the prevalence of MRSA by the ratio of patient-hours by patients that has tested positive with MRSA at the unit to the total patient hours at the unit, we conclude that there was a weak tendency for heightened prevalence for units of intermediate centrality. We also noted that the various centrality measures gave qualitatively similar results. Even though in most network models and empirical networks various centrality measures are usually positively correlated, some types of regularities can cause them to be less so, our unit network did not show any such effects. In sum, even though the healthcare system is hierarchically organized, the patient flow in our dataset is rather random. This makes the unit network inefficient in predicting units of increased MRSA prevalence. Another reason for the weak correlations is that Sweden in general [24], and this data set in particular, has a low MRSA prevalence. This suggests that most cases are community acquired (Ref. [24] argues that most Swedish MRSA cases are infected abroad). On the other hand, around the time of the test, the MRSA carriers show a rather clear tendency to move to units that are more peripheral. Another trend we observed was that the prevalences of the different types were correlated with the centrality of the unit where the patient tested positive. This correlation was strongest when the turnover of patients was used as a (dynamic) measure of centrality. We also found that patients have an exponentially increasing probability to be present in the healthcare before the date of testing positive, and a decreasing probability afterwards. These probabilities are asymmetric in time with a larger chance of being present in the health care system after the test date. The increasing presence before the test date suggests most of the contagion has occurred within the healthcare system. The increasing presence after the test date indicates that the patients' hospitalization is related to the MRSA infection.

5 Conclusions

Although there are correlations between prevalence and centrality of units, these were too weak to be practical for identifying risk units. This could probably be changed with a more structured flow, which would also restrict the outbreak sizes (cf. Ref. [14]). The trajectory of patients shows that the disease itself and the health care's response to it makes patients move to less central units, where the expected size of outbreaks they could cause is smaller.

The fact that the more dynamic aspects of our study - both the trajectories of the MRSA-positive patients and the fact that flow is the most predictive centrality measure for the outbreak sizes - showed clearer deviations from the expected results, suggests that dynamic representations of the patient flow at a unit level could be a fruitful direction for future studies. It would also be interesting to remake the analysis with more exact data - e.g. a large-scale study of people's proximity by RFID sensors accompanied by uniform and comprehensive testing of all the patients. This would probably give clearer correlations, and also results directly derived from measurable properties of the contagion process and contact patterns.

List of abbreviations used

MRSA, methicillin resistant *Staphylococcus aureus*; HAI, healthcare associated infections.

Competing interests

The authors declare that they have no competing interests.

Authors' contributions

JO, FL and PH conceived the study. JO and FL performed the analysis. JO, PH and MS wrote the manuscript.

Author details

[1]Department of Mathematics, Universität Koblenz-Landau, Koblenz, 56070, Germany. [2]Department of Sociology, Stockholm University, Stockholm, 10691, Sweden. [3]Institute for Future Studies, Stockholm, 10131, Sweden. [4]Department of Medical Epidemiology and Biostatistics, Karolinska Institutet, Stockholm, Sweden. [5]Department of Communicable Disease Control, Stockholm County Council, Stockholm, Sweden. [6]Department of Energy Science, Sungkyunkwan University, Suwon, 440-746, Korea. [7]IceLab, Department of Physics, Umeå University, Umeå, 90187, Sweden.

Authors' information

This paper is a very interdisciplinary collaboration between an applied mathematician (JO), a sociologist (FL), a medical scientist (MS) and a physicist (PH). For further information, please contact the corresponding author.

Acknowledgements

The authors thank Martin Rosvall for comments. FL was supported by Riksbankens Jubileumsfond (The Bank of Sweden Tercentenary Foundation) Grant nr. P12-0705:1. PH was supported by Basic Science Research Program through the National Research Foundation of Korea (NRF) funded by the Ministry of Education (2013R1A1A2011947) and the Swedish Research Council.

Endnote

[a] The data used was approved by the Regional Ethical Review Board in Stockholm (Record Number 2004/5:8).

References

1. Liljeros F, Edling CR, Amaral LAN (2003) Sexual networks: implication for the transmission of sexually transmitted infection. Microbes Infect 5:189-196
2. Breathnach AS (2005) Nosocomial infections. Medicine 33:22-26
3. Meyers LA, Newman MEJ, Martin M, Schrag S (2003) Applying network theory to epidemics: control measures for outbreaks of Mycoplasma pneumoniae. Emerg Infect Dis 9:204-210
4. Albrich WC, Halbarth S (2008) Health-care workers: source, vector, or victim of MRSA? Lancet Infect Dis 8:289-301
5. McBryde ES, Bradley LC, Whitby M, McElwain DLS (2004) An investigation of contact transmission of methicillin-resistant Staphylococcus aureus. J Hosp Infect 58:104-108
6. Karkada UH et al (2011) Limiting the spread of highly resistant hospital-acquired microorganisms via critical care transfers: a simulation study. Intensive Care Med 37:1633-1640
7. Lee BY et al (2013) The importance of nursing homes in the spread of methicillin-resistant Staphylococcus aureus (MRSA) among hospitals. Med Care 51:205-215
8. Liljeros F, Giesecke J, Holme P (2007) The contact network of inpatients in a regional health care system: a longitudinal case study. Math Popul Stud 14:269-284
9. Ueno T, Masuda N (2008) Controlling nosocomial infection based on structure of hospital social networks. J Theor Biol 254:655-666
10. Vanhems P et al (2013) Estimating potential infection transmission routes in hospital wards using wearable proximity sensors. PLoS ONE 8:e73970
11. Hornbeck T, Naylor D, Segre AM, Thomas G, Herman T, Polgreen PM (2012) Using sensor networks to study the effect of peripatetic healthcare workers on the spread of hospital-associated infections. J Infect Dis 206:1549-1557
12. Donker T, Wallinga J, Grundmann H (2010) Patient referral patterns and the spread of hospital-acquired infections through national health care networks. PLoS Comput Biol 6:e1000715
13. Donker T, Wallinga J, Slack R, Grundmann H (2012) Hospital networks and the dispersal of hospital-acquired pathogens by patient transfer. PLoS ONE 7:e35002
14. Donker T, Wallinga J, Grundmann H (2014) Dispersal of antibiotic-resistant high-risk clones by hospital networks: changing the patient direction can make all the difference. J Hosp Infect 86:34-41
15. Walker AS et al (2012) Characterization of Clostridium difficile hospital ward-based transmission using extensive epidemiological data and molecular typing. PLoS Med 9:e1001172
16. Newman MEJ (2010) Networks: an introduction. Oxford University Press, Oxford
17. Estrada E (2011) The structure of complex networks. Oxford University Press, Oxford
18. Jain R et al (2011) Veterans Affairs initiative to prevent methicillin-resistant Staphylococcus aureus infections. N Engl J Med 364:1419-1430
19. Huskins WC et al (2011) Intervention to reduce transmission of resistant bacteria in intensive care. N Engl J Med 364:1407-1418
20. Wang B, Cao L, Suzuki H, Aihara K (2012) Safety-information-driven human mobility patterns with metapopulation epidemic dynamics. Sci Rep 2:887
21. Melles DC, van Leeuwen WB, Snijders SV, Horst-Kreft D, Peeters JK, Verbrugh HA, van Belkum A (2007) Comparison of multilocus sequence typing (MLST), pulsed-field gel electrophoresis (PFGE), and amplified fragment length polymorphism (AFLP) for genetic typing of Staphylococcus aureus. J Microbiol Methods 69:371-375
22. Holme P (2013) Epidemiologically optimal static networks from temporal network data. PLoS Comput Biol 9:e1003142
23. Moore C, Newman MEJ (2000) Epidemics and percolation in small-world networks. Phys Rev E 61:5678-5682
24. Christenson B, Ardung B, Sylvan S (2011) Methicillin-resistant Staphylococcus aureus infections in Uppsala County, Sweden. Open Infect Dis J 5:107-114

10

Views to a war: systematic differences in media and military reporting of the war in Iraq

Karsten Donnay[1*] and Vladimir Filimonov[2]

*Correspondence: kdonnay@ethz.ch
[1] Department of Humanities, Social and Political Science, Chair of Sociology, Modeling and Simulation, ETH Zürich, Clausiusstrasse 50, Zürich, 8092, Switzerland
Full list of author information is available at the end of the article

Abstract

The quantitative study of violent conflict and its mechanisms has in recent years greatly benefited from the availability of detailed event data. With a number of highly visible studies both in the natural sciences and in political science using such data to shed light on the complex mechanisms underlying violent conflict, researchers have recently raised issues of systematic (reporting) biases. While many sources of bias are qualitatively known, biases in event data are usually not studied with quantitative methods. In this study we focus on a unique case - the conflict in Iraq - that is covered by two independently collected datasets: Iraq Body Count (IBC) reports of civilian casualties and Significant Action (SIGACT) military data. We systematically identify a number of key quantitative differences between the event reporting in the two datasets and demonstrate that even for subsets where both datasets are most consistent at an aggregate level, the daily time series and timing signatures of events differ significantly. This suggests that at any level of analysis the choice of dataset may substantially affect any inferences drawn, with attendant consequences for a number of recent studies of the conflict in Iraq. We further outline how the insights gained from our analysis of conflict event data have broader implications for studies using similar data on other social processes.

Keywords: event data; reporting bias; conflict; Iraq

1 Introduction

In recent years the increasing availability of detailed data on conflict events has led to a number of highly visible studies that explore the dynamics of violent conflict [1–4]. Taking a natural science or complex systems perspective, these studies complement a quickly growing quantitative literature in political science that heavily relies on detailed empirical records to systematically study the micro-dynamics of conflict, in particular how individual- or group-level interactions lead to the larger conflict dynamics we observe [5–9].

The conflict event datasets used in these studies primarily draw on media reports and rely to varying degrees on automatic coding as well as the expertise of country or subject experts for coding decisions and quality control [10, 11]. In specific cases - for example in studies focusing on single countries, cities or regions - data may also be based on records collected through Non-Governmental Organizations (NGOs), local newspapers or researchers' own field work [7, 9, 12]. These conflict event data, however, have been found to be prone to bias [13–16]. Even for otherwise unbiased and flawless research designs this may strongly affect any inferences with regard to conflict dynamics and mechanisms. Data biases do not only arise from variations in data quality and coding across different datasets but also from systematic uncertainties associated with the data collection efforts themselves. Unfortunately, such issues are notoriously hard to identify and difficult to eliminate in the process of data collection, even within institutionalized large-scale collection efforts. Furthermore, identification of potential biases in existing datasets is complicated by the fact that usually not more than one independently generated dataset exists, making it very difficult to infer any biases *post hoc*.

In this study, we focus specifically on a unique empirical case - the conflict in Iraq - that is covered by two independently collected datasets, one of them based on media sources (Iraq Body Count or 'IBC'), the other collected 'on the ground' by the U.S. military (Significant Action or 'SIGACT' data). We use these data to quantitatively test agreement of the event reporting in the two datasets at different temporal resolution and thus systematically identify relative biases. In particular, we find that even for subsets where both datasets are most consistent at an aggregate level the daily time series of events are significantly different. This suggests that whether analyses are based on IBC or SIGACT data may substantially affect the inferences drawn. Our findings are thus highly relevant to a number of recent studies that investigate detailed event dynamics of the war in Iraq using both IBC [2, 3, 17–19] and SIGACT data [8, 20] and contribute to the ongoing debate on issues and implications of data quality in conflict event data.

More broadly, our study speaks to a quickly growing literature that systematically analyzes highly resolved data on social processes. This includes work that uses news media articles to detect international tensions [21] or analyzes Twitter messages to detect mood changes [22]. In fact, much of 'Big Data' derived from artifacts of human interactions corresponds to time-stamped information about social processes. Studies analyzing such data, however, only very rarely consider the potentially substantive biases arising from how they are generated. In fact, these data are subject to much of the same structural limitations as conflict event data (see Section 2.2), with resulting biases that are just as hard to identify and difficult to infer from data *post hoc*. Similarly, inferences based on such data may thus also be substantially affected by the choice of dataset, its characteristics and limitations.

This study is structured as follows. Section 2 introduces the empirical case and the datasets used: IBC data and the U.S. military (SIGACT) dataset made available by *The Guardian*. In Section 3 we systematically compare the reporting of events in both datasets, starting with an aggregate comparison before turning to an in depth analysis of the time series of number of events and event severity. We further analyze the timing signatures in each dataset separately. Section 4 discusses implications of our findings for quantitative analyses of conflict and, more broadly, for studies of social processes that rely on similar data.

2 The case of Iraq

The Iraq conflict ranks among the most violent conflicts of the early 21st century and is characterized by excessive violence against civilians with fatality estimates exceeding at least 130,000 by mid-2014 [23].[a] In mid-2003 the conflict began as an insurgency directed at the U.S. military, its allies and the Iraqi central government. Attacks were initially largely carried out by forces loyal to Saddam Hussein, but by early 2004 radical religious groups and Iraqis opposed to the foreign occupation were responsible for the majority of attacks. The insurgency subsequently intensified throughout 2004 and 2005. Increasingly marked by excessive sectarian violence between the Sunni minority and Shia majority the conflict rapidly escalated in 2006 and 2007. Following the U.S.-led troop 'surge' in 2007, a massive increase of U.S. boots on the ground accompanied by a major shift in counter-insurgency tactics [24–26], the conflict eventually de-escalated significantly throughout 2008. After the U.S. withdrawal from Iraq in 2011 the country continues to experience acts of violence on a (close to) daily basis, both as a result of the continued insurgency against the central government but also increasingly again as a consequence of a renewed escalation of sectarian violence. The recent take-over of the north-western (Sunni) provinces by the Islamic State of Iraq and the Levant (ISIL), an Al-Qaeda affiliate, now even threatens the very existence of a multi-ethnic Iraq.

2.1 Data sources

In our analysis we draw on data from the two most commonly used Iraq-specific datasets: Iraq Body Count (IBC), a web-based data collection effort administered by Conflict Casualties Monitor Limited (London) [23], and U.S. military (SIGACT) data available through *The Guardian* [27]. We are very mindful of the sensitivity of the SIGACT data and the debate surrounding their use in academic studies.[b] While this debate continues studies are making use of these data, most notably a recent political science publication on Iraq [8] and an analysis published in the Proceedings of the National Academy of Science (PNAS) using data on Afghanistan [4]. Note that subsets of the SIGACT Iraq data had previously been made accessible to selected researchers and institutions [6, 17, 28] making SIGACT one of the two leading sources of data on the war in Iraq.

The IBC dataset covers violent events resulting in civilian deaths from January 1, 2003 onward until present day and is being updated continuously. We rely here on the publicly available version of the IBC records that does not disaggregate by perpetrator group [23]. The data made available through *The Guardian* contains information on all 'significant actions' (SIGACTs) reported by units of the U.S. military in Iraq that resulted in at least one casualty. The dataset covers the period January 1, 2004 until December 31, 2009 but is missing 2 intervals of 1 month each (from April 30, 2004 to June 1, 2004 and from February 28, 2009 to April 1, 2009) [27]. In order to be consistent in our dataset comparison we have selected our study period as ranging from June 1, 2004 to February 28, 2009 - a period covered by both datasets without any gaps. This period covers the main phases of the conflict described above.[c]

The two datasets differ significantly with regard to the geocoding of conflict events. IBC provides 'human description' of the location (such as 'near Birtilla, east of Mosul' or 'behind al-Faiha'a hospital, central Basra') which implies limited spatial accuracy. In comparison, SIGACT data entries are categorized by U.S. military regional command but more importantly geo-tagged with latitude and longitude coordinates. These coordinates are truncated at a tenth of a degree (about 10 km) for Iraq outside of Baghdad (Figure 1) and at a hundredth of a degree (about 1 km) for the military zone of Baghdad (Figure 1, inlay). The two datasets further differ with regard to their temporal resolution. SIGACT events carry timestamps with a resolution of minutes while IBC events are generally coded to daily precision only. Finally, in contrast to SIGACT data which reports the number of individuals

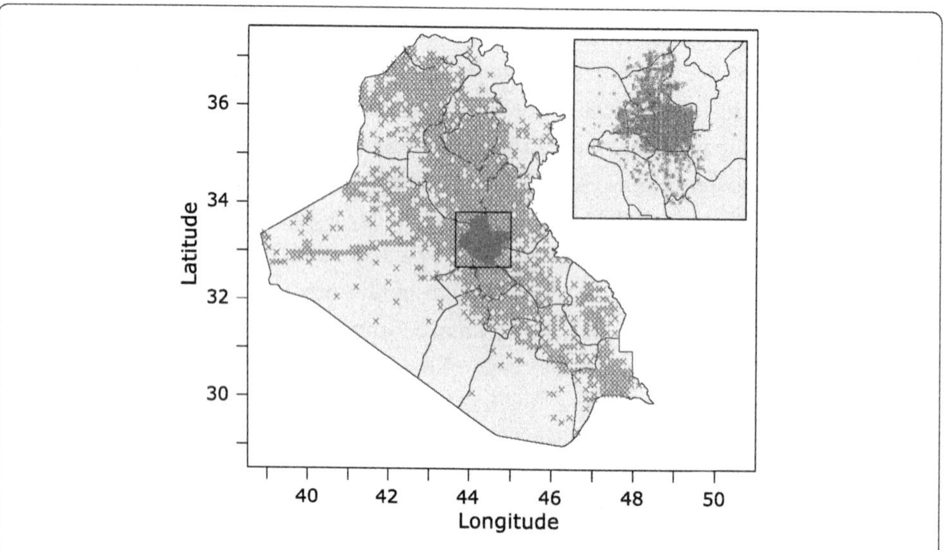

Figure 1 SIGACT data for all of Iraq and for the Baghdad regional command (inlay). Shape files for the country and district boundaries were downloaded from the database of Global Administrative Areas (GADM), http://www.gadm.org.

killed (KIA) and wounded (WIA) for both military actors and civilians, the IBC dataset exclusively covers deadly violence against civilians.[d] In order to compare the two datasets we thus restricted the SIGACT data to entries pertaining to deadly violence directed at civilians. Note that focusing on civilian casualties exclusively rather than including incidents that wounded civilians may, in fact, lead to a biased view of the violence dynamics in Iraq - simply because whether an attack lead to casualties or not may dependent more on chance than intent [29]. To control for this, we performed robustness checks where we additionally included the number of wounded civilians reported in SIGACT; these results are included in Section 3 of Additional file 1.

2.2 Structural differences in reporting

There are a number of significant differences between the reporting underlying the IBC and SIGACT datasets that may introduce systematic biases in their respective coverage of violent events. An important source of data bias in geo-referenced event datasets arises directly from the 'spatial' nature of the data, i.e., the location of where a violent event occurs may already strongly influence both its chance of reporting and how it is reported [13, 15]. Such biases may simply be structural, for example, due to the fact that newspapers and their local sources - NGOs, development agencies etc. - often only maintain a constant presence in cities or certain regions of a country. Consequently, reporting likely has a specific *urban or regional bias*, i.e., a more complete coverage of events in those areas compared to others with only limited access [15]. This is often aligned with or equivalent to a *center-periphery* bias since the access and coverage of the media and its sources generally tend to be much lower in remote, peripheral regions compared to the capital or population centers [15]. The same may apply for government or military reporting, simply because administrative infrastructures and a permanent government presence (offices, police and military installations etc.) are often much less developed in the periphery. In volatile states a central government might even effectively not have any control over large parts of the country.

In Iraq the media-based reporting of IBC is quite likely affected by issues arising from limited coverage, especially for locations outside of the main population centers. SIGACT data may also be prone to spatial bias since the U.S. military or coalition forces did not maintain a constant presence everywhere in the country [29]. This limitation, however, should be minimal in a highly patrolled region such as Baghdad. For our quantitative analyses we have thus chosen to focus exclusively on the greater Baghdad area, by far the most violent region during the entire conflict. This choice guarantees that our analysis is not systematically affected by geographic reporting bias since within Baghdad both media-based data and SIGACT's field report-based reporting are least likely to be systematically constrained in their coverage.[e] Focusing on a comparably small and coherent spatial region also avoids the fallacy of studying time series of potentially unrelated or only weakly related incidents that are geographically far apart. The violence dynamics in Kirkuk in the predominantly Kurdish north, for example, are very different from the dynamics in Baghdad. In fact, we contend that since Baghdad was the main locus of violence during the conflict but least prone to geographically biased coverage, it represents the 'best case' scenario for the reporting of violent events in Iraq and any systematic differences in reporting we uncover should also apply to the full datasets.

Notice that even when focusing exclusively on the Baghdad area, IBC's reporting may be prone to additional biases that arise from its reliance on the quality and accuracy of the media coverage. There is ample evidence that newspaper reports of incidents are subject to a number of biases including selective reporting of certain types of events [30, 31], as well as better coverage of types of events that have occurred before and of larger events compared to smaller events [32]. Such size bias should be especially pronounced in situations with a high density of incidents and only limited reporting capacity - in Iraq this would have been most relevant during the escalation of the conflict in 2006-2007. SIGACT data on the other hand is directly based on military reports from the field and should therefore, as long as military presence is high as in the case of Baghdad, cover more incidents regardless of size. Based on these structural differences in the reporting we can therefore expect that:

(I) IBC should cover systematically fewer low casualty events than SIGACT,

but also that

(II) Differences in reporting, in particular of events with few casualties, should be greater the more intense the conflict.

Note that (II) also extends beyond mere coverage - i.e., whether an incident is reported at all - to the quality of reporting. The more intense the fighting the less accurately field reports are able to reflect casualty counts, simply because soldiers may not always be able to reliably account for all casualties in such situations [29]. Similarly, media reports may also not always precisely reflect 'true' casualty counts - in fact, IBC explicitly codes for lower and upper bounds of casualty estimates.[f]

In the case of events with larger casualty counts, the reliance of SIGACT on field reports may negatively affect reporting accuracy. One key reason is that longer and intense confrontations involving multiple units may be falsely reported as several separate incidents by each unit instead of being coded as one large episode. This may lead to over-reporting of the number of incidents and under-reporting of the number of casualties per incident. Note further that the categorization of incidents and identification of victims, in particular, may sometimes be ambiguous [29]. In fact, prior quantitative research confirms that the interest of the observer tends to affect how incidents are reported [33]. Ideological biases in media reporting - such as government-directed negative reporting on the opposition or simply general limitations to press freedom - result in an inaccurate representation of the situation in a country/region and may thus bias how events are reported [15].

In Iraq, we would further generally expect coalition troops' reporting of civilian casualties to be comparably more conservative than the news media. Modern counterinsurgency doctrines emphasize the importance of 'population-centric' warfare, favoring tactics and rules of engagement that minimize collateral civilian casualties [34]. In turn, this implies strong incentives for U.S. troops to keep civilian fatality reports of operations as low as possible. These incentives are strongest for comparably larger incidents with significant unintentional ('collateral') civilian casualties. Note, too, that especially during the escalation of violence in 2006-2007 the conflict in Iraq became highly politicized along the Sunni/Shia divide. This provided strong incentives for newspapers from either side to emphasize the atrocities of the other, i.e., to provide less conservative casualty estimates, especially for large incidents. Overall we can thus expect that

(III) IBC should report comparably more events with many casualties than SIGACT.

Note that in general the timing (and location) of attacks can be expected to be more accurate when derived from field reports compared to IBC, whose coverage is fundamentally constrained here since newspaper articles usually only report approximate times and locations. However, it is also known that SIGACT reporting in Iraq did not adhere to homogenous reporting standards throughout the entire conflict, including the integration of reports (or initial lack thereof) from Iraqi military units [29]. There is also a known issue of field reports being entered with midnight timestamps if the exact reporting time is unknown. These differences should not systematically affect aggregate agreement between the two datasets but may be important when analyzing the microstructure of the data and when matching entries day-by-day. It is important to also mention that both IBC and SIGACT improved their overall reporting throughout the conflict. Taking into account that additional biases may arise from reporting during intense conflict periods as discussed before, we would therefore expect that:

(IV) The most accurate day-by-day agreement between the two datasets should be found in the later, less violent stages of the war.

We will return to these four theoretical expectations when analyzing and interpreting the results of our quantitative data comparisons.

Before turning to our analysis of the data on Iraq we would like to emphasize that issues of data bias are, of course, not unique to conflict event data. Researchers, for example, increasingly rely on social media data - such as Twitter messages - to analyze social dynamics [22]. Similar to conflict event data, these messages are time-stamped and carry location information. The same is true for data on human mobility derived from mobile phone traces that provide detailed time-resolved information about the location of users [35]. In both cases, data may be subject to biases that arise from non-uniform geographic coverage: globally Twitter is known to be heavily biased towards users from North America, Europe and Asia [36] but it also tends to be biased towards urban populations in each country [37]. Mobile phone traces rely on data released by phone companies. Since customer base and coverage of companies tend to vary across regions, they may also have a distinct geographic bias.[g] As in the case of conflict event data the character of the data source may also lead to bias. Twitter, for example, only represents a small, non-representative sam-

Table 1 Datasets

Codename	Number of events		Number of casualties	
	KIA	KIA + WIA	KIA	KIA + WIA
IBC Baghdad	9,068		29,359-31,128	
SIGACT Baghdad	18,157	18,504	33,688	59,276
SIGACT 20 km	17,533	17,854	32,522	57,151
SIGACT 30 km	18,548	18,919	34,450	60,465
SIGACT 40 km	19,369	19,782	36,061	63,215

ple of the overall population [37]. And a recent study of the web presence of scientists on Wikipedia found that influential academic scholars are poorly represented [38]. This suggests that any scientometric analyses based on Wikipedia entries would have a strong relative bias compared to studies based on Facebook and Twitter, which tend to be much more consistent with citation-based metrics of academic impact [39]. The similarities in the sources of bias thus suggest that analyzing the implications of systematic bias in conflict event data also has broader implications for analyses using similar data on other social processes.

2.3 Baghdad data

The IBC Baghdad subset we analyze comprises events location-coded as 'Baghdad' but also those that carry more precise location tags such as 'Sadr City' or 'Hurriya'. In the SIGACT dataset we rely on the U.S. military's definition of the greater Baghdad area and the corresponding regional command 'MND-BAGHDAD'. As a robustness check we then perform each of our analyses for subdatasets generated by selecting all events in SIGACT that fall within a radius of 20 km, 30 km and 40 km from the city center. These analyses confirm that the choice of dataset does not affect our substantive findings - whenever not directly reported in the manuscript the results can be found in Section 3 of Additional file 1.

Table 1 shows comparative statistics of the five Baghdad subdatasets used in our analysis: (a) IBC data filtered for events in the greater Baghdad area, (b) SIGACT data filtered by Baghdad regional command and by geo-coordinates for a radius of (c) 20 km, (d) 30 km and (e) 40 km from the city center. In the aggregate it appears as if IBC reports a much smaller number of events (approximately 2-3 times smaller than in the SIGACT data). The total number of deaths over the period of analysis also differs but is comparably more consistent. Figure 2(a) and (b) show time series of events per day and casualties per event for both datasets. Visual comparison already suggests that at a disaggregate level the datasets differ substantially with regard to the number of events per day and casualties per event reported. Note further that while both datasets capture the escalation of violence in 2006-2007, not only the number of events and casualty counts differ but also the timing of when violence escalated most.

3 Results

In recent quantitative studies casualty distributions in Iraq have been analyzed in aggregate form [1, 2], but studies mostly focus on time series of events - monthly, bi-weekly or most often daily [2, 3, 8, 17, 20]. In line with theses different levels of analysis we will compare the reporting of IBC and SIGACT at different levels of disaggregation. We start

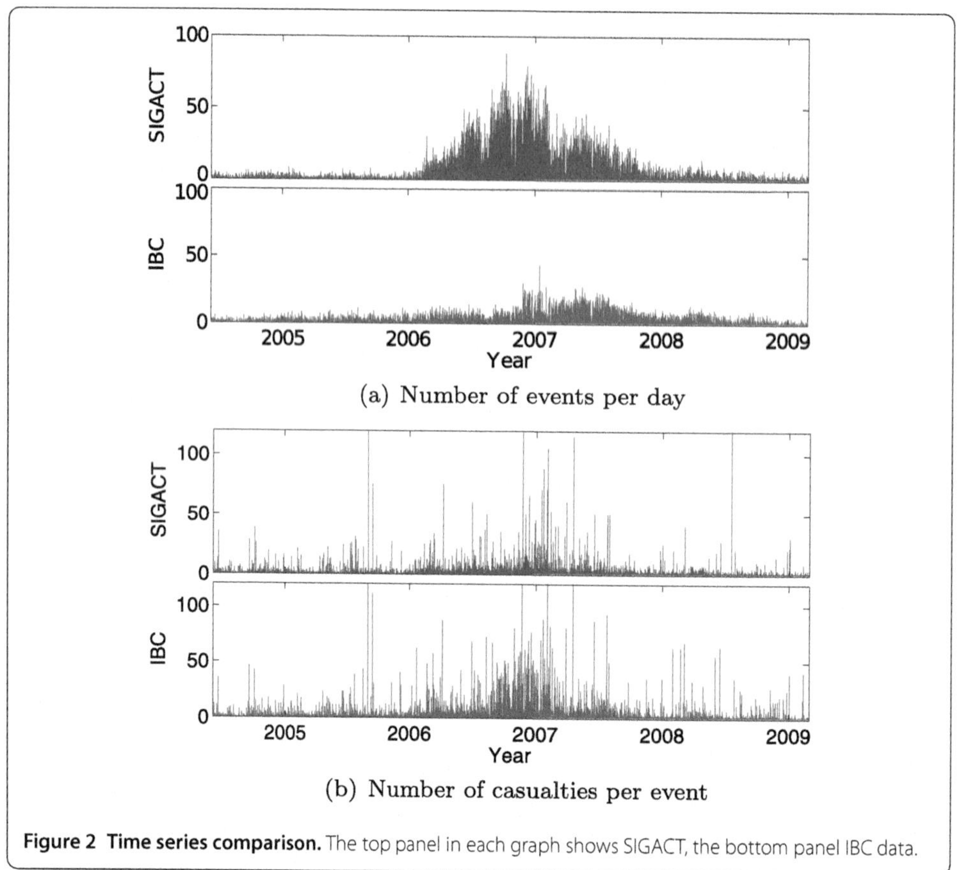

Figure 2 Time series comparison. The top panel in each graph shows SIGACT, the bottom panel IBC data.

with aggregate data and then compare the datasets at increasingly smaller temporal resolutions. The (relative) biases we identify at each level of disaggregation can then be related to our theoretical expectations on structural differences in reporting.

3.1 Aggregate comparison

The two Baghdad datasets are relatively consistent in the total number of casualties reported: 29,441-31,222 in IBC and 32,531-36,213 in SIGACT (see also Table 1). They do, however, differ noticeably in the numbers of casualties reported per event (see Figure 2(b)). These differences in overall casualty counts can be best quantified by analyzing aggregate casualty size distributions. Figure 3 shows the complementary cumulative distribution function (ccdf) of the number of casualties in the datasets 'IBC Baghdad' and 'SIGACT Baghdad' on a log-log scale. The distributions for IBC and SIGACT both appear to follow a power law distribution but differ noticeably in their slopes and their tail behavior. Note that the distributions for the geo-filtered datasets ('SIGACT 20 km', 'SIGACT 30 km' and 'SIGACT 40 km') only differ slightly from 'SIGACT Baghdad' and are therefore not discussed separately here. In the case of discrete data, such as the casualty counts analyzed here, the ccdf of a power law distribution is given by:

$$P(x) = \frac{\zeta(\alpha, x)}{\zeta(\alpha, x_0)}, \quad x \geq x_0, \tag{1}$$

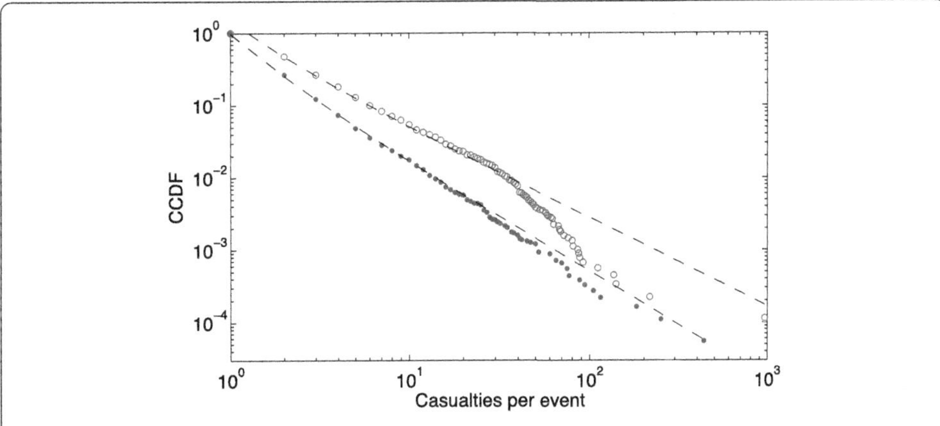

Figure 3 Complementary cumulative distribution function (ranking plot) of the number of casualties in the 'IBC Baghdad' (red circles) and 'SIGACT Baghdad' (blue dots) datasets. Dashed lines correspond to power law fits using maximum likelihood estimation (details provided in the text).

where $P(x) = \Pr(X \geq x)$ is a probability of finding event with no less than x casualties, ζ is a generalized Hurwitz zeta function [40], α is the exponent of the power law distribution and x_0 is the lower bound of the power law behavior.

To verify formally whether or not the distributions do indeed exhibit power law behavior we performed a maximum likelihood fit for a power law distribution using the methodology developed by Clauset et al. for analyzing power law behavior in empirical data [41]. The SIGACT data exhibits clear power law scaling (with exponent 2.57) starting at $x_0 = 2$, which is valid for almost 2.5 decades. In the IBC data, however, the presence of power law behavior is highly doubtful from a statistical point of view: the power law fit returns an exponent of 2.23, but the scaling is observed for only one decade and the tail clearly deviates from a power law distribution. Note that the power law shape of casualty event size statistics is a well-known empirical fact. It has been studied historically in the context of inter-state wars [42, 43] and more recently for terrorism [1] and intra-state conflict [2, 3]. We here do not intend to discuss the scaling relation of the distribution of event sizes and their possible origins but rather take these as 'stylized facts' and good quantitative indicators for marked differences between the two datasets. We would, however, like to note that in complex social or socio-economic systems deviations from power law may be indicative of incomplete data - see, for example, the discussion in [44] with respect to cyber-risk applications.

The significant upward shift of the IBC ccdf with respect to the SIGACT ccdf indicates the presence of much less small events (1-2 casualties) in the IBC data compared to SIGACT.[h] In order to quantify this difference we used a two-sample Anderson-Darling test [45, 46]. The test is a modification of the Kolmogorov-Smirnov (KS) test that gives more weight to the tail of the distribution and is thus a much better choice in the case of fat-tailed data [47]. Specifically, we use it to find the minimal threshold of casualty numbers for which the hypothesis of equal distribution of the two datasets can not be rejected. For this we proceeded as follows: For a given threshold, we select from both datasets only events with casualty counts greater or equal than a given threshold. We then apply a two-sample Anderson-Darling test (adjusted for ties) to test if both datasets were chosen from the same distribution. Varying the threshold value finally allows us to identify the minimal threshold for which the two datasets are statistically not distinguishable.

Table 2 Results of the pairwise comparison of the distributions of casualties

Threshold	Number of events					A^2 statistic			
	(i)	(ii)	(iii)	(iv)	(v)	(i)-(ii)	(i)-(iii)	(i)-(iv)	(i)-(v)
1	9,004	18,157	17,533	18,548	19,369	1,098.13	1,103.76	1,095.52	1,088.41
2	4,273	4,813	4,611	4,940	5,201	84.11	81.82	87.03	85.04
5	1163	876	851	901	952	6.60	7.11	7.81	7.92
10	484	323	310	325	340	7.25	6.72	6.63	6.82
15	296	159	154	161	169	**1.93**	**1.86**	**1.58**	**1.94**
20	206	105	100	105	108	**2.29**	**1.77**	**1.54**	**1.47**
25	159	77	75	79	82	3.09	**2.82**	**2.49**	**2.57**
30	123	47	47	51	52	**1.43**	**1.43**	**1.28**	**1.30**
40	69	29	29	31	32	**1.85**	**1.85**	**2.02**	**1.87**

The datasets are (i) 'IBC Baghdad', (ii) 'SIGACT Baghdad', (iii) 'SIGACT 20 km', (iv) 'SIGACT 30 km' and (v) 'SIGACT 40 km'. We used a two-sample Anderson-Darling tests (adjusted for ties) for comparison. Bold font marks cases where the value of the Anderson-Darling statistic A^2 is smaller than the critical level $A^2_{0.05} = 2.492$ (large-sample approximation) and the hypothesis of two datasets being sampled from the same distribution can not be rejected at a 5% significance level.

The results are shown in Table 2. The relative comparison of IBC data (i) and SIGACT data (ii)-(v) clearly shows that IBC under-reports small events and over-reports larger events compared to SIGACT. While the total number of events in the IBC dataset is almost two times smaller than in SIGACT, the number of events with 2 or more casualties in both datasets are almost equal. For larger casualty sizes IBC even reports almost twice as many events with 25 casualties and more compared to SIGACT. Note that this, of course, also implies a considerably larger absolute fraction of events with 2 and more casualties in IBC which is clearly reflected in the flatter slope of the IBC ccdf compared to SIGACT. Overall, this points to very significant differences in the aggregate casualty statistics between the two datasets.

These differences are also confirmed by our statistical tests. The hypothesis that the casualty distribution in IBC and SIGACT were sampled from the same distribution can be easily rejected for small thresholds (1-10 casualties per event, see Table 2 columns 7-10). The Anderson-Darling A^2 statistic reaches the critical value for a significance level of 0.05 and stays below it only for thresholds starting at 15 and more casualties. The hypothesis of agreement can again be rejected for threshold values between 22-28 where the value of the A^2 statistic stays slightly higher than critical level. Note, however, that a threshold of 15 casualties already selects only a very small subset of events from the whole dataset - less than 300 in IBC and less than 160 in SIGACT for the whole 5 years of data, i.e., less than 3% and 0.8% correspondingly. For thresholds greater than 25 casualties, subsets of the SIGACT datasets are even smaller (less than 100 events). In the quantitative comparisons of the two datasets in the following sections we therefore focus only on reasonably small thresholds of 1-10 casualties.

At an aggregate level, our analysis overall quantitatively confirms that IBC both reports systematically less events with few casualties (I) and more events with many casualties (III) compared to SIGACT - we can not test expectation (II) or (IV) here since these require a disaggregated comparison. It is important to point out that the differences in the casualty reporting we observe extend to the four most violent incidents in the period analyzed. In fact, their casualty counts in IBC and SIGACT disagree significantly, with IBC reporting more casualties in all four cases (Table 3).

Table 3 Most violent events and number of casualties reported by IBC and SIGACT

Date	Event	IBC report	SIGACT report
August 31, 2005	Baghdad bridge stampede*	965-1,005	436
November 23, 2006	Sadr City car and mortar bombings†	215	181
April 18, 2007	Baghdad car bombings‡	140	115
February 3, 2007	Baghdad market bombing§	136-137	105

*'A cry of suicide bomber, and 700 perish in Iraq stampede', The Guardian, http://www.guardian.co.uk/world/2005/sep/01/iraq.rorycarroll1 (accessed: 08/07/2013)
†'Iraq, Nov 23, 2006: A Day in Hell', Spiegel Online, http://www.spiegel.de/international/world/iraq-nov-23-2006-a-day-in-hell-a-722544.html (accessed: 08/07/2013)
‡'Up to 200 killed in Baghdad bombs', BBC News, http://news.bbc.co.uk/2/hi/middle_east/6567329.stm (accessed: 08/07/2013)
§'Terror takes toll on market, vendors', The Washington Times, http://www.washingtontimes.com/news/2007/feb/6/20070206-115808-3925r/ (accessed: 08/07/2013)

3.2 Monthly time series comparison

While aggregate distributional measures of conflict event signatures may already provide unique insights into conflict dynamics [1, 2], the majority of recent studies analyzing conflict mechanisms in Iraq relies on more detailed time series of incidents and their severity [3, 8, 17–20]. In this section we first focus on monthly time series. Note that we again consider a number of subsets with different minimal event sizes to account for the fact that the agreement between the two datasets may vary with the size of the events reported.

Figure 4(a) shows the number of events, Figure 4(b) the number of casualties per month in all five Baghdad datasets (see Table 1) for thresholds of 1, 2, 5, 7, 10 and 15 casualties per event. The panel in the upper left hand corner of each graph depicts the full IBC and SIGACT data (threshold equal to 1). It suggests that at the monthly level the two datasets provide distinctly different accounts of the violence dynamics in Baghdad. These differences in the number of events appear to be most substantial during the escalation of violence in 2006-2007 and for low and high thresholds. If we only exclude events with less than 5 to 10 casualties per event - i.e., intermediate thresholds - the monthly dynamics in the two datasets qualitatively agree much better (Figure 4(a)).

Before turning to a more detailed analysis of the differences in the monthly IBC and SIGACT reporting, we first tested whether at least the overall trends in both the number of events and casualties per month are consistent. A two-step Engle-Granger cointegration test [48] with an augmented Dickey-Fuller test of residuals [49, 50] can reject the null hypothesis of no-cointegration at a 5% significance level for almost all thresholds analyzed here. In other words, the differences in reporting between IBC and SIGACT generally do not affect the agreement of the coarse-grained trends. The exception are the dynamics of the number of events per month for thresholds of 1, 2 or 3 casualties per event (top panels of Figure 4(a)). Here the Engle-Granger test can not reject the null of no-cointegration (with p-values of Dickey-Fuller test equal to 0.653, 0.650 and 0.503 respectively), which suggests that even the long-term trends in the complete IBC and SIGACT datasets are statistically significantly different.

Overall, the differences in the monthly reporting of IBC and SIGACT are consistent with those observed in the aggregate statistics (Section 3.1). We also find the same casualty size dependent relative bias between the two datasets at the level of months. In particular, we again find significantly more small events in SIGACT compared to IBC in line with (I). However, this is only true during the 2006-2007 escalation of violence. In fact, before 2006 IBC even reports more small events and 2008 and onward the two datasets largely

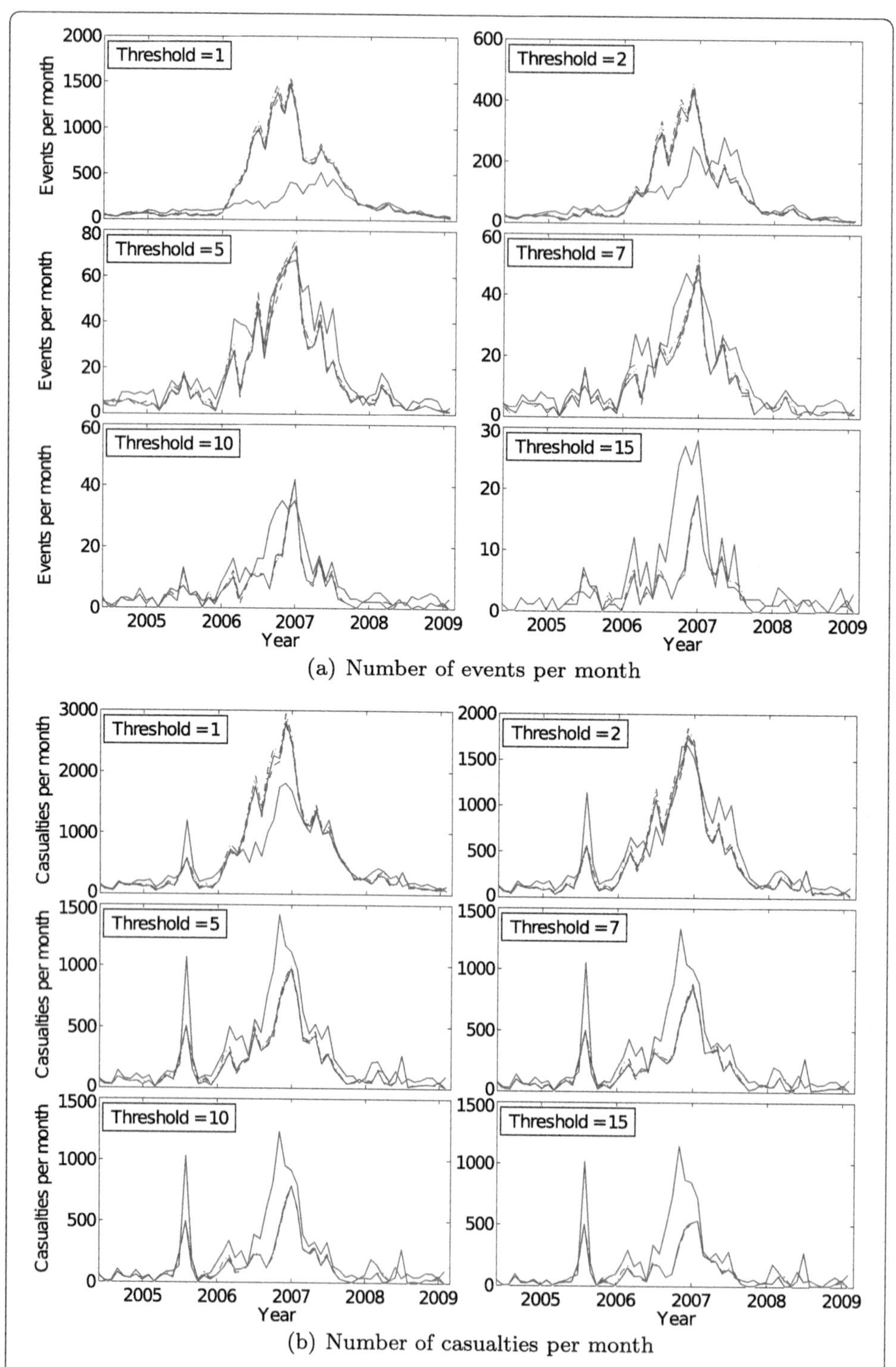

(a) Number of events per month

(b) Number of casualties per month

Figure 4 Dynamics of the number of (a) events and (b) casualties per months in 'IBC Baghdad' (red line), 'SIGACT Baghdad' (solid blue line), 'SIGACT 20 km' (dashed blue line), 'SIGACT 30 km' (dotted blue line) and 'SIGACT 40 km' (dash-dotted blue line). The panels correspond to subsets of events for thresholds of 1, 2, 5, 7, 10 and 15 casualties respectively. Note that the plots for the different SIGACT datasets (blue lines) are almost indistinguishable.

agree. This is consistent with our assertion that reporting differs more noticeably the more intense the conflict (II) and also suggests that - apart from the escalation in 2006-2007 - IBC and SIGACT reporting of small events is, in fact, quite consistent. Note, however, that we also clearly see an overall tendency of IBC to report more events with many casualties almost all throughout the conflict (III). This attests to differences in reporting also in the less intensive phases of the conflict prior to 2006 and after 2007.

Figure 4(a) and (b) also suggest that there is not one threshold value for which IBC and SIGACT reporting agrees both in terms of number of events and casualties per month. While they show the best visual agreement with respect to casualty counts for a threshold of 2 (Figure 4(b), upper right panel), the corresponding events per month statistics differ markedly (Figure 4(a), upper right panel). Recall, however, that we argued before that coverage in IBC should be much more limited for small events than in SIGACT. This implies that we should actually not expect an agreement in the number of events per months for thresholds of 1 and 2. In fact, the number of events per month are most consistent for thresholds between 5 and 10 where media-based coverage should be more complete. Since the casualty counts in IBC are significantly larger for these thresholds, this appears to suggest that overall IBC systematically reports more casualties than SIGACT.

It is important to keep in mind, however, that we previously also identified a second possible source of bias that may lead to a similar effect: the reporting of one composite episode as several incidents with less fatalities in SIGACT. In fact, for large events in the SIGACT dataset one can typically find a counterpart in the IBC dataset within the same day or two. In contrast, quite a number of events reported by IBC do not have an equally sized counterpart in the SIGACT dataset (see also Section 3.3). Since there are typically many events within a short time window one can, unfortunately, typically not convincingly establish if there are a number of smaller incidents reported in SIGACT that taken together match or approximate the total casualty count of an episode in IBC. This makes it impossible to estimate the extent to which possible mis-reporting of episodes as separate incidents may affect the reporting in SIGACT. Overall, we can therefore only say with certainty that the differences in casualty reporting observed at a monthly level are consistent with IBC systematically reporting more casualties than SIGACT, mis-reporting of episodes as separate incidents in SIGACT, and/or a combination of both.

3.3 Daily time series comparison

Many of the recent quantitative studies of the conflict in Iraq rely on detailed daily time series. We therefore now turn to a statistical analysis of deviations in the day-by-day microstructure of reporting between IBC and SIGACT. Note that in the period 2004-2009 both datasets exhibit a high degree of non-stationarity (see Figure 4(a)). In fact, the number of events in the second half of 2006 and first half of 2007 is up to 10 times larger than in 2005 or 2009. Any statistical analysis of these data thus requires us to explicitly model this non-stationarity, for instance using parametric methods. Alternatively, we can restrict our analyses to sufficiently small time windows, in which the dynamics can be assumed to be (approximately) stationary. In line with previous works (see for example [2]), we here pursue the latter approach and employ standard non-parametric tests to moving time windows. The choice of appropriate window size is subjected to trade-offs: it should be as small as possible to guarantee a stationary regime but also sufficiently large to contain sufficiently many events for robust statistical tests. We found that time windows ranging from 4 months to half a year (T = 120 days to T = 180 days) fulfill both of these conditions.[i] However, we also performed our tests for a window size of 1 year (T = 360) as a robustness check.

For every window size T we slide the moving window across the whole range of data in steps of one month and extract the subset of events in both IBC and SIGACT within each time window. For each of the (approximately) stationary periods we can then compare the distribution of events per day as a measure of the day-by-day microstructure of the data using a two-sample Anderson-Darling test. The Anderson-Darling test rejects the hypothesis of both time-series being sampled from the same distribution if the statistic A^2 is smaller than the critical level $A^2_{0.05}$ for a significance level of 0.05. Since the number of samples (window size T) is sufficiently large we use the large sample approximation for the critical level $A^2_{0.05} = 2.492$ [45]. Note that in contrast to the distribution of casualties per event (Figure 3), the distributions of events per day do not have fat-tails and typically decay almost exponentially (Figure S7 in Additional file 1). A Kolmogorov-Smirnov test would thus also in principle be applicable here [47]. However, in order to be consistent throughout our analysis and to account for the slower-than-exponential tails in case of small thresholds of 1 and 2 casualties per event, we here also rely on the more rigorous Anderson-Darling test.

Figure 5 graphically illustrates the results of the Anderson-Darling test for different thresholds and different window sizes. Color bars indicate the center of all windows of size T for which the null hypothesis of the number of events per day in both datasets being sampled from the same distribution can be rejected at a 5% significance level. The figure clearly illustrates that the two datasets significantly differ with respect to the distribution of events per day: the distributions in the two full datasets (threshold equal to 1, top panel) are statistically distinguishable from 2005 through 2007; only in the initial phase of the conflict and in the calmer phase after the U.S. military troop 'surge' in 2007 we can not detect significant differences. The higher the threshold, i.e., the more small events we exclude, the better the distributional agreement. It is important to note that in case of large differences in the numbers of events per day, the Anderson-Darling test will indicate significant deviations of one sample from another irrespective of the temporal characteristics. This certainly contributes to the strong disagreement for thresholds of 1 and 2 casualties in 2006-2007 but should not affect the results elsewhere where the numbers of events are much more similar. In general, the results for different window sizes are quite consistent and we can be confident that the exact choice of time window does not systematically drive our results.

The analysis in Figure 5 highlights that even though the average number of small events (thresholds 1 and 2) are relatively similar in IBC and SIGACT prior to 2006 and after 2007 the detailed daily reporting may still significantly differ, for example, in 2005 or in early 2008 (top panel). In the period 2006-2007 the daily structure of small events reported in the two datasets is almost everywhere significantly different except for a short episode in early 2007. For larger events (threshold 4 and larger) the average number of events per day is much more consistent throughout, but in the most intense phase of the conflict 2006-2007 the distributions of events per day remain statistically distinguishable. For events with 10 casualties and more the difference is only significant mid-2006 through early 2007 at the height of the escalation. The fact that the microstructures of the datasets become statistically indistinguishable does of course not imply that they necessarily correspond

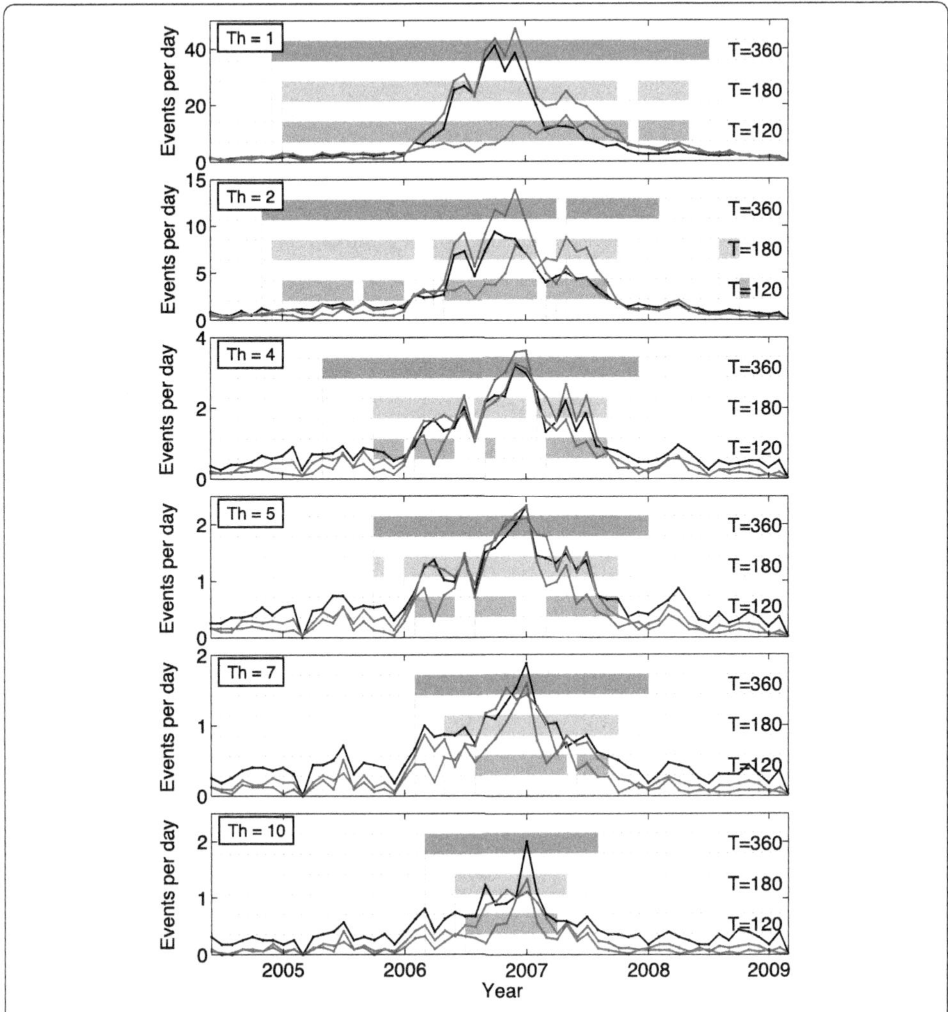

Figure 5 Distributional agreement of 'IBC Baghdad' and 'SIGACT Baghdad'. Color bars illustrate the results of a 2-sample Anderson-Darling test for the distribution of number of events for time windows of $T = 120$ days (orange bars), $T = 180$ days (green bars) and $T = 360$ days (violet bars) for thresholds equal to 1, 2, 4, 5, 7 and 10 casualties. The bars indicate the center of those time windows for which the hypothesis of agreement of the distribution of events per day can be rejected at a 5% significance level. The black line represents the RMS difference between 'IBC Baghdad' and 'SIGACT Baghdad', red and blue lines are the monthly averages of the number of events per day for the two datasets respectively.

to the same day-by-day occurrence of events. The test simply determines whether or not the overall distributions of events per day in a given (comparably large) time window are distinguishable or not. Consider, for instance, the very simple example of two time series with alternating 1 and 3 events on two subsequent days, but where the occurrence of events in the second series is shifted by one day. These time series have the same average number of events per day and are statistically absolutely not distinguishable even though each day their number of events differs by two, their average number of events per day.

In order to better quantify the actual day-by-day correspondence between IBC and SIGACT we therefore additionally consider the root mean square (RMS) difference of the number of events in IBC ($n_{\text{IBC}}(t)$) and SIGACT ($n_{\text{SIGACT}}(t)$) for a sliding window of size $T_2 - T_1 = 1$ as a simple quantitative metric of (average) daily agreement (black line in

Figure 5):

$$\mathrm{RMS} = \sqrt{\frac{1}{T_2 - T_1 + 1} \sum_{t=T_1}^{T_2} \left(n_{\mathrm{IBC}}(t) - n_{\mathrm{SIGACT}}(t)\right)^2}. \tag{2}$$

This difference can be directly compared to the average numbers of events per day in both IBC and SIGACT for the same moving time window (red and blue line in Figure 5 respectively):

$$\overline{n_{\mathrm{IBC}}} = \frac{1}{T_2 - T_1 + 1} \sum_{t=T_1}^{T_2} n_{\mathrm{IBC}}(t), \qquad \overline{n_{\mathrm{SIGACT}}} = \frac{1}{T_2 - T_1 + 1} \sum_{t=T_1}^{T_2} n_{\mathrm{SIGACT}}(t). \tag{3}$$

We find that the RMS difference is always of the order of magnitude of the average numbers of events per day for all thresholds we consider. In other words, the typical difference between two datasets is equal to the typical number of events per day. This is true even for intermediate thresholds of 5-10 casualties per event where the cumulative monthly number of events reported in IBC and SIGACT agree quite well. Note further that the RMS differences 2008 and onward is not significantly smaller than prior to 2006 contrary to our theoretical expectation that difference in reporting should be smallest in the later, less violent phases of the conflict (IV).

To test our intuition for how day-by-day differences relate to distributional agreement, we analyze the daily agreement in IBC and SIGACT in February 2006. We chose this period specifically such that the two datasets are statistically distinguishable for small and indistinguishable for large thresholds (see Figure 5). Figure 6 graphically illustrates the direct comparison of the number of events reported in each dataset. It is visually apparent that the number of events per day with thresholds of 1 and 2 casualties (upper two panels) reported in SIGACT and IBC differ. Specifically, on some days SIGACT reports more events, on others IBC does, and there are also days when one of the datasets reports no event but the other one does. For larger events (up to 4 and 5 casualties, third and fourth panel) the numbers of events per day in both datasets are much more consistent but there are still significant differences. SIGACT, for example, at a threshold of 5 reports significantly more days with one event than IBC and less days with two events. For thresholds of 7 and larger (lower two panels) the distributions of events per day are statistically not distinguishable anymore. In the day-by-day comparison we see that each daily signature is dominated by days with no, one or two events and the occurrence of these days is overall quite similar. Note, however, that at the same time for well more than 50% of the days these counts do not coincide, which explains the day-by-day mismatch represented by the comparably large RMS differences (Figure 5).

The large RMS difference we observe throughout the whole dataset should therefore be an indication that the day-by-day structure of event reporting in SIGACT and IBC does indeed significantly differ - despite the fact that they may be statistically indistinguishable at an aggregate or distributional level. In order to quantitatively estimate this daily mismatch, we compared how many events of a given size in SIGACT - the dataset with more events - can be matched to events in IBC. In matching events we allow for an uncertainty of ± 1 day. Please refer to Section 2 of Additional file 1 for the details of our automated

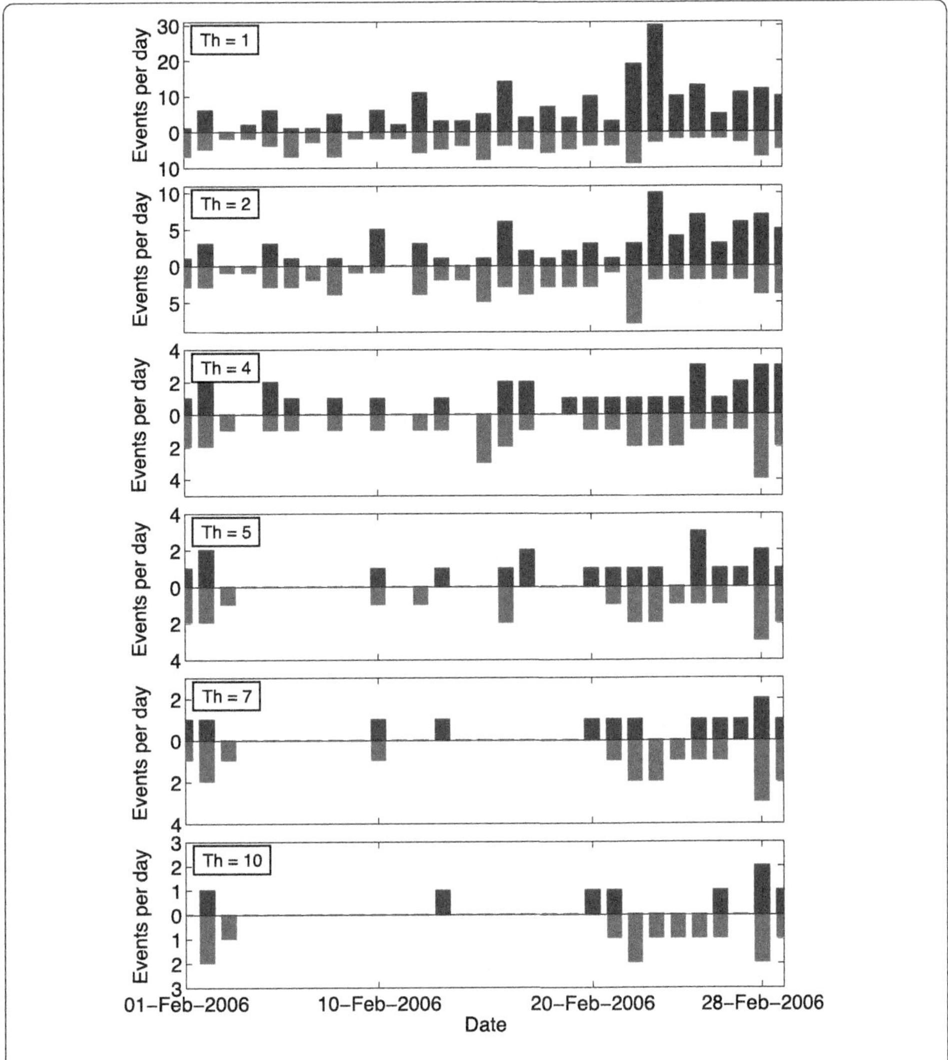

Figure 6 Dynamics of the numbers of events per day for 'IBC Baghdad' (red) and 'SIGACT Baghdad' (blue) in February 2006 for thresholds equal to 1, 2, 4, 5, 7 and 10 casualties. The vertical axis for the IBC dataset was mirrored for clarity purposes.

matching procedure. Figure 7 shows the number of matched events (blue bars) as a fraction of the total number of events in SIGACT (red line) for every month in the dataset. For simplicity we have grouped casualty sizes in categories. Note that for months with no events in a given casualty category, the fraction of matched events is set to 0 by default.

The figure suggests that daily SIGACT and IBC records are most consistent outside of the escalation of violence in 2006-2007 - this is particularly true for events with less casualties. Excluding the escalation phase 2006-2007 we find that on average 85.8% of the entries with 1 casualty and 82.3% of the entries with 2 or 3 casualties in SIGACT coincide with an entry with the same number of casualties within ± 1 day in IBC (Table 4). In contrast, during the period 2006-2007 only 24.6% of SIGACT reports with 1 casualty - by far the largest share of incidents - can be matched to IBC entries. In the same period, 50.9% of SIGACT records with 2 and 3 casualties have a corresponding entry in IBC within ± 1 day. For events with few casualties we can thus also confirm at a day-by-day resolution that differences in the reporting are generally larger the more intense the conflict (II). In con-

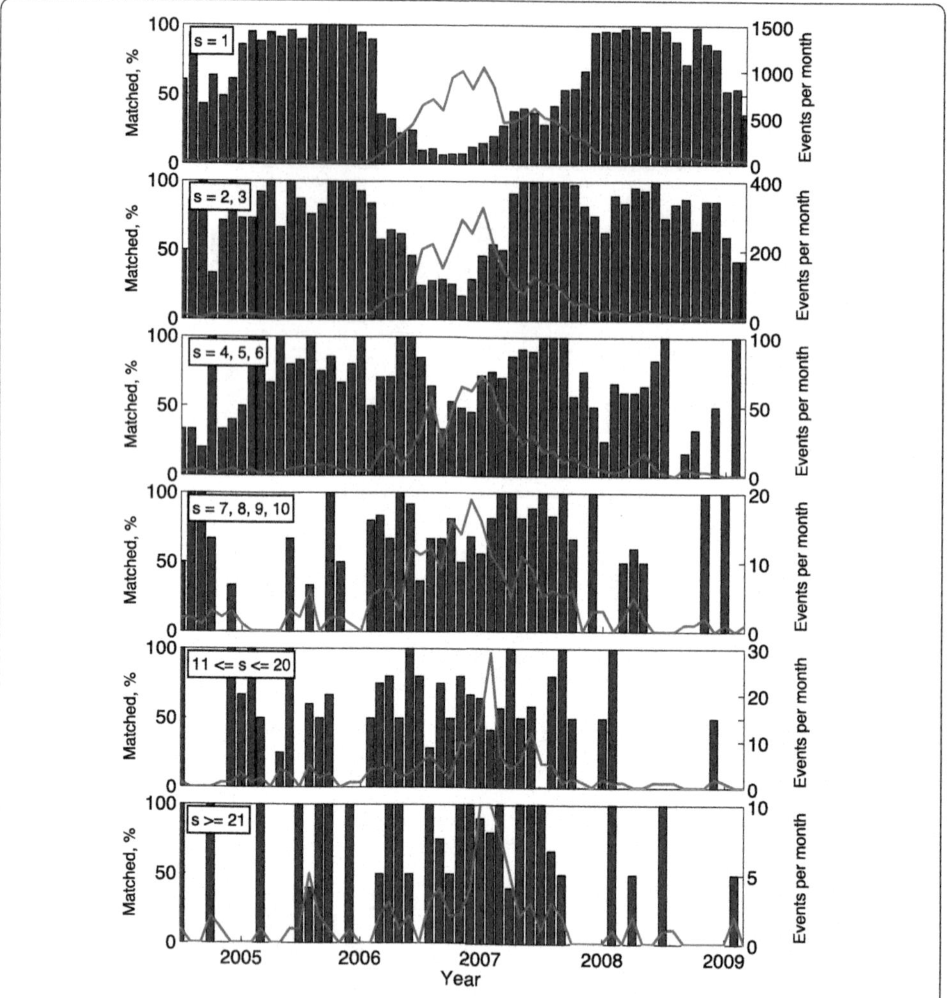

Figure 7 Day-by-day match of events of a given size *s* in 'SIGACT Baghdad' to entries in 'IBC Baghdad'. Blue bars indicate the number of matched events as a fraction of the total number of events in SIGACT for every months in the dataset (left axis), the red line illustrates the overall number events per months for the given casualty sizes (right axis). When matching events we allow for a timestamp uncertainty of ±1 day.

trast, the day-by-day agreement of events with 4 and more casualties is generally better in the 2006-2007 period (see Table 4 for details). Notice that especially the match of very large events (more than 20 casualties) is generally very good throughout (77.8% match). Finally, we do not find any systematic evidence that the detailed match of SIGACT and IBC has increased significantly after 2008, contrary to our theoretical expectation (IV).

It is important to emphasize here that we thus far only considered a one-sided comparison that matches SIGACT events to IBC. We previously observed that IBC reports more events with many casualties than SIGACT (Figure 4(a)), i.e., matching IBC to SIGACT events will yield a noticeably lower match. For example, the match of events with more than 20 casualties in this case is only 37.3% (please refer to Section 2 of Additional file 1 for the full comparison). The large RMS difference in Figure 5 reflects this mismatch. Note, too, that the RMS difference is a measure of daily agreement whereas we here allow for a timestamp uncertainty of ±1 day - it is consequently a much more conservative estimate of the agreement of the two time series than the one tested here. As we would expect, us-

Table 4 Number of SIGACT reports matched to IBC entries

Casualties	2004-05 & 2008-09			2006-07		
	matched	total	%	matched	total	%
s = 1	1,264	1,473	85.81	2,925	11,871	24.63
s = 2, 3	343	417	82.25	1,556	3,054	50.94
s = 4-6	86	133	64.66	480	693	69.26
s = 7-10	22	45	48.88	149	202	73.76
s = 11-20	18	36	50.00	83	143	58.04
s > 20	15	23	65.21	55	67	82.08

ing smaller tolerance (± 0 days) to match events generally decreases agreement while using larger tolerance (± 3 days) increases agreement of SIGACT events with IBC (see Section 2 of Additional file 1 for details). There is one notable exception though: very large events (with more than 20 casualties) are equally well matched for all tolerances suggesting that their reporting is clearly the most consistent.

We validated our day-by-day comparison by comparing it to results of a study performed at Columbia University. In the study, a small random sample of SIGACT events with civilian casualties was compared to entries in the IBC database [51]. Specifically, students were tasked to manually match SIGACT entries to IBC events following a specific detailed protocol. The analysis revealed that only 23.8% of the events in their SIGACT sample had corresponding entries in IBC. The Columbia researchers noted though that most of the events in their sample had only very few casualties - a consequence of the fact that by randomly sampling events for their study they mainly selected incidents during the period 2006-2007 where by far the most SIGACT events were recorded. In fact, the large majority of records in this period reports only one casualty per event (see Table 4). In our analysis we find an agreement of 24.6% for these events in the 2006-2007 period, which is very consistent with the Columbia estimate. For events with more than 20 casualties 94.1% of the SIGACT entries could be matched to entries in IBC in the Columbia study. The estimate of 82.1% based on our automated comparison is similar but clearly more conservative. Note that the specification of timestamp uncertainty of ± 1 day used in our automated procedure is equivalent to the matching prescription used in the Columbia study (see Section 2 of Additional file 1 for details).

It is important to emphasize two key shortcomings of the manual, in-depth comparison performed in the Columbia study. Most importantly, the random selection of events across the whole dataset effectively limits their analysis to the period 2006-2007 - the period in which all of our previous analyses find the most significant disagreement between IBC and SIGACT. Their findings thus likely systematically underestimate the overall match of events. In fact, our analysis shows that for the full period of analysis 38.5% of all SIGACT records could be matched to IBC entries with the same number of casualties. This is significantly more than the 23.8% reported in the Columbia study. Furthermore, manual comparisons are only possible for small (random) subsets of event. Having verified that we obtain results consistent with an in-depth comparison by human coders, the clear advantage of an automated comparison is its coverage, i.e., it efficiently yields estimates of the correspondence of daily reports in IBC and SIGACT for the full period of analysis.

In summary, our results strongly suggest that at any level of analysis - aggregate statistics, monthly statistics, detailed distributional level and daily time series - IBC and SIGACT reporting differ significantly, most strongly for events with few casualties but also for larger event sizes where aggregate event statistics are comparably more consistent. Consequently, we can expect that the choice of dataset would strongly affect any inference we draw from these data, simply because the conflict dynamics represented in each datasets at any level of analysis are indeed quite different.

In the following sections we complement these comparative insights with an in-depth analysis of the reporting in each dataset. Specifically, we explore if and where the two datasets contain non-trivial timing information - i.e., information about the occurrence of subsequent events - and how robust these are to uncertainty in timestamps. This is, of course, a critical precondition for the use of the datasets for any kind of timing or causal analysis. It is complementary to our prior comparative analysis in the sense that both, either or neither of the datasets may actually be suitable to study event dynamics in Baghdad, regardless of the relative differences in reporting we have already identified.

3.4 Distributional signatures

In Section 3.3 we used the distribution of events per day to characterize day-by-day event dynamics. A second very common measure that captures the micro-structure of event data is the distribution of times between incidents, or inter-event times [3]. The latter is always favorable if the data resolution is more fine-grained than days. Inter-event timing distributions at a resolution of hours, for example, provide a much more detailed characterization of the dynamics of subsequent events. We here chose to rely on the distribution of inter-event times because it also tends to be more sensitive to differences in the distribution of sparse data for which it is generally more difficult to detect deviations from a trivial timing signature. As before, we consider the dynamics in a given time window of length T within which the conflict dynamics can be assumed to be (approximately) stationary. Notice that the results for the event per day statistics are substantively equivalent; please refer to Section 5 of Additional file 1 for details.

In a structureless datasets, i.e., in datasets where the timing of events is statistically independent, the distribution of events per day simply follows a Poisson, the corresponding distribution of inter-event times an exponential distribution. The deviation of timing signatures from a Poissonian or exponential is thus mainly indicative of the usefulness of the dataset because a featureless dataset is essentially useless for any kind of quantitative (causal) inference or timing analysis. We would, however, also like to note that empirically and theoretically it is not plausible that the timing of conflict events in Iraq is completely independent. In fact, most theories of political violence prominently feature mechanisms that emphasize reciprocity and reactive dynamics [8, 52], spatial spillover effects or diffusion of violence [5].

Figure 8 shows the number of events per day for both datasets and graphically illustrates the results of a Kolmogorov-Smirnov test for a moving window of 180 days (results for larger window sizes are consistent and are discussed in Section 5 of Additional file 1). Specifically, bars indicate the center of time windows for which the Kolmogorov-Smirnov test rejects the hypothesis of agreement of the distribution of inter-event times with an exponential distribution at a 5% significance level. The analysis suggests that in the full SIGACT Baghdad dataset the timing of events deviates significantly from that of a Poisson process all throughout 2006 to mid-2008. In the much calmer periods prior to 2006 and after mid-2008 the timing signature, however, does not deviate significantly from that of a featureless process. For events larger than thresholds of 2, 4, 5, 7 and 10 casualties,

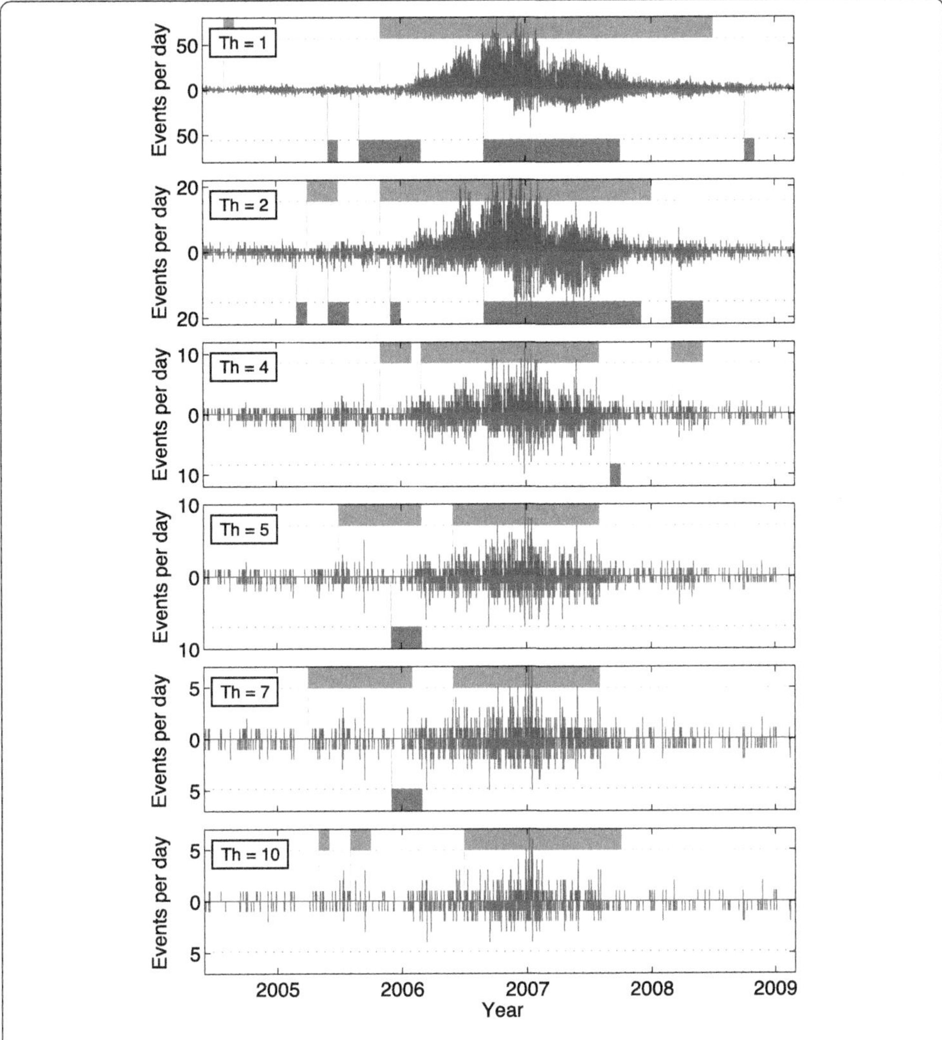

Figure 8 Inter-event timing signatures. Color bars illustrate the results of a KS-test for exponential distribution of the inter-event times in time windows of $T = 180$ days for thresholds equal to 1, 2, 4, 5, 7 and 10 casualties (see text for details). The bars indicate the center of those time windows for which the hypothesis of agreement of the distribution of inter-event times with an exponential distribution can be rejected at a 5% significance level (i.e., the datasets exhibits a non-trivial timing structure). The graph also shows the dynamics of the number of events per day in 'IBC Baghdad' (red) and 'SIGACT Baghdad' (blue). The vertical axis for the IBC dataset was mirrored for clarity purposes.

SIGACT still consistently features periods where the timing of events does not follow a featureless Poisson process, mainly in the most violent period mid-2006 to mid-2007.

In the full IBC dataset and for events with more than 2 casualties the timing of events also has a significant non-trivial timing structure that allows to reject the null hypothesis of Poisson dynamics for periods throughout late 2005 to 2007. This finding, however, is much less robust than for the SIGACT data. In fact, there is a half-year stretch in early 2006 for the full IBC dataset that features only a trivial timing signature. For a threshold of 2, the inter-event signature is also not distinguishable from a Poissonian in a period from late 2005 to late 2006; notice that in both periods the number of events per day is quite large. The differences between the signatures in IBC and SIGACT are most pronounced for subsets of events with minimally 4 or more casualties. Even though the overall number of events in SIGACT and IBC is comparable for those subsets, there is hardly any time window for which the timing signature in IBC significantly differs from that of a featureless process. This is especially obvious in the escalation phase mid-2006 to mid-2007 where the timing of events in IBC is statistically independent everywhere but deviates significantly from a featureless process in SIGACT.

As emphasized before, based on theories of political violence, we would expect that the timing of events should not be independent. The empirical narrative of the conflict in Iraq similarly suggests that events tend to be related. It is, however, in general not possible to decide whether or not the absence of non-trivial signatures in these periods is a consequence of incomplete reporting or evidence that the timing of events of a given size is indeed uncorrelated. The fact that both datasets feature time windows with trivial timing signatures thus simply suggests that it would be ill-advised to use the respective datasets in these periods to study (causal) relations between the timing of events. This is true for large parts of the IBC data - especially for larger thresholds - whereas SIGACT generally features more and longer time windows with non-trivial timing signatures (Figure 8). Notice though that in the low intensity conflict phases prior to 2006 and also after mid-2008 our statistical tests do not indicate any non-trivial timing signatures in SIGACT either.

Overall IBC appears to be much less suitable to study timing dynamics and thus to infer (causal) relationships between events. This is consistent with our observation in Section 2.2 that the reporting of timestamp in IBC may be more constrained through the use of approximate - or possibly misreported - timing of events provided in newspaper articles. It is important to keep in mind though that we only tested for non-trivial timing signatures in data drawn from the whole Baghdad area - significant correlations in the timing of events may, for example, simply be limited to smaller geographic scales.

3.5 Uncertainty of timestamps

We now turn to a systematic test of the effect of timestamp uncertainty on the distributional features analyzed in the previous section. In other words, we address the question of how robust the timing signatures we find are to uncertainties in the coding of timestamps. The robust coding of event timestamps is critically important for any quantitative technique where inferences hinge on the (causal) order of events. Examples of commonly used techniques using such time-ordered data include point process models, such as self-excited Hawkes processes [53, 54], Autoregressive Conditional Durations (ACD) [55, 56] or Autoregressive Conditional Intensity (ACI) [57]. Note that in both IBC and SIGACT the reporting of event timing may, in principle, be subject to systematic coding inaccuracies. The media sources IBC relies on may report events with a delay, provide only approximate timing information or may misreport the timing of an event altogether. SIGACT data is compiled from field reports, which may also systematically miscode the true timing of an event. Common problems include delayed reporting in situations of heavy engagement with enemy forces, reporting *post hoc* on incidents that a unit was not directly involved in and for which the timing is not precisely known, or summary reports filed at the end of a day (see also Section 2.2).

In order to statistically characterize the effect of timestamp inaccuracies on the day-by-day signatures of events, we again rely on the distribution of inter-event times $\tau_i = t_i - t_{i-1}$. We further assume that both IBC and SIGACT report events with timestamp uncertainties Δ_{IBC} and Δ_{SIGACT}. Note that the IBC dataset only codes timing of events with a precision of days, i.e., $\Delta_{\text{IBC}} \geq 1$ day. SIGACT on the other hand carries much more precise timestamps with a resolution of minutes and thus does not have this constraint. In order to account for uncertainties Δ in the timestamps we adopted the methodology proposed in [58] and assume that the difference between the real time of an event $\tilde{t}_i$ (which is unknown) and the timestamp $t_i \geq \tilde{t}_i$ is some effective 'noise' $\xi_i = t_i - \tilde{t}_i < \Delta$.

To test the impact of a given uncertainty Δ on the timing signature in each time series we then proceed as follows. For a given time window T we draw random variables $\xi_{i,\text{IBC}}$ and $\xi_{i,\text{SIGACT}}$ from the uniform distributions $U([0, \Delta_{\text{IBC}}])$ and $U([0, \Delta_{\text{SIGACT}}])$ respectively. We then construct time series $\hat{t}_{i,\text{IBC}} = t_{i,\text{IBC}} - \xi_{i,\text{IBC}}$ and $\hat{t}_{i,\text{SIGACT}} = t_{i,\text{SIGACT}} - \xi_{i,\text{SIGACT}}$, and calculate the distribution of inter-event times $\hat{\tau}_{i,\text{IBC}} = \hat{t}_{i,\text{IBC}} - \hat{t}_{i-1,\text{IBC}}$ and $\hat{\tau}_{i,\text{SIGACT}} = \hat{t}_{i,\text{SIGACT}} - \hat{t}_{i-1,\text{SIGACT}}$ for each. Note that the values $\hat{\tau}_i$ represent proxies for the unobserved real values of inter-event times $\tilde{\tau}_i$. We then apply a two sample Anderson-Darling test to the distributions of these inter-event times (for both IBC and SIGACT independently). We repeat this procedure $M = 100$ times, generating a set of binary values $\{h_{j,\text{IBC}}\}$ and $\{h_{j,\text{SIGACT}}\}$, $j = 1, \ldots, M$, where $h_j = 0$ if we can reject the null hypothesis at a 5% significance level, and $h_j = 1$ if the null hypothesis can not be rejected.

The effective measure for whether or not the timing distributions of the two time series with uncertainties are distinguishable is then simply the fraction of cases when the null hypothesis can not be rejected: $F_{\text{IBC}} = \sum_{j=1}^{M} h_{j,\text{IBC}}/M$ and $F_{\text{SIGACT}} = \sum_{j=1}^{M} h_{j,\text{SIGACT}}/M$. If the value of F_{IBC} (or F_{SIGACT}) is close to 0 we can be certain that the distributions of inter-event times $\hat{\tau}_{i,\text{IBC}}$ (or $\hat{\tau}_{i,\text{SIGACT}}$) are different from an exponential distribution - independently of particular values of the 'noise' terms $\xi_{i,\text{IBC}}$ (or $\xi_{i,\text{SIGACT}}$ respectively). This also implies that the real inter-event times $\tilde{\tau}_{i,\text{IBC}}$ (or $\tilde{\tau}_{i,\text{SIGACT}}$) exhibit non-trivial clustering. Similarly, a value of F close to 1 suggests that for most of the cases we can not reject the null hypothesis for the proxy values $\hat{\tau}_i$. This, in turn, implies that we will most likely not reject the null hypothesis at the same significance level for the real (unobserved) values $\tilde{\tau}_i$.[j] Effectively the fraction F may thus be referred to as the 'likelihood' of the time series to have been generated by a Poisson process.

From a conceptual point of views, the random time shifts $\hat{t}_i = t_i - \xi_i$ simply introduce bias to the time-series: the larger Δ, the larger the 'randomness' in our proxy time-series $\hat{t}_i$. Note that the more robust the timing signatures in the data, the larger the uncertainty Δ at which $\hat{\tau}_{i,\text{IBC}}$ and $\hat{\tau}_{i,\text{SIGACT}}$ start to only represent *iid* random samples drawn from an exponential probability distribution. The functional dependence of F on Δ is thus a quantitative measure for the robustness of the timing signatures. In particular, we will identify the critical value of Δ_c for which we can be more than 95% certain, i.e., $F < 0.05$, that uncertainties in timestamps do not destroy the non-trivial signature in $\hat{\tau}_{i,\text{IBC}}$ and $\hat{\tau}_{i,\text{SIGACT}}$.

Figure 9 shows the p-values of the KS-test and the fraction F as a function of the value of Δ for the time window October 15, 2006 to February 15, 2007 - a period specifically chosen to reflect a situation where both full datasets show non-trivial timing signatures, but where for larger thresholds this signature breaks down in IBC. For both IBC and SIGACT the figure clearly demonstrates that the non-trivial timing distributions in the full datasets are quite robust to uncertainties in timestamps with $\Delta_{c,\text{IBC}} \simeq 3$ days and $\Delta_{c,\text{SIGACT}} \simeq 2$ days respectively (Figure 9(a)). Notice, too, that the transition to Poissonian dynamics for increasing Δ is continuous and relatively slow. At uncertainties of about 5 days (IBC) and 4 days (SIGACT) 50% of the reshuffled datasets are indistinguishable from featureless data. Note that we also analyzed events with 3 or more casualties (Figure 9(b)). Here IBC clearly

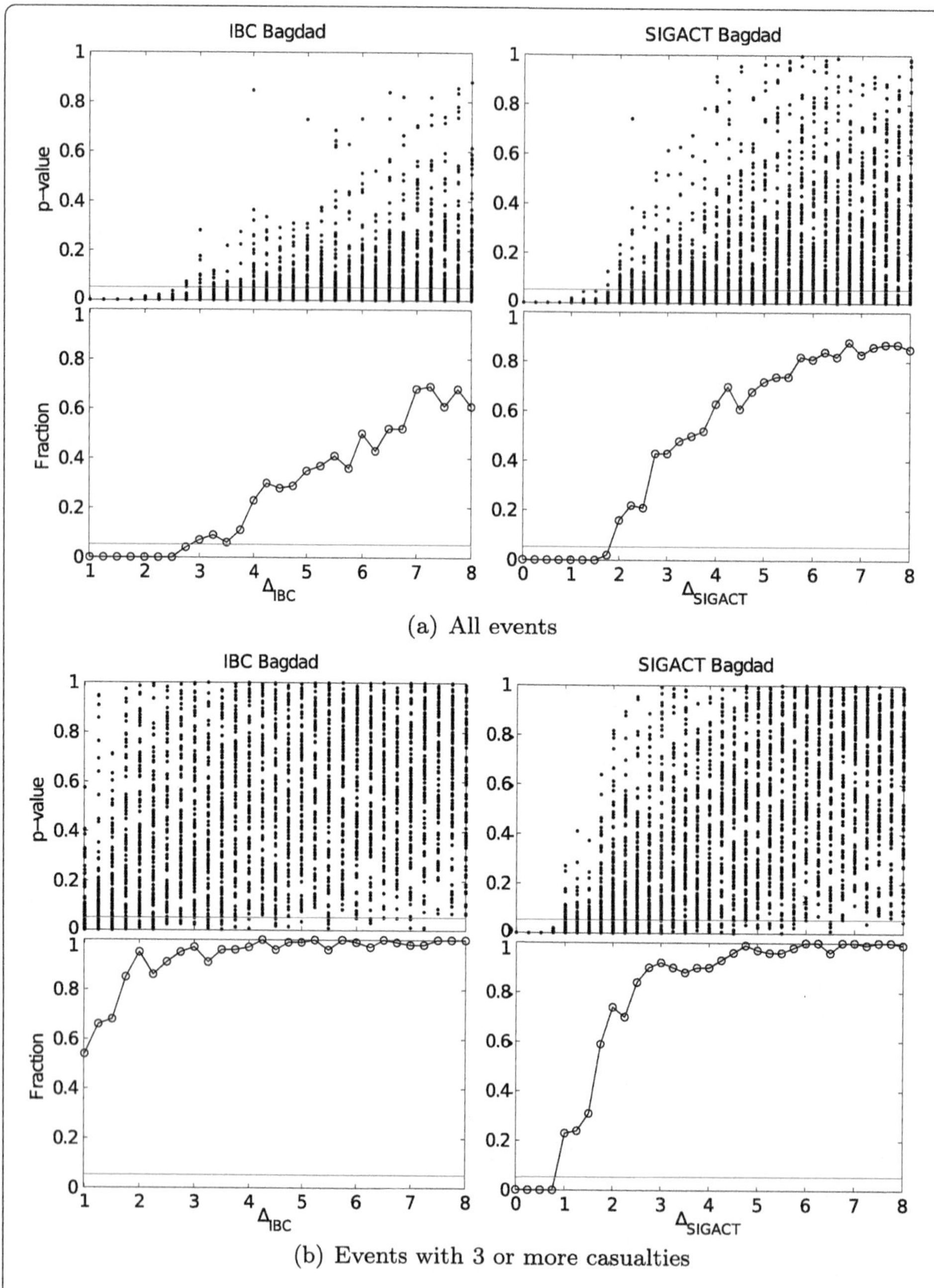

Figure 9 Robustness of timestamps. We test whether the inter-event timing distributions of 'IBC Baghdad' (left) and 'SIGACT Baghdad' (right) in the time window October 15, 2006 to February 15, 2007 exhibit non-trivial timing signatures for different timestamp uncertainty Δ. **(a)** shows the results for the full datasets and **(b)** for threshold equal to 3 casualties per event. The top panels illustrate how for 100 different redistributions (see text for details) the *p*-values for the test for exponential distribution of the inter-event times changes as a function of Δ_{IBC} and Δ_{SIGACT}. The horizontal red line corresponds to the significance level of 0.05, below which the null hypothesis of exponential distribution can be rejected. The bottom panels show the fraction *F* of realizations (out of 100) for which the exponential distribution can not be rejected.

does not feature robust non-trivial timing signature since already at the minimal uncertainty of one day F is close to 1. For SIGACT we do observe a non-trivial signature and $\Delta_{c,\text{SIGACT}} \simeq 2$ suggests that this signature is similarly robust as that observed for the full dataset.

Our analysis thus suggests that - where they exist - the non-trivial timing signatures for the full IBC and SIGACT data are indeed quite robust against uncertainty of timestamps. In fact, the signatures are robust enough that even if event timing may have been miscoded by up to 2 days, we could still expect to see non-trivial timing dynamics. Note that this does, of course, not imply that timestamp uncertainties of up to 2 days would not affect the inferences we draw from day-by-day and even distributional comparison - it only suggests that some timing information will be preserved.

4 Discussion and conclusion

In this study we systematically identified a number of key quantitative differences between the event reporting in media-based IBC data and field report-based SIGACT military data. In fact, we find significant differences in reporting at all levels of analysis: aggregate, monthly, distributional and day-by-day comparisons. These relative biases are consistent with a number of structural differences of the reporting in IBC and SIGACT. We further showed that even for subsets of events where both datasets were found to be most consistent at an aggregate level, the daily time series of events were significantly different. Overall this suggests that at any level of analysis the specific choice of dataset may have a critical impact on the quantitative inferences we draw - at the extreme using IBC or SIGACT data might, in fact, lead to substantially different results.

In an individual analysis of each dataset we further showed that SIGACT and IBC differ markedly with regard to their usefulness for event timing analyses - a key application for both datasets. In fact, IBC was found to have only trivial timing signatures, i.e., signatures indistinguishable from an *iid* random process, for much of the time period analyzed. In comparison SIGACT codes much more non-trivial timing dynamics and is thus generally more suitable for the analysis of event timing. In the low intensity conflict phases prior to 2006 and after mid-2008, however, even SIGACT generally does not feature non-trivial timing dynamics. This strongly suggests that any analysis of event timing and causal relationships between events using SIGACT should best be restricted to the period 2006 to 2008. Our analysis, however, also confirmed that where non-trivial timing signatures for the full datasets exist these signatures are quite robust against uncertainties in timestamps of events.

In order not to be systematically affected by geographically biased coverage, our quantitative analysis focused exclusively on the case of Baghdad. We contend, however, that the relative as well as absolute differences in reporting of IBC and SIGACT extend beyond this 'best case' scenario to all of Iraq. In other words, for the full Iraq datasets reporting differences are at best what we found here, but they are likely even more pronounced due to fundamentally more limited event coverage outside of the greater Baghdad area.

Our findings have a number of concrete implications for recent studies analyzing the conflict in Iraq. First, we would like to re-emphasize that the substantial disagreement between the two datasets suggests that using one or the other will likely yield substantively different results. This applies to studies using IBC data at a distributional [2] or aggregate level [17], but most notably to studies using IBC [3, 18, 19] or SIGACT [8, 20] data at a daily resolution where the differences are most substantial. The lack of simultaneous agreement with regard to number of events and casualty counts per months implies in particular that time series analysis with models that describe both event occurrence and casualties - for instance, models of marked point processes [59] - may lead to substantially different results depending on which dataset is used, even if focusing on subsets of events of certain minimal sizes.

Second, the absence of non-trivial timing signatures for significant parts of both datasets may pose a substantial problem if data is used for detailed timing (or causal) analysis. In fact, none of the above mentioned studies using either IBC or SIGACT data at a daily resolution confirmed whether they actually feature robust timing signatures. The analyses in [18, 19], for example, employ a Hawkes point process model [53, 54] to study event timing dynamics. However, our analysis suggests that the IBC data used is almost featureless at short time-scales, having only long-term non-stationary trends for long periods in 2005, 2006 and 2008. It is therefore clearly not suitable for this kind of analysis. Moreover, given the daily resolution of timestamps in IBC and the corresponding clustering of events on a given day, we strongly caution against the direct calibration of a Hawkes model even where robust timing signatures exist, simply because the resulting model fits will be (falsely) rejected by standard goodness-of-fit methods. Instead, it is better to rely on randomization techniques such as those proposed in [58] and used for the timestamp analysis in our study. Note also that the absence of non-trivial timing signatures in SIGACT prior to 2006 and after mid-2008 may affect the inferences regarding causal relationship between events in [8, 20] - this applies particularly for [20] which analyzes event dynamics exclusively in the first six months of 2005.

The growing number of recent contributions addressing issues of bias in conflict event data [13–16] points to an increased awareness for data related issues in conflict research. Our study contributes to this literature by systematically analyzing relative biases in conflict event data and relating them to structural differences in reporting. The sources of systematic bias discussed here are, however, clearly not restricted to conflict data. For researchers using data on other social processes that may be subject to similar biases our analysis suggests two important 'lessons learned.' First, the often very substantial differences between the two datasets analyzed here should raise awareness that data bias is not an afterthought but a critical issue worthy of our fullest attention. In particular, if analyses are meant to provide concrete policy advice we must be especially wary that substantive findings do not arise from biased inference. Second, we showed how structural differences in reporting directly translate into relative biases. This demonstrates, that a careful *a priori* understanding of the strength and limitations of a given dataset allows to anticipate possible biases in subsequent analyses - even if there is only one dataset that covers the case in question. If more than one comparable dataset exists one can either directly analyze their relative bias or, at least, perform the same analysis for all datasets to verify that the substantial conclusions drawn are robust and consistent. We also showed that statistical tests may help identify datasets that are more suitable than others for the analysis at hand.

To date most studies using these data unfortunately neither address potential biases nor systematically test the robustness of their findings. There is certainly not one comprehensive strategy to mitigate bias in empirical data but the present study suggests that researchers can at least actively address it. Especially with the growing availability of large and highly-resolved datasets it will be more important than ever that issues of data quality are taken seriously. As the case of the conflict in Iraq shows, if unaccounted for, we otherwise face the risk that the 'views to a war' will indeed be driving our substantial findings.

Competing interests
The authors declare that they have no competing interests.

Authors' contributions
KD and VF conceived and designed the study, KD prepared the data, VF analyzed the data and KD and VF wrote and approved the final version of the article.

Author details
[1]Department of Humanities, Social and Political Science, Chair of Sociology, Modeling and Simulation, ETH Zürich, Clausiusstrasse 50, Zürich, 8092, Switzerland. [2]Department of Management, Technology and Economics, Chair of Entrepreneurial Risks, ETH Zürich, Scheuchzerstrasse 7, Zürich, 8092, Switzerland.

Authors' information
KD is a PhD student in the Department of Humanities, Social and Political Science at ETH Zürich (Switzerland), Chair of Sociology, Modeling and Simulation. In his research he uses detailed, disaggregated empirical violence data and a range of statistical and computational modeling techniques to study micro-level conflict processes. Focusing mainly on asymmetric intra-state conflict he has worked on the Israeli-Palestinian conflict, Jerusalem in particular, and on the conflict in Iraq.
VF is a senior researcher in the Department of Management, Technology and Economics at ETH Zürich (Switzerland), Chair of Entrepreneurial Risks. His research is mainly focused on self-excited point process models for the description of dynamics in complex systems, with a particular interest in financial applications such as modeling market microstructure effects.

Acknowledgements
We are grateful to Ryohei Hisano, Spencer Wheatley, Didier Sornette, Michael Mäs, Thomas Chadefaux, Sebastian Schutte, Ryan Murphy and Dirk Helbing for fruitful discussions and comments on earlier versions of this article.

Endnotes

[a] The estimates of the total fatalities over the course of the Iraq war differ substantially. For a detailed discussion please refer to http://www.iraqbodycount.org/analysis/beyond/exaggerated-orb/.

[b] For reactions by leading conflict researchers to the release of the data see [60], for more general statements regarding their relevance and impact see [61]. We contend that the data can be used in a responsible manner for academic research, given that the empirical analysis does not in any way and under any circumstances harm or endanger individuals, institutions, or any of the political actors involved. Note in particular that all data used here has been intentionally stripped of any detailed information on specific incidents beyond information on timing, severity and location of attacks.

[c] Details on data format, preparation etc. are provided in Section 1 of Additional file 1. Data used in this study is provided as .csv files for download (see Additional file 2).

[d] We include all SIGACT events independent of perpetrator identity consistent with the coverage of IBC.

[e] Events in Baghdad make up about 35% of all events in IBC and 50% in SIGACT suggesting that there is indeed an element of relative geographic reporting bias.

[f] In our analysis we always rely on the lower bound as its is the most conservative estimate; see Section 3 of Additional file 1 for details and sensitivity analyses.

[g] In the U.S., for example, the geographic coverage of different providers varies significantly, independent of population density.

[h] Note that some of the 'missing' small events in IBC might at least be partially accounted for in the aggregated monthly (morgue or hospital) reports that were excluded from our study.

[i] A previous analysis of the number of events per day in Iraq also used a half year temporal window size [2].

[j] As a consequence of the nature of the statistical test used here we reject the correct null hypothesis in 5% of the cases by chance and we thus effectively expect to obtain $F_{max} = 0.95$ even if the dataset is completely featureless.

References

1. Clauset A, Young M, Gleditsch KS (2007) On the frequency of severe terrorist events. J Confl Resolut 51:58-87
2. Bohorquez JC, Gourley S, Dixon AR, Spagat M, Johnson NF (2009) Common ecology quantifies human insurgency. Nature 462(7275):911-914
3. Johnson N, Carran S, Botner J, Fontaine K, Laxague N, Nuetzel P, Turnley J, Tivnan B (2011) Pattern in escalations in insurgent and terrorist activity. Science 333(6038):81-84
4. Zammit-Mangion A, Dewar M, Kadirkamanathan V, Sanguinetti G (2012) Point process modelling of the Afghan war diary. Proc Natl Acad Sci USA 109(31):2414-12419
5. Schutte S, Weidmann N (2011) Diffusion patterns of violence in civil wars. Polit Geogr 30(3):143-152

6. Weidmann N, Salehyan I (2013) Violence and ethnic segregation: a computational model applied to Baghdad. Int Stud Q 57:52-64
7. Bhavnani R, Miodownik D, Choi HJ (2011) Three two tango: territorial control and selective violence in Israel, the West Bank, and Gaza. J Confl Resolut 55:133-158
8. Linke AM, Witmer FD, O'Loughlin J (2012) Space-time granger analysis of the war in Iraq: a study of coalition and insurgent action-reaction. Int Interact 38(4):402-425
9. Bhavnani R, Donnay K, Miodownik D, Mor M, Helbing D (2014) Group segregation and urban violence. Am J Polit Sci 58:226-245
10. Raleigh C, Linke A, Hegre H (2010) Introducing ACLED: an armed conflict location and event dataset. J Peace Res 47(5):651-660
11. Sundberg R, Lindgren M, Padskocimaite A (2010) UCDP GED codebook version 1.5-2011. Available online at http://www.ucdp.uu.se/ged/
12. Lyall J (2010) Are coethnics more effective counterinsurgents? Evidence from the second Chechen war. Am Polit Sci Rev 104:1-20
13. Eck K (2012) In data we trust? A comparison of UCDP GED and ACLED conflict event datasets. Coop Confl 47:124-141
14. Chojnacki S, Ickler C, Spies M, Wiesel J (2012) Event data on armed conflict and security: new perspectives, old challenges, and some solutions. Int Interact 38:382-401
15. Raleigh C (2012) Violence against civilians: a disaggregated analysis. Int Interact 38(4):462-481
16. Weidmann NB (2013) The higher the better? The limits of analytical resolution in conflict event datasets. Coop Confl 48(4):567-576
17. Condra LN, Shapiro JN (2012) Who takes the blame? The strategic effects of collateral damage. Am J Polit Sci 56:167-187
18. Lewis E, Mohler GO, Brantingham PJ, Bertozzi AL (2012) Self-exciting point process models of civilian deaths in Iraq. Secur J 25:244-264
19. Lewis E, Mohler GO (2011) A nonparametric EM algorithm for multiscale Hawkes processes. Preprint
20. Braithwaite A, Johnson SD (2012) Space-time modeling of insurgency and counterinsurgency in Iraq. J Quant Criminol 28:31-48
21. Chadefaux T (2014) Early warning signals for war in the news. J Peace Res 51:5-18
22. Golder SA, Macy MW (2011) Diurnal and seasonal mood vary with work, sleep, and daylength across diverse cultures. Science 333(6051):1878-1881
23. IBC (2014) Iraq body count. http://www.iraqbodycount.org/
24. Kagan K (2009) The surge: a military history. Encounter Books, New York
25. Petraeus D (2006) Learning counterinsurgency: observations from soldiering in Iraq. Mil Rev 86:2
26. Petraeus D (2010) Counterinsurgency concepts: what we learned in Iraq. Global Policy 1:116-117
27. Rogers S (2010) Wikileaks Iraq: data journalism maps every death. http://www.theguardian.com/news/datablog/2010/oct/23/wikileaks-iraq-data-journalism (accessed: 09/03/2013)
28. Berman E, Shapiro JN, Felter JH (2011) Can hearts and minds be bought? The economics of counterinsurgency in Iraq. J Polit Econ 119(4):766-819
29. Rogers S (2010) Wikileaks Iraq: what's wrong with the data? http://www.theguardian.com/news/datablog/2010/oct/25/wikileaks-iraq-data/ (accessed: 08/07/2013)
30. Earl J, Martin A, McCarthy JD, Soule SA (2004) The use of newspaper data in the study of collective action. Annu Rev Sociol 30:65-80
31. Oliver PE, Maney GM (2000) Political processes and local newspaper coverage of protest events: from selection bias to triadic interactions. Am J Sociol 106(2):463-505
32. McCarthy JD, McPhail C, Smith J (1996) Images of protest: dimensions of selection bias in media coverage of Washington demonstrations, 1982 and 1991. Am Sociol Rev 61(3):478-499
33. Davenport C, Ball P (2002) Views to a kill: exploring the implications of source selection in the case of Guatemala 1977-1995. J Confl Resolut 64(2):427-450
34. DoS (2009) U.S. government counterinsurgency guide. U.S. Department of State
35. González MC, Hidalgo C, Barabási AL (2008) Understanding individual human mobility patterns. Nature 453(7196):779-782
36. Leetaru KH, Wang S, Cao G, Padmanabhan A, Shook E (2013) Mapping the global Twitter hearbeat: the geography of Twitter. First Monday 2013:18(5-6). http://firstmonday.org/article/view/4366/3654
37. PewResearch (2013) 72% of online adults are social networking site users. http://www.pewinternet.org/2013/08/05/72-of-online-adults-are-social-networking-site-users/ (accessed: 06/26/2014)
38. Samoilenko A, Yasseri T (2014) The distorted mirror of Wikipedia: a quantitative analysis of Wikipedia coverage of academics. EPJ Data Sci 3:1
39. Thelwall M, Haustein S, Larivière V, Sugimoto CR (2013) Do altmetrics work? Twitter and ten other social web services. PLoS ONE 8(5):64841
40. Abramowitz M, Stegun IA (eds) (1965) Handbook of mathematical functions: with formulas, graphs, and mathematical tables. Dover Publications, New York
41. Clauset A, Shalizi CR, Newman MEJ (2009) Power-law distributions in empirical data. SIAM Rev 51(4):661
42. Richardson LF (1948) Variation of the frequency of fatal quarrels with magnitude. J Am Stat Assoc 43:523-546
43. Lars-Erik Cederman CW, Sornette D (2011) Testing Clausewitz: nationalism, mass mobilization, and the severity of war. Int Organ 65(4):605-638
44. Maillart T, Sornette D (2010) Heavy-tailed distribution of cyber-risks. Eur Phys J B 75(3):357-364
45. Pettitt AN (1976) A two-sample Anderson-Darling rank statistic. Biometrika 63:161-168
46. Scholz FW, Stephens MA (1987) K-sample Anderson–Darling tests. J Am Stat Assoc 82(399):918-924
47. Frederick J (2006) Statistical methods in experimental physics, 2nd edn. World Scientific, Singapore
48. Engle RF, Granger CWJ (1987) Co-integration and error correction: representation, estimation, and testing. Econometrica 55(2):251-276

49. Dickey DA, Fuller WA (1979) Distribution of the estimators for autoregressive time series with a unit root. J Am Stat Assoc 74(366):427-431
50. Said SE, Dickey DA (1984) Testing for unit roots in autoregressive-moving average models of unknown order. Biometrika 71(3):599-607
51. Carpenter D, Fuller T, Roberts L (2013) WikiLeaks and Iraq body count: the sum of parts may not add up to the whole - a comparison of two tallies of Iraqi civilian deaths. Prehosp Disaster Med 28(3):223-229
52. Haushofer J, Biletzki A, Kanwisher N (2010) Both sides retaliate in the Israeli-Palestinian conflict. Proc Natl Acad Sci USA 107(42):17927-17932
53. Hawkes AG (1971) Spectra of some self-exciting and mutually exciting point processes. Biometrika 58:83-90
54. Hawkes AG (1971) Point spectra of some mutually exciting point processes. J R Stat Soc, Ser B, Methodol 33(3):438-443
55. Engle RF, Russell JR (1997) Forecasting the frequency of changes in quoted foreign exchange prices with the autoregressive conditional duration model. J Empir Finance 4(2-3):187-212
56. Engle RF, Russell JR (1998) Autoregressive conditional duration: a new model for irregularly spaced transaction data. Econometrica 66(5):1127-1162
57. Russell JR (1999) Econometric modeling of multivariate irregularly-spaced high-frequency data. University of Chicago. Working paper
58. Filimonov V, Sornette D (2012) Quantifying reflexivity in financial markets: toward a prediction of flash crashes. Phys Rev E 85(5):056108
59. Daley DJ, Vere-Jones D (2008) An introduction to the theory of point processes. volume II: general theory and structure. Probability and its applications, vol 2, 2nd edn. Springer, Berlin
60. Bohannon J (2010) Leaked documents provide bonanza for researchers. Science 330(6004):575
61. The Guardian (2010) Iraq war logs: experts' views. http://www.theguardian.com/commentisfree/2010/oct/28/iraq-war-logs-experts-views/ (accessed: 08/07/2013)

11

Realities of data sharing using the genome wars as case study - an historical perspective and commentary

Barbara R Jasny*

*Correspondence:
brjasny@gmail.com
Science/AAAS, Washington, DC 20005, USA

Abstract

The importance of data sharing has become a mantra within the science research community. However, sharing has not been as easy (or as readily adopted) as advocates have suggested. Questions of privacy, individual scientist's rights to their research, and industry-academia divides have been significant hurdles. This article looks at the history of the debates and problems associated with data access that occurred during the 'human genome wars' and their aftermath as a way to explore some of the challenges facing diverse research communities.

Keywords: data sharing; data access; human genome project

Introduction

In 2009 Tim Berners-Lee, the inventor of the World Wide Web, described the power of linked data, the crucial need to get it 'unlocked from individual silos,' and the imperative to stop people, governments, and enterprises from 'database hugging' [1]. The ability to pool datasets generated by different researchers (or organizations or governments) has been considered crucial to achieving progress in areas as diverse as personalized medicine and sustainability. Those who see data sharing as providing a public good often insist that even the investigators who generate data have an obligation to their funders and the general public to release it - thus superseding their individual rights to explore the data first. As described by Alan Guttmacher *et al.* (2009), 'The model of the investigator owning data has been increasingly replaced by one in which society owns data' [2, p.1].

The reality, however, is that most researchers don't currently share their data voluntarily even when it is made easy [3–5]. Recently researchers from the National Science Foundation-funded DataONE project (5) conducted a survey of more than 1,000 scientists and concluded that 'Barriers to effective data sharing and preservation are deeply rooted in the practices and culture of the research process as well as the researchers themselves.'

The purpose of this article is to examine one process of data sharing in detail in the hope that the problems and successes can inform the system more generally. One of the arenas in which debates over this issue were especially visible and acrimonious concerned the data that represent the foundation of our genetic heritage. It is certainly true that success at delivering the first human genome sequence would have major impacts on the egos and careers of an array of aggressive, colorful people. This includes, but is not limited to leaders of the private (commercial) and public efforts, - J. Craig Venter on one side and Francis Collins and Sir John Sulston (plus a cast of associates) on the other. However, the primary focus of this article will be on the debates and discussions regarding the value of information and information access.

The so-called 'genome wars' did not occur in isolation, as events related to information access were occurring in a variety of disciplines. This focus is of much more than historical interest. As I will discuss in the concluding section, the realities of data sharing, the challenges of simultaneously fostering research and preserving individual privacy, and debates over the use of commercial data continue to pose challenges for scientists from a variety of disciplines, ranging from genomics to the social sciences.

The human genome

A genome is the sum total of all of our genetic information, encoded in an ordered sequence of 3 billion nucleotides. The information locked in that sequence has enormous symbolic value as our human inheritance. Such data also has potential value as a jumping off point to learn about the genetic pathways involved in human disease and identify potential inroads for diagnosis and therapeutics. There was a lot of money at stake for pharmaceutical and biotechnology industries in getting the first look at the human genome sequence. Money was also under the surface for the academic community as it was crucial to the publicly funded effort not to be rendered redundant in front of Congress, which would fuel the next decades of research.

The competition to present the first complete sequence of a human genome was widely seen as a battle between advocates of free access and advocates of proprietary information, but it was not that simple. At the time, the version published in *Science* magazine [6] in 2001 represented an experiment in providing the general community access to data generated by a private company.

Early history

To set the stage, it is important to go back to the Bayh-Dole Act. In an effort to spur innovation and promote public-private partnerships, Congress in 1980 declared that academic institutions and small businesses could hold on to intellectual property rights for inventions made under federally funded research programs. Universities and research institutions were being encouraged to commercialize discoveries [7]. Later, there would be debates over whether the Act had fostered a harmful anticommons [8] and the National Research Council in 2003 [9, p.23] would conclude that it had 'in some cases, impeded the unrestricted sharing of publication-related data.'

Partly as a result of the Bayh-Dole Act, the National Institutes of Health (NIH) and Venter were at the center of a controversy over publication of genetic information well before the 2001 publication. Venter, working at NIH, had developed a rapid gene-finding approach based on markers called expressed sequence tags (ests). The head of NIH's technology transfer office, Reid Adler, was contacted by an attorney at the biotechnology company Genentech Inc. because of concerns that publication of ests would result in patents being denied to the biotechnology industry 'even if the company had invested in the hard work of reading out the gene's whole sequence, identifying its protein, and figuring out what role it played in the body' [10, p.84]. Adler proposed that NIH patent the ests first; academics could use the ests without cost and companies would be able to license them for a fee. Bernadine Healy, who was NIH director at the time, supported this idea as well, and in 1991 and 1992 NIH applied for patents on 2,700 of these gene fragments.

The prospect of est patenting by NIH set off loud cries of opposition from the Pharmaceutical Manufacturers Association (PMA), biotechnology trade groups [11], and some in academia. Concern over the possibility that ests could be patented was one factor that led, in 1996, to the 'Bermuda accord,' an international agreement among the major sequencing groups mandating that sequence data be deposited in a public database within 24 hours of generation. This created prior art that could effectively render the sequence material unpatentable. It was also supposed to prevent duplication of efforts and level the playing field so that large sequencing centers would not have a monopoly on the information [12, 13], although, as I will describe, it is arguable whether a truly level playing field exists. Initially there was not an international consensus. The German research ministry had wanted to allow companies 3 months of advance access to data generated with their public funds, and only reversed themselves because of threats by US and British scientists that their German counterparts would be left out of the international community and denied access. Similar discussions occurred in France as well [14].

The beginnings of the genome wars

The Human Genome Project had originally been proposed by Charles DeLisi of the US Department of Energy (DOE) in 1986, and fit in with the DOE goals of understanding human mutation. NIH and the Wellcome Trust in the UK became the lead funders for an international consortium of publicly funded sequencing groups (which will be called the PFG here). The official start date was 1990 and, at a projected cost of $3 billion, the project was expected to take 15 years. The project was divided into mapping and sequencing phases, with the idea that maps of markers ordered along human chromosomes would guide the sequencing strategy. On May 10, 1998 at a meeting of the genome community at Cold Spring Harbor, New York, Michael Hunkapiller (representing Perkin-Elmer Corporation, which was innovating fast sequencing machinery) and Venter announced that they were forming a company (Celera Genomics) to sequence the human genome faster and cheaper than the PFG. They would use the 'shotgun sequencing' approach pioneered by Venter, which skipped the mapping step. It involved breaking the genome up into random pieces and, via algorithms, reassembling the whole thing in one step. The cost was projected to be $200-$250 million and they said they would be finished 4 years earlier than the PFG [10]. Venter announced that he would release data quarterly, which immediately raised the outcry from Robert Waterston (head of the sequencing group at Washington University, St. Louis) 'Quarterly! That's a lot different from overnight.' To which Venter reportedly replied, 'We're a company, Bob. We don't have to release the data at all. But if you think about it, quarterly is a lot closer to nightly than it is to never' [10, p.52].

The announcement at Cold Spring Harbor was the equivalent of stirring up an ant's nest with a stick. The PFG had originally envisioned producing a polished, error-free sequence but now felt pushed to generate a quick-and-dirty product to be competitive with Celera. I heard Phil Green (University of Washington, Seattle) sum up the situation graphically: 'We don't want to be the pooperscoopers for the Venterpillar' and the Welcome Trust announced that it would double the amount of money it was pouring into to the cause.

Venter was clear from the start that he planned to use the PFG data to help Celera's project. Access to public data gave Celera an advantage in assembling the sequence. Francis Collins of the NIH called it a breach of scientific ethics [15]. However, Celera received surprising support from no less than David Lipman, director of the National Center for Biotechnology Information (NCBI) who said, 'These groups understood when they deposited their data that the whole goal was to make it available without restrictions immediately' [15].

Venter was walking a tightrope between achieving the academic goal of recognition and the commercial goal of making money. Celera's initial business plan was for the data to be available by subscription. The idea was that the raw list of ordered nucleotides that make up DNA needed to be annotated, *i.e.* translated by means of computer programs into the genes and regulatory elements that could then be studied and harvested. The financial return for investors would be from the ability, for a fee, to access user-friendly tools with which to analyze the information. Pharmaceutical companies paid $5-$15 million a year and academic groups such as the Howard Hughes Medical Institute (HHMI) paid $7,500-$15,000 per lab for access to the Celera data [16].

From Celera's point of view, the genome sequence they generated could not just be released because of the concern that competing companies would repackage the data and sell it with their own tools. This concern was justified by actions of companies like Incyte Pharmaceuticals which, as early as May 1996, was selling a version of its database that included publicly available sequence data that had been analyzed with Incyte's proprietary software.

Publishing principles and database protections

The war between the public and private efforts would effectively be over if Venter couldn't publish and Venter couldn't publish if journals determined that his approach to data release violated journalistic policies.

There is a long tradition that a scientific publication must be complete enough so that other scientists can reproduce the work. Before the advent of large datasets, this meant showing the underlying data as part of the journal publication, but this became impractical as datasets grew. *Science* began making explicit statements regarding database deposition in an August 5, 1988 editorial in which Daniel E. Koshland, Jr. (1988) wrote that *Science* and other journals had developed procedures to help ensure that data would be sent to appropriate repositories [17].

For DNA sequence, the repository was the public database GenBank and its mirror sites. While data in GenBank has always been freely accessible, as of September 2012 the website still included the disclaimer that there might be patent, copyright, or other intellectual property encumbrances on the data.

In 1999 there were discussions about whether GenBank could cordon off some part of itself so that the Celera data could be viewable but not downloadable [18]. David Lipman indicated that NCBI did not have the resources to provide legal protection from copying [15] and could not even delay submission of a joint analysis to GenBank by 12 months. At one point, the PFG was willing to offer Celera a year's worth of some form of intellectual property protection as a database provider for data generated as part of a collaboration, but Celera held out for 3-5 years [19]. In 1999, no less proponents of openness than John Sulston and Tim Hubbard of the UK Sanger Center briefly considered such a model because of their concern that restrictions would be placed on reuse of the data [18].

Had Celera been operating in Europe, there would have been legal protections for its sequence database, as the European Union had enacted a database protection directive in 1996 allowing database creators 15 years of protection for the time, money, and effort they had invested. However Celera was vulnerable in the United States. In 1991 the US Supreme Court made an important decision in *Feist v. Rural Telephone*. Feist incorporated names, addresses, and phone numbers from Rural Telephone's directory into their own directory. Rural Telephone sued for copyright infringement, but the Supreme Court ruled that the information in their compilation was factual, and that facts are not protected by copyright. The reality that Rural Telephone had done the work of creating the database did not entitle it to copyright protection. The database industry responded by seeking help from Congress [19], but no legislation was passed. It was thus clear in the period between 1998 and 2001 that copyright law was not going to solve any of the issues being raised about protection for genomic databases. There was nothing to prevent a competing company from repackaging (with their own annotations) the Celera sequence and selling it.

A battle of media leaks and press announcements ensued, making the project seem less like noble science than a horse race, and splattering both sides with mud. To counter this, President Bill Clinton and Prime Minister Tony Blair issued a joint statement on March 14, 2000 in which they called the sequencing of the genome 'one of the most significant scientific projects of all time' and praised the PFG for its open release of data [20]. The statements were misinterpreted in the press as meaning that the leaders were going to come out against the patenting of genes. The result was a slide in stock prices, with Celera stock falling by 21% [21].

In another effort to shore up the public image of the field, the race to the genome was officially declared a draw. On June 26, 2000 it was announced that a draft sequence of the human genome had been completed by both Celera and the PFG. Pictures of Venter and Collins were taken with President Bill Clinton. One result was the sense that it would be an embarrassment if the two sides didn't publish side-by-side.

What was *Science* thinking?

Floyd Bloom, Editor-in-Chief of *Science* from 1995 until June 2000, focused on the lack of existing database protections. Donald Kennedy took over as Editor-in-Chief in June 2000 and felt that there could be flexibility in approaches to data access.

It was easy in 1999-2000 to find examples where guidelines for data access were being massaged to deal with realities of economics or to promote public-private interaction. One situation that formed a foundation for *Science*'s approach to commercial and academic access to data was the two-tier access existing at the time to the protein sequence archive called SWISSPROT. In 1998, SWISSPROT announced that, because its public funding could not keep up with the growing number of sequences, it would charge a yearly license fee to commercial users.[a]

Another example that was very much in Kennedy's mind was a paper that *Science* had published in 1987 that was based on a large archive of proprietary geophysical exploration data generated by EXXON Corporation [22]. The paper included summaries and not raw data; however, Kennedy felt that the research provided important insights into the history of sea-level change.

On May 25, 2000 Bloom and Kennedy, in an e-mail memorandum to both the PFG and Celera, enunciated *Science*'s position as follows: 'Access to the sequence is an essential pre-requisite for publication - However we believe that the research community is open to more than one model for database access - Restrictions that provide protection against commercial redistribution of the data can be consonant with publication in *Science*.' (personal communication, Donald Kennedy).

License negotiations

The first draft sent to *Science* by Celera in June, 2000 was not acceptable to the journal. There was a single click-through agreement for academic users, but commercial users and bioinformatics 'customers' would have to pay a fee to see any of the data. Such an agreement would have allowed users to examine the sequence only via browsing at the Celera site and to only use the analytical tool BLAST at the site to search for particular genes of interest. In addition, the first draft did not contain a provision for *Science* to keep an escrow copy, which *Science* considered vital for the archive of record. *Science* kept pushing for better access provisions and drafts were exchanged between Celera and *Science* through the fall and early winter of 2000.

A broad range of researchers (academic and commercial), bioethicists, lawyers, representatives of other journals, and experts in technology transfer from NIH and Howard Hughes Medical Institute (HHMI) were consulted. The ethics of differential access and the meaning of verification of published findings were at the center of many of the discussions. Celera was convinced to change the license terms so that for-profit users could get access to the data if they signed a material transfer agreement (MTA) that committed them to use the data for research purposes and not for commercialization. MTAs are contracts that regulate the transfer of materials (such as cell lines, plasmids, chemicals, or even software) between academic organizations and between academic organizations and industry. Some contained restrictions as to how the material could be used, and how and whether publications or commercial applications based on the material would be allowed. MTAs might require that the researcher receiving the material allow the provider a form of 'droit de Seigneur' in that the provider could review the draft of the researcher's publication or poster for a presentation, usually for 30 to 45 days.

In the agreements negotiated with Celera [23], noncommercial users would not have to sign an MTA; they would only have to execute a click-thru license and could then use the sequence to make discoveries and commercialize them without any reach-through provisions. A scientist working for a commercial organization could only get access to the sequence for purposes of basic research and to verify conclusions presented in the *Science* paper. In theory, that would make the data available to companies. However, even to confirm a result or to do basic research, it could be toxic for a company researcher to look at the data as it might be difficult to prove later that commercial advances had been made independently. Realistically, the only way commercial users would get access to the data was by paying for a subscription or getting a license from Celera.

Science received objections on philosophical grounds that any discrimination among readers was unethical. However, others commented that after facing restrictions in MTAs for clones and other materials they'd prefer to just pay for use of the data and be done with it. In addition, it was not hard for some academics, with their more limited resources, to accept the notion that the companies of the world would have to pay. Another reaction was that it was the lesser of two evils, with the greater evil being that the Celera data would not be released at all. We were told that neither NIH nor the HHMI would block their researchers from signing the agreements.

The public-private divide wasn't the only problem. For the burgeoning field of bioinformatics, which was analyzing and working out how to draw meaning from the raw sequence, verification was not enough; this community needed to be able to repost and recombine data. The ability to include chunks of data or a whole genome, not as a link to someone else's database, but as part of the actual paper was seen as crucial. The bioinformatics community did not believe that the restrictions on their ability to pool data fit a reasonable definition of 'accessible.'

The PFG decided in December 2000 to 'vote with their feet' and publish their paper in *Nature* instead of *Science*. Between December and February, when the publications appeared [6, 24] we received intense reactions - ranging from a hostile letter writing campaign to then National Academy of Sciences president Bruce Alberts' appraisal, 'If successful, this model agreement could greatly increase public access to the large amount of genome sequence data now held secret by private companies' [25].

Aftermath of the human genome publication

Celera and the Celera Genome. There was no question that the value of the Celera sequence, however well annotated, would decrease with time. Venter had said that he would put the data into GenBank in 3 years and that happened in 2005 [26]. Venter left Celera and, like other genomic data-based companies, Celera turned to pharmaceuticals and other avenues of profit [27]. As of September 7, 2012 each of the two human genome publications had received more than 10,000 citations according to Google Scholars.

Rice. In 2002 *Science* published the sequence of the rice genome produced by Syngenta's Torrey Mesa Research Institute, under essentially the same provisions as the human genome paper. Rather than downloading the sequence, academics would be sent a CD with the whole genome once they had signed a letter stating that they were using the sequence for basic research. Kennedy's rationale was that he considered rice to be the most important food crop in the world, but *Science* again received an outpouring of critical letters.

The Cech committee. In response, the National Academies of Science formed the Committee on Responsibilities of Authorship in the Biological Sciences in October 2001, headed by Thomas R. Cech. Their year-long investigation showed the existence of a general consensus about the importance of sharing but implementation varied, leading them to note 'as in many human activities, the devil is in the details' [9, p.35]. They came down hard against the idea of any exceptions to sharing upon publication, creating the acronym UPSIDE (the Uniform Principle for Sharing Integral Data and materials Expeditiously). They concluded that the access via *Science* to the human genome and rice sequence was static rather than the kind of dynamic access that would facilitate further research. However, they also recognized that lack of protection for companies who were generating databases was an issue that could impede the publication process.

Science magazine. The Information to Contributors was changed to explicitly state 'All data necessary to understand, assess, and extend the conclusions of the manuscript must be available to any reader of *Science*' [28]. It took years for the desire on the part of some of the genome community to punish *Science* to fade, but that has mostly disappeared.

Information may be free in heaven, but it's not so easy down here

During the genome wars, researchers who had to contend with the realities of the Bermuda accord were not finding it as straightforward as envisioned. If Venter was trying to 'have his cake and eat it too' by publishing in *Science* but still protecting corporate interests, some of the large scale sequencers were trying to do the same. They were advocating the high moral ground of immediate release in public while working in private to secure their publication advantage. Partial genomes, posted before the genome sequence was actually finished, were treasure-troves to scientists waiting to parse raw sequence into genes and regulatory elements and answer specific questions of biological and medical interest. As early as 1999, this tension was clear in disputes between major sequencing centers working on the genomes of agents that cause sleeping sickness or malaria and individual researchers eager to annotate genomes and use them in medical research [29].

The sequencers developed the culture of the gentlemen's agreement, which basically said that although anyone could look at and do research with the data, they could not publish until certain conditions were met. Sometimes this meant getting permission from the original sequencing group. In other cases researchers would have to refrain from publishing whole genome analyses until the originating group had published. There came to be a clear distinction between release of data to public access and the time when it was really free of encumbrances [30].

This did, however, leave a lot of grey areas. For example, the editor of *Immunology Today* asked if the sequencers had rights to sit on the data forever or if there was to be a time limit (such as a year) beyond which publication could be open to anyone [31]. Rowen and Hood [32] replied, saying that the time limit would have to start once all the data had been gathered to be fair to data producers, which could take years. Richard Hyman of the Stanford Genome Technology Center went further, responding that in the absence of written consent a third party publishing an analysis would be committing plagiarism and fraud [33].

The Fort Lauderdale meeting of January 2003 attempted to sort out some of the issues [34]. The 40 participants reaffirmed the rapid release principles but presented the case that it was in everyone's interest to nurture data producers who were involved in community resource projects. Funding agencies were called on to provide support for curation, maintenance, and distribution of the data and resources to the producers so they could analyze their data. Resource producers were asked ('when feasible') to generate and publish a project description or marker paper at the beginning of the community resource project, that would act as a citable reference and lay out the analyses for which they expected to have priority. Resource users were told that they should respect the legitimate rights of the producers by citing the marker paper, and respect the need of the producers to publish. No time limit for the prerogative of sequence producers to publish first was set. And, in a statement that sent a chill through the hearts of a number of journal editors, the Wellcome Trust report of the meeting specifically said it was the role of the journals to ensure that the system worked fairly for everyone.

This has left the journals in the middle. Sometimes publications would be moving along smoothly, with peace reigning among the analysts and junior members of the sequencing teams as co-authors, only for the journal to discover that the heads of the sequencing centers had not been consulted and were not happy with the deals that had been made. Nor is this kind of dispute old history. In August of 2009, a paper was published online at the *Proceedings of the National Academy of Science (PNAS)* that dealt with a gene associated with substance dependence in women of European descent. One of the authors had signed a Data Use Certification in which he agreed not to submit publications based on the Study of the Addiction, Genetics, and Environment dataset until September 23, 2009 but the dataset was used in the PNAS paper. The authors had to retract their paper on September 9, 2009 [35].

The National Human Genome Research Institute (NHGRI) established a 9-month moratorium on publication by third parties of data from the Encyclopedia of DNA Elements (ENCODE). An update to the policies was issued in November of 2009, extending that moratorium to 'all forms of public disclosure, including meeting abstracts, oral presentations, and formal electronic submissions to publicly accessible sites (*e.g.*, public websites, web blogs)' [36].

The Alzheimer's Disease Neuroimaging Initiative (ADNI) is an example of a public-private partnership that has been notably successful in efforts to collaborate and to have precompetitive data generated by a company made available to academic researchers. However, access to the data generated requires researchers to sign a data use agreement in which they affirm not to redistribute the data and to cite the ADNI in a manner deemed appropriate by an ADNI Data and Publications Committee [37].

The genome community has recently bumped into another problem that could affect the future of efforts to reap the fruits of the human genome project. To understand human variation, especially with regard to inherited disease, it is necessary to accumulate not just one but many genome sequences. To protect the privacy of participants in research studies, efforts have been made to deidentify the information or to present only data from pooled samples. However, the community has been shocked to learn that these approaches don't suffice - by algorithmic means or by combining anonymized sequence data with other freely available information it has been possible to reidentify certain individuals [38, 39]. Concern about this situation forced NIH and the Wellcome Trust to block public access to certain information in the databases dbGAP (The Database of Genotypes and Phenotypes) and CGEMS (a site for cancer genetics work) [40]. Certainly there are laws (*e.g.* the Health Insurance Portability and Accountability Act of 1996 (HIPAA) and the Genetic Information Nondiscrimination Act of 2008 (GINA)) that have been passed in order to protect privacy of medical data and to prevent discrimination in health insurance and employment on the basis of DNA information. However, informed consent is made more difficult by the impossibility of knowing the possible uses to which research data may be put in the future or the effects of aggregation of different kinds of personal data on privacy. Without volunteers allowing their information to be used, medical research studies that could benefit society as a whole will be impossible. Possible resolutions, such as controlled access to data that might otherwise be more freely shared, await future resolution.

Conclusions: a bigger picture

While the focus has been on the history of the 'genome wars', they did not occur in isolation, as discussions regarding information access have been occurring simultaneously in a variety of disciplines (Figure 1). Two forces are currently impacting the research community - the need to protect individual privacy regarding information and the push towards open access to data - and the outcomes are not yet clear. Data available from such sources as mobile phone calls, social media information, consumer information collected by companies, and government data have been described as revolutionizing the social sciences to an extent comparable to the effect that the microscope had on the biological sciences

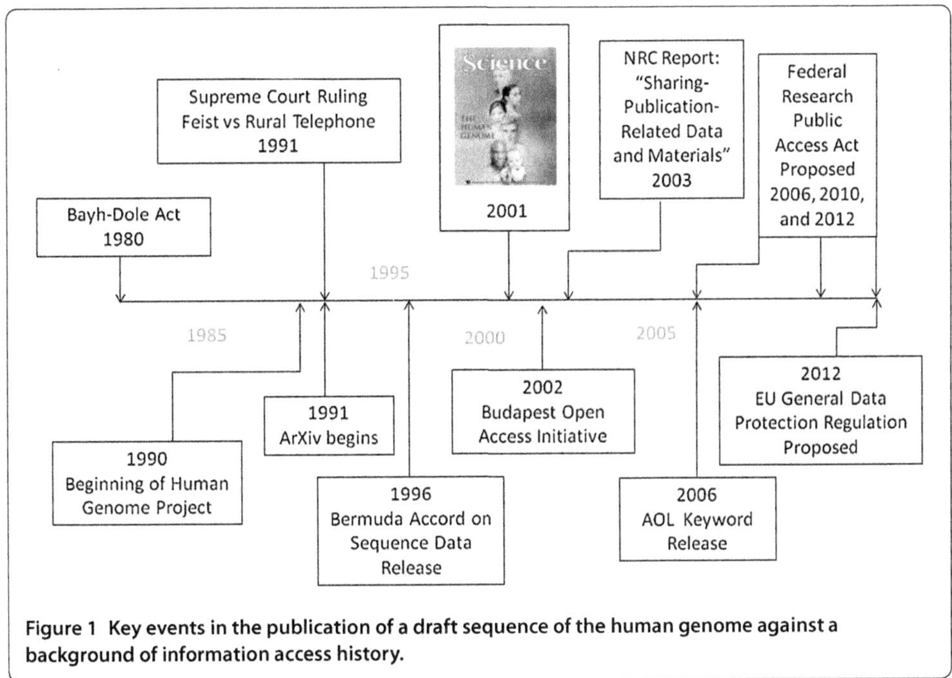

Figure 1 Key events in the publication of a draft sequence of the human genome against a background of information access history.

[41]. However such data individually (and, more importantly, in combination) could render current notions of privacy obsolete.

Large proprietary datasets have been made available to particular researchers because of the relationships or contractual agreements they have forged with the data-generating companies, which raises questions for reproducibility and review for the social science community [42]. For example, Wang *et al.* in 2009 [43] published research relating to the way that mobile viruses can spread, which has implications for the telecommunications infrastructure. Their findings were based on the anonymized billing records provided by 6.2 million mobile phone subscribers. As the privacy of the records were protected by law, the authors noted in the Supplemental Online Material that they would provide further information on request and told *Science* that as long as the researchers were willing to observe the same privacy, technological, security, and legal limitations that they were subject to at the time of the request, they would be glad to facilitate data access at their center (personal communication, A.-L. Barabasi). The motivations for some of these companies to release data to investigators are to learn more about their own clients and operations or to forge deals in which the researchers look at questions of interest to them. However, commentators have complained that such 'private' data threaten the capacity for independent replication on which science is based [44]. (As Bernardo Huberman said 'if an independent set of data fails to validate results derived from privately owned data, how do we know whether it is because those data are not universal or because the authors made a mistake?' [45].) Whether privately arranged access to data that form the basis of scientific publications or release only of aggregated data that protect company or individual privacy will continue remains to be seen. Certainly further investment in technology that can ensure control over the anonymization of data is warranted.

Nor is it easy for private companies to release such data without strings attached. Understanding how people search for information is an active area of research in the social sciences. In 2006 researchers employed by America Online, Inc. (AOL) published log files encompassing 36,389,567 searches done by users of AOL's proprietary client software on the Internet. This was done without the consent of the individuals involved and, even though screen names had been removed, New York Times reporters and others rapidly showed that it was possible to infer the identities of some of the searchers from the information that was released [46]. Even with these problems, some scientists said that the data release was a service to the research community [47]. AOL was widely criticized in the blogosphere and in mainstream media, some individuals at AOL lost their jobs, and the company was the target of a class-action lawsuit.

There is a long history of efforts to protect individual privacy in the United States and Europe covering a wide range of human activity. Some recent events should be noted as they could affect researchers' ability to gather data. In the European Union, a General Data Protection Regulation was proposed in January of 2012 and is expected to take effect by 2016 [48]. Two provisions could be especially challenging for the research community. The regulation stipulates that data can only be saved for as long as a need can be demonstrated. It also codifies a 'right to be forgotten' - that any individual has the right to have his/her data removed from a database at any time. The European Commission has stated that personal data 'is any information relating to an individual, whether it relates to his or her private, professional or public life. It can be anything from a name, a photo, an email address, bank details, your posts on social networking websites, your medical information, or your computer's IP address' [48]. In the United States, the Federal Trade Commission recently released recommendations for protecting consumer privacy, which included provisions for controls over how much data companies can collect on individuals and how long they can retain it as well as a recommendation that companies establish a 'do-not-track' mechanism for consumers who do not wish to have their information gathered [49]. There need to be consistent, transparent regulations that will safeguard the public but allow research to move forward.

While concerns about privacy could restrict data dissemination, another force is acting to promote access. The idea that sequence information should be freely available was a reflection of a much broader effort by diverse parts of the scientific community to make access to the results of scientific research faster and cost-free. The open source movement started between the 1970s and 1980s with the goal of creating, developing, and disseminating free computer operating systems that would break the hold of corporate entities [50]. While journals that are freely available to readers began to appear by the early 1980s [51] the open access movement gained momentum at about the same time as the human genome project was officially starting. In 1991, a year after the official start to the human genome project, Paul Ginsparg created ArXiv, a pre-publication server whose purpose was to facilitate rapid dissemination of scientific information, without subscription fees, page charges, or peer review [52]. It is currently possible to access more than 800,000 e-prints on ArXiv in physics, mathematics, computer science, quantitative biology, quantitative finance, and statistics.[b] The National Library of Medicine formed PubMedCentral in 2000 in order to have a free repository for NIH-funded research. Initially deposition was voluntary, but Congressional action (the Consolidated Appropriations Act of 2008 (H.R. 2764)) made deposition mandatory with release no later than a year post-publication, after statistics showed poor compliance by the fundees.

At roughly the same time as the report of the Cech committee came down hard on the idea of restrictions to data access in published papers two major manifestos of the open access movement, the Budapest open access initiative [53] and the Berlin declaration [54] appeared. Certainly some of the statements of groups and individuals who were most vociferous in their opposition to *Science*'s efforts to look for alternatives in publishing data reflect the philosophy of the open access movement. The Wellcome Trust, which has been a prime mover in supporting open access declared recently that 'Our support for open access publishing was a natural progression of our involvement in the international Human Genome Project during the 1990s and early 2000s, where the decision to place the human genetic sequence in the public domain immediately as it was generated helped to ensure this key research resource could be used by scientists the world over' [55].

There have been several attempts, via proposals in 2006, 2010, and 2012 to legislate a Federal Research Public Access Act to require that research funded by 11 federal agencies be made freely and publicly available in government sponsored repositories within 6 months of publication. While the advantages and disadvantages for researchers, funding agencies, and publishers are still being debated, the open access movement has a great deal of energy and backers willing to finance it (at least in the short term).

Does publication, whether in a repository or a journal, mean that enough information is released to form a solid foundation for future research? Despite high-minded principles, the published literature reflects the fact that many researchers do not, left to their own devices, rush to share data. Even when the *Journal of Biostatistics* offered to give formal recognition to authors who provided enough data and methods in their papers to allow an editor to replicate the findings, only a small percent complied [56]. Although the extent of sharing varies from field to field, common reasons given for withholding data are similar: it is too much work, it removes the competitive advantage from the scientists who generated the data and who require publications for their careers, or the raw data was received under confidentiality agreements. The Dataverse Network is a repository for social science data that allows depositors to note concerns and restrictions. In a 2010 survey of the conditions for use posted by more than 30,000 users, Stodden [57] found the most common were 'maintaining subject confidentiality, preventing further sharing, making a specific citation form a condition of use, restricting access by commercial or profit-making entities, and restricting use to a specific community, such as that of the researcher's home institution.'

Certainly the granting and funding and tenure cultures need to enforce good behavior, which people have been saying for years. NIH now mandates that provisions for data sharing be included in research applications for $500,000 or more of direct costs in any single year and several other agencies have similar provisions. The NSF states that to apply for a grant as of January 18, 2011 'All proposals must describe plans for data management and sharing of the products of research, or assert the absence of the need for such plans' [58]. The two-page data management plan submitted as part of the application may include 'policies and provisions for re-use, re-distribution, and the production of derivatives' and 'plans for archiving data, samples, and other research products, and for preservation of access to them.' Although the NSF-wide mandate takes precedence, there are variations within the directorates [59]. For example, the NSF Division of Earth Sciences allows up to 2 years of exclusive data use for selected principal investigators. The directorate for Social, Behavioral, and Economic Sciences allows for the possibility of ethical and legal restrictions regarding access to non-aggregated data.

Community service, whether through generation of shared data or sharing of knowledge and communication with the public needs to be formally recognized. A Data and

Informatics Working Group has recommended that NIH provide incentives for data sharing by providing information on the number of times datasets in its central repository are accessed or downloaded [60].

Even when academic communities are willing to share data, public repositories do not always exist and those that do are under siege in unstable economic environments. It can be easy to drum up funds to create databases, but not so easy to find federal or other moneys to sustain them. Data repositories need continuing support.

The momentum in academia is clearly that releasing and not hoarding data is a virtue. However, the history and examples cited in this paper show that while data sharing may become second nature, it is not an easy, seamless process and is not happening without challenges and compromises.

Competing interests

The author declares that she has no competing interests.

Additional information

This review represents the opinion of the author only and is not an official statement for *Science* magazine or the American Association for the Advancement of Science.

Author's information

The author has been on the staff of *Science* magazine for 27 years and was the manuscript editor handling the human genome paper published by *Science* and described in this review.

Acknowledgements

I would like to thank Don Kennedy for his support and unwavering sense of humor, and for comments on this manuscript.

Endnotes

[a] Important announcement concerning SWISS-PROT www.bio.net/bionet/mm/bionews/1998-July/004469.html.

[b] www.arXiv.org.

References

1. Berners-Lee T (2009) Tim Berners-Lee on the next web. www.ted.com/talks/tim_berners_lee_on_the_next_web.html. Accessed 23 Dec 2012
2. Guttmacher AE, Nabel EG, Collins FS (2009) Why data-sharing policies matter. Proc Natl Acad Sci USA 106:16894
3. Louis K, Jones L, Campbell E (2002) Sharing in science. Am Sci 90:304-309
4. Savage CJ, Vickers AJ (2009) Empirical study of data sharing by authors publishing in PLoS journals. PLoS ONE 4(9):e7078
5. Tenopir C, Allard S, Douglass K, Aydinoglu AU, Wu L, Read E, Manoff M, Frame M (2011) Data sharing by scientists: practices and perceptions. PLoS ONE 6(6):e21101
6. Venter JC et al (2001) The sequence of the human genome. Science 291:1304-1351
7. Healy B (1997) BRCA genes - bookmaking, fortunetelling, and medical care. N Engl J Med 337:788-789
8. Heller M, Eisenberg R (1985) Can patents deter innovation: the anticommons in biomedical research. Science 280:698-701
9. National Research Council (2003) Sharing publication-related data and materials: responsibilities of authorship in the life science. National Academies Press, Washington
10. Shreeve J (2004) The genome war: how Craig Venter tried to capture the code of life and save the world. Ballantine Books, New York
11. Eisenberg RS (1993) Technology transfer and the genome project: problems with patenting research pools. Risk Health Saf Environ 5:163-174
12. Dickson D (1996) NIH seeks rapid sequence release. Nature 380:279
13. Bentley DR (1996) Genomic sequence information should be released immediately and freely in the public domain. Science 274:533-534
14. Abbott A (1997) Germany rejects genome data isolation. Nature 387:536
15. Wade N (2000) Rivals on offensive as they near wire in genome race. New York Times, 7 May 2000. http://www.nytimes.com/2000/05/07/us/rivals-on-offensive-as-they-near-wire-in-genome-race.html?pagewanted=all&src=pm. Accessed 23 Dec 2012
16. Service R (2001) Can data banks tally profits? Science 291:1203
17. Koshland DE Jr (1988) The price of progress. Science 241:637
18. Sulston J, Ferry G (2002) The common thread. Joseph Henry Press, New York
19. Pike GH (2003) Database protection legislation introduced in Congress. Infotoday. http://newsbreaks.infotoday.com/nbreader.asp?ArticleID=16598. Posted 20 Oct 2003. Accessed 1 Jan 2012
20. White House Office of the Press Secretary (2000) Joint statement by president Clinton and prime minister Tony Blair of the UK, 14 March 2000. http://clinton4.nara.gov/WH/EOP/OSTP/html/00314.html

21. Schehr R, Fox J (2000) Human genome bombshell. Nat Biotechnol 18:365
22. Haq BU, Hardenbol J, Vail PR (1987) Chronology of fluctuating sea levels since the Triassic (250 million years ago to present). Science 235:1156-1167
23. Accessing the Celera human genome sequence data. http://www.sciencemag.org/site/feature/data/announcement/gsp.xhtml. Accessed 23 Dec 2012
24. International Human Genome Sequencing Consortium (2001) Initial sequencing and analysis of the human genome. Nature 409:860-921
25. Chemistry and Industry (2000) Celera makes genome data freely available. http://findarticles.com/p/articles/mi_hb5255/is_2000_Dec_18/ai_n28808580/
26. Kaiser J (2005) Celera to end subscriptions and give data to public GenBank. Science 308:5723
27. Kling J (2005) Where the future went. EMBO Rep 6:1012-1014
28. General information for authors. Science. http://www.sciencemag.org/site/feature/contribinfo/prep/gen_info.xhtml#dataavail. Accessed 3 Dec 2012
29. Macilwain C (2000) Biologists challenge sequencers on parasite genome publication. Nature 405:601-602
30. Contreras JL (2010) Prepublication data release, latency, and genome commons. Science 329:393-394
31. Bell E (2000) Publication rights for sequence data producers. Science 290:1696-1698
32. Rowen L, Hood L (2000) Response. Science 290:1696-1698
33. Hyman R (2001) Sequence data: posted vs. published. Science 291:827
34. Wellcome Trust (2003) Sharing data from large-scale biological research projects: a system of tripartite responsibility. Report of a meeting organized by the Wellcome Trust and held on 14-15 January 2003 at Fort Lauderdale, USA. http://www.genome.gov/Pages/Research/WellcomeReport0303.pdf. Accessed 23 Dec 2012
35. Schekman R (2009) PNAS takes action regarding breach of NIH embargo policy on a PNAS paper. Proc Natl Acad Sci USA 106:16893
36. ENCODE consortium data release policy summary. http://genome.ucsc.edu/ENCODE/terms.html. Accessed 8 Apr 2012
37. Alzheimer's Disease Neuroimaging Initiative (ADNI) data use agreement. http://adni.loni.ucla.edu/wp-content/uploads/how_to_apply/ADNI_Data_Use_Agreement.pdf. Accessed 8 Apr 2012
38. Gitschier J (2009) Inferential genotyping of Y chromosomes in latter-day saints founders and comparison to Utah samples in the HapMap project. Am J Hum Genet 84:251-258
39. Homer N et al (2008) Resolving individuals contributing trace amounts of DNA to highly complex mixtures using high-density SNP genotyping microarrays. PLoS Genet 4(8):e1000167. doi:10.1371/journal.pgen.1000167
40. P^3G Consortium, Church G, Heeney C, Hawkins N, de Vries J et al (2009) Public access to genome-wide data: five views on balancing research with privacy and protection. PLoS Genet 5(10):e1000665. doi:10.1371/journal.pgen.1000665
41. King G (2012) Ensuring the data-rich future of the social sciences. Science 331:719-721
42. Lazer D, Pentland A, Adamic L, Aral S, Barabási A-L, Brewer D, Christakis N, Contractor N, Fowler J, Gutmann M, Jebara T, King G, Macy M, Roy D, Van Alstyne M (2009) Life in the network: the coming age of computational social science. Science 323:721-723
43. Wang P, González MC, Hidalgo CA, Barabási A-L (2009) Understanding the spreading patterns of mobile phone viruses. Science 324:1071-1076
44. Markoff J (2012) Troves of personal data, forbidden to researchers. http://www.nytimes.com/2012/05/22/science/big-data-troves-stay-forbidden-to-social-scientists.html. Accessed 23 Dec 2012
45. Huberman B (2012) Sociology of science: big data deserve a bigger audience. Nature 482:308
46. Barbaro M, Zeller T Jr (2006) A face is exposed for AOL searcher No. 4417749. http://www.nytimes.com/2006/08/09/technology/09aol.html?pagewanted=all. Accessed 3 Dec 2012
47. Wiggins RW (2006) AOL is caught in its own long tail. http://newsbreaks.infotoday.com/nbreader.asp?ArticleID=17374. Accessed 3 Dec 2012
48. Europa press release (2012) Commission proposes a comprehensive reform of data protection rules to increase users' control of their data and to cut costs for businesses. http://europa.eu/rapid/press-release_IP-12-46_en.htm. Accessed 23 Dec 2012
49. Federal Trade Commission press release (2012) FTC issues final Commission report on protecting consumer privacy, 26 March 2012. http://www.ftc.gov/opa/2012/03/privacyframework.shtm. Accessed 23 Dec 2012
50. Wayner P (2000) Free for all: how Linux and the free software movement undercut the high-tech giants. Harper Collins, New York. http://www.jus.uio.no/sisu/free_for_all.peter_wayner/portrait.pdf. Accessed 23 Dec 2012
51. Suber P (2009) Timeline of the open access movement. www.earlham.edu/~peters/fos/timeline.htm. Accessed 23 Dec 2012
52. Ginsparg P (2001) Creating a global knowledge network. Invited contribution for conference held at UNESCO HQ, Paris, 19-23 Feb 2001, second joint ICSU press - UNESCO expert conference on electronic publishing in science, during session responses from the scientific community, Tue 20 Feb 2001. http://people.ccmr.cornell.edu/~ginsparg/blurb/pg01unesco.html. Accessed 21 Dec 2012
53. Budapest open access initiative. http://www.opensocietyfoundations.org/openaccess/read. Accessed 23 Dec 2012
54. Berlin initiative. http://oa.mpg.de/files/2010/04/berlin_declaration.pdf. Accessed 23 Dec 2012
55. Carr D, Kiley R (2012) Open access to science helps us all. http://www.newstatesman.com/blogs/economics/2012/04/open-access-science-helps-us-all. Accessed 23 Dec 2012
56. Peng RD (2011) Reproducible research in computational science. Science 334:1226-1227
57. Stodden V (2010) Data sharing in social science repositories: facilitating reproducible computational research. http://www.stanford.edu/~vcs/papers/nips2010Stodden12062010.pdf. Accessed 23 Dec 2012
58. National Science Foundation (2011) Grant proposal guide. http://www.nsf.gov/pubs/policydocs/pappguide/nsf11001/gpg_2.jsp#dmp. Accessed 23 Dec 2012

59. University of Michigan Library (2012) NSF data management plans. http://www.lib.umich.edu/research-data-management-and-publishing-support/nsf-data-management-plans#directorate_guide. Accessed 3 Dec 2012
60. Data and Informatics Working Group (2012) Draft report to the Advisory Committee to the Director, 15 June 2012. acd.od.nih.gov/Data%20and%20Informatics%20Working%20Group%20Report.PDF. Accessed 23 Dec 2012

12

Topology and evolution of the network of western classical music composers

Doheum Park[1], Arram Bae[1], Maximilian Schich[2] and Juyong Park[1*]

*Correspondence:
juyongp@kaist.ac.kr
[1]Graduate School of Culture Technology and BK21 Plus Postgraduate Organization for Content Science, Korea Advanced Institute of Science & Technology, 291 Daehak-ro, Yuseong-gu, Daejeon 305-701, Republic of Korea
Full list of author information is available at the end of the article

Abstract

The expanding availability of high-quality, large-scale data from the realm of culture and the arts promises novel opportunities for understanding and harnessing the dynamics of the creation, collaboration, and dissemination processes - fundamentally network phenomena - of artistic works and styles. To this end, in this paper we explore the complex network of western classical composers constructed from a comprehensive CD (Compact Disc) recordings data that represent the centuries-old musical tradition using modern data analysis and modeling techniques. We start with the fundamental properties of the network such as the degree distribution and various centralities, and find how they correlate with composer attributes such as artistic styles and active periods, indicating their significance in the formation and evolution of the network. We also investigate the growth dynamics of the network, identifying superlinear preferential attachment as a major growth mechanism that implies a future of the musical landscape where an increasing concentration of recordings onto highly-recorded composers coexists with the diversity represented by the growth in the sheer number of recorded composers. Our work shows how the network framework married with data can be utilized to advance our understanding of the underlying principles of complexities in cultural systems.

Keywords: complex network; classical music; network topology; network evolution

1 Introduction

Networks have been used extensively in recent years for characterizing and modeling intricate patterns found in various social, technological, and biological complex systems originating from the functional and dynamical interdependence between their components. The methodology is expanding its horizon, being eagerly adopted in new fields such as culture for exploring novel answers to new and long-standing issues [1–4]. In broad terms, the potential of the network framework for understanding culture originates from the observation that the creation and transmission of cultural products are essentially network phenomena. Networks, therefore, may lead to a new fundamental understanding of the complex nature of culture.

There are several interesting questions one can explore regarding such 'network in culture' - e.g., How does it evolve and change over time? Who are the most prominent or popular artists, and how do we measure their importance? How do the different styles combine to produce cultural products? How does information flow over network ties? [5]

- the answers to which would contribute to deepening our understanding of culture and the arts.

There have been several notable works that highlight the importance of networks on understanding various issues in culture. Suárez, Sancho and de la Rosa [6] analyzed the linkage patterns from the data of 11,443 artworks from Spain and Latin America with respect to genre and theme, identifying religious theme to be a dominant factor connecting the paintings. Gleiser and Danon [7] studied the topology and the community structure of the collaboration network of Jazz musicians, uncovering the presence of communities based on the locations of the bands correlated with the racial segregation between the musicians. Park *et al.* [8] compared two networks of contemporary popular musicians - one representing the collaboration history of the musicians, and the other representing musical similarities as judged by human experts - finding that the significant topological differences are related closely to the nature of the connections. Salganik *et al.* [9] studied the role of social influence and success of cultural products. They found that social influence has a significant effect, elevating the inequality and the unpredictability of success. Uzzi and Spiro [10] investigated the small-world property of the network of the creators of original Broadway musicals that reflect the level of their cohesion and its impact on the success of the musicals. They found that cohesion had a positive impact up to some point, but began to impede the creativity when it becomes too large. The characteristics of a system and growth or evolutionary dynamics are deeply intertwined [11]. This is likely to be the case for cultural system as well, and grasping the underlying growth principles may need a better understanding of their nature. This line of thinking is behind the work of Jeong *et al.* [12] who applied network evolution models to the movie-actor network. Recently in the field of music, Serrà *et al.* [13] constructed a time-varying network of pitch transitions in contemporary western popular music (from 1955 to 2010) and analyzed the degree distributions of pitches, pointing out the limited use of various pitch transitions.

In this paper we analyze the co-occurrence network of western classical composers constructed from the comprehensive data set of CD recordings. Using the network framework, we try to shed light on the following specific questions in order: Who are the prominent composers? What are the driving force behind composers being co-featured on a common CD? Can we characterize the temporal growth of the network and the composers? We start by measuring the fundamental network properties that give us a bird's-eye view of the general features of the network, including the size, clustering coefficient, assortativity, degree distribution, centralities, and community structure. The centralities identify influential composers with varying artistic styles, while the positive assortativity shows that period designations and artistic styles are the main driving force behind co-featured composers. This is explored further using the community structure of the composers. We characterize the growth of the composer-CD network by way of the temporal evolution of the bipartite degree distribution, and how it can be mapped to a superlinear preferential attachment model. It also allows us to forecast the future of the landscape of the composer network, where the growths of the degrees of prominent composers are accelerating and accordingly the recordings are becoming increasingly concentrated on those already well established, an effect similar to the so-called urban-scaling laws, where existing cultural centers win out over new centers [4, 14].

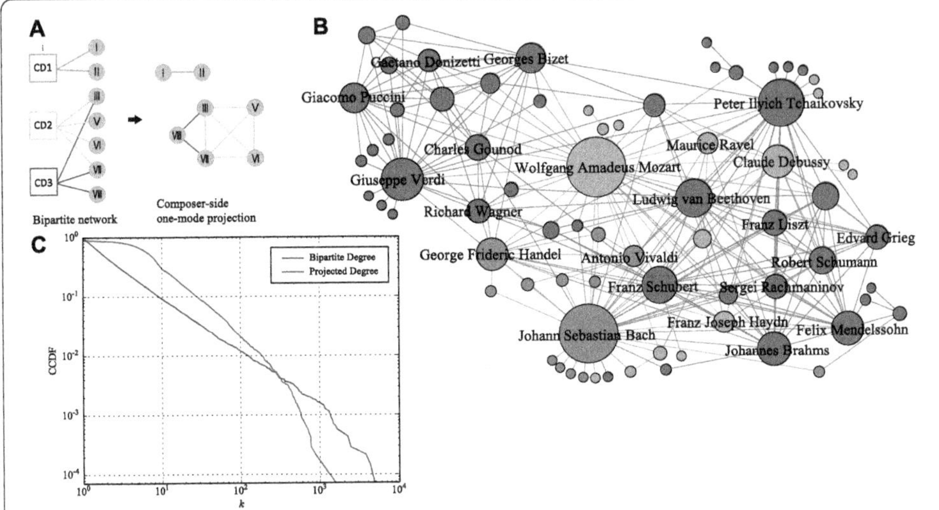

Figure 1 Construction of the network from data, and backbone of the composer network. (A) The network representation of ArkivMusic data. The association between the CDs and composers visualized as a bipartite network (left). One-mode projection of the bipartite network onto the set of composers by connecting composers when they are associated with a common CD (right). **(B)** The composer-composer network backbone, projected from the CD-composer network, reveals the major component of the network. The node sizes represent the composers' degrees, and the colors represent their active periods (violet - Baroque, pink - Classical, red - Romantic, orange - Modern). Serrano's [15] algorithm was used to extract the backbone. **(C)** The cumulative distributions for the bipartite degree q, the number of CDs in which a composer was featured (blue), and the projected degree k, the number of composers with whom a composer was co-featured on at least one CD (red). Both exhibit a right-skewed behavior.

2 Data and network construction

We utilized two online data resources: ArkivMusic (http://www.arkivmusic.com), an online music retailer, and All Music Guide (http://www.allmusic.com), a comprehensive musical information provider. As of 2013, ArkivMusic lists more than 96,000 classical music CDs and its title, release date, and the composers and performers of the music. For this work we specifically use the title, release date and the composers. As we show in Figure 1(A), the data can be represented as a *bipartite network* composed of two node classes - CDs and composers - where an edge is drawn when a composer's pieces were recorded on the CD. A *one-mode projection* onto the composer class results in a network solely of composers in which two nodes are connected if they have been co-featured on a CD (Figure 1(A)). Figure 1(B) shows the so-called network backbone (a scaled-down representation [15]). Compilation CDs (a repacked collection of previous released recordings) and the ones without release dates were weeded out from the data, resulting in 63,679 CDs and 13,981 composers for analysis.

3 Topology of the composer network

First we examine the fundamental properties of the composer network to understand its general features. We then analyze the relationship between the characteristics of connected composers to study how they affect the chances of connection, i.e. becoming featured on a common recording. We investigate the centralities, the assortativity, and the community structure of the composer-composer network to answer the question of who are the prominent composers, and what drives the formation of connection patterns.

3.1 Fundamental network properties reveal the small-world property, a high clustering, and wide differences in composer prominence

Many networks exhibit the so-called 'small-world' property [16], often expressed using 'six degree of separation' in common parlance. Mathematically defined as the mean geodesic distance (the length of the shortest path) between nodes increasing sublinearly (typically logarithmically) as a function of the size of the network, it is frequently represented by a small mean geodesic distance (a geodesic is the shortest path between two nodes. If they are directly connected, the geodesic distance is 1). Technically speaking the two definitions are unidentical [17], although for the purpose of our paper the distinction is not critical. The mean geodesic distance and the diameter (the longest geodesic) in the largest component (set of connected nodes) are 13.1 and 20 for the CD-composer network, and 3.5 and 20 for the composer-composer network, respectively.

The *clustering coefficient* C is the probability that two nodes connected to a common neighbor are themselves neighbors. It is a measure of the abundance of triangles in the network, and a high value is a hallmark of social networks [18]. In our composer-composer network we have $C = 0.648$ compared with the random expectation $\overline{C}_{\text{random}} = 0.001$, meaning that our network is indeed highly clustered. Such a clustered behavior is deeply related to patterns of mixing and community structure, which we later discuss in detail.

We now investigate the nodes' *degrees* in the network. A node's degree, the number of its neighbors, is a type of its *centrality*, a class of quantities that signify a node's importance or prominence determined from the network. The degree is the basic and most intuitive centrality, and is the principal factor behind many network properties [17]. As such, it can be useful in understanding the different roles or positions of the composers in our network. Specifically, in our study we consider two types of composer degrees: The bipartite degree q in the CD-composer network, and the projected degree k in the composer-composer network. While closely related, they carry slightly different yet interesting probable interpretations: The bipartite degree would mainly represent a composer's popularity, while the projected degree would mainly represent a composer's versatility or compatibility with others, likely in terms of musical styles. The nodes' degrees as a whole can be characterized by plotting the degree distributions $p(q)$ and $p(k)$, or the cumulative distributions $P(q) = \sum_{q'=q}^{\infty} p(q')$ and $P(k) = \sum_{k'=k}^{\infty} p(k')$ plotted in Figure 1(B) on a log-log scale. We note that both distributions exhibit heavy tails, i.e. a few composers take up the lion's share of recordings and composer-composer associations: In the CD-composer network, Wolfgang Amadeus Mozart (1756-1791) has the highest degree $q = 4{,}851$, approximately 505 times the mean $\overline{q} = 9.6$, followed by Johann Sebastian Bach (1685-1750) with $k = 4{,}292$. In the composer-composer network JS Bach has the highest degree, $k = 1{,}551$, approximately 103 times that of average degree $\overline{k} = 15.1$, followed by WA Mozart with $k = 1{,}086$. For reference, in Table 1 we show the names of composers with the twenty highest q and k values. The heavy-tailed degree distribution in Figure 1(B) tells us that there is a significant variation in the composers' prominence and popularity in the landscape of classical music, which provides us with an important clue for understanding its nature and how it would potentially evolve in time, which we discuss in a later chapter.

3.2 Composer centralities reveal the relationship between the network and composer characteristics

Next, we study further types of composer centralities in the composer-composer network that capture various 'flavors' of a node's importance in a network.

Table 1 Top 20 composers for degree, eigenvector, and betweenness centralities

Rank	Bipartite degree (q)		Projected degree (k)		Eigenvector centrality		Betweenness centrality	
	Name	Period	Name	Period	Name	Period	Name	Period
1	WA Mozart	C	JS Bach	B	JS Bach	B	JS Bach	B
2	JS Bach	B	WA Mozart	C	WA Mozart	C	WA Mozart	C
3	Beethoven	R	Handel	B	Handel	B	Handel	B
4	Brahms	R	Brahms	R	Brahms	R	Piazzolla	M
5	Schubert	R	Mendelssohn	R	Mendelssohn	R	Brahms	R
6	Verdi	R	Debussy	M	Schubert	R	Gershwin	M
7	Tchaikovsky	R	Schubert	R	Debussy	M	Debussy	M
8	R Schumann	R	Beethoven	R	Beethoven	R	Mendelssohn	R
9	Handel	B	Saint-Saëns	R	Saint-Saëns	R	Schubert	R
10	Wagner	R	Tchaikovsky	R	Tchaikovsky	R	Beethoven	R
11	Chopin	R	Ravel	M	Ravel	M	Villa-Lobos	M
12	Haydn	C	Gershwin	M	Fauré	R	Ravel	M
13	Liszt	R	R Schumann	R	R Schumann	R	Tchaikovsky	R
14	Mendelssohn	R	Fauré	R	Liszt	R	Copland	M
15	Debussy	M	Liszt	R	Chopin	R	Saint-Saëns	R
16	Puccini	R	Vivaldi	B	Vivaldi	B	Vivaldi	B
17	Vivaldi	B	Piazzolla	M	Rossini	R	Stravinsky	M
18	Dvořák	R	Rossini	R	Rachmaninoff	M	Britten	M
19	Ravel	M	Chopin	R	Haydn	C	Hindemith	M
20	R Strauss	R	Verdi	R	Gershwin	M	Bernstein	M

Each centrality can be interpreted as representing distinct composer characteristics: The bipartite degree represents a composer's popularity; the projected degree represents a composer's compatibility with others; the eigenvector centrality is a generalization of the degree that considers the quality of connections (e.g. whether a composer tends to be paired with other prominent composers); the betweenness centrality measures how often a composer acts as an intermediary between two composers. Periods are abbreviated: Baroque (B), Classical (C), Romantic (R), and Modern (M).

Besides the degree that we have already seen, the *Eigenvector Centrality* and the *Betweenness Centrality* (also called the *Freeman Centrality* after its inventor) [19, 20] are widely used. The eigenvector centrality is a generalization of the degree that considers the 'quality' of a connection: Being a neighbor to a central node in turn raises one's own eigenvector centrality. The name comes from its mathematical definition as the components of the leading eigenvector of the adjacency matrix. The betweenness centrality measures how often a node sits on the geodesic between two nodes, acting as an intermediary (e.g., in communication). One benefit of investigating different centralities is that while the centralities are often correlated, significant disagreements can point to unusual aspects of the network that in turn can lead to a deeper understanding of it. The highest-ranked composers in each centrality are given in Table 1. The lists do appear correlated, with Spearman Rank Correlations (SPR) equal to 0.753 ± 0.002 between degree k and eigenvector centrality, and 0.784 ± 0.003 between degree k and betweenness. But composers labeled 'M' for Modern (the composer's *period*, to be discussed later) are ranked significantly higher in betweenness than in other centralities. It turns out that Modern composers form a tight-knit group with many connections between them, elevating the betweenness of prominent Modern composers such as Aaron Copland (1900-1990) and Leonard Bernstein (1918-1990) although their degree is significantly lower than those from other periods. In order to understand the implications of this type of relationship between a node attribute and network topology, next we review the common period designation in western classical music and analyze them further.

3.3 Common artistic style and period designations in western classical music

As one of the oldest art forms, music has a rich history of academic research and investigation [21–24]. While not every expert would agree on one single scheme, it is common to break down the evolution of western classical music into the following several stages by distinguishable styles [25, 26] (we follow the convention employed by All Music Guide, all years are approximate and in CE):

1. *Medieval* (500-1400). The period when primeval shape of musical notation appeared, along with advances in tonal material, texture, and rhythm. Polyphony took shape in terms of tonal material [21]. Notable composers include Guillaume de Machaut (1300-1377) and Francesco Landini (1325-1397).
2. *Renaissance* (1401-1600). The period of modes and rich textures in four or more parts blending strands in the musical texture, harmony, and progression of chords [27]. Notable composers include Thomas Tallis (1505-1585), William Byrd (1540-1623), and John Dowland (1563-1626).
3. *Baroque* (1601-1750). The period distinguished by the creation of tonality. During this period, composers used elaborate musical ornamentation and made changes in musical notation. Baroque music became more complex and expanded the range of instrumental performance [23]. Notable composers include Henry Purcell (1659-1695), Antonio Vivaldi (1678-1741), Johann Sebastian Bach (1685-1750), and George Frideric Handel (1685-1759).
4. *Classical* (1730-1820). The period characterized by a lighter, clearer texture than Baroque. Variety and contrast within a piece became more pronounced than before, and melodies tended to be shorter, with clear-cut phrases and clearly marked cadences [28]. Notable composers include Wolfgang Amadeus Mozart (1756-1791) and Franz Joseph Haydn (1732-1809).
5. *Romantic* (1815-1910). The period when music was closely related with romanticism, the artistic and literary movement in Europe [29]. Romantic music is characterized by freedom of form, emotions, individuality, dynamic changes and nationalism. Notable composers include Ludwig van Beethoven (1770-1827), Franz Schubert (1797-1828), Frédéric Chopin (1810-1849), Robert Schumann (1810-1856), Franz Liszt (1811-1886), and Pyotr Ilyich Tchaikovsky (1840-1893).
6. *Modern* (1900-current). The period characterized by musical innovations in organizing and approaching harmonic, melodic, sonic, and rhythmic aspects leading to many novel styles including expressionism, abstractionism, neoclassicism, futurism, *etc.* [30]. The rise of American classical music was also significant. Notable composers from this period include Claude Debussy (1862-1918), Maurice Ravel (1875-1937), Sergei Rachmaninoff (1873-1943), Igor Stravinsky (1882-1971), George Gershwin (1898-1937) and Leonard Bernstein (1918-1990).

The composer metadata (period and active years) were available for 878 composers, leaving us with 13,667 edges between those in the composer-composer network. While accounting for 6.3% of the entire composer group, these are still the most prominent and significant ones who would be of primary interest; the average bipartite degree for this group is $\overline{q} = 64.8$, nearly twenty times larger than the remainder for which $\overline{q} = 3.5$.

3.4 Assortativity and community structures reveal artistic styles and periods as the main factor behind connections between composers

The relationship between node characteristics and network topology can be quantified by the assortativity coefficient for discrete node characteristics [31] given by $r \equiv \frac{\sum_i e_{ii} - \sum_i a_i b_i}{1 - \sum_i a_i b_i}$, where $\mathbf{e} = \{e_{ij}\}$ is a matrix whose element e_{ij} is the fraction of edges in a network that connect a node of type i to one of type j, and a_i and b_i are the fraction of each type of end of an edge that is attached to nodes of type i. For the composers' periods we have $r = 0.257 \pm 0.005$, meaning that composers belonging to a common period tend to be connected preferentially to one another. The Pearson Correlation Coefficient (PCC) between connected composers' active years (the middle point between their birth and death years) is even higher, with 0.451 ± 0.009.

The assortative mixing we see here is intimately related to the existence of *communities* or *modules* in a network. A community is commonly defined as a group of nodes of a network in which connections are denser than randomly expected or to the rest of the network. Algorithms for detecting communities have seen significant developments in recent years [32–36]. We used the Louvain algorithm of Blondel *et al.* [37] on our reduced network, among many excellent choices. We examined the five largest communities that accounted for 99% of the 878 nodes with known periods. We split Community 1 further into two (named 1A and 1B) since unlike other communities, Community 1 was ostensibly a mixture of many periods. This leaves us with the six sizable communities shown in Figure 2. We find that the communities roughly correspond to the periods introduced earlier; i.e. Community 1A to Renaissance and early Baroque, 1B to late Baroque and Classical, 2 to Romantic, and 3, 4, 5 to Modern (differentiated further among themselves as presented below). We note that, while in terms of sheer number 1B contains more Modern composers, they are rather insignificant compared with others, mainly late Baroque and Classical (the mean degree of Modern composers in the Community is 19.9, while it is 77.8 for the rest). The notable composers in each community are

- Community 1A: William Byrd (1540-1623, Renaissance) and Henry Purcell (1659-1695, Baroque)
- Community 1B: Antonio Vivaldi (1678-1741, Baroque), Johann Sebastian Bach (1685-1750, Baroque), George Frideric Handel (1685-1759, Baroque) from the Baroque period, and Wolfgang Amadeus Mozart (1756-1791, Classical), and Franz Joseph Haydn (1732-1809, Classical) from the Classical period.
- Community 2: Ludwig van Beethoven (1770-1827) and Franz Schubert (1797-1828) who are considered transitional between Classical and Romantic; Robert Schumann (1810-1856, Romantic), Frédéric Chopin (1810-1849, Romantic), Franz Liszt (1811-1886, Romantic), Johannes Brahms (1833-1897, Romantic), and Pyotr Ilyich Tchaikovsky (1840-1893, Romantic) from Romantic.
- Community 3: A US-centric Modern community, with two highest-degree Modern composers being George Gershwin (1898-1937, Modern) of *Rhapsody in Blue* and Leonard Bernstein (1918-1990, Modern) of *West Side Story*. Scott Joplin (1867-1917, Modern) and Billy Strayhorn (1915-1967, Modern), both prominent Jazz composers, and Richard Rodgers (1902-1979, Modern) and Irving Berlin (1888-1989, Modern), both Broadway composers, are also included.
- Community 4: Another US-centric community. Including the likes of Charles Ives (1874-1954, Modern) of *The Unanswered Question*, Aaron Copland (1900-1990,

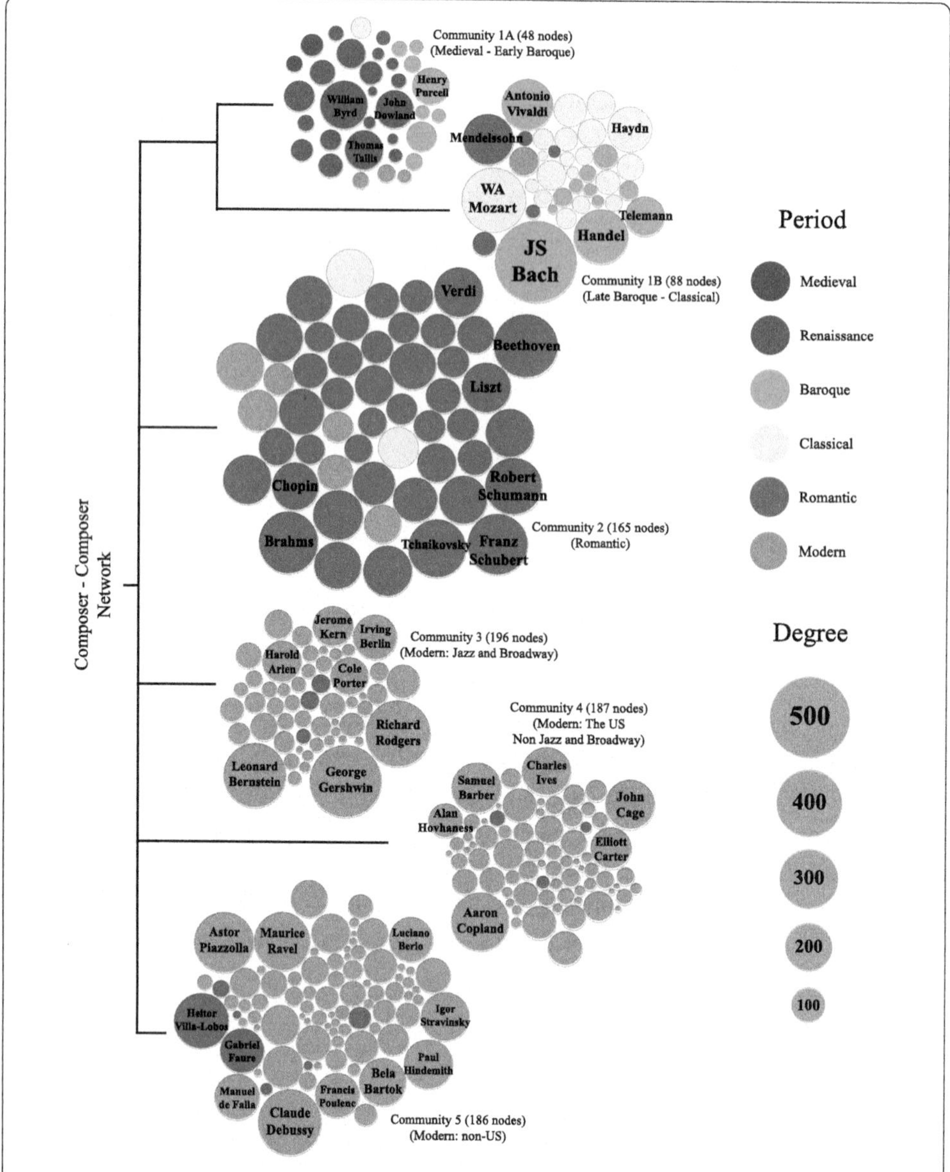

Figure 2 The community structure of the composer-composer network. The five largest composer communities identified using the Louvain method [37] (covering 6.2% of the composers who account for 60.1% of degrees) correspond well to the established period definitions in classical music history and musicological literatures. For each community we list its size and the major represented period(s). Communities 1A and 1B are subcommunities of Community 1, and correspond to the earlier and the later periods of Medieval and Classical. Community 2 represents the Romantic period, and Communities 3, 4, and 5 represent Modern composers. A closer inspection further differentiates the Modern communities: Community 3 represents US Jazz and Broadway composers, while Community 4 represents the other Modern US composers. Community 5 represents the non-US branch of Modern music.

Modern) of *Appalachian Spring*, Samuel Barber (1910-1981, Modern) of *Adagio for Strings*, and John Cage (1912-1992) of 4′33″, this can be said to represent the 20th-century American vernacular style of classical music [38]. More contemporary US composers, Terry Riley (1935-current, Modern), Steve Reich (1936-current, Modern) and Philip Glass (1937-current, Modern), are also in this module.

- Community 5: Composed of mainly Modern (89.3%) and Romantic (10.2%) composers, it includes transitional figures such as Gabriel Fauré (1845-1924, Romantic), Claude Debussy (1862-1918, Modern), and Maurice Ravel (1875-1937, Modern). In contrast with Community 4, this community represents the non-US branch of modern music, including Arnold Schoenberg (1874-1951, Modern, Austria), Manuel de Falla (1876-1946, Modern, Spain), Béla Bartók (1881-1945, Modern, Hungary), Igor Stravinsky (1882-1971, Modern, Russia), Heitor Villa-Lobos (1887-1959, Modern, Brazil), Paul Hindemith (1895-1963, Modern, Germany), Francis Poulenc (1899-1963, Modern, France), Ástor Piazzolla (1921-1992, Modern, Argentina), and Luciano Berio (1925-2003, Modern, Italy).

That the communities appear to correspond well to periods indicate the existence of correlation between the two partitions. The overlap can be quantified, for instance, via the normalized mutual information measure proposed by Danon *et al.* [36, 39]. It is given as $I_{\text{norm}}(\mathcal{X}, \mathcal{Y}) = \frac{2I(X,Y)}{H(X)+H(Y)}$, where $\mathcal{X}$ and $\mathcal{Y}$ are the partitions of the nodes by community detection and period designations, $I(X, Y)$ is the mutual information, and $H(X)$ and $H(Y)$ are the Shannon entropies of X and Y. Widely used in tests of community detection algorithms, the normalized mutual information equals 1 if the partitions are identical and 0 if the partitions are independent. In other words, in our network of composers, the normalized mutual information is 1 if the members in each community are completely identical in periods, and 0 if they are uncorrelated. The normalized mutual information of our result using Louvain method is 0.325, indicating a significant level of overlap, as was hypothesized.

Our investigation of the centralities, assortativity, and community structure shows how large-scale data built primarily for commercial purposes can yield a coherent and useful picture of the landscape of western classical music. This demonstrates that the quantitative analysis of a large collection of cultural artifacts such as CDs can indeed yield meaningful results, validated by agreements with qualitative musicology. A deeper understanding of the network of artists based on commercial cultural products may help in devising new ways of approaching the market which can in turn result in larger, more elaborate commercial data that can further help advance our understanding of the subject.

4 Growth and evolution of the composer network

The classical musical sphere is constantly evolving, with new composers entering the scene, and old composers gaining further prominence or fading out in popularity. As a consequence it is interesting to understand the dynamics of the evolution of popularity or success [40].

4.1 Network growth process hints at the uneven growth of oldboys and newbies

The network growth is microscopically driven by the creation (publication) of a new CD, as it is the only way in which new edges or new composers can be added into the network (see Figure 3(A)). Since the introduction of CD in the early 1980s, 62,537 CDs have been released, featuring compositions by 13,099 composers, with 131,706 edges connecting CDs and composers. Here we distinguish two different classes of composers, the ones first introduced before 1990 (via the older LPs, many of which were re-released as CDs after 1990) whom we call the oldboys (OBs), and the others first introduced post-1990

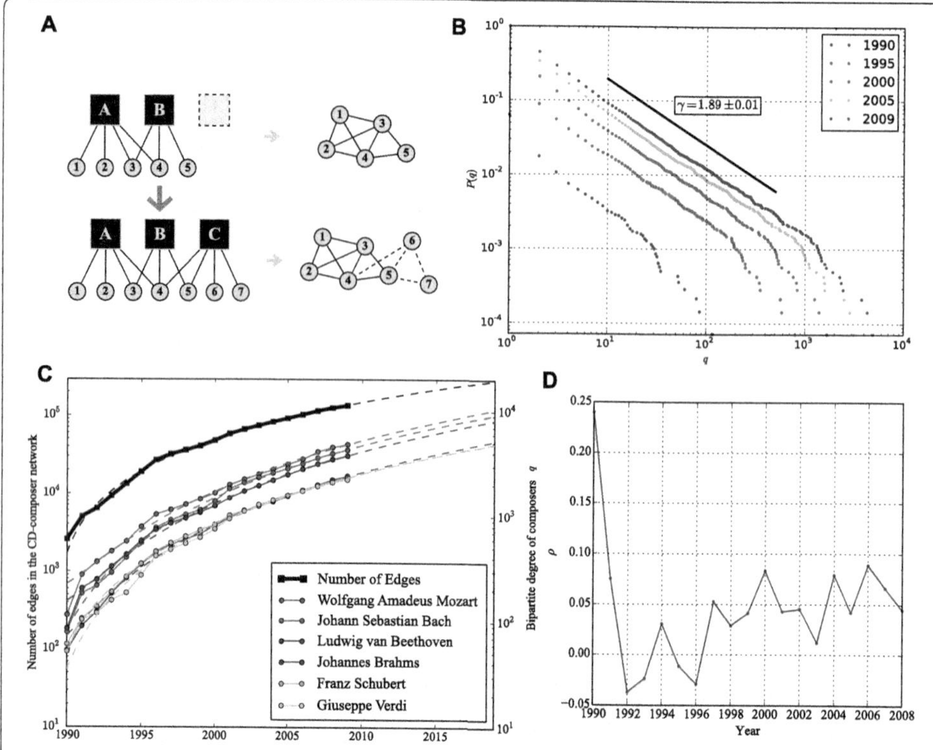

Figure 3 Growth and evolution of the composer network. (A) The fundamental process of network growth. Our network grows when a CD is created (labeled 'C', left), bringing new composers ('6' and '7') and/or new edges (dotted) into the projected network. **(B)** The evolution of the bipartite degree distribution. As the network grows the bipartite degree distribution converges to a power-law form $p(q) \sim q^{-\gamma}$ with $\gamma = 1.89 \pm 0.01$ (solid line). The color of dots indicate the different timestamps (blue - 1990, green - 1995, red - 2000, cyan - 2005, violet - 2009). The plots are cumulative. **(C)** The growth behaviors of the number of edges and the degree of six highest-degree composers indicate the predictability of top-ranked composers. The number of edges in the CD-composer network (black square) and the bipartite degrees of six highest-degree nodes (colored) show an accelerating growth rate that appears to be quadratic (dotted curves). Assuming this behavior persists, in 2019 Mozart is projected to have $q \simeq 10{,}264$, JS Bach $q \simeq 9{,}211$, Beethoven $q \simeq 8{,}119$, Brahms $q \simeq 5{,}162$, Verdi $q \simeq 4{,}897$ and Schubert $q \simeq 4{,}842$. **(D)** Estimating the non-linear preferential attachment exponent α. $\rho > 0$ indicates that the network exhibits a superlinear preferential attachment behavior, i.e. $\Pi(k) \propto k^{\alpha}$ with $\alpha > 1$, where $\Pi(k)$ is the probability that a node with degree k gets connected to a newly added link. The behaviors are observed for the majority of years (1990-1991, 1994 and 1997-2008), pointing out the disproportionately heavy concentration of new recordings onto the established composers.

whom we call the newbies (NBs). By this criterion, there are 882 oldboys and 13,099 newbies, so that the majority of composers were introduced after the advent of the CD technology. The popularity of the composers, nevertheless, are clearly skewed in the opposite direction: The total degree of the oldboys has increased from 2,553 in 1990 to 89,720 (an increase of 87,167) while only 44,539 links have been created for the newbies, for mean degrees of $\overline{q}_{\mathrm{OB}} = 101.72$ and $\overline{q}_{\mathrm{NB}} = 3.40$. This implies that, while the number of recorded composers steadily increases by introduction of new ones, the old established ones are perhaps out of their reach in terms of recordings.

4.2 Evolution of bipartite degree distribution indicates predictability for top-ranked composers and explains the rich-get-richer phenomenon in classical music industry

Extending the skewed bipartite degree distribution in the CD-composer network shown in Figure 1(B), we now focus on a more detailed figure of the temporal evolution of $P(q)$. In

Figure 3(B) we show the degree distribution of five snapshots of the network taken every five years. The degree distribution approximates a truncated power law that approaches a true power law (with power exponent $\gamma = 1.89 \pm 0.01$) as the network grows. For comparison with another example in culture, in the movie actor network the power exponent is $\gamma_{\text{actor}} = 2.3$. The highest-degree (most recorded) composers are WA Mozart, JS Bach, L van Beethoven, F Schubert, and J Brahms throughout the observational period (with final degrees 4,851, 4,292, 3,778, 2,328, and 2,429, respectively). The mean degree of the rest of the composers stays nearly constant at 3.2, again confirming the significant discrepancy between the 'major minority' and the 'minor majority' in the network landscape of classical music.

In Figure 3(C) we show the growths of the number of edges in the network and the degrees of six highest-degree composers. The curves appear to be quadratic (i.e. $\propto t^2$, dotted curves), suggesting a constant acceleration. Although it remains to be seen if the trend continues, if it does then in the year 2019 WA Mozart would have a bipartite degree of $q \simeq 10{,}264$, JS Bach would have $q \simeq 9{,}211$, and so forth (see Figure 3(C) for all six top composers). Regarding the number of edges, we find that they are becoming increasingly concentrated between the top-degree nodes: The top 1% of the nodes in 1990 (8 composers out of 882) account for 20.3% of all the degrees, while in 2009 the top 1% (139 composers of 13,981) account for 57.1%. These observations tell us that a reasonable growth dynamics of the network must incorporate at minimum two properties, namely, power-law degree distribution and the increasing concentration of degrees on the top-degree nodes.

A popular model of a growing network that exhibits a skewed degree distribution (such as the power law) is the Cumulative Advantage (CA) or Preferential Attachment (PA) [41, 42]. Our CD-composer network, too, boasts typical features that render PA a reasonable mechanism of its growth: It has a skewed distribution and a fixed fraction of the high-degree nodes take up a larger portion of the total degrees as it grows, evidenced by Figures 3(B) and 3(C).

The PA model assumes that the rate at which a node acquires new degrees is proportional to its degree, i.e. $\mathrm{d}k_i/\mathrm{d}t = \Pi(k_i)$ with $\Pi(k_i) \propto k_i$. This results in a power-law degree distribution with degree exponent 3 [42]. Different $\Pi(k)$ results in different degree distributions [43, 44]. Often studied is a polynomial form of $\Pi(k_i) \propto k_i^{\alpha}$ where $\alpha > 0$. $\alpha = 1$ is the classical PA model. In general, $\alpha < 1$ results in a stretched exponential degree distribution, and $\alpha > 1$ results in a more skewed degree distribution than the PA model, a single node linking to all other nodes asymptotically [43]. Given the power exponent of our network, $\gamma \simeq 2$, and the increasing share of the degrees by the top nodes, we estimate that for our CD-composer network, effectively $1 < \alpha < 2$, which we show as follows. Given the node degrees $\{q\}$, we calculate the mean degree $E_{\alpha}[q]$ of the node that will take the next added edge under $\Pi(k) \propto k^{\alpha}$, and also the empirical $E_{\text{data}}[q]$ from data. In Figure 3(D) we plot the quantity

$$\rho \equiv \frac{E_{\text{data}}[q] - E_{\alpha=1}[q]}{E_{\alpha=2}[q] - E_{\alpha=1}[q]}, \tag{1}$$

which shows that in the majority of years our data sits in the range $0 < \rho < 0.1$, i.e. $E_{\alpha=1}[q] < E_{\text{data}}[q] < E_{\alpha=2}[q]$. Our network indeed shows a superlinear preferential attachment behavior, which can explain the degree distribution and the growing concentration of degree portions on the highest-degree nodes.

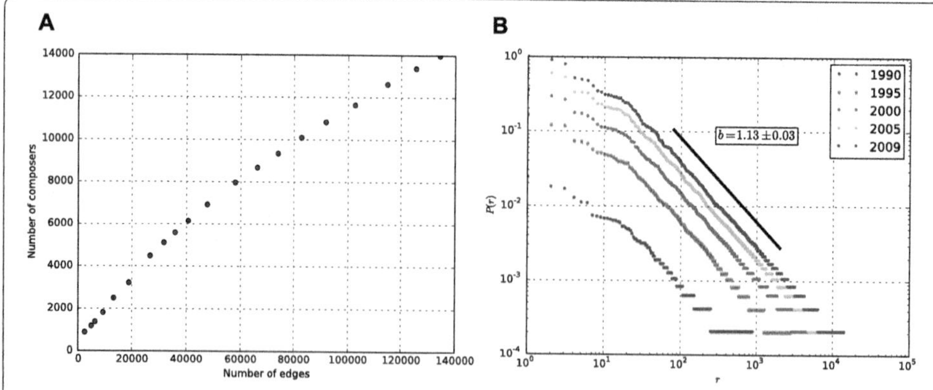

Figure 4 Growth of the composer network and its relation to Heaps' and Zipf's laws. (A) The number of composers grows sublinearly as a function of the number of edges in the network, indicating that newly-created edges are increasingly attached to pre-existing composers. **(B)** As the network grows the rank-frequency plots of the bipartite degree ranks also more clearly follow the Zipf's law, $P(r) \sim r^{-b}$ with $b = 1.13 \pm 0.03$ (solid line). This is consistent with the correlation between Heaps' law and Zipf's law [46].

Table 2 Top 10 pairs of composers for edge weights

Rank	Weight	Pair					
		Name	Period	Active year	Name	Period	Active year
1	680	Giacomo Puccini	Romantic	1891	Giuseppe Verdi	Romantic	1857
2	613	Beethoven	Romantic	1798	WA Mozart	Classical	1773
3	417	Giuseppe Verdi	Romantic	1857	Gaetano Donizetti	Romantic	1822
4	389	Beethoven	Romantic	1798	Johannes Brahms	Romantic	1865
5	384	JS Bach	Baroque	1717	WA Mozart	Classical	1773
6	381	Gioachino Rossini	Romantic	1830	Giuseppe Verdi	Romantic	1857
7	368	JS Bach	Baroque	1717	GF Handel	Baroque	1722
8	355	Giuseppe Verdi	Romantic	1857	WA Mozart	Classical	1773
9	352	Maurice Ravel	Modern	1906	Claude Debussy	Modern	1890
10	350	Franz Schubert	Romantic	1812	WA Mozart	Classical	1773

The weight of a pair indicates the number of records where they are co-featured. The pairs with high weights belong to the same period, or have similar active years.

The behavior of the bipartite degree distribution in Figure 3(B) merits further study. First, in Figure 4(A) we show the number of unique composers in the network as a function of the number of edges in the network. The growth is sublinear, meaning that the rate at which a new composer is added to the network is smaller than the rate of the increase of network edges. This is reminiscent of Heaps' law that shows that the vocabulary grows sublinearly with the document size [45]. Lü *et al.* demonstrated the connection between Zipf's law and Heaps' law [46]; we indeed observe Zipf's law for our system as well via the rank-frequency plot of the bipartite degree in Figure 4(B). Consistent with Figure 3(B), as the network grows larger, Zipf's law becomes clearer.

The sublinear growth in Figure 4(A) indicates that new edges are increasingly attached to pre-existing composers, reflecting the preferential attachment behavior that we discussed above. An interesting question to ask is between which composers (in the projected network) the new edges are created. Each added edge between two composers translates into edge weights (strength), which we believe can also shed on the growth dynamics of the network. In Table 2 we list the top ten strongest composer pairs. Here, too, we see that the newly created edges are placed between composers of similar characteristics: For example, the strongest pair is Giacomo Puccini (1858-1924) and Giuseppe Verdi (1813-1901); they not only belong to the same Romantic period, but are prominent in a common musical style, Italian opera. Their active years are nearly identical as well. Another interesting example is the pair of Giuseppe Verdi and Gaetano Donizetti (1797-1848). Although Donizetti does not appear on any list of top twenty influential composers on his own in terms of network centrality, he shows a drastic rise in prominence thanks to the number of records shared with a composer (Verdi) with an identical musical style (Romantic Italian opera) and similar active years. Likewise, other top pairs in Table 2 either share the same musical period or show similar active years.

Here we identified two main components of the evolution of the classical composer networks: growth and attachment. We observe that the power-law degree distribution becoming clearer as the network grows, which allows us to forecast the future degrees of the most recorded composers. We also find an effective superlinear preferential attachment behavior which can partially explain the observations.

5 Conclusion

In this paper, we studied the network of classical music composers constructed from the comprehensive recording data from ArkivMusic. We presented the basic properties of the CD-composer and composer-composer networks, finding that they exhibit characteristics common to many real-world networks, including the small-world property, the existence of a giant component, high clustering, and heavy-tailed degree distributions. We also explored the global association patterns of composers via centrality, assortative mixing, community structure analyses, which suggest an intriguing interplay between the networks of musicians and our musicological understanding of the western musical tradition in which both are undoubtedly continuously influencing each other. We then examined the growth of the CD-composer bipartite network over time. We identified superlinear preferential attachment as a strong candidate for explaining the increasing concentration of edges around top-degree nodes and the power-law degree distributions. The growth of edges and composer degrees exhibits a quadratic growth, allowing us to forecast the future of several prominent composers. If this behavior persists further into the future, it would suggest an interesting future research direction regarding the growth dynamics of the network.

An analytical investigation as ours on new, large-scale data can provide either new lessons or more rigorous answers to questions that are only partially understood on a subject matter (in our case classical music), although the boundary between the two can often be fuzzy: New findings challenge us to find rigorous answers to already known issues, which in turn can bring about novel discoveries about a system. In our paper we have quantified the overlap (correlation) between manually designated periods and the computationally identified communities; found the superlinear preferential attachment behavior and a quadratic growth of network edges; and showed that the growth of the composer pool is sublinear against the network size, leading to a concentration of edge weights onto specific composer pairs. These findings pose interesting possibilities and opportunities for the type of commercial databases such as the one on classical music that we have used here which, we believe, will play an increasingly important role as a source of many more academic findings than those presented here. We are living in an era where technology is greatly facilitating the consumption of culture by the public, evidenced by the increasing adoption of technology by artistic institutions worldwide for public outreach. This will lead to larger and higher-quality data that can allow us to learn more about culture and art. Classical music as presented here is merely one of many cultural subjects for this kind of investigation, and we believe that it would be interesting to apply our quantitative methodology to other subjects, e.g. visual arts and literature, and explore their nature in novel ways. Going further, it would also be interesting to compare different systems and find universal characteristics of cultural systems as well as those unique to each. We believe that our work highlights the potential of network science coupled with well-curated large-scale data in answering many pertinent questions.

Competing interests

The authors declare that they have no competing interests.

Authors' contributions

Doheum Park and Juyong Park analyzed the data and prepared the figures. All authors wrote and reviewed the manuscript.

Author details

[1]Graduate School of Culture Technology and BK21 Plus Postgraduate Organization for Content Science, Korea Advanced Institute of Science & Technology, 291 Daehak-ro, Yuseong-gu, Daejeon 305-701, Republic of Korea. [2]Arts and Technology Program, University of Texas at Dallas, 800 W. Campbell Road, Richardson, Texas 75080-3021, USA.

Acknowledgements

This work was supported by the National Research Foundation of Korea (NRF-20100004910 and NRF-2010-330-B00028), IT R&D program of MSIP/KEIT (10045459), and BK21 Plus Postgraduate Organization for Content Science.

References

1. O'Hagan J, Borowiecki KJ (2010) Birth location, migration, and clustering of important composers: historical patterns. Hist Methods 43(2):81-90
2. Malina R, Schich M, Meirelles I (eds) (2014) Arts, humanities, and complex networks. Leonardo ebook series. MIT Press, Cambridge
3. Park J (2012) Networks of contemporary popular musicians. Leonardo 45(1):78-79
4. Schich M, Song C, Ahn Y-Y, Mirsky A, Martino M, Barabási A-L, Helbing D (2014) A network framework of cultural history. Science 345(6196):558-562
5. Aiello LM, Barrat A, Cattuto C, Schifanella R, Ruffo G (2012) Link creation and information spreading over social and communication ties in an interest-based online social network. EPJ Data Sci 1(1):1
6. Suárez JL, Sancho F, de la Rosa J (2012) Sustaining a global community: art and religion in the network of Baroque Hispanic-American paintings. Leonardo 45(3):281
7. Gleiser PM, Danon L (2003) Community structure in jazz. Adv Complex Syst 6(04):565-573
8. Park J, Celma O, Koppenberger M, Cano P, Buldú JM (2007) The social network of contemporary popular musicians. Int J Bifurc Chaos 17(07):2281-2288
9. Salganik MJ, Dodds PS, Watts DJ (2006) Experimental study of inequality and unpredictability in an artificial cultural market. Science 311(5762):854-856
10. Uzzi B, Spiro J (2005) Collaboration and creativity: the small world problem. Am J Sociol 111(2):447-504
11. Newman ME (2003) The structure and function of complex networks. SIAM Rev 45(2):167-256
12. Jeong H, Néda Z, Barabási A-L (2003) Measuring preferential attachment in evolving networks. Europhys Lett 61(4):567
13. Serrà J, Corral Á, Boguñá M, Haro M, Arcos JL (2012) Measuring the evolution of contemporary western popular music. Sci Rep 2:521
14. Bettencourt LM, Lobo J, Helbing D, Kühnert C, West GB (2007) Growth, innovation, scaling, and the pace of life in cities. Proc Natl Acad Sci USA 104(17):7301-7306
15. Serrano MÁ, Boguñá M, Vespignani A (2009) Extracting the multiscale backbone of complex weighted networks. Proc Natl Acad Sci USA 106(16):6483-6488
16. Milgram S (1967) The small world problem. Psychol Today 2(1):60-67
17. Newman ME (2009) Networks: an introduction. Oxford University Press, New York
18. Newman ME, Park J (2003) Why social networks are different from other types of networks. Phys Rev E 68(3):036122
19. Newman ME (2004) Analysis of weighted networks. Phys Rev E 70(5):056131
20. Freeman LC (1977) A set of measures of centrality based on betweenness. Sociometry 40:35-41
21. Hoppin RH (1978) Medieval music. Norton, New York
22. Reese G (1959) Music in the Renaissance. Norton, New York
23. Bukofzer MF (1947) Music in the Baroque era: from Monteverdi to Bach. Norton, New York
24. Barzun J (1961) Classic, Romantic, and Modern, vol 255. University of Chicago Press, Chicago
25. Grout DJ, Palisca CV, et al (1996) A history of Western music, 5th edn. Norton, New York
26. Taruskin R (2009) The Oxford history of Western music: music in the nineteenth century, vol 3. Oxford University Press, New York

27. Atlas AW (1998) Renaissance music: music in Western Europe, 1400-1600. Norton, New York
28. Rosen C (1997) The classical style: Haydn, Mozart, Beethoven, vol 1. Norton, New York
29. Kravitt EF (1992) Romanticism today. Music Q 76(1):93-109
30. Albright D (2004) Modernism and music: an anthology of sources. University of Chicago Press, Chicago
31. Newman ME (2003) Mixing patterns in networks. Phys Rev E 67(2):026126
32. Ahn Y-Y, Bagrow JP, Lehmann S (2010) Link communities reveal multiscale complexity in networks. Nature 466(7307):761-764
33. Mucha PJ, Richardson T, Macon K, Porter MA, Onnela J-P (2010) Community structure in time-dependent, multiscale, and multiplex networks. Science 328(5980):876-878
34. Newman ME (2006) Modularity and community structure in networks. Proc Natl Acad Sci 103(23):8577-8582
35. Sales-Pardo M, Guimera R, Moreira AA, Amaral LAN (2007) Extracting the hierarchical organization of complex systems. Proc Natl Acad Sci 104(39):15224-15229
36. Fortunato S (2010) Community detection in graphs. Phys Rep 486(3):75-174
37. Blondel VD, Guillaume J-L, Lambiotte R, Lefebvre E (2008) Fast unfolding of communities in large networks. J Stat Mech Theory Exp 2008(10):10008
38. Struble JW (1995) The history of American classical music: MacDowell through minimalism. Facts on File, New York
39. Danon L, Diaz-Guilera A, Duch J, Arenas A (2005) Comparing community structure identification. J Stat Mech Theory Exp 2005(09):09008
40. Sarigol E, Pfitzner R, Scholtes I, Garas A, Schweitzer F (2014) Predicting scientific success based on coauthorship networks. ArXiv e-prints
41. Simon HA (1955) On a class of skew distribution functions. Biometrika 42:425-440
42. Barabási A-L, Albert R (1999) Emergence of scaling in random networks. Science 286(5439):509-512
43. Krapivsky PL, Redner S, Leyvraz F (2000) Connectivity of growing random networks. Phys Rev Lett 85(21):4629
44. Albert R, Jeong H, Barabási A-L (2000) Error and attack tolerance of complex networks. Nature 406(6794):378-382
45. Heaps HS (1978) Information retrieval: computational and theoretical aspects. Academic Press, Orlando
46. Lü L, Zhang Z-K, Zhou T (2010) Zipf's law leads to Heaps' law: analyzing their relation in finite-size systems. PLoS ONE 5(12):14139

13

Collective behaviors and networks

Giovanni Luca Ciampaglia, Emilio Ferrara* and Alessandro Flammini

*Correspondence:
ferrarae@indiana.edu
School of Informatics and Computing, Indiana University, Bloomington, USA

Abstract

The goal of this thematic series is to provide a discussion venue about recent advances in the study of networks and their applications to the study of collective behavior in socio-technical systems. The series includes contributions exploring the intersection between data-driven studies of complex networks and agent-based models of collective social behavior. Particular attention is devoted to topics aimed at understanding social behavior through the lens of data about technology-mediated communication. These include: modeling social dynamics of attention and collaboration, characterizing online group formation and evolution, and studying the emergence of roles and interaction patterns in social media environments.

1 Introduction

The rise in usage of online social media provides a wealth of information about social phenomena and human behavior at scale, at least to the extent to which interactions, intentions and beliefs measured online reflect their real-world counterparts [1, 2]. Data about online traces of activity from Twitter, Facebook, Wikipedia, blogs, etc., have been used to predict elections and political opinions [3, 4], movie revenues at the box office [5, 6], fluctuations in the stock market [7], and the spreading of influenza [8–12], to cite a few examples. Similar data have shed light on the mechanisms behind social influence [12, 13] and spread of behavior [14, 15], or to study the diffusion of viral information [16–18], and the dynamics of social protests [19, 20].

Even preceding the surge of scholarly attention toward social media and online social networks, the use of Agent-based Models (ABM) has grown in scope, percolating to several disciplines within the social sciences from economics to environmental policy, sociology, and psychology. One major appeal of the agent based approach is the possibility to test *in silico* hypotheses about the emergence of macroscopic behavior as result of simple interaction rules among stylized agents [21, 22]. In recent years the focus has started to shift from testing the plausibility of specific theories to the development of quantitatively accurate models; rather than just testing ?what-if? scenarios, ABMs are now being used to provide quantitative forecasts in social systems.

Although the Network Science community, which studies interconnected socio-technical systems, and the ABM community, which simulates artificial societies as groups of interacting agents, have similar focus and a large overlap in interests, they are still separated from a profound chasm in their methodological approach. We believe that each community would greatly benefit by a larger degree of acquaintance with the methodological approaches of the other. Agent-based models that are strongly informed by empirical facts and capable of producing predictions at multiple scales and resolutions - predictions for which empirical data are presently available - could be a highly desirable outcome of the increased interaction among the two communities.

These are the driving motivations behind our series of workshops ?*Covenant: Collective Behaviors and Networks*? that have been held in conjunction with the European Conference and Complex Systems (ECCS). The great success of the first edition, which was held in Barcelona (Spain) in September 2013, set a milestone by bringing together these two communities, and brought us to expand even further our objectives for a second edition, held in Lucca (Italy) in September 2014. This event replicated the success of the first and surpassed our wildest expectations, with a peak attendance of a hundred participants, and close to 50 original submissions by researchers and practitioners from all over the world.

The goal of the present thematic series is twofold: showcase the most outstanding contributions presented at these two meetings, and provide a discussion venue about recent advances in the study of networks and their application to the study of collective behaviors. The first five contributions published here have been carefully selected among those presented at Covenant 2013, and they present advances in three areas: (i) modeling social dynamics of attention [23] and collaboration [24]; (ii) characterizing online group formation and evolution [25]; (iii) studying the emergence of sharing habits patterns [26] and roles [27] in social media environments.

2 Contributions

The first contribution, by Ruiz *et al.* [23], investigates the dynamics of content production in an online microblogging community, and in particular the interplay between user activity and the attention she receives. In online social network (OSN) media content (such as photos, stories, news, etc.) is produced by the same set of people. As a consequence, the evolution of OSN sites is driven by the complex interplay between individual activity and attention received from others. This has important implications for the online communities. Receiving attention is a non-monetary reward that is crucial to sustain user engagement and prevent churn; therefore understanding what strategies are employed by the most successful users is likely of interest to anybody who wishes to promote socially sustainable communities, both online and offline. Proxies for collective attention are easy to measure in the digital world, and several works have approached the issue from different angles. Here the authors analyse a novel and interesting dimension of collective attention, the efficiency, defined as the ratio between the volume of collective attention received and the volume of content produced by a single user. They find that 56% of users in the system have very well-defined efficiency patterns over time, exhibiting either an increasing/decreasing, or peaking behavior. Further analyses lead the authors to conclude that increases in efficiency are determined by the creation of high-quality content, but that the attention acquired in this way has to be sustained by means of social exchanges (such as commenting or liking) to maintain high efficiency. Whenever this form of social activity is missing, efficiency quickly drops.

The second paper, contributed by Iñiguez *et al.* [24], also looks at a content-producing online community. In contrast to Ruiz *et al.* [23] that focused on a system, where contents is exchanged over social connections, here the authors investigate the free online encyclopedia Wikipedia, a strictly collaborative environment, where social connections arguably play a lesser role. Wikipedia is famous for allowing everyone to alter its content. This policy of low participation barrier has resulted in a surprisingly fast growth in its first decade of existence. The other side of the coin is, however, the occurrence of conflicts among contributors with differing viewpoints. Wikipedia, with its detailed records about the history of edits on each article, provides an ideal ground to study how conflict arise and are solved. Indeed data about conflicts in other systems are usually difficult to find, possibly for the negative social connotation of the subject. Iñiguez *et al.* make an original contribution to this line of research by proposing a stylized agent-based model of fictitious Wikipedia editors that compete for control of an article (the medium). All editors and the medium are endowed with an internal opinion-like variable. For editors this represents their own viewpoint on the topic of the medium, and for the medium this can be thought as the most recent viewpoint contributed to it. Opinions are continuous variables and their dynamics follows the so-called Bounded Confidence (BC) rule from opinion dynamics. Such a stylized model, while simplifying several important aspects of Wikipedia?s editorial process, still features, as the authors report, a rich dynamic. In particular, different regimes, corresponding to empirical observation of conflict on real Wikipedia pages, can be found for different ranges of key model parameters.

The third work, by Martin-Borregon *et al.* [25], studies Flickr, the popular photo-sharing platform, to understand how social groups form and evolve in time, space, and across the socio-topical dimension. The authors propose a general model to characterize groups through several metrics of reciprocity, activity and topical diversity (which embody the theory of *common identity and common bond*). The model clusters groups according to their temporal activity into three categories: evergreen, short-lived, and bursty ones. The authors? analysis shows that their model predicts accurately the type of a groups when compared with the manually-generated ground truth. The model also demonstrates that: (i) geographically-wide groups are longer-lived than local ones; (ii) topical groups are more robust to user churn than other types and tend to exhibit constant activity; and, (iii) social groups have bursty activity patterns, with most members joining at the beginning and then interacting only occasionally. The definition of groups according to this framework provides a more nuanced description of community if compared with that obtained solely by clustering the user social graph, better capturing user behaviors and group activities. In fact, the authors show that groups identified by the framework and clusters obtained from community detection don?t overlap much, and are more often social than the declared ones. This agrees with the increasing body of literature that highlights the limitations of traditional topology-based network clustering to identify dynamical characteristics of socio-technical systems. The work finally concludes that information diffusion is affected by the grouping, with social and bursty groups spreading information across the boundaries more efficiently than topical and evergreen ones.

The fourth and fifth contributions selected from ?Covenant 2013? both make use of Twitter data to study socio-technical environments: the former aims to model content sharing habits, and the latter at understanding the emergence of roles on the platform.

The work by An *et al.* [26] explores four different dynamics that contribute to the sharing behavior of news on social media: gratification, selective exposure, socialization, and trust. Traditional literature explored these dimensions independently, and without making use of datasets containing real social interactions and behaviors at scale. An *et al.* explore in particular whether the theories of *selective exposure* and *echo chamber* can be observed in a non-controlled environment (as done in the past by traditional psychologists). They also discuss what factors drive users to predominantly consume information that is aligned with their pre-existing views. The work focuses on political news, as political leaning has been identified as one the critical factors making people with different viewpoints drift apart. The authors first collected a large longitudinal dataset of tweets - produced during eight months in 2009 - from users sharing links to news articles selected from a list of 22 news agencies. They propose a model based on 12 features called PoNS (*Political News Sharing*), featuring the four social factors mentioned above. They then carefully design a protocol to evaluate their model. In particular, they determine which features contribute the most to the likelihood of rebroadcasting (retweeting) a news item based on its political inclination (either in line or opposing one?s political views), and provided that the news story comes from an *official channel* or through friends. After adjusting for various confounding factors and possible sources of bias, they observe that homophily strongly limits who connects to whom on Twitter. Users are disproportionately more likely to connect with and retweet from others who share their same political views. The emergence of this polarization effect, which was first observed for Twitter in previous studies [28], makes it difficult for ideas to spread from one group to another. This work also highlights for the first time that individuals are much more likely to retweet news that oppose their views when they come from their contacts, compared to official accounts. This contrasts the broadly regarded theory of *cognitive dissonance*, which posits that individuals tend to stick even more to their views when they are faced with opposing ones. Finally, the authors ranked the predictive power of the twelve features they selected. They find that, when one controls for the number of exposures, other variables become important, although not uniformly for all users: some prefer popular stories, while others value those coming from trusted friends.

The fifth and last contribution, by González-Bailón *et al.* [27], focuses on the sociological theory of *brokerage* and extends it to complex, large-scale social networks. The goal of this work is to provide a method to identify user roles in inter-personal communication dynamics, leveraging information about network topology and, in particular the community structure that characterizes online social networks like Facebook and Twitter [29, 30]. The assumption is that roles respond to a division of labor that reflects different functions or behaviors, within the network. Network features, the authors hypothesize, may help detecting structurally similar positions and communication dynamics. The authors collect data on discussions about the Spanish political protest of May 2012 from Twitter, and pair this data with the classic Zachary?s Karate Club dataset as a baseline. The question they aim to answer is whether individuals who exhibit similar network roles also behave similarly in terms of communication patterns. Additionally, they identify the most significant roles in this context. The authors proposed a hybrid local-global method (HM) based on clustering the network via a community detection algorithm. Once the community structure is obtained, the two classic schemes of GF (local role inference based on paths of length two around each node) and GA (global role inference based on the density of the membership community) can be computed and combined for each node. Based on their analysis, the authors observe that in Twitter most individuals play a representative role, are peripheral and exhibit low levels of brokerage, both at the local and global level. There is little opportunity for information to flow from community to community, and that most users don?t control direct diffusion channels. The work finally shows that similar roles trigger similar behavior. By measuring number of retweets and mentions received by each user as proxy for authority and salience, the authors show that local and global brokers are consistently the most retweeted users (therefore, essential conduits for global information flow), while the most salient users are brokers only at local level.

3 Conclusions

Technology-mediated social collectives are taking an important role in the design of social structures. Yet, our understanding of the complex mechanisms governing networks and collective behavior is still shallow. Social systems are often viewed as instances of entirely unpredictable systems, their future bound to be dominated by contingency and happenstance. Agent-based models and complex networks methods are relatively novel items in the toolbox of computational social scientists, and as any tool they have their strengths and limitations. In this thematic series we aimed to show that combining these two approaches may help formulate better models and perhaps open up the possibility of entirely novel modeling approaches. Thank to the ubiquity of big data about social interactions, computational models of social phenomena are becoming more accurate in forecasting complex social phenomena. We foresee an intense growth of synergistic interactions between ABM and network based approaches in the future of computational social science.

Competing interests

The authors declare that they have no competing interests.

Authors? contributions

All authors contributed equally to the writing of this paper. All authors read and approved the final manuscript.

References

1. Lazer D, Pentland AS, Adamic L, Aral S, Barabasi AL, Brewer D, Van Alstyne M, et al (2009) Life in the network: the coming age of computational social science. Science 323(5915):721
2. Vespignani A (2009) Predicting the behavior of techno-social systems. Science 325(5939):425
3. Metaxas PT, Mustafaraj E (2012) Social media and the elections. Science 338(6106):472-473
4. Conover MD, Gonçalves B, Flammini A, Menczer F (2012) Partisan asymmetries in online political activity. EPJ Data Sci 1:6
5. Asur S, Huberman BA (2010) Predicting the future with social media. In: 2010 IEEE/WIC/ACM international conference on web intelligence and intelligent agent technology (WI-IAT), Vol 1. IEEE, pp 492-499
6. Mestyán M, Yasseri T, Kertész J (2013) Early prediction of movie box office success based on Wikipedia activity big data. PLoS ONE 8(8):e71226
7. Bollen J, Mao H, Zeng X (2011) Twitter mood predicts the stock market. J Comput Sci 2(1):1-8
8. Culotta A (2010) Towards detecting influenza epidemics by analyzing Twitter messages. In: Proceedings of the first workshop on social media analytics. ACM, New York, pp 115-122
9. Signorini A, Segre AM, Polgreen PM (2011) The use of Twitter to track levels of disease activity and public concern in the US during the influenza A H1N1 pandemic. PLoS ONE 6(5):e19467
10. Chew C, Eysenbach G (2010) Pandemics in the age of Twitter: content analysis of Tweets during the 2009 H1N1 outbreak. PLoS ONE 5(11):e14118
11. Lazer D, Kennedy R, King G, Vespignani A (2014) Big data. The parable of google flu: traps in big data analysis. Science 343(6176):1203
12. Aral S, Walker D (2012) Identifying influential and susceptible members of social networks. Science 337(6092):337-341
13. Bond RM, Fariss CJ, Jones JJ, Kramer AD, Marlow C, Settle JE, Fowler JH (2012) A 61-million-person experiment in social influence and political mobilization. Nature 489(7415):295-298
14. Centola D (2010) The spread of behavior in an online social network experiment. Science 329(5996):1194-1197
15. Golder SA, Macy MW (2011) Diurnal and seasonal mood vary with work, sleep, and daylength across diverse cultures. Science 333(6051):1878-1881
16. Salganik MJ, Dodds PS, Watts DJ (2006) Experimental study of inequality and unpredictability in an artificial cultural market. Science 311(5762):854-856
17. Szabo G, Huberman BA (2010) Predicting the popularity of online content. Commun ACM 53(8):80-88
18. Weng L, Menczer F, Ahn YY (2013) Virality prediction and community structure in social networks. Sci Rep 3:2522
19. Conover MD, Davis C, Ferrara E, McKelvey K, Menczer F, Flammini A (2013) The geospatial characteristics of a social movement communication network. PLoS ONE 8(3):e55957
20. Conover MD, Ferrara E, Menczer F, Flammini A (2013) The digital evolution of Occupy Wall Street. PLoS ONE 8(5):e64679
21. Vespignani A (2012) Modelling dynamical processes in complex socio-technical systems. Nat Phys 8(1):32-39
22. Epstein JM (1996) Growing artificial societies: social science from the bottom up. Brookings Institution Press

23. Ruiz CV, Aiello LM, Jaimes A (2014) Modeling dynamics of attention in social media with user efficiency. EPJ Data Sci 3:5
24. Iñiguez G, Török J, Yasseri T, Kaski K, Kertész J (2014) Modeling social dynamics in a collaborative environment. EPJ Data Sci 3:7
25. Martin-Borregon D, Aiello LM, Grabowicz P, Jaimes A, Baeza-Yates R (2014) Characterization of online groups along space, time, and social dimensions. EPJ Data Sci 3:8
26. An J, Quercia D, Cha M, Gummadi K, Crowcroft J (2014) Sharing political news: the balancing act of intimacy and socialization in selective exposure. EPJ Data Sci 3:12
27. González-Bailón S, Wang N, Borge-Holthoefer J (2014) The emergence of roles in large-scale networks of communication. EPJ Data Sci 3:32
28. Conover M, Ratkiewicz J, Francisco M, Gonçalves B, Menczer F, Flammini A (2011). Political polarization on twitter. In: ICWSM
29. Ferrara E (2012) A large-scale community structure analysis in Facebook. EPJ Data Sci 1:9
30. De Meo P, Ferrara E, Fiumara G, Provetti A (2014) On Facebook, most ties are weak. Commun ACM 57(11):78-84

14

The nature and evolution of online food preferences

Claudia Wagner[1,2*], Philipp Singer[1] and Markus Strohmaier[1,2]

*Correspondence: claudia.wagner@gesis.org
[1] GESIS - Leibniz Institute for the Social Sciences, Unter Sachsenhausen 5-8, Cologne, Germany
[2] University of Koblenz-Landau, Koblenz, Germany

Abstract

Food is a central element of humans? life, and food preferences are amongst others manifestations of social, cultural and economic forces that influence the way we view, prepare and consume food. Historically, data for studies of food preferences stems from consumer panels which continuously capture food consumption and preference patterns from individuals and households. In this work we look at a new source of data, i.e., server log data from a large recipe platform on the World Wide Web, and explore its usefulness for understanding online food preferences. The main findings of this work are: (i) recipe preferences are *partly driven* by ingredients, (ii) recipe preference distributions exhibit *more regional differences* than ingredient preference distributions, and (iii) weekday preferences are *clearly distinct* from weekend preferences.

Keywords: food; online preferences; server logs

1 Introduction

Italians are ?*Macaronis*", the English are ?*Roastbeef*", the French are ?*Frogs*" and the Germans are ?*Krauts*" [1]. In other words, food is often used to define and differentiate social groups. Claude Fischler [1] points out that human beings mark their membership of a culture or social group by asserting the specificity of what they eat or by defining differences with others. Eric B. Ross describes diet as an ?*evolutionary product of environmental conditions and of the basic forces, especially social institutions and social relations, that determine their use*" [2]. Work by Manuel Calvo [3] observed that in situations of migration, certain features of cuisine are sometimes retained even when the original culture and language have already been forgotten. This suggests that culture and diet are deeply connected. Understanding dietary patterns and food preferences[a] of humans is therefore central to several research communities. It is not only relevant from an anthropological and sociological view point, but also from a medical point of view since food preferences and diet obviously impact health.

Predominantly, studies of offline food preferences are based on surveys and consumer panels which continuously produce longitudinal behavioral data on the consumption behavior and preferences of individuals and households [4]. However, generating this data is a time-consuming and costly process and despite its strengths it also suffers from limitations such as high drop-out rates, high latency or *Hawthorne effects*.

Research objectives and methods. By contrast, in this work we leverage server log data from a large online recipe platform which is frequently used in the German speaking regions and present a multi-dimensional approach for exploring users? online food preferences. We infer the popularity of recipes and ingredients by counting the number of times each recipe or ingredient is visited from a certain geographic region within a certain time window.[b] These region- and time-specific popularity distributions are treated as the observable outcome of users? online food preferences and allow us to explore the nature and evolution of online food preferences using well established statistical methods. Amongst others, we apply (i) power law fitting methods by Clauset et al. [5] for explaining the intrinsic statistical properties of recipe and ingredient popularity distributions, (ii) correlation and similarity measures for explaining spatial food preferences and (iii) a stability measures [6] for exploring dynamics of temporal food preferences.

Concretely, we use these methods to explore the online food preferences of users on the following four dimensions:

- *Recipe preferences.* What are the intrinsic statistical properties of recipe popularity distributions? How general are those properties - i.e., do the recipe popularity distributions of different geographic regions reveal similar statistical properties? How do recipe popularity distributions differ from the popularity distributions of other types of online content (e.g., YouTube videos or websites in general)?
- *Ingredient preferences.* Do the ingredient popularity distributions of different regions reveal information about users? food preferences or are they just an artifact of users? recipe preferences and ingredient distribution over recipes? What are the intrinsic statistical properties of ingredient popularity distributions? How general are those properties - i.e., do the ingredient popularity distributions of different geographic regions reveal essentially the same statistical properties?
- *Spatial food preferences.* What is the relation between the geographic distance of regions and their online food preferences? Are online food preferences of geographically close regions more similar than those of distant regions?
- *Temporal food preferences.* To what extent do online food preferences change over time - i.e., change during the week or over seasons?

Contributions. The main findings of this work are: (i) Recipe and ingredient popularity distributions are heavy tail distributions and can be best approximated by truncated power law functions. The truncation is stronger for very popular recipes compared to popular ingredients. We can observe this behavior on a macro level (i.e., in the aggregation of all German-speaking regions in Europe) as well as on a meso level (i.e., in individual regions). (ii) Recipe preference distributions exhibit *more regional differences* than ingredient preference distributions. This suggests that food cultures manifest themselves more via the way food is combined and prepared, rather than what a culture ingests. (iii) Recipe preferences are *partly driven* by ingredients and (iv) weekday preferences are *clearly distinct* from weekend preferences.

Our work thereby shows that recipe visits as well as the inferred ingredient visits represent a preliminary, yet promising, *signal* for food preferences of human populations, since (a) our observations can in part be linked to real-world events, such as the asparagus season, and findings from offline studies and (b) our observations are fairly consistent on a macro and meso level which suggests that the observed online preference distributions can be reproduced at different scales.

Outline. We begin by describing our dataset in Section 2. In Section 3 we focus on investigating the nature of online food preferences on the four different dimensions described above. We discuss our main findings in Section 4, present a review of related work in Section 5 and finally conclude our work in Section 6.

2 Description of the dataset

We analyze server log data from the largest online recipe platform in Austria, ichkoche.at. The server logs describe how frequently a recipe has been visited within a certain region. A visit is defined as one or several page requests from the same IP address within the same session. We use visits rather than page hits or views to get a more accurate picture about users? recipe interests rather than their browsing practices. The 184,296 recipes have been visited by 1,695 different regions around 24 million times between August 2012 until November 2013. In addition to the log data, our dataset also contains information about the ingredients of recipes.

Even though the platform is from Austria, other German-speaking countries such as regions in Germany and Switzerland are prominently included (Bavaria, Zurich, Stuttgart, Hessen, Berlin, Worms, Bern and Saxony belong to the top 20 most active regions). Hence, we focus on data from the main German speaking regions in Europe - i.e., 50 federal states in Austria (AT), Germany (DE) and Switzerland (CH).

Figure 1 shows the number of visits for each of the 50 German speaking regions in our dataset on a log scale and the normalized entropy of the recipe and ingredient frequency vector per region. In order to be able to compare the visits of recipes and ingredients, we normalize the entropy by the logarithmic length of the vector since the number of recipes is much higher than the number of ingredients. A low entropy indicates that clear preferences have emerged (i.e., some recipes or ingredients are much more popular than others), while a high entropy indicates a more even distribution (i.e., many recipes or ingredients are equally popular). We can see that ingredient preferences are more focused than recipe preferences according to their lower entropy values. However, the list of regions ranked by their normalized recipe and ingredient entropy are strongly correlated (Kendall τ = 0.95). This is not surprising since it simply shows that regions which have

Figure 1 How active are different regions and how focused are their recipe/ingredient preferences? This figure shows the normalized entropy of the recipe and ingredient frequency vectors per region versus the number of visits per region on a log scale. Low entropy means that there is a high regional focus on just a few recipes/ingredients while a large entropy indicates a more even distribution. We see that ingredient preferences are more focused than recipe preferences according to their lower entropy values; however, they are strongly correlated (Kendall τ = 0.95 for the list of regions ranked by their recipe entropy and ingredient entropy). Furthermore, we can observe that the most active regions are in Austria (due to their higher number of clicks) and that the more active a region is, the less random their recipe and ingredient preferences are (according to their lower entropy values).

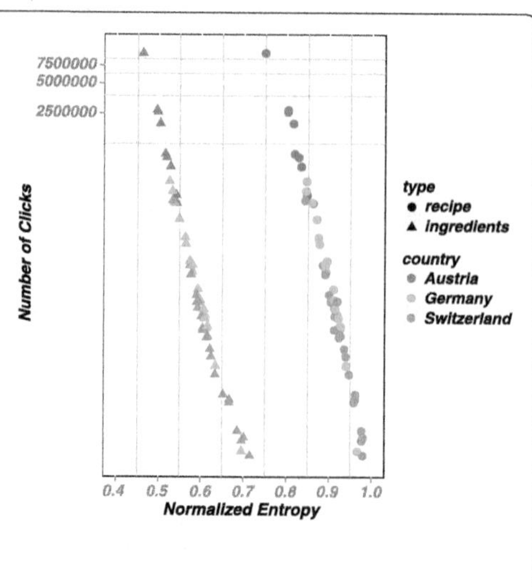

a narrow recipe focus also have a narrow ingredient focus. Furthermore, we can observe almost prefect linear relationship between the activity of a region and its recipe and ingredient entropy. This indicates that the more active a region, the less random its recipe and ingredient preferences. One potential explanation is that the platform ranks popular recipes higher which will make them even more popular. Therefore, the more users from a region use the platform the more skewed the preference distribution which we observe. The most active regions are in Austria since the platform originates from this country.

3 Online food preferences

In this section we investigate online food preferences along the four introduced dimensions - i.e., recipe preferences, ingredient preferences, spatial food preferences and temporal food preferences.

3.1 Recipe preferences

Approach. To approximate the recipe preferences of one or several region(s) we count the number of times users from that region(s) have visited each recipe. We explore the intrinsic statistical properties of the popularity distributions of recipes, since the exact form of the popularity distribution often allows to infer which mechanisms might have generated the data [7, 8] and may therefore allow to gain insight into the underlying process which drives the evolution of recipe preferences. We do not only explore the properties of these distributions on a *macro level* (i.e., recipe preferences aggregated over all German-speaking regions in Europe), but also on a *meso level* (i.e., recipe preferences per region). The latter can help us to answer the question whether the shape of online recipe preferences of individual regions differs from each other and from the global, accumulated recipe preferences. That means, we explore whether different geographical regions produce popularity distributions with similar intrinsic statistical properties.

In the past, many researchers found that the *power law model* can best explain these distributions which emerge when users engage with content on the Web (cf. [6, 9–11]). Power laws are frequently appearing in social sciences, physics, biology or other sciences [12] and the probability density (mass) function of the power law distribution is defined as $f(x) = x^{-\alpha}$. Hence, we can hypothesize that our distributions at hand are also heavy tailed distributions that will most likely follow a power law model. We test this hypothesis as follows:

A simple approach to fit a power law function to data is using a least-squares linear regression. However, this method can introduce strong biases and hence, we use *maximum likelihood estimation*[c] as suggested by Clauset et al. [5] and implemented and extended by Alstott et al. [13]. Since for empirical distributions it is often difficult to find a good fit for the complete range of values, Clauset et al. [5] suggest that the power law might only hold for values that are greater than some given $x_{\min}$ value - i.e., the part of the distribution that captures popular items. Thus, we specifically focus on investigating the tail (popular recipes and ingredients) of the distribution. We use the *Kolmogorov-Smirnov statistic* as suggested by Clauset et al. [5] to find the appropriate $x_{\min}$ value that is the lowest value for which the power law model produces a good fit. Nevertheless, other candidate functions that produce heavy-tailed distributions exist. Hence, we do not only fit the power law function to our empirical data, but also other candidate functions: (a) the truncated power law function which has an exponential cut-off and is defined as $f(x) = x^{-\alpha} \exp(-\lambda x)$,

(b) the lognormal function defined as $f(x) = \frac{1}{x}\exp[-\frac{(\ln(x)-\mu)^2}{2\sigma^2}]$ and (c) the exponential function defined as $f(x) = \exp(-\lambda x)$ which represents the lower boundary for heavy-tailed distributions. Note that for each distribution the appropriate normalization constant C is necessary such that $\sum_{x=x_{\min}}^{\infty} Cf(x) = 1$. We would like to point the interested reader to [5] and [13] for corresponding normalization definitions. In case of the lognormal distribution no discrete form for the theoretical distribution is known. Thus, we resort to the continuous counterpart for approximation by utilizing a rounding method that sums the probability mass from $x - 0.5$ to $x + 0.5$ for each data point. For comparing the candidate functions with each other - regarding their statistically significant differences - we use *likelihood ratio tests*.

One needs to note that power law fitting has some limitations (see, e.g., [6]). First of all, it is often difficult to determine which distribution has generated the data since several candidate functions might produce equally good fits. Secondly, we can only assess the goodness of fit in relative terms - i.e., we only say that a function A fits better than a function B. Thirdly, by automatically calculating $x_{\min}$ we potentially reduce the distribution to a small portion of the tail. If the tail is small enough, the power law function will always produce a good fit, but a large portion of the data will be ignored. In order to tackle this issue, we try to contrast the best fit for the whole distribution with the best fit for the tail. Finally, many different hypotheses exist that may explain why power law distributions emerge. Nevertheless, in our context some hypotheses are more plausible than others.

Macro results. Figure 2A shows a clear heavy-tailed behavior for the empirical popularity distribution of recipes since the tail of the complementary cumulative distribution function (CCDF) is heavier than one would expect by an exponential function. The figure also shows that the recipe popularity distribution does not follow a power law for the whole range of values but can best be approximated by a truncated power law function compared to other candidate functions. This is imminent as the truncated power law function is a statistically significant better fit to the empirical data compared to the pure powerlaw or lognormal function. The likelihood ratio tests between the fit of the truncated power law function and the pure powerlaw function (normalized log-likelihood ratio[d] of $R = 38.19$ with a p-value < 0.05) as well as between the truncated power law function and the lognormal function ($R = 23.60$ with a p-value < 0.05) indicate that the truncated power law function best approximates the observed distribution.

When limiting the range of values for finding the best power law fit ($\geq x_{\min}$) we see that the best $x_{\min}$ value is very high ($x_{\min} = 20{,}784$) which again indicates that power law distributions do not fit well for the whole range of values (cf. Figure 2B). Since the remaining tail of the distribution is short, we can not find statistically significant differences between the fits of the power law, the lognormal and the exponential function.

Several mechanisms such as the aging [14], information filtering [15] and content-fetching behavior [16] have been proposed to explain the sharp decay from the straight power law in the tail. In [11] the authors investigated the statistical properties of the popularity distributions of YouTube and Daum videos and argue that the so-called ?fetch-at-once" model originally introduced by Gummadi et al. [16] is most likely to explain the truncation. The model suggests that in a power-fetching scenario where users request the same content item millions of times (e.g., popular websites such as CNN) no truncation can be observed; however, if the same content is only fetched once or a limited number of times a cutoff can be observed. Cha et al. [11] conclude that it is plausible that users do

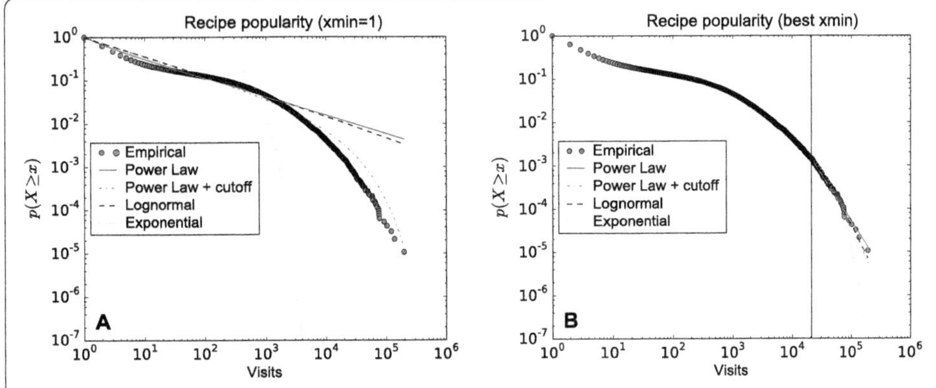

Figure 2 What are the intrinsic statistical properties of recipes? popularity distributions? The figure visualizes the CCDF of the empirical popularity distributions of recipes as well as the best fits for several candidate functions. The truncated power law function is the best fit for the whole empirical distribution (cf. panel **A**). When analyzing only the tail of the empirical distribution (cf. panel **B**) we can see that the best x_{min} is very high (x_{min} = 20,784), which indicates that power law is not a good fit for the whole range of values. Since the remaining tail of the distribution is short, we can not find statistical significant differences between the fits of the power law, lognormal and exponential function.

not watch the same video millions of times and that the limited fetching effect produces the truncation. It seems to be plausible that users of recipe platforms also fetch the same recipe a limited number of times, since the recipes do not change. If this holds true, the truncation in Figure 2 may also be explained by the *finite-size effect* [17] meaning that there is some upper limit (e.g., the number of users) that prevents the most popular recipes to be as popular as a power law distribution would suggest. A recipe can never be more popular than the number of users of the platform.

Meso results. Figure 4A shows the CCDF of the recipe popularity distribution of 50 different regions in Germany, Austria and Switzerland. We fit our candidate functions (lognormal, exponential, power law and truncated power law) to the region-specific popularity distributions. First, we use a fixed x_{min} ($x_{min} = 1$) to cover the whole range of values for each region separately. We depict the corresponding power law fit parameters in the first row of Table 1. By comparing the power law fits of each region to the corresponding candidate functions, we can see that in almost all cases the truncated as well as the lognormal function are better fits to the data than the power law function (in 49 out of 50 cases the likelihood ratio test exhibits a p-value below the significance level of 0.05). This confirms our macro results on a regional (meso) level.

Next, we extend our analysis by finding the best x_{min} parameter for each region separately (second row of Table 1). Similar as in the macro-level analysis we again end up with extraordinary high x_{min} values. On average x_{min} is so high that the remaining tail only covers around 9% of all potential x_{min} values (i.e., bins). Again, this indicates that the power law function can only explain a very small part of the tail of the region-specific distributions.

3.2 Ingredient preferences

Approach. For analyzing ingredient preferences we infer the popularity of ingredients from the popularity of recipes - e.g., if two users visit two distinct recipes which both contain salt, than each recipe would have the popularity 1 since it received one visit, while salt would have a popularity of 2 since it received two visits. Therefore, recipe and ingredient

Table 1 Parameters of the best power law fits for the recipe and ingredient preference distributions

	α	std	x_{min}	std
Recipes (all)	1.678	0.224	1.0	0.0
Recipes (best x_{min})	2.762	0.277	342.3	1428.403
Ingredients (all)	1.523	0.077	1.0	0.0
Ingredients (best x_{min})	1.883	0.712	720.94	3914.296

The fits are calculated for each region independently in two ways: (i) setting $x_{min} = 1$ and fitting on the whole range of values and (ii) finding the best x_{min} value for the best power law fit. We report the average values over all regions and the corresponding standard deviation.

popularity distributions are obviously interdependent and it is unclear if the inferred popularity distribution of ingredients reveals information about the online food preferences of users or if it is just an artifact of the ingredient universality distribution (i.e., in how many recipes ingredients are used) and the recipe popularity distribution (i.e., how often each recipe was visited). To address this question we (i) analyze the universality distribution of ingredients and (ii) simulate the ingredient preferences of a synthetic region as follows: A synthetic region consists of a set of agents who randomly select recipes from a randomly generated recipe-popularity distribution with the same shape as our empirical recipe distribution. For each selected recipe we extract all its ingredients from our data and increase the visit count of those ingredients. Repeating this process allows generating a synthetic ingredient preference distribution which reflects how the visits would be distributed over ingredients if the recipe selection process would be random. We assume that visits are independent and use the median number of visits of all regions as the activity level of the synthetic region.

We contrast the ingredient preference distribution which is generated by the synthetic region with the empirically observed ingredient distributions. If the shapes of the two distributions do not differ significantly, we can conclude that ingredient popularity preferences are an artifact of recipe popularity and the distribution of ingredients over recipes. Otherwise, we may conclude that external forces such as users? ingredient preferences or seasonality of ingredients impact the recipe selection process. In other words, if users recipe selection process is partly driven by ingredients, we expect the empirical ingredient distributions to differ from the synthetically generated one in the sense that they should be more focused towards fewer ingredients than the synthetic one.

To investigate the shape of the popularity distribution of ingredients on a meso and macro level we adapt the same approach as for recipes which we described in the previous section.

Macro results. In the previous section we have shown that the recipe popularity distribution is best approximated by a severely truncated power law (cf. Figure 2). However, it is unclear how the ingredients are distributed over recipes (i.e., in how many recipes each ingredient is used). That means, how many ingredients are so universal that they are used in almost all recipes and how does this universality decrease? Figure 3D shows that the universality distribution of ingredients follows a truncated power law (at least for the most universal ingredients with $x_{min} \geq 15$). This is also imminent by the results of the likelihood ratio test which indicates that the fit of the truncated power law function is a statistically significant better fit than the pure powerlaw, the lognormal and the exponential function; all p-values are below the significance level of 0.05. This observation is

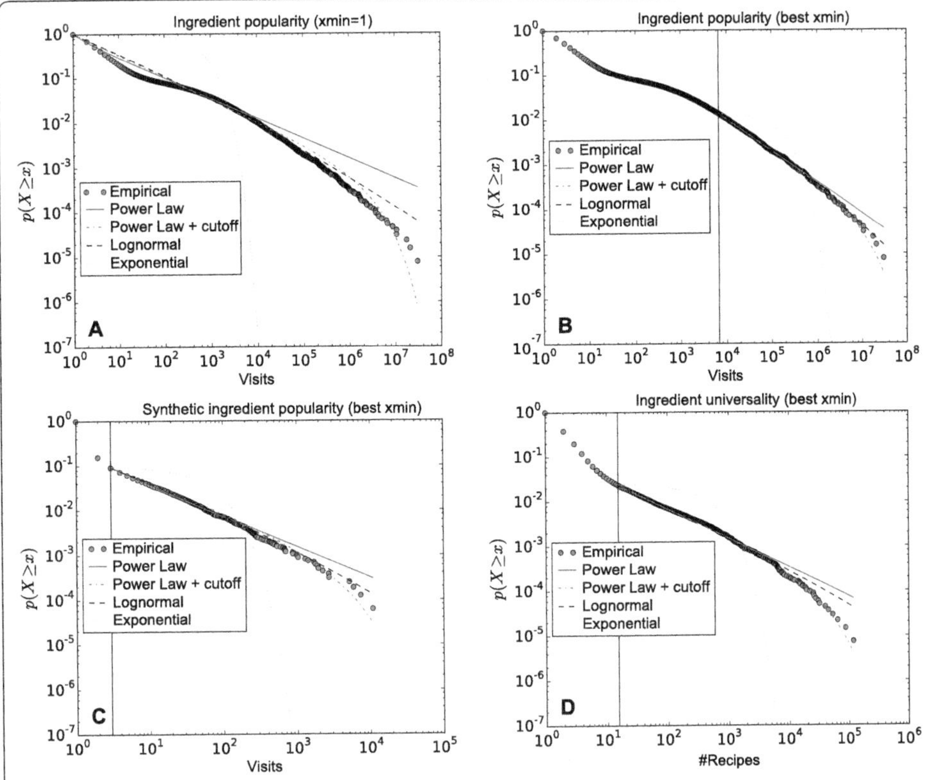

Figure 3 What are the intrinsic statistical properties of ingredients? popularity distributions?We visualize the empirical CCDFs coupled with corresponding candidate function fits. The popularity of ingredients clearly follows a truncated power law when looking at the whole range of values (cf. panel **A**). When only focusing on the most popular ingredients (> x_{min}) the truncated power law function as well as the log-normal function fit best as visible in panel **B**. For the synthetic ingredient popularity distribution which we obtained by simulating a region with a random recipe selection behavior also the truncated power law and the lognormal function are the best fits (cf. panel **C**). The universality distribution of ingredients follows as well a truncated power law (cf. panel **D**).

in line with a study looking at the distribution of ingredients over recipes in cook books [18] as the truncation captures finite size effects (i.e., number of recipes is finite). We also find that the mean number of ingredients per recipe is 11 and the median is 10, which is similar to what was found in previous studies of cookbooks (mean number of ingredients per recipe was found to be between 8 and 10 [19] or between 7 and 11 [18] for different cookbooks and cuisines).

For the empirical ingredient popularity distribution we can clearly see that it follows a truncated power law for the whole range of values (cf. Figure 3A, the likelihood ratio tests between the distinct distributions all result in p-values below 0.05 indicating that the truncated power law fit is the best one out of those we tested). We also find a truncation in the ingredient popularity distribution, but the truncation is less sharp for ingredients than for recipes (cf. Figure 2). This can be derived from looking at the exponential cutoff of both truncated fits: $\lambda = 1.74e{-}05$ ($1/\lambda = 57.303$)[e] for recipes and $\lambda = 1.14e{-}07$ ($1/\lambda = 8{,}752.642$) for ingredients. One potential explanation for this might be that the popularity of recipes is limited by the number of users of the platform, especially if they only fetch each recipe a limited number of time. The popularity of an ingredient depends on the number of recipes in which it is used (i.e., its universality) and the popularity of all recipes. Therefore, the finite-size effect is less pronounced in the ingredient popularity distributions than in the recipe popularity distributions. When only focusing on the most popular ingredients with $x_{\min} = 6{,}711$ (see Figure 3B), we again find that the truncated power law is a statistically significant better fit to the data than the power law function ($R = 2.55$ with p-value 0.002). The likelihood ratio test between the truncated power law function and the lognormal function indicates similar good fits (p-value above 0.05).

For the synthetically generated ingredient popularity distribution we find that the truncated power law function is a better fit than the power law function (p-value below 0.05). The lognormal and truncated power law function are similar good fits (p-value of 0.036). This indicates, that on the first glance our synthetic ingredient popularity distribution which is generated by a random recipe selection process does not differ from our empirical observations. However, this is only true for the most popular ingredients (such as salt, sugar, butter or oil). When taking a closer look one can see two interesting differences: the two distributions differ in (1) how unpopular ingredients are accessed by users and (2) the growth rate of popularity. Concretely, we can see in Figure 3B and C that the best $x_{\min}$ value is much smaller for the synthetic popularity distribution than for the empirical ones. This indicates, in our empirical data the shape of the distribution which also contains unpopular ingredients is different from the part which only contains more popular ingredients. We can further see that the distributions as well as corresponding fits are slightly steeper for the empirically observed ingredient preferences compared to the synthetically generated ones - the α parameter of the power law function is 1.70 for Figure 3B while it is 1.68 for the synthetic data. From these two observations we can derive that *the recipe selection process of users seems to be at least partly driven by the ingredient preferences of users,* since the ingredient preferences which are generated via the recipe selection process are more focused towards few ingredients and less focused towards others than one would expect if the process would be random. This means that users? ingredient preferences reveal stronger favor or disgust for selected ingredients than we would expect to observe if the recipe selection process would be random.

Meso results. Finally, to gain insight into the potential universality of the pattern which we observed in our macro analysis, we repeated the analysis for each region separately. We first fitted the power law and several other candidate function to the whole range of values (i.e., $x_{\min} = 1$) of region-specific ingredient preference distributions (cf. third row in Table 1). By comparing candidate functions, we can see that for all regions the truncated as well as the lognormal function fit the data better than the power law function (p-values below 0.05). Next, we estimated the best $x_{\min}$ value for each region and fitted different candidate functions to the part of the distribution which exceeds $x_{\min}$ (cf. fourth row in Table 1). Our results show that in 46 cases the truncated power law function fits statistically significantly better our data than the power law function (positive likelihood ratio, p-values below 0.05) while in 3 regions it is worse (negative likelihood ratio, p-values below 0.05). In one case the fits are equal (p-values above 0.05). The lognormal function equals the power law function in nearly all cases (46) (p-values above 0.05). This indicates that it is indeed likely that *the ingredient distributions of different regions have been generated by the same underlying process,* since we observe the same patterns on the macro and meso level. Finally, we also observe that *the popularity distributions of different ingredients tend to be very similar, while for recipes we observe slightly more regional variability.* This observation becomes not only apparent when comparing the different regional CCDF plots

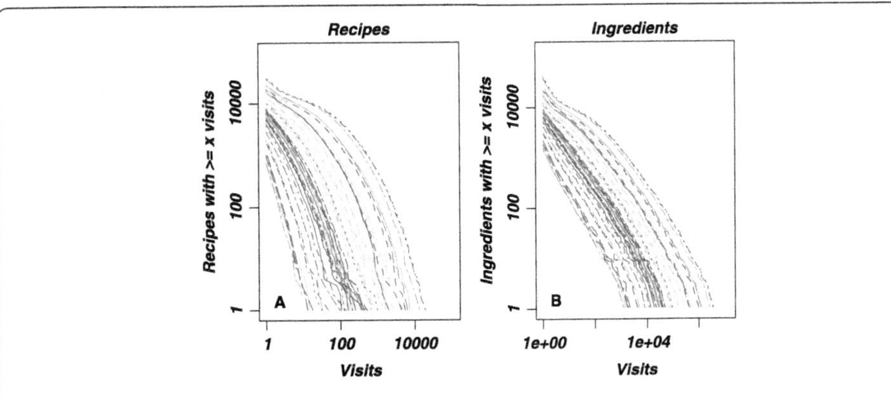

Figure 4 Are the recipe and ingredient preferences of different regions generated by the same process? The figure shows the CCDF of the ingredient and recipe popularity distributions of individual regions. The variable x on the x-axis corresponds to the number of visits, while the y-axis shows the number of recipes/ingredients that have received equal or more than x visits. One can see that the ingredient popularity distributions of different regions tend to be very similar, while for recipes we can observe slightly more regional variability. This observation is also apparent when comparing the standard deviations of the fitted α slopes (cf. Table 1) - higher for recipes (all) compared to ingredients (all).

in Figure 4, but also when comparing the standard deviations of the fitted α parameters (cf. Table 1) which is higher for recipes (all) compared to ingredients (all).

3.3 Spatial food preferences

One potential cause of shared online food preferences is geographical proximity since frequent communication and migration may explain the adoption of food preferences [20]. In the following, we test the hypothesis that geographically nearby regions are more similar regarding their online food preferences than geographically distant regions.

Approach. We compute the recipe and ingredient similarity between different regions using cosine similarity. Cosine similarity is a measure of similarity between two vectors that measures the cosine of the angle between them. Two vectors (in our case recipe or ingredient frequency vectors) with the same orientation have a cosine similarity of 1, while vectors with opposite orientation have a cosine similarity of -1.

We test the hypothesis that geographical distant regions reveal more distinct online food preferences than geographic close regions by measuring Spearman rank correlation between the geographical distance of region pairs and their recipe similarity and ingredient similarity. We use 10k bootstrap samples to estimate the confidence interval of the correlation coefficient.

We further compare the difference in the means (recipe-similarity and ingredient-similarity means) of geographical distant regions (i.e., regions which are more distant than the median distance) and geographical nearby regions (i.e., regions which are closer than the median distance) using a permutation test. For Austria, the median distance of all region pairs is 167 km, for Germany it is 283 km and for Switzerland it is 84 km. The overall median distance is 385 km. We created two groups of region pairs, distant ones D and close ones C whose sample means are $\bar{x}_D$ and $\bar{x}_C$. Let n_D and n_C be the sample size corresponding to each group. The permutation test is designed to determine whether the observed difference $T(obs)$ between the sample means is large enough to reject the null hypothesis H_0 which states that the two groups have identical probability distribution.

First, the difference in means between the two samples is calculated as $T(obs) = \bar{x}_D - \bar{x}_C$. Then, the observations of groups D and C are pooled and subsequently, the difference in sample means is calculated and recorded for every possible way of dividing these pooled values into two groups of size n_D and n_C (i.e., for every permutation of the group labels D and C). The set of the calculated differences is the exact distribution of possible differences under the null hypothesis that group labels do not matter.

Results. When analyzing all three countries together, we find a slightly negative correlation between geographic distance and the cosine similarity of the recipe and ingredient frequency vectors of different regions (Spearman?s $\rho = -0.19$, standard error $SE_\rho = 0.03$ and confidence interval CI at 95% is (−0.2535, −0.1259) for recipes and Spearman?s $\rho = -0.22$, $SE_\rho = 0.03$ and CI at 95% is (−0.2804, −0.1551) for ingredients). When only looking at Austria, we observe a much stronger correlation but with higher standard error especially for ingredients (Spearman?s$\rho = -0.74$, standard error $SE_\rho = 0.16$ and confidence interval CI at 95% is (−0.9242, −0.2340) for recipes and Spearman?s$\rho = -0.21$, $SE_\rho = 0.31$ and CI at 95% is (−0.7505, 0.4891) for ingredients).

Figures 5 and 6 show that at least in Austria and in Germany the recipe preferences of geographic close regions tend to be more similar than those of geographic distant ones. Ingredient preferences are very similar for both geographic close and distant regions (cf. Figure 6). For Switzerland we cannot observe the same pattern since geographic distances in Switzerland are very small and the diversity in the country is very large (see Figure 6). When looking at all three countries, we can still see the tendency of geographic close regions to be more similar than geographic distant ones. However, the differences are not significant and our permutation test results suggest that we cannot reject the null hypothesis - i.e., the differences within all groups can potentially be generated from the same underlying distribution. In previous work [21] the authors tested the same hypothesis for China and were able to reject the null hypothesis. However, one needs to note that our study focuses on a much smaller geographic area and therefore geographic distances may play a minor role.

3.4 Temporal food preferences

Food preferences are not static and may change over time. Therefore, we next explore the temporal evolution of human?s online food preferences and how potential temporal regularities relate to what we know about food and dietary patterns observed in offline studies.

Approach. First, we explore the normalized number of visits per day or month for selected ingredients using z-scores. The rationale behind z-score normalization is to mitigate the effect of anomalous days [22].

Next, we compute the average popularity change rate of two consecutive days or months d_i and d_{i+1} for selected ingredients as follows:

$$R(d_i, d_{i+1}) = \frac{|F(d_i) - F(d_{i+1})|}{\sum_{j=1}^{N} |F(d_j) - F(d_{j+1})|}. \quad (1)$$

N refers to the number of consecutive pairs (which is e.g., 7 in the case of a week) and $F(d)$ refers to the total access volume at day or month d.

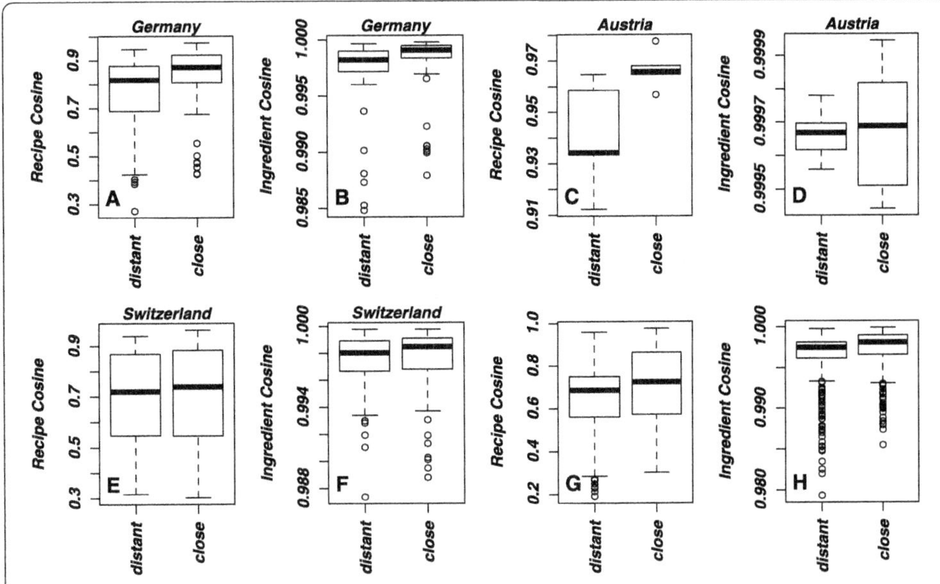

Figure 5 Do geographic nearby regions reveal more similar online food preferences than distant ones? This figure shows the cosine similarity distribution of two groups of region-pairs within each country and across countries, distant ones (which are above the median distance) and nearby ones (which are equal or below median distance). One can see that in Austria and Germany geographic close regions tend to reveal more similar recipe and ingredient preferences than distant regions; however, in Switzerland we do not observe this tendency.

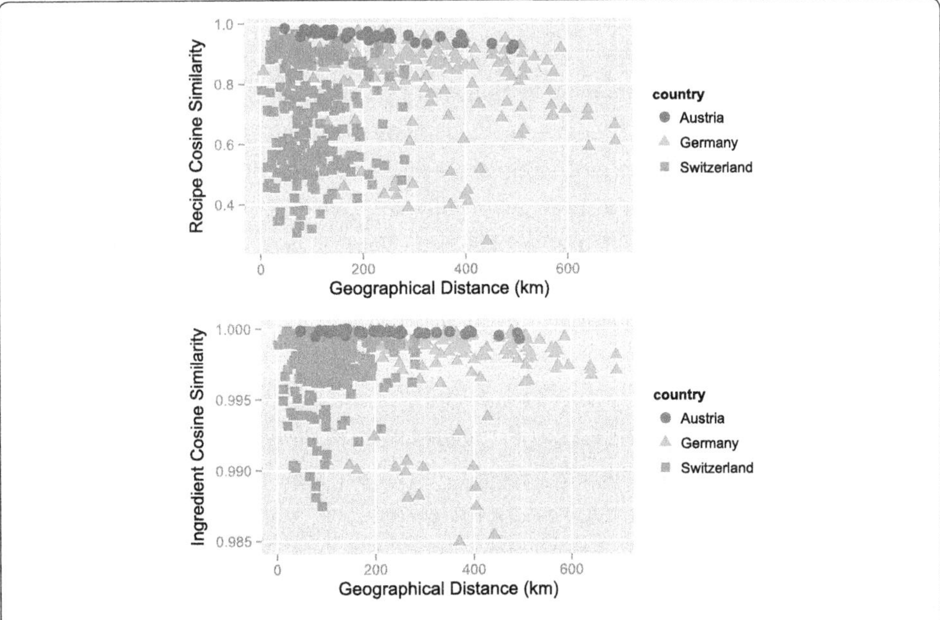

Figure 6 Do geographic nearby regions reveal more similar online food preferences than distant ones? This figure shows the cosine similarity of region pairs in relation to their physical distance. One can see that ingredient preferences tend to be very similar independent of the geographical distance in all three countries. Recipe similarity slightly decreases with increasing distance, at least in Austria and Germany.

To go beyond the exploration of the popularity of selected ingredients, we next explore the dynamics (i.e., stability and changes) of the recipe and ingredient frequency vectors between consecutive weekdays and months using the rank biased overlap (RBO) metric

[23]. RBO measures the correlation between two ranked lists of recipes/ingredients that represent the popularity of recipes/ingredients in different regions. Recipes and ingredients are ranked by the number of visits they obtained during that weekday/month within one year. RBO is a top weighted metric which means that it is more important that the ranking of the most popular recipes/ingredients does not change from one day/month to the next day/month than the ranking of recipes/ingredients in the long tail of unpopular recipes/ingredients. This makes sense, since we know that the popularity distributions of recipes and ingredients are heavy tail distribution and one might argue that recipes and ingredients which have been accessed very few times during a day or month do not reflect the online food preferences of that day or month. Therefore, we do not care if the ranking of those recipes/ingredients changes. RBO is defined as follows:

$$\mathrm{RBO}(\sigma 1, \sigma 2, p) = (1-p)\sum_{d=1}^{\infty} \frac{\sigma 1_{1:d} \cap \sigma 2_{1:d}}{d} p^{(d-1)}. \tag{2}$$

Let $\sigma 1$ and $\sigma 2$ be two not necessarily conjoint lists of ranking. Let $\sigma 1_{1:d}$ and $\sigma 2_{1:d}$ be the ranked lists at depth d. The RBO falls in the range $[0,1]$, where 0 means disjoint, and 1 means identical. The parameter p $(0 \leq p < 1)$ determines how steep the decline in weights is. The smaller p, the more top-weighted the metric.

Results by week day. Figure 7 shows the normalized access volume of sample ingredients ordered by group (meat, carbohydrates, fish, vegetables and alcohol). We can see that different groups of ingredients indeed reveal similar temporal trends regarding their popularity. Meat (e.g., pork and steak) is mainly requested during the weekend with a peak on Sunday. This confirms offline observations (gained via questionnaires) which reveal that Austrians consume meat products more frequently on Sundays compared to other days in the week [24]. Carbohydrate-rich, cheap and healthy food such as pasta, vegetables and potatoes is more frequently requested at the beginning of the week and less frequently during weekends. We also observe that fish is most popular on Thursday and Friday and alcohol is more popular at weekends than during the week.

Our preliminary results raise the question whether online preferences of certain ingredients show a clear shift from weekdays to weekends. Figure 8 shows that indeed most changes happen before and after the weekend, suggesting that *online preferences for ingredients during the week are starkly different from weekend preferences.* Changes in online food preferences over the course of a week slowly accumulate, with noticeable changes starting around Thu/Fri. The end of the weekend period is clearly demarcated, evident in a high change rate across most ingredients on Sun-Mon. This means that online food preferences tend to change slowly towards weekend preferences during the week, but they change abruptly back to weekday preferences over Sun-Mon.

Finally, to complement our analysis of selected ingredients and ingredients groups, we study the dynamics of all recipes and ingredients collectively. Figure 9 shows the stability of ingredient and recipe preferences during the course of a week using the RBO metric with different top weightiness (i.e., p-values). One can see that users? ingredient preferences are very stable which can be explained by the fact that many of the most popular ingredients (such as butter, salt and pepper) are equally important on different weekdays. The shifts in

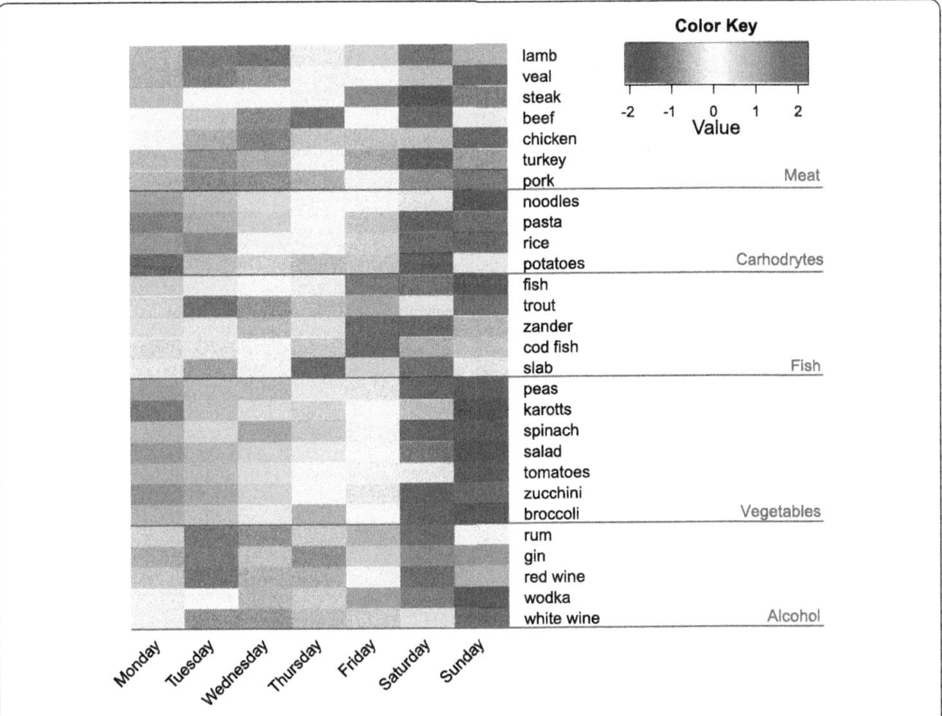

Figure 7 How popular are different ingredients over the course of a week? The figure shows *z*-scores of the request volume per weekday. One can see that fish is mainly requested Friday, meat during the weekend and carbohydrate-rich and cheap food such as pasta or potatoes during the week.

the ingredient preferences only become visible when one focuses on selected ingredients but not when analyzing the aggregation of all ingredients. For users? recipe preferences we can see that they are relatively stable during the week, but major shifts in the preferences happen during the weekends. This confirms our hypothesis that *users? online food preferences change during the weekend* which becomes visible in their recipe selection process which is in part driven by ingredient preferences as we have shown before. However, not all ingredients have the same function in the recipe selection process and it is unlikely that the most popular ingredients impact the recipe selection process since those are mainly staple food. We leave the question about which types of ingredients may drive the recipe selection process for future research.

Results by month. To characterize a typical year, we compute for a sample of ingredients their normalized access volume and the change rate between consecutive months. Figure 10 shows that the access volume of ingredients indeed allows to identify ingredients with strong seasonal prevalence such as asparagus, since recipes with asparagus are mainly requested during the asparagus season which starts at the end of April and ends in June.

Again, so far we have only explored selected ingredients. To further extend and complement our analysis we investigate the dynamics (i.e., stability and changes) of the recipe and ingredient frequency vectors between consecutive months using the rank biased overlap (RBO) metric. Figure 11 shows the RBO value between the ranked lists of recipes or ingredients of consecutive months. Recipe and ingredients are ranked by the number of

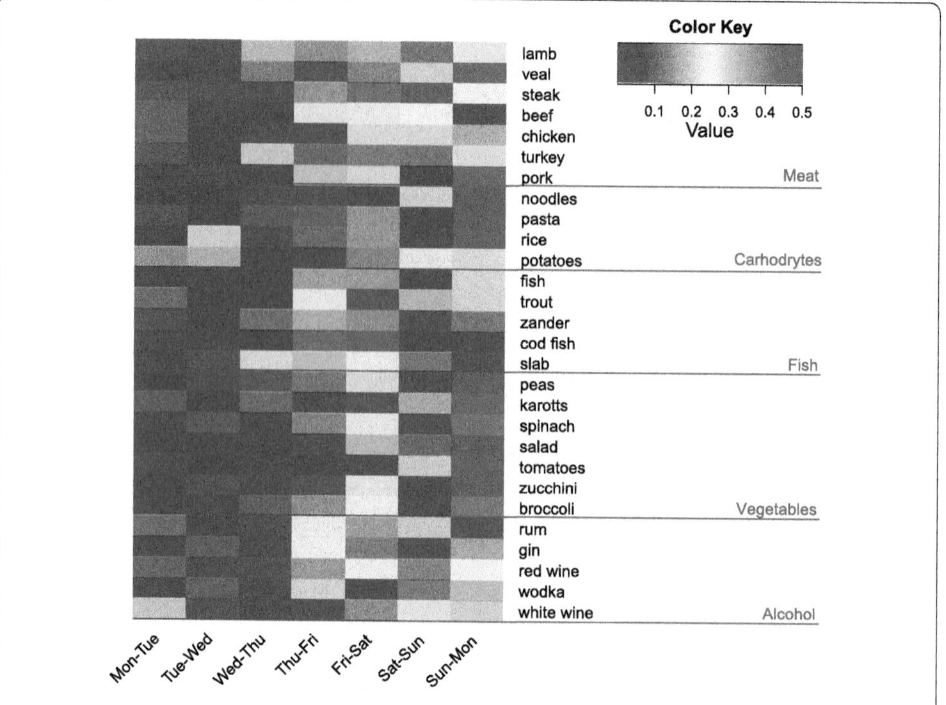

Figure 8 How do preferences change over the course of a week? The figure shows the average change rate from one day to the next one. One can see that most changes happen before and after the weekend. That means that the weekday-preferences are different from weekend-preferences.

visits they obtained during that month within one year. One can see that the recipe preferences are pretty unstable and change a lot during the course of a year. Only November and December and January, February and March seem to be exceptions since the recipe preferences remain pretty stable during these periods. However, to further dig into these patterns data collections which span over several years are required.

4 Discussion

In the following we will discuss the main findings of our work and their implications. This work is based on data stemming from one single recipe platform with unknown biases. In future work we plan to extend this study on additional log data from other recipe platforms.

Recipe and ingredient preferences. We observe that both the popularity distributions of recipes and ingredients are heavy tailed. Both can be best approximated by a truncated power law distribution, while the truncation is stronger for the recipe popularity distribution (cf. Figure 2) compared to the ingredient popularity distribution (cf. Figure 3). Our results also indicate that the recipe selection process of users is at least partly driven by their preferences towards ingredients since the empirically observed ingredient preferences are more focused towards few ingredients and less focused towards others than one would expect if the recipe selection process would be random. By investigating the online food preferences of each region separately (meso level), we obtained similar results as for the accumulated analysis (macro level). However, we see slightly more regional variability for the recipe preference distributions than for the ingredient preference distributions.

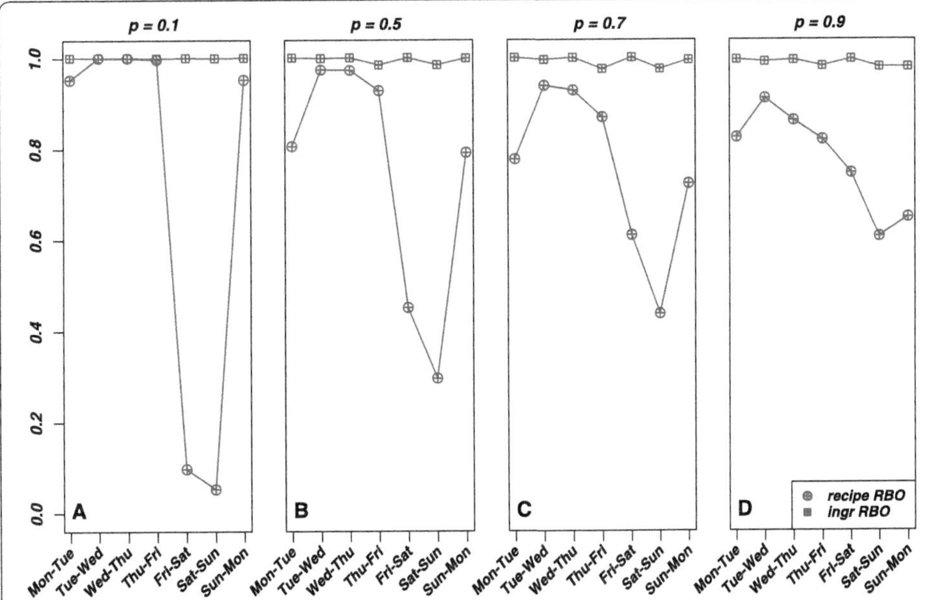

Figure 9 How stable are users? online food preferences during the course of a week? This figure shows the RBO values between the ranked lists of recipes or ingredients of two consecutive days. Recipe and ingredients are ranked by the number of visits they obtained during that weekday within one year. One can see that users online food preferences are relatively stable during the week, but major shifts in the preferences happen during weekends.

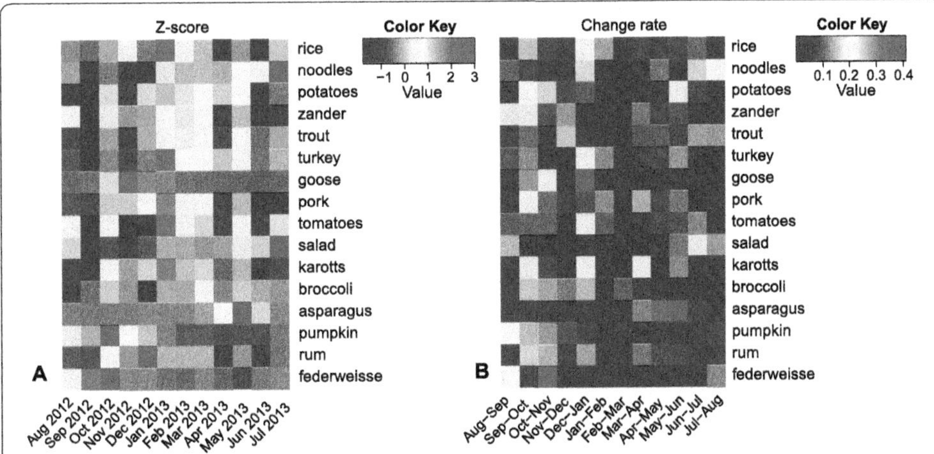

Figure 10 How seasonal are the preferences for different ingredients? This figure shows the *z*-score per month and the average change rate from one month to the next one. One can see that the popularity of certain ingredients such as asparagus can clearly be mapped to its seasonal availability in central Europe.

This indicates, that the process which generated the ingredient preferences in different regions is more similar across different regions than the process which generated the recipe preferences.

In the literature several mechanisms have been proposed and described that may produce heavy tailed and specifically power law distributions (e.g., [8, 25, 26]). The most prominent one is the so-called *Yule process* [27] (also known as preferential attachment or the rich get richer phenomenon) which can only explain certain parts of online food

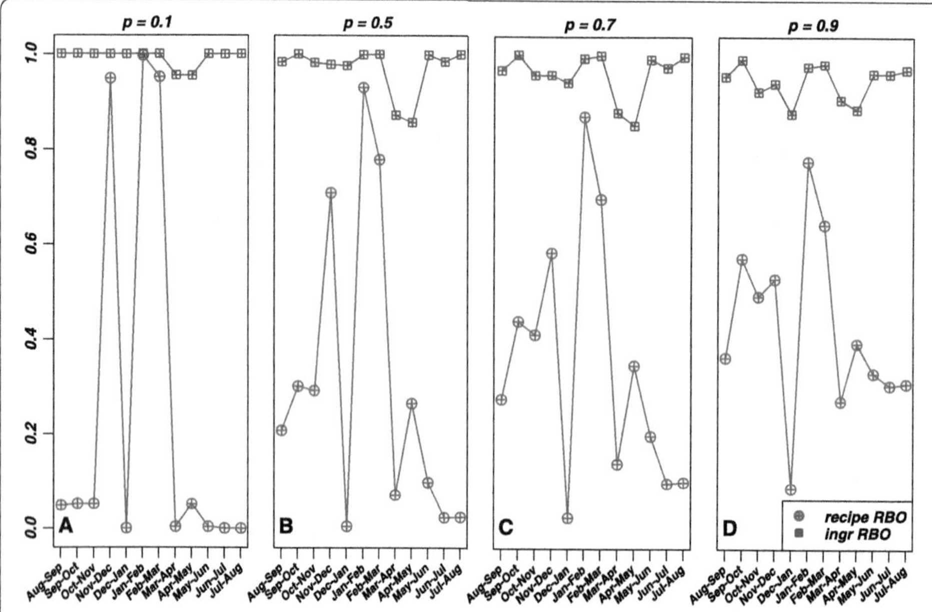

Figure 11 How stable are users? online food preferences during the course of a year?This figure shows the RBO values between the ranked lists of recipes or ingredients of consecutive months. Recipe and ingredients are ranked by the number of visits they obtained during that month within one year. One can see that the recipe preferences are pretty unstable and change a lot during the course of a year. Only November and December and January, February and March seem to be exceptions since the recipe preferences remain pretty stable during these periods.

preference distributions. As mentioned before, our results indicate that the most popular recipe and ingredient popularities are truncated (i.e., they are lower than one would expect if the power law distribution would explain the whole distribution). Several hypotheses exists that aim to explain what causes this truncation (see e.g., [11, 15, 17, 28]). In this work we presented two potential explanations of why the Yule process fails to explain the evolution of online food preferences and why we can observe a truncation for the popularity of the most popular recipes: (i) We can expect that the static nature of recipes has an influence on how they are viewed; the fact that recipes do not change and are therefore most likely only fetched a limited number of times by each user leads to the *fetch-at-once effect* which can causes the truncation of the most popular recipes. (ii) If this holds true the truncation is further impacted by the *finite-size effect* - i.e., that a physical upper limit of the maximum popularity of recipes exists which corresponds to the number of users on the platform. For ingredients, the truncation is also visible but less pronounced since universal ingredients like salt or butter are included in almost all recipes. Therefore, even if a finite number of users fetches every recipe only once or a very small number of times, universal ingredients are fetched repeatedly.

Spatial preferences. Anderson et al. [20] point out that ?*our basic nutritional needs, and some very broad preferences, are set by biology, but preferences are notoriously subject to cultural and social forces*". Therefore, it seems to be a plausible assumption, that geographic close regions have more similar food preferences than distant ones since they are more likely to be subjects of the same cultural forces. Zhu et al. [21] further point out that frequent communication and migration may explain the adoption of food preferences and their empirical findings support this hypothesis. Our spatial preference analysis (cf. Figures 5 and 6) shows that there exists a slight tendency of geographic close regions to reveal more similar recipe and ingredient patterns; however, the differences in the German speaking part of Europe are not significant as it was observed for China [21]. One potential explanation for that is that distances in German speaking part of Europe are much smaller and also the mobility of people living in this area might be higher. Therefore, other factors like cultural similarities and transportation infrastructure might be more suitable alternatives to explain the similarities of food preferences between different regions in central Europa.

Temporal preferences. Food preferences are not static and change over time and our results clearly show that users? online food preferences change during the weekend, which becomes visible in their recipe selection process which is in part driven by ingredient preferences. Selected ingredients show a prevalence for specific seasons (cf. Figure 10) and weekdays (cf. Figure 7) which can be related with phenomena from the offline world such as the seasonal availability of some ingredients or results from reactive diet studies which showed that users tend to eat more meat during the weekend than other days in the week [4]. However, when looking at the aggregation of all ingredients we observe that the ingredient preferences are relatively stable during the course of the week, while the recipe preferences clearly change during the weekend (cf. Figure 9). This can be explained by the fact that not all ingredients have the same function in the recipe selection process and especially the most popular ingredients like salt, sugar or butter are so common that they probably do not impact the recipe selection process. Therefore, when analyzing the collection of all ingredients, their popularity appears to be very stable (cf. Figure 9), while for selected ingredients we can observe interesting changes and temporal regularities (cf. Figures 8 and 10) which can be related with the offline world (cf. Figures 7 and 10). We leave the question about which types of ingredients may drive the recipe selection process for future research.

5 Related work

Dietary trends and culinary evolution. Previous research suggests that dietary trends are affected by behavioral, socio-cultural and economic variables [29, 30], while the impact of taste factors is for adult?s food intake less apparent [31]. A question which has been of long lasting interest is: *which variables can explain the culinary variety to what extent?* Researchers, for example, found culinary regularities that are functions of the climate. The work of [32] shows that the usage of spices in a given region is highly correlated with its annual temperature. The work of West et al. [22] also suggests that climate impacts dietary patterns. Zhu et al. [21] investigate the effect of climate and geographic distance on the cuisine of different regions in China and show that geographic distance plays a more important role than climate conditions. Concretely, they showed that climate does not show any correlation with the ingredient usage similarities when controlling for geographic distance (PCC = 0.116), while geographic distance remains correlated with ingredient usage similarities also when they control for climate (PCC = −0.280).

In [18] the authors analyze the ingredient distributions of six different cookbooks. They found that the universality of ingredients varies over four orders of magnitude documenting huge differences in how frequently various ingredients are used in recipes. The authors further find that the rank-ordered ingredient distribution (i.e., ingredients are ranked by the number of recipes in which they appear) follows a power law with an exponential cut-off to capture finite size effects. The slope of the power law parameter $\alpha = 1.72$ which cannot be explained by a general Yule process which would produce a power law with $\alpha \geq 2$. To model cuisine growth the authors propose a copy-mutate algorithm which preservers idiosyncratic ingredients in a manner akin to the founder effect in biology.

In [19] the authors empirically tested the *food pairing hypothesis* originally proposed by Benzi and Blumenthal which states that ?two ingredients which share important flavor compounds will go well together". They found that shared flavors compounds effect ingredient combinations very differently in Western and Eastern cuisines. While in Western cuisines ingredients that share flavor compounds are more frequently combined then one would expect from randomly generated recipes (with the same ingredient frequencies), in the Eastern cuisines ingredients with distinct flavor compounds are combined much more frequently than for random recipes. The authors further reveal that the food preparing differences between the Western and Eastern cuisine is due to few outliers which are frequently used in a particular cuisine, such as butter, cocoa or vanilla in North America.

While our work focuses on studying the popularity of recipes in different regions, previous work on the culinary evolution relied on a regional categorization schema of recipes to define what is typical for a region. However, it remains unclear if typical recipes of a region reflect the preferences of that region.

Online food preferences. Despite the fact that online recipe databases and community sites gain a lot of attention in the online world, little research exists today on the nature and evolution of users? online food preferences and how those preferences relate to their offline preferences (i.e., their preferences in the real world). A very inspiring piece of work was published by West et al. [22] who analyze temporal patterns and regional differences in dietary patterns online and relate them with observations from the world. Unlike in our work, West et al. use web logs recorded by a Web browser add-on provided by Bing and use the access statistics of recipes a user clicks on from a search query result page to approximate the food consumption of different regions in the US. Their user study suggests that it is a reasonable assumption that users who search for a dish and click on the recipe afterwards, are likely to cook it. Their results indicate that the online access volume of food related information may potentially allow to predict offline medical needs. They found a significant correlation between the hospital admissions of patients admitted with a diagnosis related to congestive heart failure over time and the sodium intake over time approximated via recipe visits. The curves indeed follow each other closely, however the causal relationship cannot be proved. High sodium intake may e.g. be linked to holidays which might be linked to higher traveling activities leading to a loss of compliance with medication.

Another interesting work by Teng et al. [33] shows that structural properties of nodes in ingredient networks (co-occurrence and substitution networks) can be used to improve the prediction performance of recipe ratings. The authors make the assumption that the ratings of recipes reflect the online food preferences of users, which can be inaccurate especially if only a small fraction of users uses the rating feature while most of them are lurkers.

Our work overcomes this issue by focusing on the consumption of content rather than the production of content. Unlike West et al. we focus on a rather small area in central Europe (Austria, Germany and Switzerland), while they focus on the US. Further, we use the access volume of recipes as a proxy for food preferences rather than for food consumption.

Popularity of online content. Since we analyze the popularity of recipes and ingredients over time and space, also research about the popularity of other types of online content is relevant for our work. For example, in [11] The authors found that the popularity distribution of videos on YouTube and Daum follows a power law but with a sharp decay from the straight line for the most popular videos. The curve fitting results show that the decay at the heavy tail is best fitted by adding an exponential cutoff to the power law distribution. The power law part of the distribution can be explained by the Yule process (also known as preferential attachment or the rich-get-richer phenomenon), while the sharp decay for the most popular videos can be explained by *the aging effect* [14] (i.e., high degree nodes will eventually stop receiving more links because every node ages and will stop being active at some point), *the information filtering effect* [15] (i.e., users cannot receive information about all available videos but only about a fraction of them and therefore preferential attachment is hindered), and finally *the limited fetching phenomenon* [16] (i.e., users may fetch popular videos only once or few times since they do not change, while they may fetch popular websites such as news sites million of times). In [11] the authors show via simulations that the limited-fetching phenomenon can indeed explain the sharp decay from the straight power law line for very popular videos. The higher the number of requests per users in their simulations the more visible the decay.

Server logs. In our work we use server logs as a proxy for users? online food preferences. In previous work, logs of search engine use have been successfully used to identify temporal trends (cf. [34]), geographic differences (cf. [35]) and to predict real world medical phenomena (cf. [36]). However, to our best knowledge this is the first work which analyzes server log data from recipe platforms to analyze the evolution of online food preferences.

6 Conclusions

To the best of our knowledge, our work is the first to study online food preferences of users via log data obtained from recipe websites and presents a comprehensive multi-dimensional approach which allows to dig into the nature and evolution of users? online food preferences. We find that recipe visits (as well as the inferred ingredient visits) may represent a plausible *signal* for food preferences of human populations, since (i) our observations can in part be linked to real-world events, such as the asparagus season, and findings from studies which e.g., showed that people eat more meat at weekends than at other days of the week and (ii) our observations are fairly consistent on a macro and meso level which suggests that the observed online preference distributions can be reproduced at different scales. We hope that this work contributes to understanding the nature and evolution of online food preferences by analyzing the observable outcome of such preferences on four different dimensions.

The main findings of this work are: (i) Recipe and ingredient popularity distributions are heavy tailed and can be approximated well by a severely truncated power law function (recipes) and a truncated power law function (ingredients). These effects can both be found on a meso level (i.e., in individual regions) as well as on a macro level (i.e., in the aggregation of all German-speaking regions in Europe). (ii) Recipe preference distributions exhibit *more regional differences* than ingredient preference distributions. (iii) Recipe preferences are *partly driven* by ingredient preferences and (iv) weekday preferences are *clearly distinct* from weekend preferences.

Competing interests

The authors declare that they have no competing interests.

Authors? contributions

All authors designed the methodology and conceived the experiments. CW collected the data and performed the spatial and temporal analysis. PS analyzed the statistical properties of recipe and ingredient popularity distributions. All authors wrote and revised the manuscript.

Acknowledgements

We thank ichkoche.at for sharing their data with us and the anonymous reviewers for their valuable comments.

Endnotes

[a] Food preferences may not only expose what is liked but also what is disliked and avoided. Preferences assume a situation of choice but do not necessarily reflect use. One might prefer lobster over shrimps but eat more shrimps.

[b] Ingredient visits are inferred from the recipe visits in which the ingredients are used.

[c] Note that we work with discrete and not continuous data and hence, also use the exact methods necessary to cope with discrete data. For fitting the discrete power law function we use the faster analytical methods, instead of using the slow exact numerical variants.

[d] A positive value of R means that the log-likelihood of the first distribution (in this case the truncated power law function) is higher than that of the second (in this case the power law function).

[e] We also report $1/\lambda$ as it roughly tells us where the cutoff is.

References

1. Fischler C (1988) Food, self and identity. Soc Sci Inf 27(2):275-292
2. Harris M, Ross EB (1987) Food and evolution: toward a theory of human food habits. Temple University Press, Philadelphia
3. Calvo M (1982) Migration et alimentation. Soc Sci Inf 21(3):383-446
4. Prester H-G (2001) Consumer panel research at GfK. In: Social and economic analyses of consumer panel data. ZUMA-Nachrichten Spezial, vol 7
5. Clauset A, Shalizi CR, Newman MEJ (2009) Power-law distributions in empirical data. SIAM Rev 51(4):661-703
6. Wagner C, Singer P, Strohmaier M, Huberman BA (2014) Semantic stability in social tagging streams. In: Proceedings of the 23rd international conference on World Wide Web, pp 735-746
7. Mitzenmacher M (2003) A brief history of generative models for power law and lognormal distributions. Internet Math 1:226-251
8. Andriani P, McKelvey B (2009) Perspective - from Gaussian to Paretian thinking: causes and implications of power laws in organizations. Organ Sci 20(6):1053-1071
9. Adamic LA, Huberman BA (2000) Power-law distribution of the World Wide Web. Science 287(5461):2115
10. Sen S, Lam SK, Rashid AM, Cosley D, Frankowski D, Osterhouse J, Harper FM, Riedl J (2006) Tagging, communities, vocabulary, evolution. In: Proceedings of the 2006 20th anniversary conference on computer supported cooperative work, pp 181-190
11. Cha M, Kwak H, Rodriguez P, Ahn Y-Y, Moon S (2009) Analyzing the video popularity characteristics of large-scale user generated content systems. IEEE/ACM Trans Netw 17(5):1357-1370.
12. Newman ME (2005) Power laws, Pareto distributions and Zipf?s law. Contemp Phys 46(5):323-351
13. Alstott J, Bullmore E, Plenz D (2014) powerlaw: a Python package for analysis of heavy-tailed distributions. PLoS ONE 9(1):e85777
14. Amaral LA, Scala A, Barthelemy M, Stanley HE (2000) Classes of small-world networks. Proc Natl Acad Sci USA 97(21):11149-11152
15. Mossa S, Barthelemy M, Stanley EH, Amaral LA (2002) Truncation of power law behavior in ?scale-free" network models due to information filtering. Phys Rev Lett 88(13):138701
16. Gummadi KP, Dunn RJ, Saroiu S, Gribble SD, Levy HM, Zahorjan J (2003) Measurement, modeling, and analysis of a peer-to-peer file-sharing workload. In: Proceedings of the nineteenth ACM symposium on operating systems principles. SOSP?03, pp 314-329
17. Bak P, Tang C, Wiesenfeld K (1988) Self-organized criticality. Phys Rev A 38(1):364
18. Kinouchi O, Diez-Garcia RW, Holanda AJ, Zambianchi P, Roque AC (2008) The non-equilibrium nature of culinary evolution. New J Phys 10(7):073020
19. Ahn Y-Y, Ahnert SE, Bagrow JP, Barabási A-L (2011) Flavor network and the principles of food pairing. Sci Rep 1:196
20. Anderson EN (2005) Everyone eats. Understanding food and culture. New York University Press, New York
21. Zhu Y-X, Huang J, Zhang Z-K, Zhang Q-M, Zhou T, Ahn Y-Y (2013) Geography and similarity of regional cuisines in China. PLoS ONE 8(11):e79161

22. West R, White RW, Horvitz E (2013) From cookies to cooks: insights on dietary patterns via analysis of web usage logs. In: Word Wide Web conference (WWW)
23. Webber W, Moffat A, Zobel J (2010) A similarity measure for indefinite rankings. ACM Trans Inf Syst 28(4):20
24. Kiefer I, Haberzettl C, Rieder C (2000) Ernährungsverhalten und Einstellung zum Essen der ÖsterreicherInnen. J Ernährmed 2(5):2-7
25. Mitzenmacher M (2004) A brief history of generative models for power law and lognormal distributions. Internet Math 1(2):226-251
26. Sornette D (1998) Multiplicative processes and power laws. Phys Rev E 57(4):4811
27. Yule GU (1925) A mathematical theory of evolution, based on the conclusions of Dr. J. C. Willis, F.R.S. Philos Trans R Soc Lond B 213:21-87
28. Sornette D, Cont R (1997) Convergent multiplicative processes repelled from zero: power laws and truncated power laws. J Phys I 7(3):431-444
29. Logue AW (2004) The psychology of eating and drinking. Psychology Press, New York
30. Sanjur D (1982) Social and cultural perspectives in nutrition. Prentice Hall, New York
31. Drewnowski A (1997) Taste preferences and food intake. Annu Rev Nutr 17:237–253
32. Sherman PW, Billing J (1999) Darwinian gastronomy: why we use spices. BioScience J 49(6):453–463
33. Teng C-Y, Lin Y-R, Adamic LA (2012) Recipe recommendation using ingredient networks. In: Proceedings of the 3rd annual ACM web science conference. WebSci?12, pp 298-307
34. Vlachos M, Meek C, Vagena Z, Gunopulos D (2004) Identifying similarities, periodicities and bursts for online search queries. In: Proceedings of the 2004 ACM SIGMOD international conference on management of data. SIGMOD?04, pp 131-142
35. Bennett PN, Radlinski F, White RW, Yilmaz E (2011) Inferring and using location metadata to personalize web search. In: Proceedings of the 34th international ACM SIGIR conference on research and development in information retrieval. SIGIR?11, pp 135-144
36. Ginsberg J, Mohebbi MH, Patel RS, Brammer L, Smolinski MS, Brilliant L (2009) Detecting influenza epidemics using search engine query data. Nature 457(7232):1012-1014

15

Personalized routing for multitudes in smart cities

Manlio De Domenico[1*], Antonio Lima[2], Marta C González[3] and Alex Arenas[1]

[*]Correspondence: manlio.dedomenico@urv.cat
[1]Departament d'Enginyeria Informàtica i Matemàtiques, Universitat Rovira i Virgili, Av.da Països Catalans, 26, Tarragona, 43007, Spain
Full list of author information is available at the end of the article

Abstract

Human mobility in a city represents a fascinating complex system that combines social interactions, daily constraints and random explorations. New collections of data that capture human mobility not only help us to understand their underlying patterns but also to design intelligent systems. Bringing us the opportunity to reduce traffic and to develop other applications that make cities more adaptable to human needs. In this paper, we propose an adaptive routing strategy which accounts for individual constraints to recommend personalized routes and, at the same time, for constraints imposed by the collectivity as a whole. Using big data sets recently released during the Telecom Italia Big Data Challenge, we show that our algorithm allows us to reduce the overall traffic in a smart city thanks to synergetic effects, with the participation of individuals in the system, playing a crucial role.

Keywords: personalized routing; collective behavior; smart city; potential energy landscape; big data

1 Introduction

Rapid development of wireless communication and mobile computing technologies call new research that explores the responses of urban systems to the flow of instant information. Thus, the analysis of spatial signals becomes an increasingly important research theme.

The required four steps to model trips consist of calculating trip generation, trip distribution, modal split and route assignments. The sources to inform these steps traditionally have come from travel diaries and census data [1]. However, the presence of new information and communication technologies (ICT) provide big data sources that are allowing novel research and applications related to human mobility. Recent studies have advanced the knowledge on trip generation by studying the number of different locations visited by individuals through mobile phones and quantifying their frequent return to previously visited locations. These have demonstrated that the majority of travels occur between a limited number of places, with less frequent trips to new places outside an individual radius [2, 3]. In the domain of trip distributions, new models have helped us to predict number of commuting trips when lacking data for calibration [4].

An important topic is to explore route assignments in the context of smart multimodal systems [5, 6], where individual daily trips follow recommendations based on personal and global constraints. This is of special interest towards efficient cities, where individuals could be automatically routed reducing the probability of traffic congestion and at the same time reducing the environmental impact. From the individual's point of view, for instance, one might want to choose a trip which minimizes the amount of traffic along the route, or to avoid routes across areas with high criminality level, or to favorite routes across more touristic areas, *etc.* On the other hand, the choices of certain routes at individual level, without accounting for the *state of the system*, often leads to traffic congestion [7, 8] which, in turn, is responsible for increasing pollution while decreasing the quality of the environment, with evident impact on the community.

In this work we model the trips in an urban system as interacting particles with data-driven origin-destination pairs that can be routed in their trips. Their route choices are based in a time-varying potential energy landscape that seeks to satisfy individual's and community's requirements simultaneously. Main streams methods for distributed routing seek to avoid congestion by global travel time reduction based on optimization methods [7, 9]. More recently, adaptive path optimization on networks (London underground network and global airport network) related the problem to physics of interacting polymers [10]. In this work we go one step forward in that direction and use a framework based on potential energy landscapes to integrate diverse layers of constraints to favor certain routes and to study the effects of the level of adoption of the proposed recommendations. In this work our main focus is to explore a new framework of analysis to study routing strategies for urban mobility, while the road network constrains are left to further studies.

2 Data-driven routing of human mobility

We consider a geographic area of interest (e.g., a city, a district, *etc.*) and we discretize it into a grid $\mathcal{G}$ with size $L \times L'$. In the following, for sake of simplicity, we will consider squared grids with size L.

We model individuals moving within the grid as a complex system of interacting sentient particles whose goal is to move between two geographic points according to certain criteria. Each criterion is encoded by a matrix $\mathbf{C}$, with the same dimension of the grid, where each entry indicates the state of the corresponding cell in $\mathcal{G}$. In the same spirit of physical models of an electromagnetic surface, we use the convention that $C_{ij} > 0$ indicates a *repelling* cell, i.e., a geographic area that should be avoided. Similarly, $C_{ij} < 0$ indicates an *attracting* cell, i.e., a geographic area that should be involved for routing. Areas where $C_{ij} = 0$ are considered as neutral.

The origin of a constraint can be of different nature. In fact, there are constraints at individual level, i.e., the ones corresponding to requirements of the single user (*e.g.*, avoid areas with high criminality level), and at global level, i.e., the ones corresponding to the requirement of the whole community (e.g., keep minimum the pollution level). Moreover, there are *static (or quasi-static) constraints* corresponding to restrictions that do not change over time or change over large temporal scales, and *dynamic constraints* corresponding to rapid changes within the system itself, like the traffic flow or the weather. On one hand we should account for individuals' goals and requirements, while on the other hand it is crucial to satisfy constraints imposed for the wealth of the community.

In the following, we consider the set of all constraints, static and dynamic at individual and collective level, and we assign to each of them a time-varying matrix $\mathbf{C}^{(\alpha)}(t)$, where $\alpha = 1, 2, \ldots, M$ and M is the total number of constraints. In the case of static constraints, the matrix is considered constant over time. Moreover, the entries of each matrix are rescaled to the range $0 \leq C_{ij}^{(\alpha)} \leq 1$, for all values of i, j and α to assign a relative importance to each constraint and to settle on a common scale. Finally, the total constraint matrix is defined by the linear combination of such constraints at each time step:

$$\mathbf{C}(t) = \sum_{\alpha=1}^{M} w_\alpha(t)\mathbf{C}^\alpha(t), \quad \sum_{\alpha=1}^{M} w_\alpha(t) = 1, \tag{1}$$

where the coefficients $w_\alpha(t)$ are empirical and define a trade-off between individual's and global constraints. It is worth remarking that these coefficient might vary over time because, depending on the circumstances (special events, incidents, *etc.*), it could be necessary to change their value to satisfy different priorities.

We define another matrix, $\mathbf{D}_\ell(t)$ ($\ell = 1, 2, \ldots, N(t)$), encoding the starting and destination cells of each individual in the system, where the starting point is considered to be a repelling or neutral area and the destination point is an attractor. The number of individuals $N(t)$ is allowed to change over time. The matrix $\mathbf{D}_\ell(t)$ might change over time because, in principle, the individual might change destination during his or her travel, and for simplicity we assume that $-1 \leq D_{ij} \leq 0$ for each individual. It is worth remarking that attracting cells are in general associated to destinations and should be encoded in the set of matrices $D_\ell(t)$, whereas repelling cells are associated to constraints and should be encoded only in the set of matrices $C^\alpha(t)$.

We interpret the set of matrices $\mathbf{C}(t)$ and $\mathbf{D}_\ell(t)$ as potential energy landscapes and the routing of individuals is performed by means of a gradient descent, where each user moves along geodesics while reducing his or her potential energy until he or she reaches the destination. For simplicity, we assume no dependence on time for matrices $\mathbf{D}_\ell(t)$. We consider the case of a gravitational field in two dimensions permeating the areas encoded by $\mathbf{D}_\ell(t)$. More specifically, let (i_ℓ, j_ℓ) and $(i_\ell^{(d)}, j_\ell^{(d)})$ denote the cells of the underlying grid and destination point of the journey of individual ℓ, respectively, and let $r = \sqrt{(i_\ell^{(d)} - i_\ell)^2 + (j_\ell^{(d)} - j_\ell)^2}$ indicate their distance. The potential energy landscape is defined by

$$D_\ell(r) = \begin{cases} -\frac{\Omega}{\sqrt{r}}, & (i_\ell, j_\ell) \neq (i_\ell^{(d)}, j_\ell^{(d)}), \\ -\frac{\Omega}{\sqrt{1-10^{-4}}}, & (i_\ell, j_\ell) = (i_\ell^{(d)}, j_\ell^{(d)}), \end{cases} \tag{2}$$

where Ω is a constant factor, defining the scale of the potential which should guarantee that the potential is strong enough in each cell. In our simulations, we considered $\Omega = 30L\sqrt{2}$.

The choice of the value of the potential at the destination is somehow arbitrary and, as a rule of thumb, it should be a number smaller than the potential of the neighbors (whose distance is $r = 1$ or $r = \sqrt{2}$, the latter if movements along diagonals are allowed), but not so small to avoid a potential well so deep that the rest of the landscape is almost flat.

To guarantee the convergence of the gradient descent even in presence of constraints or noise resulting in potential wells, we weight the overall landscape for each particle by

$$V_\ell(r,t) = \gamma(t)D_\ell(r) + \big(1 - \gamma(t)\big)C(r,t), \tag{3}$$

where $C(r,t)$ is the potential energy landscape corresponding to constraints encoded by matrix $\mathbf{C}(t)$. The weighting factor $\gamma(t)$ should be a function ranging between 0 and 1 accounting for the importance given to the constraints with respect to the destination. The key to ensure the convergence of the gradient descent, while accounting at the same time for the constraints, is to make this function changing over time from an initial value up to 1. A candidate function is given by

$$\gamma(t; a, b) = 1 - (1 - b)e^{-at}, \tag{4}$$

where a is a non-negative number whose inverse $\tau = a^{-1}$ defines the time scale for convergence to 1 and b is the relative importance to be assigned at time $t = 0$ to constraints and destination. A reasonable choice is to balance the two potential energy landscapes to allow the particles to be routed according to the constraints *and* the destination up to a time scale τ, above which the influence of the destination becomes more important. Small values of b might give more importance to the constraints rather than destination, leading to a routing less oriented to the final destination during the first time steps. Therefore, we require $\gamma(0) \geq 1 - \gamma(0)$ leading to $b \geq 0.5$.

We rewrite Eq. (3) to put in evidence the terms corresponding to different constraints. Let $C_\sigma(r)$ and $C_\delta(r, t)$ denote the potential due to all static and dynamical constraints, respectively, which are not related to the state of the other particles of the system. For instance, $C_\sigma(r)$ might encode the landscape corresponding to crimes, supposed to change over very long time scales, while $C_\delta(r, t)$ might encode the areas where it is raining, snowing or being affected by other meteorological events. On the other hand, we make the realistic assumption that not all individuals follows the routing provided by the smart system. While the information about the traffic of all individuals can be available by sensors properly disseminated across the grid, it is not possible to predict the behavior of a certain fraction p of individuals. To account for such a fraction p of individuals, we consider a set of $N(1 - p)$ individuals moving along shortest paths between pairs of origin and destination, sampled from real data as discussed further in the text, and a set Np of individuals moving randomly in the city, i.e., following random walks instead of shortest paths. We indicate by $F_{\text{in}}(r, t)$ the potential corresponding to the flow of individuals *within* the system, i.e., those ones following suggestions from the smart system, and by $F_{\text{out}}(r, t)$ the potential corresponding to the flow of individuals *out* of the system. The latter is modeled by a noisy flow in terms of random walking individuals, although other mobility models can be used. In order to preserve conservation of the flow, we rescale each term by the number of particles in the most visited cell, i.e., by a weight $m(t) = \max[\mathbf{F}(t)]$, being $\mathbf{F}(t)$ the matrix accounting for the flow of individuals in the city at time t, with $\sum_{\text{cell}\in\mathcal{G}} \mathbf{F}(t) = N(t)$. The matrix $\mathbf{F}(t)$ is not weighted by the factor $[1 - \gamma(t)]$ as in the case of $C_\sigma(r)$ and $C_\delta(r, t)$, because it would wash out the contribution of $\mathbf{F}(t)$ to the potential landscape for increasing time. This choice makes our model more realistic: in fact, while it is possible to decide to traverse an undesirable area to balance the time spent looking for alternatives, it is not possible to traverse those areas which are congested or overcrowded. Therefore, the potential energy landscape accounting for the traffic flow should not be weighted by the function $1 - \gamma(t)$, whose existence is justified only to introduce a trade-off between the needing to reach the destination and the time spent to achieve this goal while accounting for personalized constraints. Finally, Eq. (3) maps to

$$\begin{aligned} V_\ell(r, t) &= \gamma(t)D_\ell(r) + \left(1 - \gamma(t)\right)\left[C_\sigma(r) + C_\delta(r, t)\right] \\ &\quad + m(t)\left[(1 - p)F_{\text{in}}(r, t) + pF_{\text{out}}(r, t)\right]. \end{aligned} \tag{5}$$

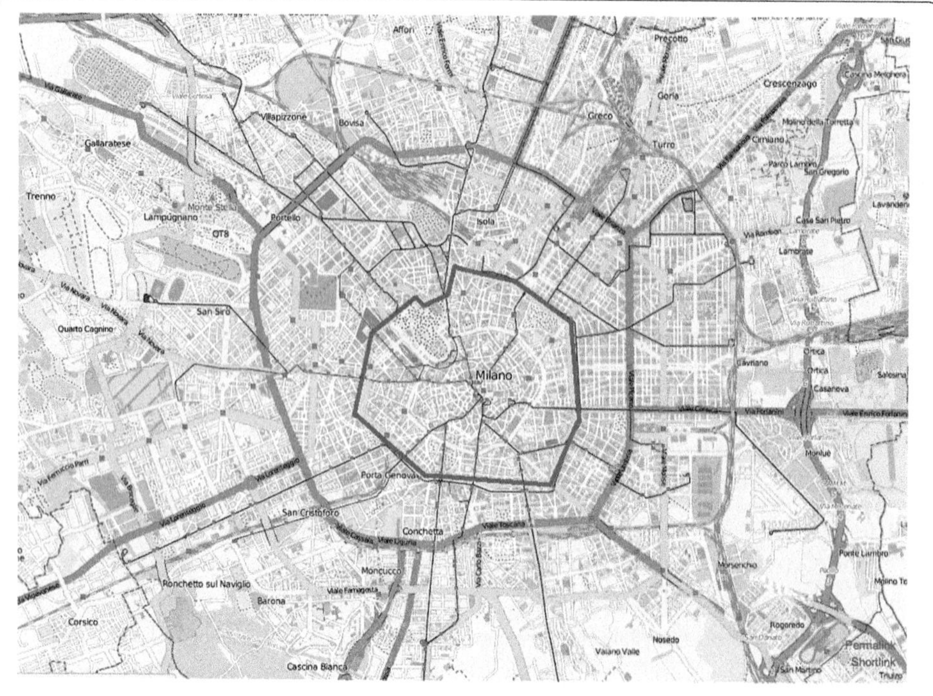

Figure 1 City of Milan. Area of Milan (Italy) considered in the present study. The area is divided into a squared grid with 10,000 cells of size 55,225 m^2.

This model is rather general, accounting for the presence of traffic and, simultaneously, for personalized and collective, static and dynamic, constraints. However, in this study we focused only on static constraints and we aggregated time-varying constraints for simplicity. It is worth remarking here that the potential landscape $V_\ell(r,t)$ experienced by individual ℓ still changes over time, because of the traffic flow term. Moreover, if agents are distributed in the grid according to the underlying population distribution and they move along shortest-path adapting over time in the evolving potential landscape, it is not possible to perform quantitative predictions about the state of the full system at a given time without numerical simulations.

3 Overview of the dataset

Most of the datasets used in this work were acquired as part of the Telecom 'Big Data Challenge' and all of them are related to the city of Milan, Italy (see Figure 1).

The constraints encoded by matrices $\mathbf{C}^\alpha(t)$ can be represented as different 'layers' of the city, as shown in Figure 2. The weighted combination of such layers, as in Eq. (1), allows to build the potential energy landscapes $C_\sigma(r)$, $C_\delta(r,t)$, $F_{\text{in}}(r,t)$ and $F_{\text{out}}(r,t)$ influencing the overall landscape defined by Eq. (5).

For simplicity, we considered four static layers obtained from the provided datasets and here we explain how the layers were generated. The 'pollution' layer was generated from readings of 7 sensors scattered around the city, taken hourly over the course of 2 months. Because these sensors are very sparse in space, we smoothed their readings conveniently. The 'events' layer was generated by looking at the number of tweets coming from each grid of the city. It contains 100,000 geolocated tweets generated over a 30-day period. Lastly, the 'crime' layer was generated from a list of crimes, manually curated, and sourced from

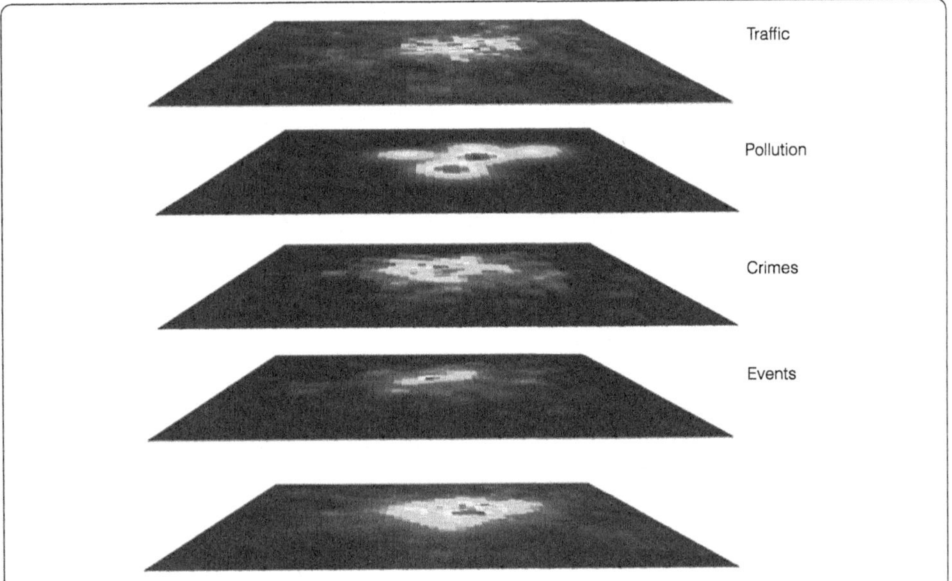

Figure 2 Layered potential energy landscapes. Each layer represents a potential energy landscape corresponding to a specific individual or collective constraint. The potential energy landscape in the bottom of the figure represents an example of weighted combination of such potentials.

newspaper articles.[a] It contains 1276 crimes happened during the course of 12 months in Milan and reported by newspapers and local media.

Finally, we used data about the total number of calls and texts generated in Milan by all users of a mobile carrier, over a period of two months. We used the aggregated fraction of calls and texts between areas of the city, aggregated over the whole 2-month period, to determine the distribution of trip origin and destination, as detailed in the next session.

4 Simulation of personalized routing

We performed massive simulations of personalized routing in Milan to gain insights about which factors influence the time required to complete a journey.

We started by exploring different ways to sample origin and destination cells for each individual in the city. The simplest strategy would be to choose both origin and destination with uniform probability on the grid. Of course, this strategy can not be realistic for several reasons. On one hand, the population is never uniformly distributed over metropolitan areas like Milan, where there is a high concentration of individuals in the 'core' of the city, while the population density decreases for increasing distance from the city centre [11]. In fact, assuming a uniform distribution of origins implicitly considers a population uniformly distributed. On the other hand, the choice of a random destination, regardless of the origin, is not representative of real urban mobility, where individual's journeys show a high degree of spatio-temporal regularity, with a few highly frequented locations [12–14] and high predictability of the underlying trajectories [3, 15, 16].

For this reason, we employed a data-driven approach accounting for intrinsic correlations in human mobility and leading to a more realistic distribution of origin-destination pairs. As a proxy for the population distribution, we have used the human activity measured by calls and texts generated by mobile phones. The calls dataset also provided information about the distribution of calls across all the pairs of grids; we exploited this infor-

Figure 3 Simulation of origin and destination. Different strategies for the simulation of origin and destination affect the distribution of time required to complete a journey. 'Approximated' indicates a random geographical area, whereas 'data-driven' indicates a simulation where origin is sampled from the population distribution and destination is sampled according to the origin-destination probability matrix.

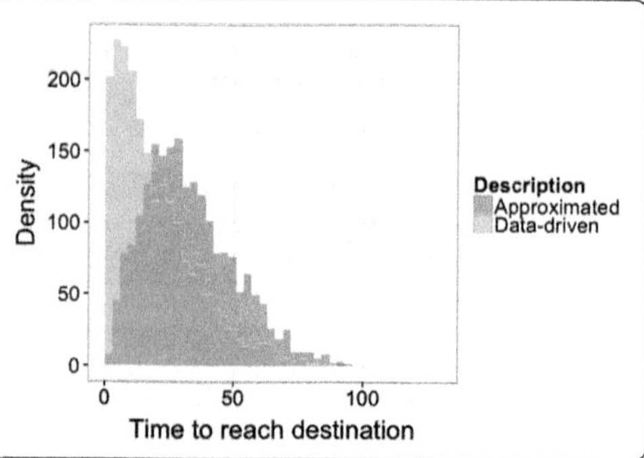

Figure 4 Simulation of personalized routing in Milan. Data-driven simulations where a certain fraction of individuals traveling in the city are routed by our system. The average time required to complete a journey decreases for increasing synergy, i.e., for increasing adoption of the personalized routing. The distribution of journey duration is shown in the ideal case, i.e., the non-physical scenario where each individual travels without constraints of any type, such as traffic, *etc.*

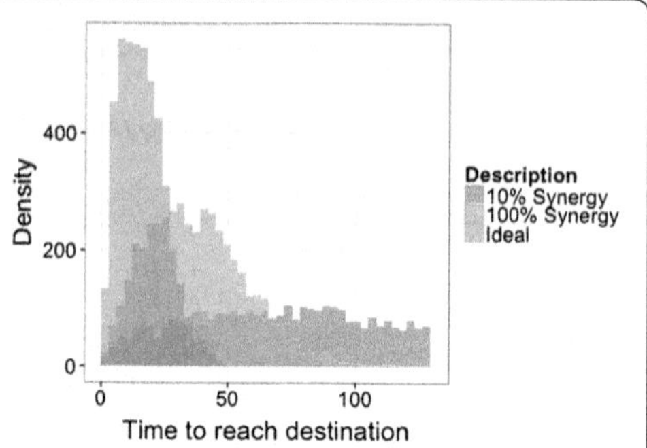

mation to sample a realistic ensemble of origin-destination pairs and to build an origin-destination probability matrix. Although this is a strong assumption, recent works [17–19] show how one of these quantities can be used to measure the other. Our simulations, summarized in Figure 3, show that the time required to complete a journey is, on average, faster when a data-driven strategy is employed vs. the one approximated by random origin and destinations.

We capitalized on this result to perform data-driven simulations by varying the fractions of individuals traveling by adopting our routing system. For each individual, we calculated again the time required to complete his or her journey, sampled according to the origin-destination probability matrix. To understand how the efficiency of our re-routing algorithm is affected by the fraction of individuals adopting the recommended routes, we define this fraction $(1 - p)$ as the *synergy* of the system and we calculate the time required to reach the destination for each individual. The remaining fraction p of individuals does not follow the recommended routes. We found that the underlying synergy has a non-negligible effect on the way individuals experience mobility the city. Our results, shown in Figure 4, put in evidence that the average time required to complete a journey decreases for increasing synergy, i.e., for increasing adoption of the personalized routing. This result was expected: when only a small fraction of individuals moves along the routes suggested by our system, it is not possible to calculate efficient trajectories because the only information available to the system is about the traffic generated by other people, while the information about their origin and destination is unknown. Conversely, when a large number of individuals adopts the suggested routes the potential energy landscape is less subjected to noisy fluctuations and a more efficient calculation of trajectories can be performed. For comparison, we show in the same figure the distribution of journey duration in the non-physical scenario where each individual travels without constraints of any type, such as traffic, *etc.* This optimal case, shown in figure for comparison, is a free-flow scenario where every person goes to their destination undisturbed by other people. Individuals' routes were sampled according to origin-destination matrix also in this case. While it is not possible to fit the distribution of the ideal journey duration, our results show that a 100% synergy produces a distribution close to the ideal one. It is worth remarking that this analysis would be able to quantify the benefits of synergy for urban traffic if information on the individual adoption of routing technology could be available to researchers.

Our routing system also allows to monitor mobility of the city from a new point of view. Interpreting individuals as particles moving in a thermodynamical system, it is possible to calculate the 'temperature' of the city. For each particle ℓ we calculate the mean speed at time t by

$$v_\ell\left(t;t_\ell^{(0)}\right) = \frac{\sqrt{[i_\ell(t) - i_\ell(t_\ell^{(0)})]^2 + [j_\ell(t) - j_\ell(t_\ell^{(0)})]^2}}{t - t_\ell^{(0)}}, \tag{6}$$

i.e., as the ratio between the distance travelled up to time t and the time required to travel. Here $t_\ell^{(0)}$ indicates the time at which the particle has been injected into the system, i.e., the time at which the individuals leaves the origin of his or her route. The temperature of this system can be defined as the mean squared speed $\langle v_\ell^2 \rangle_\ell$. This measure is better understood in terms of permeability (or connectivity) of the city, as defined in urban studies allowing us to quantify how fast individuals flow through the city. Therefore, we define the permeability by

$$\mathcal{P}(t) = \left\langle v_\ell^2(t) \right\rangle_\ell = \frac{1}{N_{\text{in}}(t)} \sum_{\ell=1}^{N_{\text{in}}(t)} v_\ell^2(t), \tag{7}$$

where the sum and the average are limited to individuals adopting the routing system, because of the lack of information about origin-destination of the others. Nevertheless, $\mathcal{P}(t)$ is indirectly affected by the traffic generated by $N_{\text{out}}(t)$ individuals, therefore it is a robust measure of permeability. Higher the value of $\mathcal{P}(t)$ faster the flow of individuals trough the city and, conversely, lower the value of $\mathcal{P}(t)$ and slower the movements in the city, i.e., higher the probability that there are congested areas or, in the worst case, 'frozen' cells in the grid. In the upper panel of Figure 5 we show how the permeability changes over time for a data-driven simulation with $N = 100$ individuals, $a = 0.1$, $b = 0.5$ and $p = 0$, i.e., for 100% synergy. The color gradient codes the status of the city with respect to its historical permeability. The existence of congested areas is more evident when the time series of anomaly $\mathcal{A}(t)$ is observed. The anomaly is defined as the departure of $\mathcal{P}(t)$ from the historical average $\mu_{\mathcal{P}}(t)$ with respect to the historical standard deviation $\sigma_{\mathcal{P}}(t)$

$$\mathcal{A}(t) = \frac{\mathcal{P}(t) - \mu_{\mathcal{P}}(t)}{\sigma_{\mathcal{P}}(t)}, \tag{8}$$

where

$$\mu_{\mathcal{P}}(t) = \frac{1}{t} \sum_{\tau=1}^{t} \mathcal{P}(\tau), \tag{9}$$

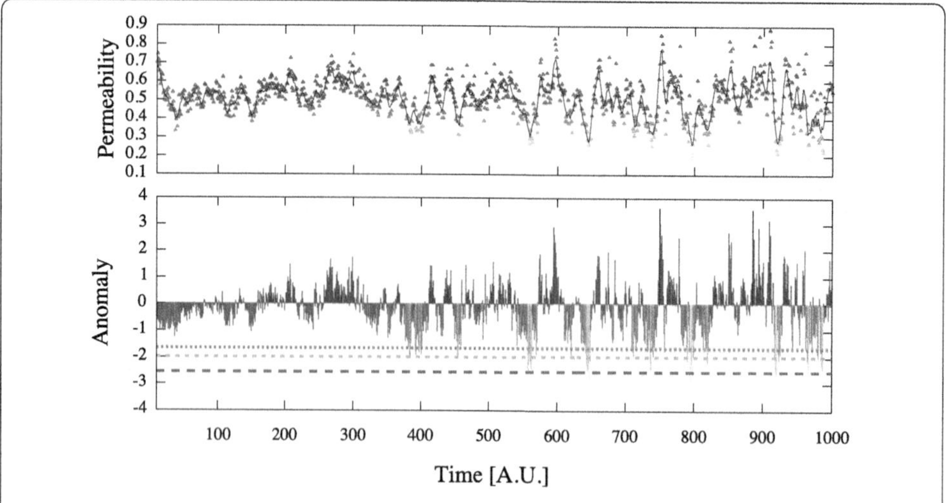

Figure 5 Monitoring traffic congestion in the city. Permeability of the city and corresponding anomaly *versus* time in the case of a data-driven simulation with $N = 100$ individuals, $a = 0.1$, $b = 0.5$ and $p = 0$. The horizontal lines in the bottom panel corresponds to different possible levels of 'traffic congestion alert'. The color gradient codes the status of the city with respect to its historical permeability (see the text for further detail).

$$\sigma_{\mathcal{P}}(t) = \sqrt{\frac{1}{t}\sum_{\tau=1}^{t}\mathcal{P}(\tau)^2 - \left[\frac{1}{t}\sum_{\tau=1}^{t}\mathcal{P}(\tau)\right]^2}. \tag{10}$$

In the bottom panel of Figure 5 we show the anomaly changing over time. The traffic experiences large fluctuations for large values of t, positive and negative ones, alternating periods of high permeability with a few periods of low permeability. This is due to a few overcrowded cells that are quickly and automatically uncrowded by the system itself. Therefore, it is possible to monitor the traffic of the city by looking at the permeability and its anomaly over time, programming different alert levels such as low ($-2 \leq \mathcal{A}(t) < -1.7$), medium ($-2.6 \leq \mathcal{A}(t) < -2$) or critical $\mathcal{A}(t) < -2.6$.

5 Discussion and conclusions

We have presented a strategy to route individuals between pairs of points of interest according to constraints of different type. Our method accounts for the simultaneous interplaying between personalized constraints, as avoiding specific areas of the city because of personal choices, and collective constraints, from pollution reduction in certain areas of the city to the presence of adverse atmospherical conditions requiring targeted intervention. We have shown that the synergy plays a fundamental role in designing a smart city: only when all individuals take part in the routing system and move according to the recommended routes, the overall traffic in the city is closer to the most ideal mobility scenario. In the presence of real time information, our method allows to monitor the state of the city in real time, automatically identifying areas that are experiencing a temporary congestion and giving authorities the possibility to intervene timely.

Finally, the potential applications of our routing strategy are multiple. For instance, for certain values of the parameters (i.e., $a = b = 0$, leading to $\gamma(t) = 0$), we obtain a routing strategy from an origin and without a fixed destination, while accounting for specified constraints. This case could be useful to perform automated routing of objects or individuals through the city. For instance, it would be possible to route cars or drones which are collecting data about the city (as Google cars) and to route people in charge of social services like cleaning the streets or performing targeted intervention, as disseminating salt in areas with snow. An additional application could be in the field of social security, to route police cars in areas with high crimes rate. Finally, our framework can help decision-makers to real-time application of urban mobility policies in responses to crisis, e.g. the emergence of hotspots of infection in specific areas of the city (or a larger area) can be incorporated into the model to avoid people passing through dangerous areas before physical quarantine is employed.

Competing interests
The authors declare that they have no competing interests.

Authors' contributions
MDD, AL, MCG and AA devised the study and wrote the manuscript. MDD and AL performed the data analysis and data-driven simulations. All authors reviewed and approved the complete manuscript.

Author details
[1]Departament d'Enginyeria Informàtica i Matemàtiques, Universitat Rovira i Virgili, Av.da Països Catalans, 26, Tarragona, 43007, Spain. [2]School of Computer Science, University of Birmingham, Edgbaston, Birmingham, B15 2TT, UK. [3]Department of Civil and Environmental Engineering, Massachusetts Institute of Technology, 77 Massachusetts Avenue, Cambridge, MA 02139, USA.

Acknowledgements
MDD is supported by the European Commission FET-Proactive project PLEXMATH (Grant No. 317614), AA by the MULTIPLEX (grant 317532) and the Generalitat de Catalunya 2009-SGR-838. AA also acknowledges financial support from the ICREA Academia, the James S. McDonnell Foundation, and FIS2012-38266. MCG acknowledges Accenture and the KACST-Center for Complex Engineering Systems.

Endnote
[a] http://www.linkiesta.it/reati-a-milano.

References

1. Hazelton ML (2008) Statistical inference for time varying origin-destination matrices. Transp Res, Part B, Methodol 42(6):542-552
2. Schneider CM, Belik V, Couronné T, Smoreda Z, González MC (2013) Unravelling daily human mobility motifs. J R Soc Interface 10(84):20130246
3. Song C, Qu Z, Blumm N, Barabási A-L (2010) Limits of predictability in human mobility. Science 327(5968):1018-1021
4. Simini F, González MC, Maritan A, Barabási A-L (2012) A universal model for mobility and migration patterns. Nature 484:96-100
5. De Domenico M, Solé-Ribalta A, Gómez S, Arenas A (2014) Navigability of interconnected networks under random failures. Proc Natl Acad Sci USA 111(23):8351-8356
6. Gallotti R, Barthelemy M (2014) Anatomy and efficiency of urban multimodal mobility. Sci Rep 4:6911
7. Youn H, Gastner MT, Jeong H (2008) Price of anarchy in transportation networks: efficiency and optimality control. Phys Rev Lett 101(12):128701
8. Wang P, Hunter T, Bayen AM, Schechtner K, González MC (2012) Understanding road usage patterns in urban areas. Sci Rep 2:1001
9. Delling D, Goldberg AV, Pajor T, Werneck RF (2011) Customizable route planning. In: Experimental algorithms. Springer, Berlin, pp 376-387
10. Yeung CH, Saad D, Wong KM (2013) From the physics of interacting polymers to optimizing routes on the London underground. Proc Natl Acad Sci USA 110(34):13717-13722
11. Makse HA, Havlin H, Stanley H (1995) Modelling urban growth. Nature 377:19
12. Gonzalez MC, Hidalgo CA, Barabasi A-L (2008) Understanding individual human mobility patterns. Nature 453(7196):779-782
13. Lima A, De Domenico M, Pejovic V, Musolesi M (2013) Exploiting cellular data for disease containment and information campaigns strategies in country-wide epidemics. arXiv:1306.4534
14. Salnikov V, Schien D, Youn H, Lambiotte R, Gastner M (2014) The geography and carbon footprint of mobile phone use in cote d'ivoire. EPJ Data Sci 3(1):3
15. Song C, Koren T, Wang P, Barabási A-L (2010) Modelling the scaling properties of human mobility. Nat Phys 6(10):818-823
16. De Domenico M, Lima A, Musolesi M (2013) Interdependence and predictability of human mobility and social interactions. Pervasive Mob Comput 9(6):798-807
17. Crandall DJ, Backstrom L, Cosley D, Suri S, Huttenlocher D, Kleinberg J (2010) Inferring social ties from geographic coincidences. Proc Natl Acad Sci USA 107(52):22436-22441

18. Farrahi K, Emonet R, Cebrian M (2014) Epidemic contact tracing via communication traces. PLoS ONE 9(5):95133
19. Palchykov V, Mitrović M, Jo H-H, Saramäki J, Pan RK (2014) Inferring human mobility using communication patterns. Sci Rep 4:6174

Permissions

All chapters in this book were first published in EPJ-DS, by Springer; hereby published with permission under the Creative Commons Attribution License or equivalent. Every chapter published in this book has been scrutinized by our experts. Their significance has been extensively debated. The topics covered herein carry significant findings which will fuel the growth of the discipline. They may even be implemented as practical applications or may be referred to as a beginning point for another development.

The contributors of this book come from diverse backgrounds, making this book a truly international effort. This book will bring forth new frontiers with its revolutionizing research information and detailed analysis of the nascent developments around the world.

We would like to thank all the contributing authors for lending their expertise to make the book truly unique. They have played a crucial role in the development of this book. Without their invaluable contributions this book wouldn't have been possible. They have made vital efforts to compile up to date information on the varied aspects of this subject to make this book a valuable addition to the collection of many professionals and students.

This book was conceptualized with the vision of imparting up-to-date information and advanced data in this field. To ensure the same, a matchless editorial board was set up. Every individual on the board went through rigorous rounds of assessment to prove their worth. After which they invested a large part of their time researching and compiling the most relevant data for our readers.

The editorial board has been involved in producing this book since its inception. They have spent rigorous hours researching and exploring the diverse topics which have resulted in the successful publishing of this book. They have passed on their knowledge of decades through this book. To expedite this challenging task, the publisher supported the team at every step. A small team of assistant editors was also appointed to further simplify the editing procedure and attain best results for the readers.

Apart from the editorial board, the designing team has also invested a significant amount of their time in understanding the subject and creating the most relevant covers. They scrutinized every image to scout for the most suitable representation of the subject and create an appropriate cover for the book.

The publishing team has been an ardent support to the editorial, designing and production team. Their endless efforts to recruit the best for this project, has resulted in the accomplishment of this book. They are a veteran in the field of academics and their pool of knowledge is as vast as their experience in printing. Their expertise and guidance has proved useful at every step. Their uncompromising quality standards have made this book an exceptional effort. Their encouragement from time to time has been an inspiration for everyone.

The publisher and the editorial board hope that this book will prove to be a valuable piece of knowledge for researchers, students, practitioners and scholars across the globe.

List of Contributors

Gautier Krings
ICTEAM Institute, Université catholique de Louvain, Avenue Georges Lemaître, 4, 1348, Louvain-la-Neuve, Belgium

Márton Karsai
Department of Biomedical Engineering and Computational Science, Aalto University School of Science, P.O. Box 12200, FI-00076, Aalto, Finland

Sebastian Bernhardsson
Swedish Defence Research Agency, SE-147 25 Tumba, Sweden

Vincent D Blondel
ICTEAM Institute, Université catholique de Louvain, Avenue Georges Lemaître, 4, 1348, Louvain-la-Neuve, Belgium

Jari Saramäki
Department of Biomedical Engineering and Computational Science, Aalto University School of Science, P.O. Box 12200, FI-00076, Aalto, Finland

A Paolo Masucci
Centre for Advanced Spatial Analysis, University College of London, London, UK

Sophie Arnaud-Haond
Département Étude des Ecosystèmes Profonds-DEEP, Laboratoire Environnement Profond-LEP, Institut Français de Recherche pour l'Exploitation de la MER, Centre de Brest, France

Víctor M Eguíluz
IFISC (CSIC-UIB), Instituto de Física Interdisciplinar y Sistemas Complejos, Consejo Superior de Investigaciones Científicas - Universitat de les Illes Balears, Palma de Mallorca, Spain

Emilio Hernández-García
IFISC (CSIC-UIB), Instituto de Física Interdisciplinar y Sistemas Complejos, Consejo Superior de Investigaciones Científicas - Universitat de les Illes Balears, Palma de Mallorca, Spain

Ester A Serrão
CCMAR, CIMAR-Laboratório Associado, Universidade do Algarve, Gambelas, Faro, 8005-139, Portugal

Martin Wirz
Wearable Computing Laboratory, ETH Zürich, Zürich, Switzerland

Tobias Franke
Embedded Intelligence Group, DFKI Kaiserslautern, Kaiserslautern, Germany

Daniel Roggen
Wearable Computing Laboratory, ETH Zürich, Zürich, Switzerland

Eve Mitleton-Kelly
Complexity Research Programme, London School of Economics and Political Science, London, United Kingdom

Paul Lukowicz
Embedded Intelligence Group, DFKI Kaiserslautern, Kaiserslautern, Germany

Gerhard Tröster
Wearable Computing Laboratory, ETH Zürich, Zürich, Switzerland

Tad Hogg
Institute for Molecular Manufacturing, Palo Alto, CA, USA

Kristina Lerman
USC Information Sciences Institute, Marina del Rey, CA, USA

Silvia Paldino
Department of Physics, University of Calabria, Via Pietro Bucci, 87036 Arcavacata, Rende CS, Italy

Iva Bojic
SENSEable City Laboratory, Massachusetts Institute of Technology, 77 Massachusetts Avenue 9-209, Cambridge, MA 02139, USA

Stanislav Sobolevsky
SENSEable City Laboratory, Massachusetts Institute of Technology, 77 Massachusetts Avenue 9-209, Cambridge, MA 02139, USA

Carlo Ratti
SENSEable City Laboratory, Massachusetts Institute of Technology, 77 Massachusetts Avenue 9-209, Cambridge, MA 02139, USA

Marta C González
Department of Civil and Environmental Engineering, Massachusetts Institute of Technology, 77 Massachusetts Avenue, Cambridge, MA 02139, USA

Anna Samoilenko
Oxford Internet Institute, University of Oxford, 1 St Giles', Oxford, OX1 3JS, UK

Taha Yasseri
Oxford Internet Institute, University of Oxford, 1 St Giles', Oxford, OX1 3JS, UK

Peter Cauwels
Department of Management, Technology and Economics, ETH Zurich, Scheuchzerstrasse 7, Zurich, CH-8092, Switzerland

Nicola Pestalozzi
Department of Management, Technology and Economics, ETH Zurich, Scheuchzerstrasse 7, Zurich, CH-8092, Switzerland

Didier Sornette
Department of Management, Technology and Economics, ETH Zurich, Scheuchzerstrasse 7, Zurich, CH-8092, Switzerland

Raquel A Baños
Institute for Biocomputation and Physics of Complex Systems (BIFI), University of Zaragoza, Zaragoza, 50018, Spain

Javier Borge-Holthoefer
Institute for Biocomputation and Physics of Complex Systems (BIFI), University of Zaragoza, Zaragoza, 50018, Spain

Yamir Moreno
Institute for Biocomputation and Physics of Complex Systems (BIFI), University of Zaragoza, Zaragoza, 50018, Spain
Department of Theoretical Physics, Faculty of Sciences, University of Zaragoza, Zaragoza, 50009, Spain

Jan Ohst
Department of Mathematics, Universität Koblenz-Landau, Koblenz, 56070, Germany

Fredrik Liljeros
Department of Sociology, Stockholm University, Stockholm, 10691, Sweden
Institute for Future Studies, Stockholm, 10131, Sweden

Mikael Stenhem
Department of Medical Epidemiology and Biostatistics, Karolinska Institutet, Stockholm, Sweden
Department of Communicable Disease Control, Stockholm County Council, Stockholm, Sweden

Petter Holme
Institute for Future Studies, Stockholm, 10131, Sweden
Department of Energy Science, Sungkyunkwan University, Suwon, 440-746, Korea
IceLab, Department of Physics, Umeå University, Umeå, 90187, Sweden

Karsten Donnay
Department of Humanities, Social and Political Science, Chair of Sociology, Modeling and Simulation, ETH Zürich, Clausiusstrasse 50, Zürich, 8092, Switzerland

Vladimir Filimonov
Department of Management, Technology and Economics, Chair of Entrepreneurial Risks, ETH Zürich, Scheuchzerstrasse 7, Zürich, 8092, Switzerland

Barbara R Jasny
Science/AAAS, Washington, DC 20005, USA

Doheum Park
Graduate School of Culture Technology and BK21 Plus Postgraduate Organization for Content Science, Korea Advanced Institute of Science & Technology, 291 Daehak-ro, Yuseong-gu, Daejeon 305-701, Republic of Korea

ArramBae
Graduate School of Culture Technology and BK21 Plus Postgraduate Organization for Content Science, Korea Advanced Institute of Science & Technology, 291 Daehak-ro, Yuseong-gu, Daejeon 305-701, Republic of Korea

Maximilian Schich
Arts and Technology Program, University of Texas at Dallas, 800 W. Campbell Road, Richardson, Texas 75080-3021, USA

Juyong Park
Graduate School of Culture Technology and BK21 Plus Postgraduate Organization for Content Science, Korea Advanced Institute of Science & Technology, 291 Daehak-ro, Yuseong-gu, Daejeon 305-701, Republic of Korea

Giovanni Luca Ciampaglia
School of Informatics and Computing, Indiana University, Bloomington, USA

Emilio Ferrara
School of Informatics and Computing, Indiana University, Bloomington, USA

Alessandro Flammini
School of Informatics and Computing, Indiana University, Bloomington, USA

Claudia Wagner
GESIS - Leibniz Institute for the Social Sciences, Unter Sachsenhausen 5-8, Cologne, Germany
University of Koblenz-Landau, Koblenz, Germany

Philipp Singer
GESIS - Leibniz Institute for the Social Sciences, Unter Sachsenhausen 5-8, Cologne, Germany

Markus Strohmaier
GESIS - Leibniz Institute for the Social Sciences, Unter Sachsenhausen 5-8, Cologne, Germany
University of Koblenz-Landau, Koblenz, Germany

Manlio De Domenico
Departament d'Enginyeria Informàtica i Matemàtiques, Universitat Rovira i Virgili, Av.da Països Catalans, 26, Tarragona, 43007, Spain

Antonio Lima
School of Computer Science, University of Birmingham, Edgbaston, Birmingham, B15 2TT, UK

Marta C González
Department of Civil and Environmental Engineering, Massachusetts Institute of Technology, 77 Massachusetts Avenue, Cambridge, MA 02139, USA

Alex Arenas
Departament d'Enginyeria Informàtica i Matemàtiques, Universitat Rovira i Virgili, Av.da Països Catalans, 26, Tarragona, 43007, Spain

CPSIA information can be obtained
at www.ICGtesting.com
Printed in the USA
BVOW10*1103040716
454361BV00002B/228/P